The **M**athematics **C**urriculum and **T**eaching **P**rogram

Professional development package

Activity Bank–
Volume 1

Charles Lovitt & Doug Clarke

Assisting teachers, advisers and systems to explore new educational territory by providing:

• documented classroom images of that new territory,

• professional development structures to facilitate the exploration.

Curriculum
CORPORATION

Acknowledgements

THE PROJECT TEAM: Charles Lovitt and Doug Clarke.

CDC PROJECT OFFICER (1985-8): Laurie Howell.

PRODUCTION, DESIGN and TYPESETTING: Ray and Betty Smith Publications.

CLERICAL STAFF: Pauline Poulter and Susan Vaughan.

MCTP MANAGEMENT COMMITTEE: Vin Faulkner (Chairperson), Brent Corish, Amos Dixon, David Francis, Cheryl Praeger, Max Stephens, Dahle Suggett.

MCTP ADVISORY COMMITTEE: Max Stephens (Chairperson), Rowan Barnsley, John Connell, Barrie Fenby, John Gaffney, Neville Grace, John Hamilton, Frank Hickey, John Hutchins, Jim Moule, Kevin Nener, Bill Newton, Howard Reeves, Noelene Reeves, Phil Rofe, Kaye Stacey, Vicki Stokes.

MAJOR CONTRIBUTORS TO MCTP'S ACTIVITY BANK AND PROFESSIONAL DEVELOPMENT MATERIALS:

The MCTP was originally conceived by CDC and the Directors of Curriculum as a collaborative venture by the States and Territories. The following list indicates the extent of the involvement of a large number of people from the mathematics community:

Nick Alexopoulos, Rod Barry, Barry Bastow, Jeff Baxter, Donna Carlton, Wendy Caughey, Richard Cavanagh, David Clarke, Ken Clements, Margaret Clyne, Richard Cooney, Trish Corcoran, Pat Costello, Peter Cribb, Robyn Crompton, Murray Cropley, Gina Del Campo, Paul Ganderton, Rob Gell, Rachel Griffiths, Peter Howe, Robert Hunting, Neville Johnson, Beth Lee, Bruce Llewellyn, Ian Lowe, Bruce McAvaney, Ted McCoy, Alistair McIntosh, Colin Marriott, Linn Maskell, Tom Maxwell, Will Morony, Joanne Mulligan, Kevin Olssen, John Owen, Michael Palmer, Neil Pateman, Kim Peterson, John Pegg, Alan Pitman, Maureen Price, Ben Pritchard, Cyril Quinlan, Carlene Riley, Ian Robinson, Tom Romberg, Barry Salmon, Sol Sigurdson, Penny Snow, Suzanne Steiner, Jan Stone, Peter Sullivan, Jan Thomas, Vern Treilibs, Coleen Vale, Tony Walker, Vivienne Willis.

In addition we wish to acknowledge the hundreds of teachers whose classroom wisdom is reflected in these pages.

Heptathlon and Decathlon tables reproduced by courtesy of International Amateur Athletics Federation.

CARTOONS: Ron Tandberg and Ray Smith. Also on page 3 by Geoff Coleman and Peter Cole, reprinted by kind permission of VCAB from AdVISE, 1983.

PHOTOGRAPHY: Claude Sironi and Richard Crompton, Monash University, Victoria. Rowing photo courtesy of Hebfotos.

VIDEOTAPE DEVELOPMENT and PRODUCTION: Michael Ryan (Educational Technology Services) and Dudley Blane (Mathematics Education Centre), Monash University. Also *Real Maths - School Maths* by Bill Newton, Victorian Ministry of Education.

COMPUTER DISK DEVELOPMENT AND PRODUCTION: Ian Searle and Jonathan Searle.

ISBN: 0 642 53278 8

First published by the Curriculum Development Centre, Canberra, 1988
Reprinted by Curriculum Corporation, Carlton, 1992, 1994

© Curriculum Corporation, 1992

Curriculum Corporation
St Nicholas Place
141 Rathdowne Street
Carlton Vic 3053

Telephone: (03) 639 0699
Facsimile: (03) 639 1616

Printed in Australia by Impact Printing, Brunswick, Victoria

Foreword

This book and its companion volume, *Activity Bank Volume 2*, are the flag carriers of the successful Mathematics Curriculum and Teaching Program (MCTP).

This program, initiated by the former Curriculum Development Centre, has captured the spirit and nature of exciting and exemplary classroom practices. By presenting resources in ways that encourage learner and teacher alike, MCTP has been and continues to be instrumental in enhancing teacher development and student outcomes.

By supporting continuing improvement in teaching mathematics, by documenting the collective "wisdom of classroom practice", MCTP is consonant with (although it predates) the emphasis and directions of the *National Statement on Mathematics for Australian Schools*.

MCTP has been a truly collaborative venture involving input from all States and Territories, from both Government and non-Government sectors and from tertiary institutions. The model of development followed, and particularly the widespread acceptance of the materials amongst practitioners, is strongly mirrored in the concept and conduct of current national collaborative mathematics activities being managed by Curriculum Corporation.

MCTP is successful and directly relevant to mathematics learning and teaching in our classrooms. It is also attracting considerable international attention.

I commend this book and indeed the other titles that comprise MCTP to all teachers of mathematics, to education systems, to tertiary institutions and to all groups concerned with the professional development of teachers.

David Francis
Executive Director

MCTP professional development package

Activity Bank – Volume 1

Chapter four:
Physical involvement in mathematics learning

Chapter five:
Pupils writing about mathematics

Chapter six:
Mental arithmetic

Other publications in the MCTP professional development package

- *MCTP Activity Bank Volume 2.* Chapters 7 to 13.
- *Guidelines for Consultants and Curriculum Leaders.*
- Assessment Kit - 3 volume set.
- Software - available in Apple 2, Apple Macintosh, BBC and IBM.
- Videos - available as set or 6 individual videos.

A sample double-page spread, showing the various levels of communication.
From *Volume of a room*, (pages 152-3).

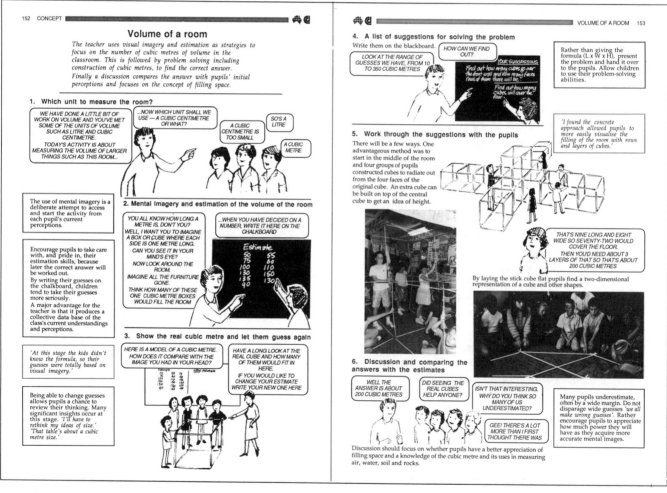

Overview, purpose and structure of the MCTP

THE PURPOSE OF THE MCTP

T*eachers throughout Australia are responding to widespread desires for continued improvement within mathematics teaching.....Can we 'capture', document and share the 'wisdom of practice'?*

It is an exciting time in mathematics education in Australia. Around the country, there is growing agreement at the 'chalkface' and in the wider community about a range of directions and opportunities for improvement within mathematics education. There is growing consensus about the sorts of classroom experiences most likely to be successful in enriching and improving the mathematical development of pupils.

In many classrooms across Australia, as teachers discover more about how children learn, excellent examples of appropriate teaching practice are emerging.

In a nutshell, MCTP seeks to *collect* some of these, the best examples of Australian classroom teaching. It further seeks to *share* this *wisdom of practice* using the best available approaches to professional development.

The MCTP was established for this purpose with a K-10 focus by the Curriculum Development Centre, in consultation with State and Territory Education Departments.

A glimpse into the wisdom of practice

Consider the example on page vi showing a part of the activity *Volume of a room* (Ch. 3).

In this activity, drawn from 'the field', traditional treatment of this topic has been greatly modified by the deliberate inclusion of teaching strategies such as:

- visual imagery
- estimation
- problem solving
- cooperative group work
- physical involvement

The question remains as to whether the quality of the learning environment is improved as a result of these additions.

Results from extensive trialling in schools suggest that teachers are in no doubt whatever that it is a significant improvement.

MCTP seeks:

- to provide resources for all interested teachers to explore such alternative approaches in their classrooms;
- to facilitate debate about the effectiveness of, and theoretical support for such approaches;
- to assist teachers towards an expanded teaching repertoire through selective adoption by them of the principles underpinning the changes.

Hence MCTP aims to assist teachers to move towards greater understandings about teaching and learning, thereby informing their practice.

Authors Charles Lovitt and Doug Clarke.

AREAS FOR GROWTH AND IMPROVEMENT IN MATHEMATICS TEACHING

Teaching strategies such as those described on page 5 are a positive response to some of the areas of teaching and learning identified by teachers as in need of continued improvement.

Ask a group of teachers, pupils, or even parents to reflect on current practice or their own school experience and some consistent images arise.

'Irrelevant...authoritarian'

Teachers readily identify two of the most commonly-asked questions — 'What are we doing this for?' 'When are we ever going to have to use this?'

Perceptive pupils tend to question the relevance of maths studies at times when such questions are most difficult to answer. One (authoritarian) answer tends to be of the type 'because you've got a test on it next week!'

Henry Schoenheimer (1975) reflected on his experiences in mathematics teaching:

I solved, and conscientiously dragooned kids into solving, complicated problems about lunatics named A, B and C who poured water with astonishingly mechanical regularity into leaking cisterns from which it flowed out twice as fast as it flowed in. I and my students have papered enough imaginary walls to outstretch the great wall of China..., calculated the areas of the surfaces of spheres smaller than positrons and larger than Alpha Centauri. Ours not to reason why, ours but to cube and Pi. It was the era of unquestioned authoritarianism, and if a teacher asked you how long it took a limbless cassowary to swim backwards across the Sahara Desert at 300 miles an hour, you did the calculation and you gave the arithmetical answer. And they marked it correct (p. 5).

'Boring'

Invited to offer one word which summarises their views of maths teaching, this is easily the most common response of pupils (and teachers!)

'I'd like my students to be more independent thinkers in maths'

Many children see maths as a set of rules to be applied to exercises, thirty at a time, and more if you finish quickly! On the contrary, mathematics is a powerful way of thinking that can provide considerable enjoyment and satisfaction through its inherent beauty and its ability to aid the solution of 'real' problems. Teachers are looking for ways to convey this to students.

'Maths is so competitive.....you sit at your desk and work by yourself '

While so much of the maths that is done outside the classroom involves people working together, this is sometimes not evident in classrooms. Too much competition can lead to considerable anxiety among students, rarely conducive to effective learning.

> *If you are in a field and are being chased by a bull you will probably perform above your your usual level at jumping the gate, but below usual at undoing the combination lock. Anxiety may enhance motor skills, but it depresses complex intellectual performances.*
> > (Skemp, as cited in Bell et al, 1983).

On the other hand, skills related to cooperative problem solving are of long-term value vocationally and of immediate value through facilitating effective learning.

'When I think of maths, I think of the 'Maths Test'

There has been an urgent need for a range of assessment alternatives to complement the pen and paper test. The need has become more pressing as teachers are adopting a range of new teaching approaches in their classrooms.

Copyright VISE 1983.

'Many of my students withhold their participation for fear of failure'

There is growing recognition that more open, positive and encouraging learning environments will increase the access to, and opportunities for, success of more pupils.

'Many girls can't wait to drop mathematics!'

The content of school maths and the way in which mathematics has traditionally been taught and assessed is under fire for the way in which it has been shown to disadvantage the performance, attitudes and expectations of girls in the subject.

In asking teachers (the criteria for excellence), the answers almost invariably relate not to the mathematics content but to what the teacher does.

WHAT REPRESENTS A QUALITY LEARNING ENVIRONMENT?

Across Australia on any given school day, we estimate that about 170,000 times teachers enter classrooms to create, orchestrate or manage a mathematics learning environment. Many, many of these will be experiences of the highest quality. Yet arguably few if any of these are being recognised or recorded as illustrations for others to consider, analyse and reflect upon.

Shulman (1987, p. 11) argued this when he wrote:

Teaching is characterised by a collective and individual amnesia — the consistency with which the best creations of its practitioners are constantly being lost to both current and future peers... It is devoid of a history of practice.

If we could float over those 170,000 maths classrooms how would we know when we are witnesses to the art of quality maths teaching? What are the criteria by which we identify excellence?

In asking teachers this question, the answers almost invariably relate not to the mathematics content but *to what the teacher does*. Shulman calls this feature *pedagogical reasoning*. It is *the intellectualization of what good teachers do and why they do it.*

MCTP has sought to find a means of recognising and recording the best teaching practice available, and to create structures whereby we can all learn from these.

This identification of excellence has come from practising teachers. There does exist in the actions and professional beliefs of these teachers a coherent and substantive theory about teaching and learning. Recording this theory remains a major challenge.

Discussion with teachers about quality teaching has identified the following (non-exhaustive) list of variables.

Quality teaching is characterised to the extent that the learning environment:

- starts from 'where the pupil is at'
- recognises that pupils learn at different rates and in different ways
- allows pupils time to reflect on their own thinking and learning
- involves pupils physically in the learning process
- encourages pupils to expand their mode of communicating mathematics
- responds to the interests, concerns and personal world of the pupil
- conveys the wholeness of mathematics, rather than presenting it as a disjointed collection of topics
- recognises the importance of risk-taking for effective learning
- encourages pupils to learn together in cooperative small groups
- invokes the power of visual imagery
- recognises the power of story-shells
- is non-threatening and encourages participation of all pupils
- encourages a wide variety of strategies in problem solving and investigation
- recognises the key role parents play in the pupil's development
- uses the full range of available and appropriate technology
- recognises the special needs of particular pupils
- uses a range of assessment procedures which reflect the approaches to teaching and learning mentioned above.

The activities identified to the MCTP by teachers as exemplary are those where one or more of the above features have been evident to some significant degree. In general, the more evident these features, the greater the quality of the learning environment.

... it is these innovative teachers who have provided the vignettes within the MCTP Activity Bank

A MODEL OF OPERATION FOR EXPLORING NEW EDUCATIONAL TERRITORY

Central to the operation of MCTP is the concept of the individual teacher recognising and reflecting upon his or her own personal repertoire of understandings about teaching and learning. Let us label this repertoire

CURRENT PRACTICE

It is unique to each individual and it has fluid boundaries which vary with those intangible qualities of experience and confidence. It seems axiomatic that the richer this repertoire the greater the quality of learning environments the teacher can offer to pupils.

Many teachers are seeking to improve and expand the quality and range of their current practice. This entails exploring new ideas and theories which may currently, for that teacher, lie outside their confidence or comfort zone.

For such a teacher this is *new educational territory*. The MCTP seeks to be an agency, along with others, to help the teacher explore this new territory. Central to the exploration are the notions of trialling, reflecting, adapting and hence gradually reshaping current practice.

What represents new educational territory?

Teachers, in analysing current practice, have generated a relatively large list of themes, issues or concerns that warrant exploration. Many of these are represented on the diagram.

* Group investigations and problem solving
* Writing mathematics
* Mathematical modelling
* Story-shell frameworks
* Physical/Outdoors
* Mental arithmetic
* Concept learning
* Applications
* Social issues
CURRENT PRACTICE
* Computers
* Video
* Estimation
* Calculators
* Equity
* Concrete materials
* Visual imagery
* Personal
* Iteration and numerical methods
* Non-threatening learning environments

These aspects lie outside current practice for many teachers who admit they lack the confidence, experience or resources to make them a part of their regular repertoire.

It is not suggested that these represent new educational territory for all teachers. For many teachers, these lie firmly within their current practice. Indeed, it is these innovative teachers who have provided the vignettes illustrated within the *MCTP Activity Bank* upon which others can reflect.

This activity actually <u>encourages</u> pupils to toss chalk into a rubbish bin in determining trajectory parameters and modelling these using the computer. (Projectiles, Ch. 8)

*... single classroom experiences,
illustrations of a quality learning
environment*

The MCTP Activity Bank

For each of thirteen major themes, the MCTP
has endeavoured to find and document about
five or six illustrations of exemplary practice.
These are in the form of single classroom
experiences in which the particular theme is
evident and which could be described as
illustrations of a quality learning environment.

The themes are organised into thirteen chapters
in the *Activity Bank.*

VOLUME 1	VOLUME 2
• Video	• Visual imagery
• Social issues	• Computers
• Concept learning	• Estimation
• Physical/Outdoors	• Story-shell frameworks
• Writing mathematics	• Group investigations and
• Mental arithmetic	problem solving
	• Mathematical modelling
	• Iteration and numerical
	methods

Each chapter has an introductory rationale
discussing the educational potential of the
particular theme.

This is followed by five or six fully annotated
classroom activities. In addition, some brief
outlines of possible activities have been
included, with a view to providing a starting
point for interested teachers to develop.

Classification into chapters is often difficult as
an excellent activity might exhibit many
themes all integrated together in one learning
experience. For example, the activity *Algebra
walk (Ch. 4)* could be equally classified as
Physical, Concept or *Visual imagery.* Thus the
chapters are only a first level of classification.

Other themes

A number of other themes, also valued by
teachers, are illustrated within activities. The
use of calculators, concrete materials and
applications are prominent features which
might well have formed chapters in their own
right. Others of a more pedagogical nature are
the creation of a non-threatening learning
environment and making the learning
personally meaningful to pupils. These and
other features are recognised as critical
ingredients of a quality learning environment
and attention is drawn to their existence on the
list at the beginning of many activities.

One feature of particular importance is that of an
inclusive curriculum.

Children from non-English speaking backgrounds
are faced with the dual task of learning English
as their second language and learning through
English as the medium of instruction across all
areas. As an example for discussion, the activity
Dice cricket (Ch. 12) has been additionally
annotated in order to highlight appropriate
intervention strategies.

The reader is also referred to two useful
publications for teachers of NESB children:
Thomas (1986) and Grigson and Johns (1987).
These indicate that approaches to teaching and
learning outlined throughout the *Activity Bank*
find strong support from those working in this
area.

Anyon (1981) and others have demonstrated that
pupils from different socio-economic backgrounds
have different aspirations and interpret their
maths education as serving different purposes.
The relevance of an activity in one context
therefore does not necessarily imply relevance in
another.

Girls and mathematics

The participation rates of girls in senior
secondary mathematics are well below that of
boys. (See, for example, Morgan, 1986). As most
work and tertiary study options requires a level
of senior maths, many girls are therefore closing
off many of their post-school options. At the
same time, technology is making its greatest
inroads in the area of 'traditional' female work,
further restricting women's career and life
options.

Intervention strategies that assist girls to make
more informed selections of subjects and career
paths are necessary, but only form part of the
picture.

*If the quality of mathematics (and science)
education is improved in ways that are
sensitive to the needs, experience and interests
of girls, then girls can achieve success and
acquire knowledge and skills which are
mathematical and scientific.* (Vale, 1987, p. 4)

Girls are then in a position to make real choices
about study and work and are more confident to
participate in an increasingly technological
society.

Teachers are identifying strategies that appear
to improve the attitudes and achievement of
girls in mathematics. Lee (1986) provides an
excellent resource for interested teachers.

Providing opportunities for pupils to become informed and analytical about ... the relevance and significance of mathematics education.

The MCTP would argue that the following strategies are based on sound learning principles, and are therefore of great importance in *all* teaching situations:

- Encouraging pupils to talk and write about mathematics.

- Providing opportunities for pupils to work in cooperative groups.

- Observing and collecting data about the participation of girls in mathematical activities

- Setting learning tasks that require pupils to manipulate materials to solve real problems.

- Encouraging pupils to link knowledge and skills with 'real things' and to see their relationship to social issues and personal or living concerns in particular.

- Encouraging pupils to participate in decision-making about the course. This will enable girls' interests and experiences to be included, raising self-esteem and commitment to learning and reducing their anxiety.

- Ensuring that the timetable, subject composition and the process for subject selection is not obstructive to girls.

- Ensuring that assessment strategies and process are consistent with the learning tasks, content and method.

- Creating an atmosphere for learning which is caring, personal and without harassment and sexist attitudes.

- Providing opportunities for pupils to become informed and analytical about the structure of the paid workforce, women's role in both paid and unpaid work and the relevance and significance of mathematics education.

- Challenging stereotypes.

- Determining clear, achievable goals which can be acknowledged.

There is still a need for further research to confirm (or deny) the intuitive wisdom of many of these strategies.

We will now discuss the first two of these in some detail.

1. The role of language

Language has a significant part to play in the learning process. Pupils being able to describe or explain a mathematical experience in their own language is seen as a vital step in the progress to understanding and the acquisition of formal mathematical language.

> *The productive value of talk in the context of group activity is especially challenging for mathematics teachers because of a long tradition of quiet, busy work. In fact, 'talk' and 'work' can seem at odds with each other. 'How can you be working? You're talking. "'*

(Snow, 1988)

Tell me a story – Primary (Ch. 5) is an MCTP activity which draws on pupils' experience, imagination, cooperation and discussion to develop the concept of 'explaining' a graph. Pupils are presented with a graph which shows the depth of water in a bath over a period of time.

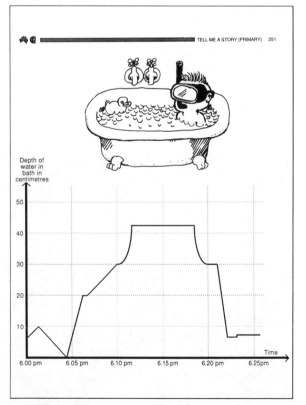

TELL ME A STORY (PRIMARY)   251

In pairs, pupils write a story which could 'explain the graph'. This is then acted out, as the rest of the class listen to the story and follow the graph, looking for mathematical accuracy.

> Most writers advocate a balance
> between competition and
> cooperation.

Teachers who have tried this activity report that the discussion between pupils and with the whole class, and the opportunity to write about mathematics, drawing on experience and imagination, are all aspects of the activity which provide successful and enjoyable experiences for pupils and which lead to greater understanding of the underlying formal concepts.

The language used in pupil resource materials should be non-sexist and not promoting sex-role stereotyping. The activity *Tinker Tailor Soldier Sailor — Male or Female* (Ch. 12), encourages pupils to investigate classroom materials in a statistical way, with discussion as to inclusiveness or the lack of it. (See Steiner 1985 for detailed research in this area).

2. Cooperative group work

The collaborative working in small groups seems to be a more comfortable way for girls to work, supporting each other, exploring ideas verbally... A study of primary children in Denmark with problems that can be solved using a computer has found that if a small group of boys is given a problem, they will tend to negotiate time and each work independently, but quickly to solve the problem. Whereas the girls will work collaboratively and explore verbally a lot more implications about the problem.

Harding (1986, pp. 7-8)

Owens and Barnes (1982) investigated competitive, cooperative and individualised teaching modes. They found that girls of all ages expressed stronger preferences for cooperative learning than boys, while secondary teachers of mathematics and science preferred to teach in a competitive style.

Most writers advocate a balance between competition and cooperation.

One advantage of group work is the opportunity to pool existing knowledge of pupils. But often this valuable resource is largely unrecognised and untapped.

The activity *Fermi problems* (Ch. 11) powerfully demonstrates this feature directly to pupils.

In the activity, groups of pupils are presented with problems which at first appear insoluble. (A typical problem might be 'how many German Shepherd dogs are there in your town?').

As the group 'teases out' the problem, they begin to realise all the knowledge needed to find a reasonable solution already resides within the group.

Teachers trialling this activity report that pupils react enthusiastically to solving what at first appear quite off-beat problems, and learn a valuable lesson about the power of group work in the process.

Group 'scribes' report on the assumptions made and final estimates for the problem 'How many piano tuners are there in Sydney?' (Fermi problems, Ch.11).

> *More is learnt from a single success than from multiple failures. A single success proves it can be done — what is, is possible.*

Capturing the wisdom of practice

The MCTP's documentation of quality activities is an attempt to capture the *pedagogical reasoning,* or wisdom of what good teachers do and why they do it. To use an art metaphor, each activity is a small piece of the art of excellent teaching. The *MCTP Activity Bank* is an attempt to build a gallery of the wisdom of practice.

To capture the spirit as well as the substance of a quality learning environment, has been a particular challenge for the MCTP. We want the activity documentation to function for the reader as *a window into the mind of the teacher.*

Consider particularly the commentary in the side boxes which is a tentative attempt to paraphrase the pedagogical thinking of the creators of the activity. Readers will make their own judgements as to whether this experience represents quality teaching. We claim that it does, the actions of the teacher arising from learning principles that do have demonstrable support in both the literature and among the general teaching community.

The change process and an emphasis on the single experience.

The MCTP has chosen to focus on the single classroom activity as a means of promoting discussion and reflection on good practice.

One crucial principle of the MCTP approach is that changes in the *attitudes* or *beliefs* about new approaches *follow* changes in teaching *behaviour;* new practices which lead to improved learning outcomes have a particularly profound effect on changing teachers' attitudes.

> *More is learnt from a single success than from multiple failures. A single success proves it can be done — what is, is possible.*
>
> Merton, as cited in Fullan (1982, p. 208)

The aggregation of the single experiences makes a collective statement about quality teaching and learning and is a major resource for teachers wishing to explore a particular theme. We believe that a teacher can learn from the collection in the same way that an artist learns through visiting an art gallery to observe a work of art? Whether the study begets shallow imitation or new conceptualisations in the learner is a function of purpose and intensity of the observation.

From page 147 – This goes with this.

3. Group work

Each group needs a piece of butcher's paper (or A3), a 100-bead ring, and a cardboard strip and sticky tape.

If there are 27 in the class, rule up a large piece of cardboard into 27 rows (plus extra for overlap) and then cut off one strip for each group.

'I felt it was very valuable for each group to physically handle the concrete aids — it seemed to help generate a lasting mental image.'

'I prepared some "100-bead rings" with the colours mixed at random. In others, for easy counting, I grouped the colours (in twos, fives or tens).'

The teacher moving around the groups can observe organisation, cooperation and initiative. Let groups organise themselves, but encourage all pupils to physically handle the material.

4. Reporting

9 OUT OF 27 WOULD LIKE TO HOLIDAY IN NEW ZEALAND

THAT IS SHADED IN BLUE HERE ON THE STRIP GRAPH

HERE IT IS ON THE PIE CHART

IT'S A '33-BEAD' CHOICE. THAT IS, 33 OUT OF EVERY 100 PEOPLE

There are enough tasks in the reporting to require every member of the group to participate in many ways.

'The groups were reporting back the class's own data.'

Listening to the language (not always formal) gives interesting insight into pupils' understandings.

The completed graphs and charts could be displayed on a board (and used for reference in the future) or made into a class activity book.

Conclusion

Ask pupils their reactions to the use of the concrete aids.

One benefit of the repetition of the use of the 27 is that pupils nearly all realised that each vote was worth about 4 beads and saw relationships such as $^{10}/_{27}$ as about 10 lots of 4 beads — approximately 40%.

'I sent the project material home with pupils to show their families as a form of reporting.'

'I wanted to strengthen in pupils, the value of using concrete aids to get away from seeing maths as very abstract.'

> *... attaining clarity of vision of this new territory by trying some appropriate teaching activities.*

PROFESSIONAL DEVELOPMENT WITHIN THE MCTP

This section is written for people such as consultants and curriculum leaders who have a responsibility for the professional development of teachers of mathematics. The term curriculum leaders includes curriculum coordinators, heads of mathematics departments and other personnel who have a key role in professional development in schools.

MCTP PROFESSIONAL DEVELOPMENT IN A NUTSHELL

Consider the following hypothetical scenarios:

CONSULTANT TO MCTP: I've got a group of schools interested in exploring cooperative group work. Can you assist?

MATHS COORDINATOR TO MCTP: The new maths guidelines advocate the use of problem solving and also computers, but we have little experience in these areas. Can you assist?

MCTP's response:

We can offer
(i) a collection of illustrative activities (the very best we have been able to find) highlighting your chosen features in action,

(ii) a range of structures for supporting teachers to explore and learn from these illustrative activities (the very best models of professional development we have been able to find).

Issues in educational change

An effective professional development strategy is dependent on:

- assessing the needs of teachers.
- developing a professional development program to meet those needs.
- having resources available which reflect existing good practice to use in the program.

This section is designed to assist you with the first two of these activities. *The MCTP Activity Bank* is designed to help you with the third.

The 13 chapters in the *Activity Bank* reflect many of the needs for professional development identified by teachers.

Consider one of those themes, for example using a computer in the maths classroom. Teachers might be involved in three curriculum-related processes:

- attaining clarity of vision of this new territory by trying some appropriate teaching activities which are included in the *MCTP Activity Bank*;
- developing and trying teaching activities they write themselves which are based on the principles underpinning these examples;
- designing and trying whole units which incorporate ideas which are contained in the *Activity Bank*. (This may include integrating ideas from one or more chapters.)

These are processes which will take place, as much as possible, in the teachers' own classrooms and schools, and as such will impinge on the ongoing or existing mathematics programs in the schools. In that they affect pupils, the activities themselves are part of a curriculum change process in their own right. Thus there is a link between the professional development of teachers and the development of better curricula in the schools.

We have given these three stages the titles *initial trialling, implementation,* and *continuation.* To state this more formally:

1. *Initial trialling*

This would entail, after reflection on current practice, a decision to undertake substantive trialling of some of the available MCTP resources on a chosen theme. Central to the notion of trialling is the teacher's willingness to *suspend judgement,* while being committed to exploring a new dimension of teaching. Hopefully, subsequent discussion can then be based on the realities of a successful classroom experience, rather than on pre-conceived ideas.

2. *Implementation*

We suggest that implementation consists of the writing and trialling of school-based activities around that theme. This would normally follow initial trialling.

3. *Continuation*

Continuation or institutionalisation is concerned with sustaining the approach in the school. We suggest that an indicator of continuation is the incorporation of the theme in a unit or subject in the maths curriculum (or perhaps in other programs in the school of an interdisciplinary nature). This would normally mean that the school develops documentation which reflects this incorporation.

As part of a professional development program, teachers workshop the activity Tell me a story.

We have called these different parts *stages* because there is an element of increased commitment to good mathematics teaching as one moves from stage to stage. However, in some cases the third stage could be happening in conjunction with earlier stages.

MCTP SANDWICH MODEL —
HOW A GROUP OF TEACHERS IN A SCHOOL OR CLUSTER OF SCHOOLS MIGHT USE MCTP RESOURCES TO EXPLORE A THEME OF THEIR CHOOSING

1. Workshop using MCTP and other activities developed around the chosen theme.

2. School-based trialling of these activities.

3. Reflection and sharing following classroom trialling. Plans for further exploration.

Professional development models

Now that we have outlined three stages within which teachers might consider the incorporation of new approaches to their own practice and the school mathematics curricula, the challenge remains as to how schools and school support personnel might operate in practice to encourage the uptake of new skills and understandings.

An important part of the response lies in the establishment of a comprehensive professional development program.

The question is: how can this be encouraged by those responsible for planning, developing and implementing school mathematics curriculum policy; and by consultants with a brief to support teachers in this task?

Part of the answer is that there are a number of approaches or models by which teachers might be assisted and in which consultants might operate. The models are a synthesis of good professional development practice drawn from theoretical perspectives and practical experience: the best we have been able to find operating across the country.

At the outset, we would like to point out that the 'one-shot' inservice is not included as one of the models. This approach is in conflict with many established principles of professional development. We do not recommend this approach, as it is unlikely to lead to lasting change.

On the following pages, we describe briefly each of eight models as a basis for selecting between the approaches.

We present a more expanded description of each model in the *Guidelines for Mathematics Consultants and Curriculum Leaders* (a separate publication of the MCTP), which could be consulted in preparation for the use of a specific model.

Structured Course

Here many of the processes are formalised into an organised course over a fixed time frame, perhaps a ten week period. Teachers commit themselves, (hopefully with school support in the form of regular time release from school responsibilities) to attend sessions, and to incorporate course content into their classroom practice. Discussion of themes and the results of trials and developments which teachers undertake in their classrooms between sessions, form the basis of the sessions.

The roles of the consultant/curriculum leaders are to organise the course and to arrange for and/or participate in the presentation or sharing of new approaches with teachers.

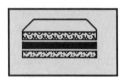

Sandwich

This generally consists of two sessions, between which school level trials of themes presented in the first session are 'sandwiched'. These are discussed at the second session. Because of the relatively short time span of the model, the emphasis is on the initial trialling stage.

Broadly, the roles of the consultant/curriculum leader are to organise the course and to arrange for and/or participate in the presentation of new approaches to teachers.

The sandwich model is an attempt to make a small but important extension beyond the limitations of the 'one-shot' inservice. Specifically it aims to build in classroom trialling and a structured opportunity for reflection.

In-School Intensive

This model is conducted within a school with a group of staff, preferably the whole of the mathematics staff. The consultant /curriculum leader develops a plan with the staff, to which they make a commitment over a given period. Depending on the length of this commitment the staff may consider all three stages; namely initial trialling, implementation and continuation.

The roles of the consultant/curriculum leader are to support a school to become involved, to facilitate a program for the school, and to arrange and/or provide presentations of illustrative classroom practice when necessary.

School Cluster Groups

Groups of schools form a network to consider new approaches. The group provides feedback to each other on the trials via regular group meetings of staff drawn from the cluster. Progression through the stages depends on the life of the cluster and the preferences of the cluster members.

Broadly, the roles of the consultant/curriculum leader are to set up and provide maintenance activities for the group, and to arrange for and/or provide presentations when necessary.

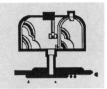

Postal

Teachers receive and trial new materials through the post and comprehensive feedback is provided to a central or regional consultant who is responsible for the mailing. This model is designed to support teachers in remote regions to try new strategies and to reflect on their effectiveness.. The consultant may assist in organising occasional sharing sessions for teachers if these are possible.

The roles of the consultant/curriculum leader are to keep in touch with the teachers concerned, and to arrange for and/or provide presentations if sessions are possible.

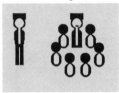

Pre-Service

Using arrangements in pre-service teacher education, student teachers trial a small number of activities while in schools, and in conjunction with supervising teachers and lecturers they analyse the impact of the approaches. In this way preservice teachers can be exposed to a range of new ideas by using the best creations of experienced teachers.

Broadly, the role of the consultant/curriculum leader is to liaise with teacher education institutions and encourage them to use the model.

Peer Tutoring

This relies on the availability of a colleague within the school to provide support for the use and incorporation of new approaches. Effective use of peer tutoring requires the systematic collection of data about teaching activities and the non-threatening support of a 'critical friend.'

The role of the consultant/curriculum leader is to encourage groups of teachers to use the approach if appropriate, inform them of its characteristics and provide input about new approaches as a basis for their deliberations.

Activity Documentation

This involves the creation of networks of teachers who have progressed in the use of new approaches, perhaps to the implementation and continuation stages. The networks are designed to gather and share the documents and activities so developed.

Broadly, the roles of the consultant/curriculum leader are to set up the networks and maintain them.

Choosing the right model

An important decision for a consultant/curriculum leader is to decide which of the models is the most appropriate one to use in a given situation. This should be decided in conjunction with the clients of the professional development activity.

It may well be that over an extended period of time more than one model or a hybrid will be used with the same group of teachers.

The descriptions above should be a first source of information in this regard. The table below is a second source in that it compares the models on a number of criteria. These criteria are based on some recent research which suggests that there is a consistent set of professional development principles needed to achieve lasting educational change.

Professional development should:

❖ address *issues of concern* recognised by the teachers themselves,

❖ take place as close as possible to the *teacher's own working environment*,

❖ take place over an *extended period of time*,

❖ have the *support* of both colleagues and the school administration,

❖ provide opportunities for *reflection and feedback*,

❖ enable participating teachers to feel a substantial degree of *ownership*,

❖ involve a conscious *commitment* on the part of the teacher,

❖ involves *groups* of teachers rather than *individuals* from a school,

❖ use the *services of a consultant* and/or *critical friend*.

Each model has been been assessed for the degree to which it contains each of these characteristics, given that the model is used in its 'ideal form'.

The far right-hand column of the table describes the services of the

consultant/curriculum leader in the use of the model. We have used terms here which need to be explained.

The first is *interactive strategies*. By this we mean involvement in tasks designed to assist teachers to come to grips with the content and processes of the proposed area of change.

Demonstrating a particular approach in a classroom with participant teachers watching is an example of an interactive strategy. Such demonstrations are a particularly powerful strategy for generating meaningful discussion about any underlying learning principles.

Leading a group discussion on the underlying principles of an activity is a further example of a consultant or curriculum leader being involved in an interactive strategy.

The second is *logistics*. By this we mean organisational and administrative roles of the consultant/curriculum leader in setting up and maintaining a model. Planning the details of a session and ensuring that teachers know what to expect are examples of logistics.

Table 1. A comparision of the MCTP models with respect to professional development principles.

MODEL	PROGRESSION THROUGH STAGES	ADDRESSES TEACHER ISSUES	IN TEACHERS' ENVIRONMENT	ON-GOING OVER TIME	SUPPORT OF COLLEAGUES IN SCHOOLS	OPPORTUNITY FOR FEEDBACK	OWNERSHIP DEVELOPED	DEVELOPS COMMITMENT	CONSULTANT'S ROLE
1. Structured Course	all stages can be covered if course is of sufficient length	yes	school-level practice encouraged	strong feature of model	between sessions	yes, feature of sessions	develops over time	develops over time	interactive strategies (sessions), logistics
2. Sandwich Course	concentration on initial trialling	yes	school-level practice between sessions encouraged	limited to early stages	restricted to participating teachers	yes, in sessions	to a limited extent	to a limited extent	interactive strategies (sessions), logistics
3. In-school Intensive	concentration on initial trialling and implementation, but all stages could be considered	yes	yes	strong feature, of model	strong feature, relies on school support for on-going activities	yes, if sessions well-structured	yes	yes	(maybe) interactive strategies, logistics
4. School Cluster Groups	concentration on initial trialling and implementation, but all stages could be considered	yes	yes	yes	between sessions	yes, if sessions well-structured	yes, strong feature	particularly those involved in cluster meetings	(maybe) interactive strategies, logistics
5. Postal Model	probable concentration on initial trialling	yes	not necessarily present	yes	possible, but not influenced by consultant	no	yes	possible, but not influenced by consultant	interactive strategies unlikely, logistics
6. Pre-service Model	probable concentration on initial trialling	yes	yes	limited to teaching rounds	support of teachers and lecturers	yes	to some extent	to some extent	liaison with institutions
7. Peer Tutoring	may involve all stages	yes	yes	yes	yes	depends on the sessions	yes	yes	limited to invitation
8. Activity Documentation	concentration on implementation and continuation	yes	yes	yes	not necessarily present	yes	probably already developed	yes	acts a cog in a wheel, logistics
One-shot Model	unlikely to consider initial trialling (or other stages)	to some extent	maybe	no	maybe	no	unlikely	maybe	information giving

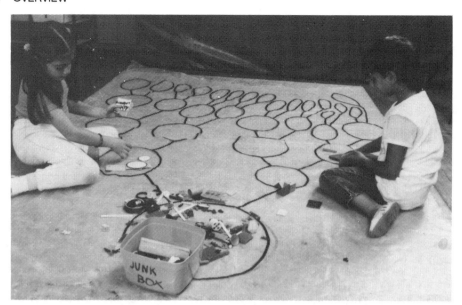

Junior primary school children construct their own classification tree and classify familiar objects.

Conclusion

While the information in the Table should be considered, it should also be said at this point that the local conditions and restrictions will almost certainly be a factor in choosing the model(s) you can use. It may also be necessary to use a variation of one of the models we have presented.

Again, we do urge you to avoid the one-shot approaches to professional development.

Change is generally a slow process given the complex naure of the teaching task and all the inhibitors to change. We would encourage consultants, curriculum leaders and teachers to concentrate on relatively small areas of growth at one time and build on the successes that occur The evidence is overwhelming that teachers must have the benefit of time to reflect on the new MCTP approaches and to use it in their schools, and to interact with school colleagues if real change is to take place in mathematics teaching.

As we said earlier this section is just an introduction to the models of professional development. For more extensive information on each of the models, please refer to the separate MCTP publication; *Professional Development — Guidelines for Mathematics Consultants and Curriculum Leaders.*

REFERENCES

Anyon, J. (1981). Social class and school knowledge. *Curriculum Inquiry 11*(1), 3-42.

Bell, A.W., Costello, J., & Kuchemann, D.E. (1984). *A review of research in mathematical education: Part A, Research on teaching and learning.* London: NFER-Nelson.

Fullan, M. (1982). *The meaning of educational change.* New York: Teachers College Press.

Grigson, D. & Johns, L. (1987). *Mathspack* (draft material). Canberra: Curriculum Development Centre.

Harding J. (1986). Girls and science. Address presented to Girls and Science Seminar, The Age Education Unit, Melbourne.

Lee, B. (1986). *Girls (and boys) and mathematics: discussion paper and strategies.* Canberra: ACT Schools Authority.

Morgan, D. (1986). *Girls education and careers: what the research says.* Sydney: Non-Government Schools Participation and Equity Committee for New South Wales.

Owens, L. & Barnes, J. (1982). The relationship between cooperative, competitive, and individualised learning preferences and students' perceptions of classroom learning atmosphere. *American Educational Research Journal, 19,* 182-200.

Shoenheimer, H. (1975). Maths could be vital. In D. Williams (Ed.), *Perspectives in teaching mathematics.* Melbourne: Mathematical Association of Victoria, 1-13.

Shulman, L.S. (1987). Knowledge and learning: foundations of the new reform. *Harvard Educational Review, 7*(1), 1-22.

Snow, P. (1988). Girls in mathematics. In *Mathematics frameworks – a forward look.* Melbourne: Victorian Ministry of Education.

Steiner, S. (1985). Sex differences in mathematics learning and related features. Masters Thesis, Monash University, Clayton.

Thomas, J. (1986). *Number ≠ Maths.* Melbourne: Child Migrant Education Centre.

Vale, C. (1987). Introduction. *Recreating maths and science for girls.* Melbourne: Participation and Equity Program.

The major maths features and recommended-year levels of the activities

Volume 1

Volume 2

Title of activity	Appropriate grades are shaded	Mathematical features

Chapter 7 — Visual imagery

Title of activity	Appropriate grades (shaded in **bold**)	Mathematical features
Krazy kennels.	**K 1 2 3** 4 5 6 7 8 9 10	Length, polyhedra, estimation.
Silence.	**K 1 2 3** 4 5 6 7 8 9 10	Geometric shapes.
Footsteps over Australia.	K 1 2 3 **4 5 6 7** 8 9 10	Scale, distance, compass direction.
Map of Australia.	K 1 2 3 4 5 **6 7 8 9 10**	Estimation, calculators, area, proportion, mental computation.
Introductory Pythagoras.	K 1 2 3 4 5 6 7 **8 9 10**	Estimation, calculators, Pythagoras.
Venus.	K 1 2 3 4 5 6 7 8 **9 10**	Measurement, coordinates, computers.

Brief descriptions

Title of activity	Appropriate grades (shaded in **bold**)	Mathematical features
Draw my house.	**K 1 2 3** 4 5 6 7 8 9 10	Scale, proportion.
Photo sort.	K 1 2 3 **4 5 6 7 8 9 10**	Spatial logic, seriation.
Mental map.	K 1 2 3 4 5 **6 7 8 9 10**	Map reading, scale.
Belt around the earth.	K 1 2 3 4 5 6 7 **8 9 10**	Circumference, estimation.
How far can you go?	K 1 2 3 4 5 6 7 **8 9 10**	Geometric properties.

Chapter 8 — Computers

Title of activity	Appropriate grades (shaded in **bold**)	Mathematical features
Five modem activities.	**K 1 2 3 4 5 6 7** 8 9 10	Measurement, visual imagery, problem solving.
Billiard ball bounces.	K 1 2 3 4 5 **6 7 8 9 10**	Angles, number patterns, problem solving.
Eight queens.	K 1 2 3 4 5 **6 7 8 9 10**	Visual imagery, problem solving.
Biggest volume.	K 1 2 3 4 5 6 **7 8 9 10**	Visual imagery, calculators, volume, limits.
Eratosthenes revisited.	K 1 2 3 4 5 6 7 **8 9 10**	Trigonometry, length, calculators, spherical geometry.
How close ... painting?	K 1 2 3 4 5 6 7 **8 9 10**	Trigonometry, calculators, limits
Projectiles.	K 1 2 3 4 5 6 7 8 **9 10**	Modelling, speed, angles,

Brief descriptions

Title of activity	Appropriate grades (shaded in **bold**)	Mathematical features
Cones.	K 1 2 3 4 5 6 7 **8 9 10**	Angle, volume and limits.
The human computer.	K 1 2 3 4 5 6 **7 8 9 10**	Binary notation, computation.
Pythagoras - area proof.	K 1 2 3 4 5 6 7 **8 9 10**	Pythagoras, visual imagery, area.

Chapter 9 — Estimation

Title of activity	Appropriate grades (shaded in **bold**)	Mathematical features
Mallet.	**K 1 2 3** 4 5 6 7 8 9 10	Length.
Pupil growth.	K 1 2 3 4 **5 6 7 8 9 10**	Mass, height, data collection and analysis.
Estimation - a general structure.	K 1 2 3 4 **5 6 7 8 9 10**	Angles, decimals, time, error.
Estimation of percentages.	K 1 2 3 4 5 6 **7 8 9** 10	Percentages, error.

Brief descriptions

Title of activity	Appropriate grades (shaded in **bold**)	Mathematical features
Tailor made.	K 1 2 **3 4 5 6** 7 8 9 10	Surface area, proportion.
There and back.	K 1 2 **3 4 5 6** 7 8 9 10	Distance, map reading.
Calculator snooker.	K 1 2 3 4 5 6 **7 8 9 10**	Mental computation.

Chapter 10 — Story-shell frameworks

Title of activity	Appropriate grades (shaded in **bold**)	Mathematical features
Licorice factory.	K 1 2 3 4 5 **6 7 8** 9 10	Prime numbers, factors.
How many ... stand ... classroom?	K 1 2 3 4 5 **6 7 8 9** 10	Fractions, area, estimation, visual imagery, problem solving.
Mirror bounce.	K 1 2 3 4 5 **6 7 8 9** 10	Angles, indices, symmetry, visual imagery, problem solving.

Brief descriptions

Title of activity	Appropriate grades (shaded in **bold**)	Mathematical features
Stories as springboards.	**K 1 2 3 4 5 6 7 8 9 10**	(Many major areas)

THE MAJOR MATHS FEATURES AND RECOMMENDED-YEAR LEVELS OF THE ACTIVITIES(continued).

Title of activity	Appropriate grades are shaded	Mathematical features

Chapter 11 — Group investigations and problem solving

Title of activity	Appropriate grades (shaded)	Mathematical features
Money trails.	K 1 2 3 4 **5 6 7 8** 9 10	Calculators, length, estimation.
Spirolateral walk.	K 1 2 3 4 **5 6 7** 8 9 10	Visual imagery, geometric patterns, symmetry, computers.
The shape of things.	K 1 2 3 4 **5 6 7** 8 9 10	Proportions, length.
Mindreader.	K 1 2 3 4 **5 6 7** 8 9 10	Number patterns, computers.
Fermi problems.	K 1 2 3 4 **5 6 7 8 9 10**	Estimation, computation.
Four cube houses	K 1 2 3 4 **5 6 7 8 9 10**	Volume, surface area, combinations.
Soma cube.	K 1 2 3 4 5 6 **7 8 9** 10	Volume, combinations, 3–D drawing.
Add the numbers 1 to 100.	K 1 2 3 4 5 6 7 **8 9** 10	Computation, computers, calculators.
Tinker, tailor – male or female?	K 1 2 3 4 5 6 7 **8 9 10**	Data collection and analysis.

Brief descriptions

Title of activity	Appropriate grades (shaded)	Mathematical features
Balancing act.	**K 1 2 3** 4 5 6 7 8 9 10	Mass, number properties.
What's my number?	**K 1 2 3 4 5 6 7 8** 9 10	Number properties
Cooperative logic.	K 1 2 3 4 5 **6 7 8 9 10**	Logic.
How long to see a million dollars?	K 1 2 3 4 5 6 7 **8 9 10**	Data collection and analysis.

Chapter 12 — Mathematical modelling

Title of activity	Appropriate grades (shaded)	Mathematical features
Carrot patch people.	K 1 2 3 4 **5 6** 7 8 9 10	Permutations and combinations, problem solving.
Final five.	K 1 2 3 4 **5 6 7** 8 9 10	Probability, computers.
Only a matter of time!	K 1 2 3 4 5 **6 7 8 9 10**	Probability, averages, computers.
Dice cricket.	K 1 2 3 4 5 6 **7 8 9 10**	Probability, averages, calculators, computers.
Speed graphs.	K 1 2 3 4 5 6 7 **8 9 10**	Speed, data collection, linear algebra.
Head turning.	K 1 2 3 4 5 6 7 8 **9 10**	Speed, trigonometry, calculators, computers
Nails.	K 1 2 3 4 5 6 7 8 **9 10**	Measurement, indices.
Irregular areas.	K 1 2 3 4 5 6 7 8 **9 10**	Area, length.

Brief descriptions

Title of activity	Appropriate grades (shaded)	Mathematical features
Iceberg towing.	K 1 2 3 4 5 6 7 **8 9 10**	Volume, estimation, problem solving.
Triple dead heat.	K 1 2 3 4 5 6 7 **8 9 10**	Probability, computers.

Chapter 13 — Iteration — numerical methods

Title of activity	Appropriate grades (shaded)	Mathematical features
A calculator search for √2.	K 1 2 3 4 5 6 **7 8** 9 10	Calculators, estimation.
Area of a circle.	K 1 2 3 4 5 6 7 **8 9** 10	Area, estimation, calculators.
Quadratics.	K 1 2 3 4 5 6 7 8 **9 10**	Quadratic equations, calculators, estimation.

Brief descriptions

Title of activity	Appropriate grades (shaded)	Mathematical features
Number problems.	K 1 2 3 **4 5 6** 7 8 9 10	Whole number operations.
Find my side.	K 1 2 3 4 5 **6 7 8** 9 10	Area, calculators.
Drink can design.	K 1 2 3 4 5 6 7 **8 9 10**	Volume, surface area, calculators, visual imagery.

Outlines of the activities

Chapter 1
VIDEO

Snippets

This series of activities and the accompanying video clips are designed to illustrate ways in which mathematics is used in sporting and others events in the 'real world'. Pupils are encouraged to be actively involved in collecting information from the screen and discussing and working with the data. It is designed to illustrate how a short video clip can complement current classroom work across years three to twelve.

Heptathlon and Decathlon scoring systems

A videotape of highlights of the Heptathlon and Decathlon events in the 1984 Olympic Games at Los Angeles shows the interesting way in which mathematics is used in the scoring system for these events. Pupils learn the method of calculation and practise it. At the same time, they enjoy the excitement of world-class athletic performances by Glynis Nunn of Australia and Daley Thompson of the United Kingdom. There is one version for years 4 to 7 and another for years 8 to 12.

Maths of darts and Darts2

Videotapes of the 1986 Pacific Masters Darts Championship and 1986 Embassy World Darts Championships are used as highly motivating sources for learning mathematics. Children gain appreciation of the game of Darts, the scoring, mathematical strategies and logic needed. There is an important emphasis on quick mental calculation. The personalities of the game, in particular World Champion Eric Bristow, are also of great interest to pupils.

The mathematics of diving

Using videotape of the final of the women's 3 m Springboard event from the Los Angeles Olympic Games, pupils are introduced to the interesting scoring system used in Diving events. Pupils master and apply the scoring system, discover the important aspects of good diving, and enjoy the world-class athletic performances.

Simulation of the TAB

This lesson encourages pupils to gain a greater awareness of the way the TAB operates so their expectations are realistic if they decide in the future to 'invest' on the TAB. A full meeting of Harness Racing and Greyhound Racing is made available on the accompanying tape and teachers are encouraged to use this tape or similar material to confront the social issue of gambling. Pupils see how mathematics can empower them to have realistic expectations.

The mathematics of rowing

This activity uses videos from world championship events to involve pupils in some of the mathematics of rowing. Data that can be obtained directly from the screen allows pupils to calculate such things as stroke rating, speed of the boat and distance moved per stroke.

Ten pin bowling

This activity encourages pupils to learn the scoring system of Ten Pin Bowling, observe top class male and females bowlers, consider scoring implications in the event of consecutive 'strikes' and 'spares', and gain an insight into the skill of the game itself.

Chapter 2.
SOCIAL ISSUES

Everybody wins

By developing a mathematical model of the well known show game 'Clown', pupils discover that carnival games are usually more difficult than they first appear and that the odds are heavily stacked in favour of the operator. Pupils also see the way in which a computer can simulate the real experience, and consider the dilemma of the carnival operator who must offer tempting prizes, while still making a profit.

Danger distance

How far away does an oncoming car have to be before a person can safely cross the road? This activity challenges children to estimate, measure, calculate and cooperate in group tasks. As a result of their investigations, they can extend their thinking through thoughtful discussion. The purpose of the activity therefore is to use mathematics to explore the serious social issue of road safety, and in particular the judgment of speed and distances needed by pedestrians.

Baby in the car

Each summer, many infants suffer when well-meaning parents lock them in motor cars on hot days. This activity explores the reasons why babies suffer more than adults would in the same situation. By creating and improving a mathematical models of babies and adults using cubes, pupils are able to discover that the reasons lie in the relationship between volume and surface area.

Maths and Lotto

If a person pays to participate in any scheme they should know what to expect. Do pupils who are tomorrow's investors have a realistic idea of their chances of winning and the probability of losses? This activity, through a simplified version of the real game, is designed to enable pupils to gain more realistic expectations if they choose to participate.

Coin in the square

In this activity, children model the popular fairground game 'Coin in the Square'. Pupils investigate, through experiment, their chances of landing a coin strictly within the squares on the table. It also investigate the appropriate payouts for the game, and older pupils are encouraged to explore probability aspects.

Mortality quiz

Should Life Insurance statistics be used to teach mathematical probability or should the figures be used in the hope and expectation that pupils will be more aware of road realities and that this knowledge will make them safer road users. Both approaches are educationally sound, but this activity strongly presents the latter. Using a five question quiz, pupils draw on their collective experiences to discuss a range of social issues, including road safety and smoking.

The mathematics of hunger

The availability and distribution of essential foodstuffs such as protein or calories across our planet, is not equitable. Pupils use a mathematics analysis of the way resources are used to produce foodstuffs to confront the value systems that underpin this inequity.

Public versus private transport

Public transport is frequently criticized, but if all the train passengers used cars how far would this line of cars reach? This activity encourages pupils to investigate the social issue of the impact of this on traffic levels, fuel usage, costs and other areas.

Chapter 3
CONCEPT LEARNING — A FIRST PRINCIPLES APPROACH

Cats and kittens

This activity builds on the natural interest children have in cats and kittens, by exploring possible combinations of coloured kittens from single coloured parents. Children classify the various kittens and discuss and justify their conclusions. The well known story *The Three Little Kittens* is used as a 'springboard' for the work that follows.

This goes with this

This activity demonstrates the power of concrete aids in illustrating important mathematical concepts such as fractions, strip graphs, pie charts and percentages. The organisation and group work is such that a large amount of the pupils' personal data can be presented in an interesting and innovative way.

Volume of a room

This activity focuses on the concept of volume and illustrates how adding a variety of additional teaching strategies can enhance the quality of the learning environment. Pupils are encouraged to visualise a cubic metre, and then through instruction using sticks and plastic joins they actually "fill" the room with cubic metres. Mental imagery and a sense of estimation are evoked in this group activity.

Estimation with fractions

Much of the work traditionally tackled in fractions focuses almost entirely on skills. This activity, through concentrating on the concept of a fraction, seeks to improve both the understanding of the meaning of fractions and the pupils' estimates of these through whole group and individual activities. Pupils almost always demonstrate a considerable improvement through the activity.

First principles percentage

Pupils are often presented with 'rules without reasons'. This activity encourages the first principles understanding of the concept of percentage through carefully graded problems. For each problem the pupils are encouraged to carefully set out their work, verbalise their reasoning within a group of four and then several pupils are chosen to explain the steps to the rest of the group.

Backtracking

The solution of linear equations frequently takes several weeks' work at the end of which many pupils remain confused. The process of 'backtracking' where pupils are able to link equations to a form of 'reality' is highly successful in giving greater meaning and enjoyment to this topic.

Sliding ladder

This activity introduces sines and cosines using concrete experiences. Through small group activity and some historical background, this activity provides a suitable introduction to trigonometry, as pupils gain a 'feeling' for the changes in sines and cosines as angles increase.

419

How many subtraction problems have the answer 419? This challenge is posed to small groups of pupils. Important concepts of subtraction are exposed through this variation to 'traditional' approaches. Strategy development and discussion are additional features of this activity.

Weighing it up

This activity requires young children to sort a variety of objects using simple scales into order from lightest to heaviest. Pupils work in pairs on this task.

Cordial relations

Ratio is a difficult concept to understand. Much of the mathematics used at the school and in the community assumes that children understand it. This primary activity uses the experience of children as frequent cordial drinkers and encourages them to verbalise their thinking on a range of problems, to devise further problems and to illustrate and provide solutions to these for the rest of the group.

Chapter 4
PHYSICAL/ OUTDOORS

Maths in motion

This range of activities has as a central idea children being (representing) numbers moving around and being physically involved. They are presented with a range of number problems and groups of children act out the roles involved in these tasks while the rest of the class encourages and offers advice.

Bingo bodies

This version of Bingo encourages teachers to involve their pupils as physical 'counters' playing the game Bingo. Quick mental computation, estimation, number facts and the use of calculator all combine in an enjoyable problem solving activity. With both an indoor and outdoor component, a traditional skill-based task is enriched through an injection of a range of interesting features.

Platonic solids

Platonic solids have all faces and angles the same. In this activity children develop their visual imagery and an appreciation of basic structures, their stability and properties through constructing models using large sticks and plastic joins. Euler's rule is also introduced.

How far is it around a circle?

This outdoor activity provides an excellent introduction to the concept of pi and the way in which it is involved in the relationship between ratio and circumference. Pupils make predictions about the circumference of circles for various radii and paste these out. A rough approximation of pi is developed in an easily retained, straightforward way.

Algebra walk

Using outdoor axes, pupils are placed on the x axis, and through a variety of operations on the number between their feet, striking images of straight lines emerge. This activity promotes interesting discussion and develops and creates 'episodes' in the pupils' minds. These episodes can be successfully drawn upon during later pencil and paper work.

Trigonometry walk

Through pupils' physical experience of walking the sine and later the cosine of various angles a strong mental image of the relationship between the angle and length is created. These cognitive images can then be used in formal situations back in the classroom. They provide a concrete basis for understanding sine and cosine.

Outdoor Pythagoras

This activity uses estimation, the outdoors, careful measurement and calculators to demonstrate the accuracy of Pythagoras' Theorem. The triangles formed and worked with are 'real' and this activity provides a refreshing alternative to the typical textbook approach.

Estimating lengths

Pupils' concepts of metric length are assessed and improved through this enjoyable outdoor activity where pupils see that their error in estimation decreases over time.

Regular polygons

Using a long piece of string, groups of pupils create various regular polygons, carrying out appropriate checks using blackboard protractors to investigate the accuracy of these.

How long is your pace?

This activity encourages pupils to observe the way in which pace lengths change under various conditions. Most pupils greatly underestimate their pace lengths. The data is collected outside and pupils plot their results on a graph and discuss them.

The 40 second walk

Pupils are challenged to walk to a distant object (for example, a tree), arriving there in exactly 40 seconds. The task is therefore to judge the pace (as this must be constant), in such a way to arrive as near as possible to the time. This can be tried for a range of distances.

Walk the plank

The concept of positive and negative numbers is often a difficult one for pupils to grasp. This outdoor activity provides a gradual and enjoyable introduction to the topic.

Incentre of a triangle & Circumcentre of a triangle

In these activities, one pupil places a hidden object (for example, a coin) at the incentre/circumcentre of a triangle. Through the use of mirrors and other strategies, groups of pupils attempt to find the missing object.

The three-way tug of war

This outdoor activity provides the sort of experience from which understandings about angles and vectors develop. Whilst the normal tug of war relies largely on brute strength, this three-way version is a contest of tactics and ability, which presents important vector properties in a memorable, if exhausting way.

Chapter 5

WRITING ABOUT MATHEMATICS

Children writing about calculators

Young children are provided with calculators and are encouraged, in a non-structured way, to explore the calculator, its physical features and its capabilities. Through discussion with other pupils and the teacher and through writing about the experience, their discoveries can be shared, modified as necessary and consolidated.

Tell me a story (Primary)

In this activity pupils learn that most graphs tell a story. A graph is presented showing the depth of water in a bath over a period of time. Pupils work in pairs to write a story that could explain the graph and then act this out for the rest of the group. The other pupils are encouraged to check each story for its accuracy in explaining the actual graph.

Tell me a story (Post-Primary)

This secondary activity illustrates the way in which Distance-Time graphs can tell a story. Pupils are presented with a graph showing the movement of a variety of cars along a straight road. In small groups they each write a story or dialogue which relates to the experiences of the passengers in a designated car. Having prepared the story, pupils read and/or act it out, while the rest of the class assesses its fidelity to the graph.

Favourite number

In this activity, young children are asked to select their favourite number or are presented with one of a number of mathematical concepts such as 'equals', 'odd', 'even', 'one half', and so on. Given this as a basis the pupils are asked to write about things they know — their mathematical understandings about this number or concept. These are shared with the rest of the group, providing the teacher with an opportunity to discuss the properties or meanings of these for the information of all.

Inflationary language

In this activity, children are encouraged to use Victor Borge's *Inflationary Language* as a stimulus for creative writing. They generate a list of 'number words', perform 'operations' on them, and challenge the rest of the class to crack the code. The mathematical content is fairly minimal, but it's a lot of fun!

Chapter 6
MENTAL ARITHMETIC

Sum stories

In this middle primary mental arithmetic activity, pupils are presented with a mathematical operation and asked to verbalise a range of situations where such a calculation might occur. This discussion is directed by the teacher and pupils see the wide variety of applications of a given calculation.

Today's number is ...

The teacher provides the answer, and the pupils are required to come up with a range of questions that would give this answer. These are carefully classified on the board and a particular class of these is drawn upon for particular consideration by the teacher and the class.

How did you do it?

This activity encourages pupils to verbalise their reasonings as they mentally solve the problem. Pupils (and teachers) are frequently amazed by the variety and sophistication of the methods articulated by this process. Pupils are able to watch themselves thinking, discover that there are many successful ways to tackle problems, and that they use different sorts of approaches when pen and paper are not available or necessary.

Think of a number

Children are asked to think of a number between 1 and 10. The teachers gives a succession of mathematical operations to perform on that number and to the amazement of children immediately tells them their answer. The beauty of these exercises is that they can be tackled at many levels, the analyses are fascinating and they can be used as a very motivating introduction to algebra.

More than, less than

Pupils estimate a variety of distances and other measures by 'bracketing' their estimates. Group consensus is required at each stage. Pupils are encouraged to articulate their reasoning. The power of outer limits when estimating is exposed. This activity has potential for extensions into time, volume, capacity and area and so encourages teachers to take a structured detailed approach and apply it in a range of areas.

Find my number

The teacher has a number in mind that only he or she knows. Through carefully thought out questions, the children attempt to narrow down the possibilities. The teacher can initially only answer yes or no. The notion of good questions is highlighted, as pupils problem solving ability develops through the task.

Hangman

Hangman, which is normally thought of as a language game, can also be an excellent way to involve children in mathematics. This activity uses a code making machine to convert words by mathematical processes to code and vice versa. Using mental arithmetic and group and individual work, pupils also discover the frequency with which various letters occur in common words.

Brief descriptions of other mental activities

These brief activities challenge many of the assumptions that underlie the' traditional' approach to mental arithmetic. Through a variety of simple yet powerful hints, teachers are encouraged to approach mental arithmetic in a new, enjoyable and involving way.

VOLUME TWO

Chapter 7.
VISUAL IMAGERY

Krazy kennels

In this junior primary activity, children are challenged to use sticks and plastic joins to build a variety of dog kennels in preparation for a Dog Show. As well as working from the diagram to create a model, they are encouraged to build other structures using the equipment. Children work in groups and there is a lot of discussion surrounding the results of their efforts and the mathematics involved.

Silence

In this group activity, a series of standard shapes are cut into either two or three pieces each. The resulting pieces are distributed amongst the players of the game. In absolute silence, children are encouraged to pass one of their pieces across to another person in order that the other person may eventually complete their own shape. Cooperation is essential as pupils may give but never take. The rule of silence ensures that all pupils are actively involved, and this activity can be presented at a variety of levels.

Footsteps over Australia

This scale drawing and estimation activity assigns a capital city to each pupil in the group. Using a suggested scale they are encouraged to visually memorise the position of this state relative to Melbourne. Outdoors, the Map of Australia is reproduced as pupils use the position of Melbourne and an appropriate scale to determine the location of their city.

Map of Australia

This activity illustrates the way in which different people form different mental images. The ability to estimate areas and proportions is a vital mathematical skill. Our preconceived ideas of sizes and proportions of even familiar objects is quite often nothing like reality. This activity encourages pupils to compare their images with the reality of the relative sizes of the states of Australia. This is followed by problem solving where the children are challenged to validate the figures that the teacher has provided.

Introductory Pythagoras

This secondary activity assists pupils to develop a concept of the relationships between sides of right angled triangles. The historical problem that was originally posed on a Babylonian clay tablet around 300 B.C. is used to stimulate interest in the activity to follow. Imagery, estimation and cooperative group work are used to improve measuring and graphing skills and the ability to interpret graphically-represented relationships.

Venus

NASA scientists were confronted with a challenging job when given the task of finding a suitable landing spot for their short range motor car because they couldn't see the target area. In a similar way, in this lesson the pupils are presented with a sealed box inside which flat and sloping surfaces and simple geometric shapes are placed. They are then challenged to chart the 'surface' in a logical way, assisted by a computer. The aim is to chart the most cost efficient route from one point to another. This activity illustrates the power of mathematical models, as well as presenting an historical background to the task.

Draw my house

Young children are asked to imagine themselves at the front door of their home. They are then asked to imagine a walk through their house and sketch an overall map labelling various rooms. This is checked by parents who carry out a similar task, with follow-up discussion.

Photo sort

A range of photographs are taken as the viewer moves around an object. These are shuffled and children are asked to order them as they might have been taken.

Mental map

People frequently instruct each other over the phone as to directions between places. In this activity, one person with a street directory writes down or describes a possible way of getting between A and B. This is then 'acted upon' by the second person sketching their image of the described journey. Discussion follows.

Belt around the earth

In this activity, pupils are asked to visualise a steel belt around the equator of the Earth. They are told that approximately six metres have been added to the length of this belt and they are asked to indicate their perceptions of how high above the Earth the belt would now rise. This question is then investigated mathematically.

How far can you go?

Pupils are challenged to (mentally) follow a series of instructions with their eyes closed, constructing a detailed diagram in their mind. They are asked to raise their hand at the stage at which they lose track of it in their mind and immediately draw as much as they can of it. The resulting diagrams are discussed, and pupils who have followed all nine steps discover that they have created Tangram pieces.

Chapter 8
COMPUTERS

Five modem activities

This activity explores one segment of the potential of computers and modems in creating learning environments. Specifically, activities are arranged between two schools requiring an interchange of data necessary to the activity. This data is only accessible in one or other location, necessitating its sharing. A typical question that is posed is 'Is our class heavier than yours?'

Billiard ball bounces

Pupils are given the task of finding how many bounces a billiard ball will make before it goes into a pocket on a range of different size tables. Then the problem is posed - can the pupils predict the number of bounces for any size table? This requires a collection of data which is analysed by small groups and a formula is generated. Having found the rule, pupils use it to make and test predictions.

Eight queens

Placing eight queens on a chess board so that none can capture any of the others is quite a challenge. In this outdoor activity, pupils work cooperatively on a large grid and discover that they must employ a systematic approach in order to solve a challenging puzzle.

Biggest volume

Pupils create different sized boxes from the same size rectangular paper by cutting different size squares from the corners. When compared it is clear that the volumes of the boxes vary. In small groups, the whole class then systematically investigates methods in finding the dimensions of the box that has the biggest volume, by experiment, using calculators and computers. The hands-on approach is particularly helpful to non abstract thinkers.

Eratosthenes revisited

During 1985, several schools across Australia were linked electronically in order to replicate the famous historical experiment by Eratosthenes. When the sun was directly overhead one of the schools, each other school measured the angles of the sun's rays and transmitted their results to all other schools by computer-linked electronic mail. Each group of pupils then used the data to make calculations of the circumference of the earth just as Eratosthenes did. These can be averaged to produce a final result. Pupils can be linked with other schools interstate, or use the data provided in the lesson.

How close can you stand to a painting?

When viewing a painting a person can be too close or alternatively too far away. Where is the ideal spot? In this activity calculators and computers are used to model the situation mathematically as the distance that gives maximum viewing angle is determined.

Projectiles

This lesson actually *encourages* pupils to toss chalk into a rubbish bin as the basis of a mathematics lesson. Pupils enjoy testing their skills at throwing but also the mathematical challenge of determining a typical projectile path, considering angle, speed and time. A computer is used to model the path also.

Cones

Pupils create various cones from the same sized circles by cutting out different sized sectors. When compared, it is clear that the cones vary in volume. An investigation, by experiment, and the use of a computer follows to determine which sized angle cutout produces the cone with the biggest volume.

The human computer

This activity involves pupils physically simulating a computer and shows that the sum of the computer is greater than its parts. A team of five or six pupils faces the class and using a conversion sheet of binary and decimal numbers, by raising and lowering hands they carry out a number of calculations.

Pythagoras — area proof

The computer gives a visual proof of Pythagoras Theorem. Pupils, using triangular cardboard cutouts can physically transform one diagram into another thereby using imagery to 'prove' the theorem. The role of the computer is that of an electronic blackboard in generating a dynamic 'cartoon affect' of the transformation of one diagram into another.

Chapter 9
ESTIMATION

Mallet

This activity, using a mixture of maths and ballet (hence the title), encourages teachers to integrate mathematics with other areas of curriculum. Estimation, an increasingly essential skill, is approached through practical activity where pupils in pairs carry out a range of tasks involving estimation and testing of estimates.

Pupil growth

Physical growth patterns of pupils over the years are quite fascinating and present a great opportunity for interesting analysis. Which year level will grow the most during the school year? If all the pupils in year 5 were placed head to toe how far would they stretch? How much would they weigh? How much **more** would they weigh at the end of the year? In small groups, pupils take the measurements required to answer these and other questions. The results are generally quite surprising.

Estimation — a general structure

A range of different activities which use the same 3-part organisational structure.

Pupils are challenged to make **estimates** of measures such as length, angle or time. The correct answers are provided, errors calculated and the students ability is qualified.

Different methods of estimation are discussed and then practised.

A second set of estimation challenges is given. Pupils' performance is again qualified and any improvement is noted.

Estimation of percentages

In this junior secondary activity, pupils focus on the concept of percentage in an interesting and enjoyable estimation activity. A glass measuring cylinder with a graduated scale is filled to a variety of levels and pupils are challenged to estimate the percentage that the measuring cylinder is full. Pupils find that as the lesson proceeds their discrimination improves considerably as well as their understanding of the concept of percentages. This is best illustrated by a graph showing their errors during that lesson.

Tailor made

Pupils are shown 200 milligrams of rice on a table. They are asked to make a container of any shape they wish that would hold exactly that amount of rice. By trial and error pupils used cardboard and masking tape and refine their containers until they hold very close to 200 milligrams. The wide variety of shapes so generated provides a basis for a good discussion. A second part of the activity involves pupils preparing 'jackets' for a variety of wooden solids and recording the capacity of the solids that emerge.

There and back

Pupils are challenged to visualise themselves being at the front of the school gate. Pupils asked to visualise themselves walking exactly one kilometre in an agreed direction, and predict where they would finish. The range of responses are then discussed. The pupils mark their images of one kilometre on a photocopy on a map of the local area, on which the scale is hidden. Pupils then, under parent supervision, travel exactly a kilometre and compare their perceptions with reality.

Calculator snooker

Following a brief introduction in which a basic understanding of snooker is developed using on pupils' experiences and possibly videotape of a snooker game, pupils take part in an activity which simulates a game of snooker. They have to estimate the result of calculations and make decisions which correspond with the selection of a particular coloured ball to be potted. There is a considerable emphasis here on mental computation and estimation.

Chapter 10
STORY-SHELL FRAMEWORKS

Licorice factory

Using a fantasy story about a factory in which licorice is produced, pupils are presented with a concept lesson on prime numbers. Pupils develop logical strategies for concluding the investigation. Strong links to the story-shell increase the chances of long-term retention of the concept of prime numbers.

How many can stand in your classroom?

Pupils are asked to imagine a situation in which they are responsible for selling tickets to either a sporting event or a pop concert for an area of standing room about the size of the classroom. Pupils are asked to predict the number of people that they could reasonably accommodate in this space, and then to suggest and explore a range of possible strategies for testing these predictions. Pupils are frequently staggered by the number of people that could comfortably stand in their classroom.

Mirror bounce

How did the artists who decorated the pharaoh's tomb have enough light to work? We know it wasn't oil lamps or candles because there are no deposits of carbon on the walls or ceiling. Possibly it was by highly polished metal mirrors reflecting sunlight. This story-shell introduces some interesting mathematical problems. What angles would you need to hold the mirrors? What size mirrors would be needed? What loss of intensity would there be? Pupils are physically involved in simulating the bouncing of light by mirrors with the eventual aim of hitting a target on the blackboard and discussing the results.

Stories as springboards

Children's stories have considerable potential for use as a springboard for mathematics activities. There are several brief examples outlining how a simple story can provide rich mathematical experiences. The section also provides a bibliography of such stories indicating the particular mathematical topics covered.

Chapter 11
GROUP INVESTIGATIONS AND PROBLEM SOLVING

Money trails

Money trails are frequently used by schools and other organisations for fund-raising. In this activity the question is posed as to how far a money trail which goes from the classroom to the school gate would raise. Following the pupils' estimates, pupils work in groups to discover what the actual value of the money trail would be.

Spirolateral walk

Spirolaterals are a well known mathematical concept. This activity, through the addition of the physical outdoor component enriches the experience for children. Children move through a series of spirolaterals in an attempt to reproduce these on paper. The question is posed as to whether pupils can predict for a spirolateral of any order whether it will be open or closed. The same process can be simulated using the computer.

The shape of things

In the three activities that form this unit, pupils are discovering a lot about the various measurements of their body. The emphasis is on measurement in small groups, prediction and discovery.

Mindreader

In this activity, a clever number trick is presented to the pupils, and they are then empowered to use the same trick. Some pupils are also able to investigate why the trick works in an interesting way.

Fermi problems

The essence of a Fermi problem is that a reasonably well-informed person can solve it approximately by a series of estimates. These problems also have the characteristic that most people who encounter them instantly respond that it is a problem that they could not possibly solve without recourse to some reference material. Pupils see that through a series of simple steps using only common sense and their experience they can quite often come up with reasonable estimates for the problems. Pupils work in small groups to create and solve such problems.

Four cube houses

The task here is find all the possible combinations of four cube houses that can be created with the provision that the blocks touch face to face. Pupils create a variety of models and then investigate the cost of each of these given a range of criteria.

Soma cube

This problem-solving activity examines the history and mathematical basis of this popular puzzle. Pupils are given an initial set of conditions for joining unit cubes together. By experiment and then by analysis all possible pieces are discovered. The dimensional drawing is a feature of the activity. Finally a range of soma-cube puzzles are presented.

Add the numbers 1 – 100

This lessons begins with a promise that at the end of the lesson all pupils will be able to add the numbers from 1 to 100 or 1 to 1000 or even 1 to 1 million within 30 seconds. The promise is fulfilled as pupils are introduced to the simple yet powerful technique developed by Carl Frederick Gauss, and explore a range of problems of increasing complexity. A race with the computer is also a feature of this activity.

Tinker, tailor — male or female?

In this activity pupils discuss their perceptions of the relative proportions of males and females in particular occupations, consider the actual figures, and then explore the extent to which the reality is reflected in the subjects and the problems in textbooks. It is frequently the case that textbooks do not reflect the increasing extent to which females are working in non-traditional occupations.

Balancing act

Using the common primary school balance children are challenged with a series of problems to balance a range of weights on one side with a number of weights on the other. Useful discussion and mathematical concepts arise from this experience.

What's my number?

Using sticky paper, children each have a number that is not known to them stuck on their back. Through asking their friends one question each, to which the answer can only be yes or no, they eventually determine their number. Children learn that some questions are far more powerful and useful to ask than others.

Cooperative logic

This activity encourages pupils to work in groups, where each member of the group has an important aspect of the information necessary for the solution of the problem. This 'forced' cooperation has proved quite powerful in encouraging groups to share the load.

How long to see a million dollars?

Pupils discuss their perceptions on how long it would take a million dollars of cars to pass the school gate. The survey work then takes place in front of the school with pupils making a note of the type of cars that pass during a fixed period. Using newspaper advertisements for new and used cars and the data collected from outside, pupils are able to discover the value of cars passing the school.

Chapter 12
MATHEMATICAL MODELLING

Carrot patch people

The claim is frequently made that every *Cabbage Patch* person is unique. Pupils model the real situation and investigate the number of combinations that are possible, concluding with the fact that it is certainly theoretically possible for all *Cabbage Patch* people to be different.

Final five

In the Australian Rules Final Five ladder arrangements, it is the case that teams in different positions have vastly different chances of reaching the Grand Final and winning the premiership. Pupils model this activity through the role of the dice and the movement of counters. The assumptions of the model are then discussed.

Only a matter of time!

Pupils frequently collect 'free' swap cards with the challenge being to collect the full set. This activity models such a process and pupils' perceptions are contrasted with mathematical reality. The assumptions of the model are then considered in the light of pupils' experiences.

Dice cricket

Pupils play an enjoyable game of *Dice cricket* using dice to generate their run scores. As well as discussing the results and those that are produced by a computer simulation, they discover that mathematics can predict fairly closely the sort of results they are likely to get. An interesting discussion then follows on the strengths and weaknesses of the model, and pupils have the opportunity to improve and test variations of the model.

Speed graphs

In this application of linear graphs pupils use their understanding of linear graphs to model their movement when walking and jogging. An outdoor experiment is followed by its representation on a distance time graph and certain key features are taken from the graph. Predictions of the model are further tested by outdoor activity.

Head turning

In this activity, pupils discover how the physical act of turning your head to watch a car go past can be modelled mathematically. An outdoor experience, use of computer, and the idea of a limit are notable features of the activity. Once the initial model has been created it can be systematically explore in a variety of levels of complexity.

Nails

If a manufacturer was wanting to produce a range of nails, one might expect him or her to make each length a linear measure a regular amount more than the previous length. In fact this is not the case as pupils discover when they measure it. This activity leads to a study of percentage increases the mathematics of exponential growth and the notion of mathematical modelling.

Irregular areas

Pupils are used to carrying out a range of calculations to find the area of *regular* figures. This activity considers irregular areas such as golf greens and pupils are challenged to develop strategies for measuring such areas. As well as the pupils' methods, two other formal methods are also presented to them.

Triple dead heat

Triple dead heats have only occurred four times in the history of Australian racing. In this activity pupils develop a model of a race in order that the chances of a dead heat can be considered and the mathematical predictions compared to reality.

Iceberg towing

In recent years, there has been considerable discussion about the feasibility of towing an iceberg from the Antarctic to Australia, with a view to using the water that this would produce. Pupils investigate the feasibility of this with considerations of volume, size and cost.

Chapter 13
ITERATION — NUMERICAL METHODS

A calculator search for √2

Situations are created here in which pupils can appreciate something of the historical development of mathematics through considering some of the problems faced by ancient mathematicians. Pupils come to appreciate something of the toolbox of mathematical techniques which are available to contemporary mathematicians.

Area of a circle

Given the area of a circle, many pupils have difficulty determining the radius of the circle. By applying the first principle' or numericals method approach and with the extensive use of calculators, the concept of iteration is developed and pupils with a range of abilities are able to solve a series of problems.

Quadratics

The typical algebraic problem such as $x^2 + 4x - 10 = 0$ can be thought of as 'a number multiplied by a number four bigger gives ten'. Using a calculator in an iterative approach pupils can find solutions in an increasingly efficient way, and one more closely tied to their intuitions.

Number problems

In this primary activity, pupils are challenged to find two numbers which add to a particular number and multiply to give another particular number. Calculators are used to enable pupils to get closer and closer to the actual answers.

Find my side

Given the area of a square, pupils are asked (without using the square root key) to iteratively 'zoom in' on the correct value of the side length. Considerable discussion and the development of useful concepts can occur.

Drink-can design

Pupils are presented with the situation of a company hiring a mathematician to design a drink can. Using a range of practical criteria and a fixed volume, the pupils are asked to develop a range of possible drink cans, and to discuss the most feasible and agreeable size.

Real maths — school maths, a videotape of a very different style, a discussion starter for teachers and parents, is available from the same address.

VIDEO

Chapter one

The role of video in the mathematics classroom

Purpose

This chapter and the related video programs illustrate and encourage teachers to explore particular styles of video use. In this way, teachers can evaluate and adopt such styles, where appropriate, as part of their regular teaching practice. The particular aspects of video use that MCTP has chosen to emphasise are those that

(a) involve students actively;

(b) bring data from real contexts into the classroom.

(a) The active component is achieved partly by the deliberate organisation of the video so that data or information required by the pupil is supplied directly from the screen, often requiring direct pupil participation by counting, measuring or timing.

(b) The 'real data' aspect is achieved partly by using video footage (with permission) from news telecasts, sporting events or television advertisements. By using such contexts, a major outcome is learning about those

> **(Videos) demonstrate many uses and applications of mathematics that influence our lifestyles and surround our daily living.**

contexts and an appreciation of the role mathematics plays within them. For example, in *The mathematics of diving* pupils learn about the sport of diving and the role mathematics plays within the scoring system. It is not a contrived situation, merely to teach the skills relating to decimals or averages.

Rationale

In spite of the availability of over 400 mathematical films for a number of years, less than half of primary and secondary teachers have ever used a maths film (Bestgen & Reys, 1982). For those who have, the overwhelming majority cited *Donald in Mathemagic Land* as the one film they had used.

Videotapes are proving to be a far more satisfactory medium than film, in ease and cost of production, and convenience in their presentation to audiences. The growing interest in the use of videos in mathematics education is confirmed by the establishment of the Television, Video and Film division of the Technology Theme Group at the 1984 conference of the International Congress on Mathematics Education, held in Adelaide.

The recent emphasis in videos on the active involvement of pupils was identified as a key element in classroom videos by Koumi, as quoted by Roseveare (1986) — *'active (mindful) learning'*. In recent years, the availability of VHS video recorders in both primary and secondary schools and pre-service education institutions has resulted in a dramatic increase in the production of videotapes in the mathematics education community, with considerable variation in purpose and quality.

The videos currently available can be categorised as follows:

• **Videos showing teachers 'in action',** to create discussion on appropriate teaching and learning styles.

• **Videos showing children at work in classrooms.** These enable teachers to observe children as they engage in planned or unplanned learning experiences. They also enable children to see themselves at work in the classroom and, therefore, to reflect on what they did (and what they could have done).

• **Videos showing noted maths educators discussing their views** of mathematics education.

• **Instructional videos designed to be used by individuals** to focus on particular mathematical techniques.

• **Videos to stimulate discussion on particular issues or themes** within mathematics education.

• **Videos produced for direct use with children in classrooms.** These videos bring real data into the classroom, to enable maths learning to have a more active and relevant context.

All of these types of videos have their place in education, according to circumstances. However, as described above, it is the last type that MCTP has chosen to emphasise. *The mathematics of diving* is a good example of this inter-active type of use.

While the dominant theme of the MCTP tapes is mathematics as it is used in sport, this was not originally intended, but arose because of availability of footage and because of the positive response from teachers and subsequent suggestions for other videos to be produced in the sporting area. As De Mestre has stated there is much potential in allowing children to develop and solve sports-oriented problems (De Mestre, 1987). Other areas that may well be developed in the future include social issues in cities such as traffic and populations counts and wildlife and conservation issues.

Research indicates that audio-visual presentations in the classroom setting strongly influence the kind of visual imagery which children store in their memories for future use (Salomon, 1972, 1974). Jaworski and Gates (1987, p. 98) have drawn special attention to the power of the video replay facility in enabling pupils and teachers to share events and concerns and to discuss pertinent issues immediately. They have also pointed out that if children establish a 'resonance' with what they view, then this provides an excellent basis for future classroom discussion. In explaining the term 'resonance' Jaworski and Gates (p. 99) gave the following fourth century quotation from St Augustine's *De Magister* which, they said, captured beautifully what the term meant in the context of video:

If anyone hears me speak of them (images of things once perceived), provided he has seen them himself, he does not learn from my words, but recognises the truth of what I say by the images which he has in his own memory. But if he has not had these sensations, obviously he believes my words rather than learns from them. When we have to do with things which we behold with the mind, ... we speak of things which we look upon directly in the inner light of truth.

Our experiences in trialling the MCTP videos in classrooms has led us to believe that they resonate with school learners. By viewing them children are given a stimulating basis for future learning.

An example illustrating the features of the use of these types of videos

In *The mathematics of diving*, the Women's Springboard Diving event from the Los Angeles Olympic Games is used to highlight the interesting way mathematics is used in the scoring system. This tape exemplifies a number of powerful features of the use of videos in classrooms:

• They provide informative and entertaining opportunities for explorations into mathematics by presenting data from 'the real world'. The diving tape presents top class sporting competition involving real data.

• They demonstrate many uses and applications of mathematics that influence our life-styles and surround our daily living. Pupils are encouraged to see that the mathematics of decimals and averages has effective application outside the classroom.

• They supply a concrete visual basis for conceptual thinking and thereby reduce the emphasis on textbook presentations, which too often have a level of reading and communication standards which prohibit some pupils from learning. Presenting diving scores on the screen and having the scoring system explained to the pupils by an authority on the sport, with opportunities to pause the tape for clarification, has meant that all pupils can participate and succeed.

• Since much of the instruction is on the videotape, the teacher is freed to concentrate on observing the pupils and giving assistance where necessary. Teachers who trialled the diving tape commented that they were able to move around the classroom as the tape explained the process, spotting and resolving any misconceptions and taking time to observe the pupils in action.

Experiences from trialling — some important points to consider when using MCTP videos

• It is essential that each video is previewed prior to use by the teacher, and the calculations involved (if any), worked through.

• Pause or stop the tape as required in order to clear up any misconceptions or difficulties. However, teachers should resist the temptation to intervene for lengthy periods, as this often disrupts the continuity of the activity.

• The videos should not be used as a teacher-substitute. Effective use of video requires comprehensive teacher involvement, before, sometimes during, and certainly after the viewing.

• Explaining to pupils the purpose of the use of video encourages students to see video as a legitimate, and growing aspect of mathematics education and not just trivial entertainment.

References

Bestgen, B.J., & Reys, R.E. (1982). *Films in the mathematics classroom.* Virginia: National Council of Teachers of Mathematics.

De Mestre, N. (1987). Mathematics and sport. *Australian Mathematics Teacher,* 43(4), 2-6.

Jaworski, B., & Gates, P. (1987). Use of classroom video for teacher inservice education. In J.C. Bergeron, N. Herscovics, & C. Kieran (Eds.), *Proceedings of the Eleventh International Conference on the Psychology of Mathematics Education, Vol. 2,* 93-99.

Roseveare, D. (1986). Television and video report. In J. Moyla (Ed.), *The role of technology (Theme Group 3 Report).* Adelaide: Fifth International Congress on Mathematical Education, 89.

Salomon, G. (1972). Can we affect cognitive skills through visual media? An hypothesis and initial findings. AV *Communication Review, 20,* 401-422.

Salomon, G. (1974). Internalization of filmic schematic operations in interaction with learners' aptitudes. *Journal of Educational Psychology, 66*(4), 499-511.

Activities in other chapters with video components

Danger distance (Ch. 2).
Mallet (Ch. 9).
Calculator snooker (Ch. 9).

Bob Beamon breaks the world record for the long jump. Children can mark their estimate of a world-class jump, and then compare it with the reality of 8.90 metres. (See Snippet 4, page 34).

Snippets

The variety of video clips we have put together here show how mathematics is used in sporting and other events in the real world.

As in the other video material, the purpose is to illustrate the capacity of video to bring the real world into the classroom, and do this in a way that actively involves pupils in collecting information from the screen.

With each video clip, there are suggested classroom activities. These are examples only. We encourage you to further develop any aspects that will enrich your teaching programs.

These snippets are designed to complement current classroom work and are not intended as 'one-offs'. For example, the first two snippets could be a good application for the topic of linear measurement.

Years 4 ↓ 10   VIDEO

Features of this activity

- Realistic application of mathematics.
- Pupils are involved actively in obtaining data directly from the screen.
- Outdoor activities in several snippets.
- The Eratosthenes' experiment provides an interesting historical background to a mathematical task.
- Involves estimation, measurement, perception, decimals and calculator use.

SUGGESTED LEVELS

OUTDOOR ACTIVITIES

SNIPPET NUMBER	1	2	3	4	5	6	7	8	9	10	11	12	13
MIDDLE / UPPER PRIMARY	✔	✔	✔	✔			✔			✔	✔	✔	
JUNIOR SECONDARY	✔	✔	✔	✔	✔	✔	✔	✔	✔	✔	✔	✔	
MIDDLE / UPPER SECONDARY	✔	✔	✔	✔	✔	✔	✔	✔	✔	✔	✔	✔	✔

EXTENSIVE CLASS WORK

THIS ACTIVITY IS PART OF THE MCTP PROFESSIONAL DEVELOPMENT PACKAGE FROM THE CURRICULUM DEVELOPMENT CENTRE, CANBERRA

We gratefully acknowledge the considerable assistance of the Ten Television Network in making much of the footage available for classroom use. We also thank Mr Michael Ryan of the Monash University Educational Technology Service for his highly skilled contributions in the development of the finished products.

SNIPPET 1   How long is a running pace?

Pupils are shown a video clip of the final of the men's 100 metres race at the 1984 Olympic Games at Los Angeles and are challenged to calculate the average length of the winner's (Carl Lewis') pace, by counting the number of paces and dividing that number into 100 metres.

THIS ACTIVITY RELATES CLOSELY TO THE ACTIVITY *'HOW LONG IS YOUR PACE?'* (page 233) AND SNIPPETS 2 AND 3.

> PREPARATION
> A tape or metre rule for measuring up to three metres.

'The 100 metres is considered by many as the purest of all athletic events; no need for tactical considerations of concern about conserving energy here. It is just one mighty explosion of speed from gun to finish, with time perhaps for only three huge lungfuls of air along the way.'

from: D. Emery and S. Greenberg, *World Sporting Records*, The Bodley Head, London, 1986.

Counting at normal speed is a real challenge. Even at slow motion, some people have difficulty. Ask the pupils who find the task straightforward to share their methods.
Some methods found in trials schools were:
• Counting every pace.
• Counting only the right foot (1, 3, 5...).
• Counting only the left foot (2, 4, 6...).
Note: Children found that the rate of counting could be maintained even when the view is obscured.

The answer is 43½ paces although some would argue for greater accuracy.
Therefore the average pace length is 100 ÷ 43.5 ≈ 2.3 m .

METHOD

1. Gather the class around the video monitor. Participation is greatly enhanced if all pupils have a clear and close view of the screen.

2. Count the paces. Show the men's 100 metres race. Pupils focus on the eventual winner, Carl Lewis of the United States. The challenge is to count his paces for 100 metres.

first play the tape at normal speed, then pausing after the run for class discussion,

second tell the class that this next time they will see the race in slow motion, thereby making counting easier using whichever strategy they decide.

3. Mark out the distance 2.3 metres. Pupils are often quite surprised at how great is this distance.

EXTENSIONS

The 'average' pace. Does that mean all paces are the same size?

a. There is a line across the track 20 metres from the start. This could be used to discriminate between the paces for the first 20 metres and the paces for the last 80 metres.

b. There is also a line 10 metres before the finish, and the last five metres are marked on the track. With slow motion and estimation, interesting analyses can be made.

c. Mark out five lines 2.3 metres apart and see if pupils can stride at this length.

SNIPPET 2

Does pace length relate to finishing position?

Using the same video clip as in Snippet 1 pupils select different runners and calculate their average pace length. These are then tabled and the pace length is compared to the position the runner finished.

1. Ask the pupils to speculate on the results

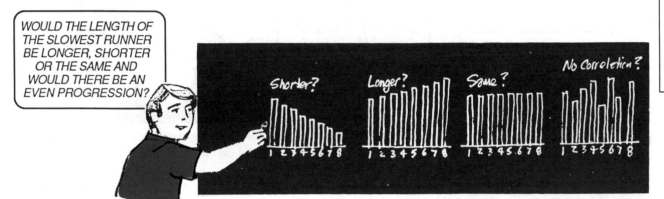

WOULD THE LENGTH OF THE SLOWEST RUNNER BE LONGER, SHORTER OR THE SAME AND WOULD THERE BE AN EVEN PROGRESSION?

Shorter?   Longer?   Same?   No Correlation?

Years 4 ↓ 10

VIDEO

2. Select a runner

Groups of children could 'own' a runner.

Be sure that every runner is covered. The nearest runner to the camera is in lane 8.

3. Calculate the average length of each runner's pace

Sometimes the runners are obscured and the counting is difficult. A few replays may be necessary.

4. Make a table of the results like in the table below.

Lane	Name	Country	Time	Place	Paces	Av. Pace
1	Ron Brown	U.S.A.	10.26 s	4th	46.5	2.15 m
2	Mike McFarlane	G.B.	10.27 s	5th	49.0	2.04 m
3	Tony Sharpe	Canada	!0.35 s	8th	46.0	2.17 m
4	Ben Johnson	Canada	10.22 s	3rd	47.0	2.13 m
5	Sam Graddy	U.S.A.	10.19 s	2nd	45.0	2.22 m
6	Donovan Reid	G.B.	10.33 s	7th	48.0	2.08 m
7	Carl Lewis	U.S.A.	9.99 s	1st	43.5	2.30 m
8	Roy Stewart	Jamaica	10.29 s	6th	45.5	2.20 m

Pupils may recall the incident in the film *Chariots of Fire* where the coach of Harold Abrahams points out that he is overstriding. He reduces the length of stride and wins the Gold Medal.

5. Compare the results with the original speculations

SNIPPET 3

Lewis takes 84 paces to cover the 200 metres. His average pace is therefore 200 ÷ 84 = 2.38 metres (approximately) — slightly longer than in the 100 metres.

PHOTO COURTESY REUTERS NEWS PICTURES.

Bob Beamon's world-record jump of 8.9 m at the 1968 Olympic Games in the high altitude at Mexico City.

'It was simply the most astonishing single exploit in track and field history..... a giant leap forward for mankind that was generations ahead of its' time'.

D. Emery and S. Greenberg, *World Sporting Records*, The Bodley Head, London, 1986.

Beamon beat the existing world record of 8.35 set the previous year. When Jessie Owens (USA) set the world record in 1935 (8.13 m), it then stood for 25 years, the longest time for a world record in a standard event to remain unbeaten. Will Bob Beamon's outlast him?

Pace length for 200 metres — Would you expect it to be longer or shorter than for 100 metres?

METHOD

1. Pose the question and tell pupils that you will be showing the final of the 200 metres race featuring Carl Lewis in lane 7, second front position at the start.

2. Invite the children to predict the answers and give reasons.

> I THINK THEY WILL BE LONGER BECAUSE IN THE 100 METRES HIS PACE GOT LONGER THE FURTHER HE RAN

> I THINK IT WILL BE SHORTER BECAUSE BEING FURTHER HE WOULD GET TIRED

> WHAT ABOUT THE BEND?

3. Play the video tape. The race is shown in both normal speed and in slow motion. Each child should do his or her own counting and calculation.

4. Discuss the reasons for this result (in hindsight).
Speculate on whether there would be a different result if the track were straight rather than around a bend.

PREPARATION
A tape measure or rule to measure up to ten metres.

SNIPPET 4   Long jump — perception and reality

Pupils are challenged to estimate how long world class athletes could possibly jump. These estimates are then compared with the performances shown on the video clip of Glynis Nunn (Australia), Daley Thompson (Great Britain), Carl Lewis (USA) and Gary Honey (Australia) and also the world record jump of 8.9 m by Bob Beamon in 1968.

METHOD

1. Pupils explore (preferably outside) **how far they can jump** and extrapolate this to how long a world-class athlete might jump. Record their estimates.

> WE CAN JUMP THIS FAR. I THINK A WORLD- CLASS ATHLETE SHOULD BE ABLE TO JUMP TWICE AS FAR

> YES! ABOUT TO HERE

2. Play the videotape. After watching the tape, ask students to mark out their perceptions of how far the athletes are jumping.

3. Tell students about Bob Beamon's world record

4. Have children mark out that distance and compare it with their estimates.
The highlight of this activity is often the visual impact of marking out the 8.9 m and comparing this to initial perceptions.

SNIPPET 5

Speed — 4000 metres team pursuit (cycling)

Children watch the event and estimate the average speed of the race, then calculate to check their estimations.

METHOD

1. **Tell pupils** that after the screening they will be calculating the actual speed, but as they watch the tape they are challenged to estimate the speed.
2. **Show the video tape** and record the estimations.
3. **Calculate the speed.** This may be done as a class activity or by pupils individually. Probably the easiest method is to use a calculator as follows:

Australia's winning pursuit cycling team.

4000 m in 4 : 25.9

= 4000 m in 265.99 seconds

= $\frac{4000}{265.99}$ m in one second

= 15.038 m in one second

= 15.038 x 3600 m in one hour

= 54137 m in one hour

= 54.137 km/h

SNIPPET 6

Speed — women's 4 x 100 metres relay — How fast do the winners move the baton?

The smooth baton changeover between Cheeseborough (third leg) and Ashford (final leg) for the U.S.A.

METHOD

1. **Let the children watch and enjoy the event**

   In particular, note the acceleration of Cheeseborough and Ashford for the U.S.A.
2. **After the event pupils estimate the speed**
3. **Calculate the speed**

   This may be done as a class activity or by pupils individually.

   400 m in 41.65 seconds

   = $\frac{400}{41.65}$ m in one second

   ≈ 9.604 m in one second

   = 9.604 x 3600 m in one hour

   ≈ 34570 m in one hour

   = 34.570 km /h

> The fastest average speed attained in an individual world record for running is 36.92 km/h when Tommie Smith (U.S.A.) ran 19.5 seconds for 220 yards straight in 1966.

SNIPPET 7

Speed — 100 metres freestyle—
Can you walk as fast as these people can swim?

Pupils are shown a video clip of the race.
Then they are challenged to match the speed of the winner by walking at that speed.

METHOD .

1. Get a feeling of the speed

Show the videotape of the final of the men's 100 metres freestyle which features the then world record holder, Rowdy Gains (USA) and Mark Stockwell (Australia), who won the silver medal.

As the children watch, tell them to try to get a feeling of the speed, for later they will be trying to walk at the speed of the winner.

2. Walk at that speed

Set up a 50 metre 'pool' — two lines 50 metres apart. Challenge children to walk at an even rate to the other line, do a 'tumble turn' and return in 49.8 seconds.

> PREPARATION
> A trundle wheel tape measure to measure 50 metres.

> At a swimming pool children could walk alongside the pool of swimmers in training to *get a better feeling* of swimming speed.

> Trials schools found it was worthwhile to ask the pupils to walk to their estimate of 50 m first. Estimates ranged from 30 m to 75 m.

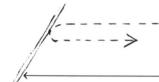

GO!

⟵——————— 50 m ———————⟶

SNIPPET 8

10 metre diving tower —
How long are they in the air?
How fast do they hit the water?

> PREPARATION
> Stopwatches.

Pupils watch finalists in the tower diving event, and estimate the time the contestants are in the air and the velocity at which they hit the water.

> The first three divers shown are Val Beddoe (Australia), Stephen Foley (Australia) and Greg Louganis (USA).

> Accurate timing technique is quite a challenge. You will probably have a wide variation at first.

> Pupils could speculate on why the time should not be the theoretical 1.428 seconds.

METHOD

1. **Pose the questions** and explain that we will be seeing the divers and estimating the time they are in the air and the velocity at which they hit the water.

2. **Play the tape twice.** The first time to simply enjoy the quality of the dive and the second, to estimate the velocity and to find (as accurately as possibly using a stopwatch) the time they are in the air.

3. **Calculate the entry speed** using the formula $V = 9.8\,t$ (This gives the answers in metres per second which can then be converted to km/h.) The answer is about 50 km/h.

4. **The formula $S = 4.9\,t^2$** relating height and time, could also be explored. For example, given the measured time, calculate the tower height. Since the tower is known to be 10 m, explain any differences.

SNIPPET 9   Speed versus endurance —
Do you think speed changes much as the distance of the event increases?

Children find out that the longer the race distance, the more the average speed decreases.

METHOD

1. **Show the videotape** introduction which features world-class performances by women and men in the 100 m, 400 m and the marathon to give a visual comparison of speeds.

2. **Each pupil copies the times** from the screen into the fourth column (headed *time*) of the worksheet as they watch highlights from the Los Angeles Olympic events.

3. **Calculate the average times** for each 100 m in each event and enter it in the last column (headed *Av. time/100 m*).

4. **Compare the times for the different events.**

QUESTIONS FOR THE CLASS

- Beside the obvious difference in speed, what does the graph tell you about the performances of women compared with men?
- What is the percentage drop off in speed from event to event?
- Between which two events is this change the greatest?
- Is the change the same for men as for women?

  Pupils could calculate the percentage difference between the speeds for men and for women and find out the events which have the greatest and the least difference.

PREPARATION
Give one copy of the worksheet on the following page to each pupil.
Be careful not to copy the answer strip at the side.

Years 4 ↓ 10

VIDEO

You could construct a histogram, or graph the results this way.

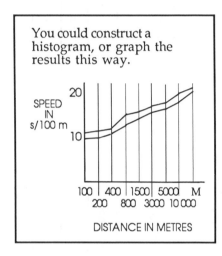

SNIPPET 10   The perfect 10

To be honest, the maths in this activity is a bit thin. But we couldn't leave out such excellent performances from the selection of material we had.

Simply let children enjoy the 'perfect' performances which score a 'perfect' 10. Of course to a mathematician, 10 is certainly *not* a perfect number.

METHOD

1. Give pupils the definition of a perfect number.

'A perfect number is one for which the sum of divisors (including 1) is equal to the number itself.'

For example 6, with divisors 1, 2 and 3 is a 'perfect' number.

2. With tongue firmly planted in cheek, ask 'So, is 10 a perfect number?'

Worksheet for Snippet 9

Using the following tables, complete the WORLD RECORD TIMES and the average time for each 100 m.

DISTANCE	COMPETITOR	COUNTRY	TIME	AV. TIME / 100 m
100 m	Evelyn Ashford	USA		
	Ben Johnson	Canada		
200 m	Marita Koch	E. Germany		
	Pietro Mennea	Italy		
400 m	Marita Koch	E. Germany		
	Lee Evans	USA		
800 m	J. Kratochvilova	Czech.		
	Sebastian Coe	GB		
1500 m	Tatyana Kazankina	USSR		
	Said Aouita	Morocco		
3000 m	Tatyana Kazankina	USSR		
	Henry Rono	Kenya		
5000 m	Zola Budd	GB		
	Said Aouita	Morocco		
10 000 m	Ingrid Kristiansen	Norway		
	Fernando Mameda	Portugal		
Marathon (41.2 km)	Ingrid Kristiansen	Norway		
	Carlos Lopez	Portugal		

The answers

Do NOT photocopy.

TIME	AV. TIME / 100 m
10.76 s	10.76 s
9.83 s	9.83 s
21.71 s	10.86 s
19.72 s	9.86 s
47.60 s	11.90 s
43.86 s	10.97 s
1:52.28	14.03 s
1:41.73	12.72 s
3:52.47	15.50 s
3:29.45	13.96 s
8:22.62	16.75 s
7:32.21	15.07 s
14:48.07	17.76 s
13:00.14	15.61 s
30:59.42	18.59 s
27:13.81	16.30 s
2:21.06	20.05 s
2:07.12	18.50 s

Marathon running—
SNIPPET **Can you stand the pace?**

11   *The video shows several stages of the women's marathon at the Los Angeles Olympic Games. To most children the running speed doesn't look too difficult to maintain. Most children can match the speed. But for how long?*

METHOD

1. Show the video tape which features the eventual gold-medal winner, Joan Benoit of the USA. Point out that, in winning, Joan had to average a speed of 20 seconds every 100 metres for 43.2 kilometres.

2. Challenge the pupils to keep up this pace

You could do this on a 400 m circular track or by going back and forth between two lines 100 m or 50 m apart.
Every 20 seconds (10 secs. for 50 m), children would have to run 100 m. So every 20 seconds signal with a flag or whistle. See if pupils can adjust their speed to keep up with the world record pace.

The winner, Joan Benoit of the USA.

Years 4 ↓ 10   VIDEO

IF YOU KEEP THAT PACE UP FOR ANOTHER 238 LAPS SMITH, YOU'LL BE A WORLD CHAMPION

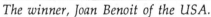

SNIPPET   **High jump—**
12   **Perception and reality**

The gold medalist, Ulrike Meyforth is shown winning the medal. The videotape is paused and pupils are challenged to mark their estimations of the height of the jump on the classroom wall. The world record of 2.09 m* is then marked and compared with the estimates.

*As of the 31st August, 1987, the world record was held by Stefka Kostadinova of Bulgaria. (1987 World Cup, Rome)

Circumference of the earth —
Eratosthenes' experiment revisited.

This activity follows a 1986 experiment which involved six schools in different places across Australia. At exactly the same time they measured the angle the sun made to the vertical. And since the distances between the places were known, the circumference of the earth could be calculated.

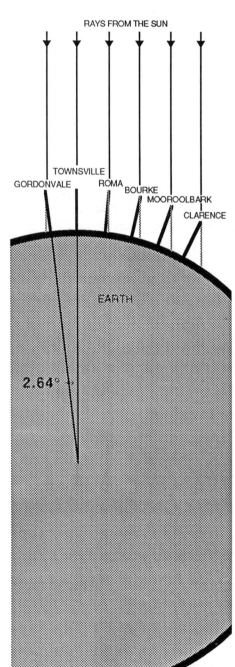

RAYS FROM THE SUN

TOWNSVILLE
GORDONVALE   ROMA
                    BOURKE
                       MOOROOLBARK
                          CLARENCE

EARTH

2.64°

The method of calculation is outlined on the videotape. In summary it is as follows:

Eratosthenes (275–194 B.C.), while in Alexandria, noticed one day the Sun reflected at the bottom of a well, and realised the Sun must be directly overhead. Exactly one year later, at a place approximately 800 km south, (a distance he knew, because he paid a man to pace it out!) he noticed the Sun was not overhead, but cast a shadow.

By measuring the angle of the Sun's rays, he calculated the circumference of the Earth. His calculation was accurate to within 80km of the accepted value today.

With the cooperation of several schools across Australia, pupils were able to obtain the data shown on the tape and included in the worksheet.

When the Sun was directly overhead of the Townsville school, each other school measured the length of the shadow cast by a stick of known length. From this, an approximation to the circumference of the Earth could be determined as follows:

Finding the angle of the Sun's rays

Here are the figures and calculations from Gordonvale High School, 288 km north of Townsville. The vertical stick was 130 cm long and had a shadow of 6 cm. The angle of the Sun's rays can be determined by scale drawing or by trigonometry as follows:

$$\text{Tan } \theta = \frac{6}{130}$$

$$\theta \approx 0.046$$

$$\theta \approx 2.64°$$

Finding the approximate circumference of the Earth

Every 2.64° will be 288 km. There are $\frac{360}{2.64}$ lots of 288 km around the Earth.

$$\frac{360}{2.64} \times 288 \approx 39\ 273 \text{ km}$$

The generally accepted value of the circumference of the Earth is 40 008 km north–south (as applies here) or 40 075 km around the equator. Source: *World Book Encyclopædi*a, Volume 6, USA, 1975, p. 5.

Challenge your pupils to calculate the Earth's circumference
using the data from the schools. This can be done individually or as a group activity.

EXTENSIONS

1. Since only two schools' measurements are needed, 15 (being $^6C_2$) different 'circumferences' could be calculated from the six measurements provided.

2. Choose one school roughly north or south from you. Ring them up and replicate the experiment.

Worksheet for Snippet 13

TOWN	DISTANCE FROM TOWNSVILLE (km)	HEIGHT OF STICK (cm)	LENGTH OF SHADOW (cm)	ANGLE OF SUN'S RAYS (°)	CALCULATION OF EARTH'S CIRCUMFERENCE (km)
Townsville (Qld)	0	100	0	0°	N/A
Gordonvale (Qld)	288 (N)	130	6		
Roma (Qld)	786 (S)	190	24.5		
Bourke (NSW)	1158 (S)	100	18		
Mooroolbark (Vic.)	1986 (S)	100	34.4		
Clarence (Tas.)	2574 (S)	61	27		

Eratosthenes' experiment solutions

TOWN	DISTANCE FROM TOWNSVILLE (km)	HEIGHT OF STICK (cm)	LENGTH OF SHADOW (cm)	ANGLE OF SUN'S RAYS (°)	CALCULATION OF EARTH'S CIRCUMFERENCE (km)
Townsville (Qld)	0	100	0	0°	N/A
Gordonvale (Qld)	288 (N)	130	6	2.64°	39273
Roma (Qld)	786 (S)	190	24.5	7.20°	39300
Bourke (NSW)	1158 (S)	100	18	10.20°	40871
Mooroolbark (Vic.)	1986 (S)	100	34.4	18.98°	37669
Clarence (Tas.)	2574 (S)	61	27	23.88°	38804

Stride length of a race horse — using any video of a horse race

Using videotape of any horse race, pupils can calculate such things as the stride length, by getting the data they need directly from the screen.

Features of this activity

- Pupils are actively involved with video to obtain data.
- An interesting application.
- Contrasts pupils' perceptions with reality.

A stride is the distance between successive footprints of the same hoof.

Pupils usually underestimate and are often surprised at the answer.

Distances worked out from the end of races usually are about seven to eight metres. A fresh horse without the impediment of a rider can have a stride length in excess of nine metres.

A possible outline

1. Just how long do you think is a horse's stride?

Pupils are invited to 'visualise' a horse race and to mark out their estimates of the length of one complete stride. Record these estimates.

2. How could we find out?

Play the videotape showing the last stages of a race. One solution is to count the strides over the last 200 metres. The race could be shown at normal speed and slow motion.

3. Show how long that is

Mark the distance on the ground and compare it to the estimates.

Apart from being informative, the value for pupil seems to be in the surprise of how big is a full-stride length.

4. Extensions

Pupils could investigate differences between long and short events, or between the starts and finishes of races.

MATHS AT THE OLYMPICS

Heptathlon and Decathlon scoring systems

This videotape of the Heptathlon and Decathlon events at the 1984 Olympic Games at Los Angeles shows the interesting way mathematics is used in the scoring system. Pupils learn the method of calculation and practise it (using a calculator if required). At the same time they enjoy the excitement of world-class athletic performances.

Two different approaches to the calculation are given, one, using linear proportion for years 8-12 and another using prepared tables for years 4-7.

These activities could be done in conjunction with your school's Physical Education program. Adjoining periods could be used. See Ideas for extensions, page 51.

Features of this activity
- A realistic application.
- The data is provided on the video.
- Use of calculators.
- Excellence in Olympic competition.
- Ratio and decimals in the years 8-12 version.
- Decimals, place value and addition in the years 4-7 version.
- Reading and interpreting tables.

Years 4 → 10

VIDEO

STRUCTURE OF THE VIDEOTAPE

1. Heptathlon — 20 minutes

Glynis Nunn of Australia, the eventual Gold Medal winner, is followed through the various events, as are her main rivals, Jackie Joyner (USA) and Sabine Everts (West Germany).
There is:
- a lively introduction, showing a variety of Olympic events,
- an explanation of the scoring system,
- an invitation to try out the system, and
- the conclusion, leading up to the Gold Medal.

2. Decathlon — 20 minutes

Daley Thompson from Great Britain attempts to win the Gold Medal and break the world record for the event. It includes:
- an introduction to the Decathlon,
- an explanation of the scoring system,
- an invitation to practise this method,
- calculations, using Daley Thompson's performances, and
- the Olympic Closing Ceremony.

The mathematics of the scoring tables

The tables are based a progressive curve which provides increased reward for performance nearer to the theoretical limit. For example, in the high jump, an improvement from 1.9 to 2.0 m is more significant than between 1.8 and 1.9 m, and is rewarded accordingly.

We have taken a mathematical liberty with the tables on page 47. For this exercise we will assume that the graph is straight between two close points and we therefore use linear proportion.

The judges at the Olympics do not perform the calculations — they simply look up the points score from a complete set of tables, which are worked out by mathematicians. (The book of tables has 112 pages).

Time required

Two sessions are required for the Heptathlon and at least one for the Decathlon. Have a break of at least two days between sessions. Apart from the physical exhaustion (?), this will promote a high interest level.

MCTP acknowledges the considerable expertise and assistance of Bruce McAvaney (Ten Network) in the production of the videotape.

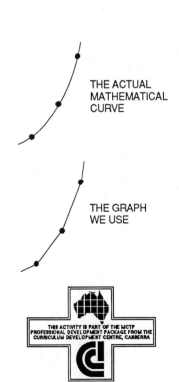

THE ACTUAL MATHEMATICAL CURVE

THE GRAPH WE USE

THIS ACTIVITY IS PART OF THE MCTP PROFESSIONAL DEVELOPMENT PACKAGE FROM THE CURRICULUM DEVELOPMENT CENTRE, CANBERRA

The Heptathlon scoring system

Children follow Glynis Nunn and two other finalists in their exciting struggle for the gold medal, calculating* their points and totaling their scores.

*(For years 4-7, children read the points from the tables.)

PREPARATION
• One worksheet (page 46) per pupil.
• A scoring table (page 46).
• A videotape player and prepared tape.
Preview the videotape and familiarise yourself with the calculations.

1. Preview the videotape and give the background to the event

HOW MANY OF YOU SAW THE LAST OLYMPIC GAMES IN LOS ANGELES ON TV?

WHO KNOWS WHAT THE HEPTATHLON INVOLVES?

DO YOU REMEMBER THE NAME OF THE AUSTRALIAN COMPETITOR?

THE HEPTATHLON STARTED IN 1981, EVOLVING FROM THE PENTATHLON, A COMPETITION OF FIVE EVENTS WHICH IN TURN WERE MADE UP FROM ELEVEN EVENTS IN NINE FORMS OVER THE YEARS.

FOR INSTANCE, IN 1851 THE PENTATHLON INCLUDED CLIMBING A 16.7 METRE ROPE!

TODAY'S HEPTATHLON IS A TWO DAY COMPETITION WITH SEVEN EVENTS.
ON THE FIRST DAY IT'S THE 100 m HURDLES, HIGH JUMP, SHOT PUT AND 200 m.
ON THE SECOND DAY IT'S THE LONG JUMP, JAVELIN AND 800 m

IN 1984 AT LOS ANGELES , THE COMPETITION WAS VERY CLOSE AND THE SCORING SYSTEM MADE IT VERY EXCITING.
IN TODAY'S LESSON WE'LL BE USING MATHS TO KEEP UP WITH THE SCORES LEADING TO THE GOLD MEDAL

SCORING METHOD
The instructions are given on the videotape. However, after the explanations of Glynis Nunn's score in the 100 m Hurdles, and again after Joyner and Evert's scores are explained, the teacher would be advised to revise the method.

Emphasise that the answer must lie between 1002 and 987.

Alternatively, with the increasing use of calculators, decimals and the metric system, a more appropriate series of steps would be
.2 of 15 = 3
So subtract 3 from 1002

2. The 100m Hurdles

The following method is for years 8–12. For years 4–7, use the tables on page 47.

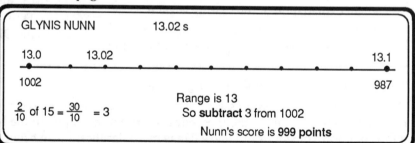

GLYNIS NUNN   13.02 s

13.0   13.02   13.1
1002   987

$\frac{2}{10}$ of 15 = $\frac{30}{10}$ = 3

Range is 13
So **subtract** 3 from 1002

Nunn's score is **999 points**

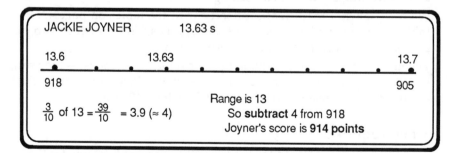

JACKIE JOYNER   13.63 s

13.6   13.63   13.7
918   905

$\frac{3}{10}$ of 13 = $\frac{39}{10}$ = 3.9 ($\approx$ 4)

Range is 13
So **subtract** 4 from 918
Joyner's score is **914 points**

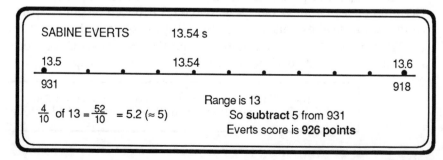

SABINE EVERTS   13.54 s

13.5   13.54   13.6
931   918

$\frac{4}{10}$ of 13 = $\frac{52}{10}$ = 5.2 ($\approx$ 5)

Range is 13
So **subtract** 5 from 931
Everts score is **926 points**

3. The High Jump and Shot Put

In the next two events a difficulty in concept may arise. Whereas in the 100 m Hurdles, an *increase* in time gives a *decrease* in score, in the next two events, an *increase* in length of jump or put, gives an *increase* in score. So pupils must *add* to the low figure when doing the calculations in the second and third events.

For example, the calculations for Sabine Everts' high jump are below.

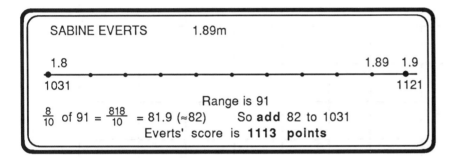

SABINE EVERTS   1.89m

1.8   1.89 1.9
1031   1121

Range is 91

$\frac{8}{10}$ of 91 = $\frac{818}{10}$ = 81.9 (≈82)   So **add** 82 to 1031

Everts' score is **1113 points**

THE SHOT PUT

Years 4 ↓ 10   VIDEO

PROGRESS SCORES AFTER THREE EVENTS

Nunn 2799   Joyner 2806   Everts 2788

4. The 200 m, the Long Jump and the Javelin

PROGRESS SCORES AFTER SIX EVENTS

Nunn 5473   Joyner 5504   Everts 5424

5. Final Scores

Nunn 6390   Joyner 6385   Everts 6363

Always do your homework

After the first day's competition, Glynis went home and as most athletes would do, checked her results and found a judge's error of three points. These were given to her the next day.

To get 1000 points

The scoring tables have changed considerably over the years. Factors considered in the derivation of the tables include the results of the 100 top performers in each event. These are averaged, the average being given 1000 points.

Recent changes in the scoring tables

The latest changes were implemented after the Los Angeles Olympics. The tables for the field events were regressive, that is, there was a diminishing yield in points for each improvement in performance. This coupled with considerable improvements in some of the events, particularly the high jump, brought about the changes in August, 1984.

Closeness of the results

Glynis wins by just five points. To give a visual image of how close the result was, go back to the first event and freeze the picture as Glynis crosses the finishing line. The girl who comes second earns *eight points less.*

WOULD YOU LIKE EIGHT-POINT SHOES OR SIX-POINT SHOES

Holding a world record for 0.4 seconds

In the 800 m, the last event of the Woman's Pentathlon at the 1980 Olympic Games in Moscow, Olga Rukavishnikova (URS) finished second in 2 : 04.80 s. This gave her an overall point score of 4937, more than the then world record. In the third place behind her came team mate Nadyezda Tkachenko in a time of 2 : 04.20 s, bringing her total to an even higher score of 5083 points. So for 0.4 seconds Rukavishnikova held the current world record — *the shortest reign ever in any event.*

For ideas for extension activities, see page 51.

The current world record

This is held by Sabine Praetz (GDR). Using the latest tables, her score is 6946. Her results were:

100 m hurdles — 12.64 s	1179
High jump — 1.80 m	978
Shot put — 15.37 m	886
200 m — 23.37 s	1042
Long jump — 6.86 m	1125
Javelin — 44.62 m	756
800 m — 2 : 08.93	980
Total score:	6946

HEPTATHLON WORKSHEET

EVENT	GLYNIS NUNN			JACKIE JOINER			SABINE EVERTS		
	Perf.	Pts.	Total	Perf.	Pts.	Total	Perf.	Pts.	Total
1. 100 m Hurdles									
2. High Jump									
3. Shot Put									
4. 200 m									
5. Long Jump									
6. Javelin									
7. 800 m									
FINAL POINTS									

HEPTATHLON POINTS   (Correct values)

EVENT	GLYNNIS NUNN			JACKIE JOINER			SABINE EVERTS		
	Perf.	Pts.	Total	Perf.	Pts.	Total	Perf.	Pts.	Total
1. 100 m Hurdles	13.02	999	999	13.63	914	914	13.54	926	926
2. High Jump	1.80	1031	2030	1.80	1031	1945	1.89	1113	2039
3. Shot Put	12.82	769	2799	14.39	861	2806	12.49	749	2788
4. 200 m	24.06	932	3731	24.05	933	3739	24.05	933	3721
5. Long Jump	6.66	1047	4778	6.11	930	4669	6.71	1058	4779
6. Javelin	35.60	695	5473	44.50	835	5504	32.62	645	5424
7. 800 m	2:10.6	917	6390	2:13.0	881	6385	2:09.1	939	6363
FINAL POINTS	6390			6385			6363		

HEPTATHLON SCORING TABLE — DAY ONE | DAY TWO (Years 8-12 version)

100 m Hurdles

s	pts.
13.0	1002
13.1	987
13.2	973
13.3	959
13.4	945
13.5	931
13.6	918
13.7	905
13.8	891
13.9	879
14.0	866
......	......
15.0	748
16.0	645
......	......
25.0	91
26.0	53
27.0	18
27.5	1

High Jump

m	pts.
1.9	1122
1.8	1031
1.7	935
1.6	834
1.5	726
1.4	612
1.3	488
1.2	353
1.1	201
1.0	1

Shot Put

m	pts.
18.0	1053
17.0	1002
16.0	949
15.0	895
......	......
14.5	867
14.4	862
14.3	856
14.2	850
14.1	844
14.0	838
......	......
13.0	780
12.9	774
12.8	768
12.7	762
12.6	756
12.5	750
12.4	744
12.3	738
12.2	731
12.1	735
12.0	719
......	......
4.0	90
3.5	34
3.4	23
3.3	11

200 m

s	pts.
22.0	1145
23.0	1037
24.0	938
24.1	928
24.2	919
24.3	909
24.4	900
24.5	891
24.6	882
24.7	873
24.8	864
24.9	855
25.0	846
......	......
26.0	762
27.0	684
28.0	612
29.0	545
30.0	484
......	......
35.0	223
36.0	180
37.0	133
38.0	99
39.0	63
40.0	27
40.8	1

Long Jump

m	pts.
7.0	1117
6.9	1097
6.8	1076
6.7	1056
6.6	1034
6.5	1014
6.4	992
6.3	971
6.2	950
6.1	928
6.0	906
5.9	884
5.8	862
5.7	839
5.6	817
5.5	794
5.4	771
......	......
4.0	423
3.5	284
3.0	135
2.9	103
2.8	72
2.7	39
2.6	6

Javelin

m	pts.
70.0	1170
60.0	1047
50.0	914
49.0	900
48.0	885
47.0	871
46.0	857
45.0	842
44.0	828
43.0	813
42.0	797
41.0	782
40.0	766
39.0	750
38.0	735
37.0	719
36.0	702
35.0	685
34.0	669
33.0	652
32.0	635
31.0	617
30.0	599
......	......
20.0	400
15.0	285
10.0	141
9.0	109
8.0	75
7.0	39
6.0	1

800 m

m	pts.
2:00.0	1084
2:01.0	1067
2:02.0	1051
2:03.0	1034
2:04.0	1018
2:05.0	1002
2:06.0	986
2:07.0	971
2:08.0	955
2:09.0	941
2:10.0	926
11.0	911
12.0	897
13.0	881
14.0	869
15.0	855
16.0	842
......	......
20.0	790
30.0	672
40.0	569
50.0	478
3:00.0	397
10.0	325
20.0	260
30.0	201
40.0	147
50.0	99
4:00.0	54
10.0	13
11.0	9
12.9	1

✂ -

HEPTATHLON SCORING TABLE — DAY ONE | DAY TWO (Years 4-7 version — no linear proportion)

100 m Hurdles

s	pts.
13.00	1002
13.01	1000
13.02	999
13.03	997
13.04	996
13.05	994
13.06	993
13.07	992
------	----
13.52	929
13.53	927
13.54	926
13.55	925
13.56	923
13.57	922
13.58	920
13.59	919
13.60	918
13.61	916
13.62	915
13.63	914
13.64	912
13.65	911
13.66	910
13.67	909
------	----
25.00	91
26.00	53
27.00	18
27.50	1

High Jump

m	pts.
1.92	1140
1.91	1131
1.90	1122
1.89	1113
1.88	1104
1.87	1095
1.86	1086
1.85	1077
1.84	1068
1.83	1059
1.82	1049
1.81	1040
1.80	1031
1.79	1021
1.78	1012
-----	------
1.20	353
1.10	201
1.00	1

Shot Put

m	pts.
14.45	864
14.43	863
14.41	862
14.39	861
14.38	860
14.36	859
------	----
12.88	773
12.87	772
12.85	771
12.83	770
12.82	769
12.80	768
12.78	767
12.77	766
-----	----
12.57	754
12.55	753
12.53	752
12.52	751
12.50	750
12.48	749
12.47	748
------	----
4.00	90
3.50	34
3.40	23
3.30	11

200 m

s	pts.
23.99	938
24.00	938
24.01	937
24.02	936
24.03	935
24.04	934
24.05	933
24.06	932
24.07	931
24.08	930
------	----
35.00	223
36.00	180
37.00	133
38.00	99
39.00	63
40.00	27
40.80	1

Long Jump

m	pts.
6.74	1064
6.73	1062
6.72	1060
6.71	1058
6.70	1056
6.69	1053
6.68	1051
6.67	1049
6.66	1047
6.65	1045
6.64	1043
6.63	1041
6.62	1039
----	-----
6.15	939
6.14	937
6.13	934
6.12	932
6.11	930
6.10	928
6.09	926
----	----
4.00	423
3.50	284
3.00	135
2.90	103
2.80	72
2.70	39
2.60	1

Javelin

m	pts.
44.72	838
44.64	837
44.58	836
44.50	835
44.44	834
44.38	833
44.30	832
------	----
35.80	699
35.74	698
35.68	697
35.62	696
35.56	695
35.50	694
35.44	693
------	----
32.72	647
32.66	646
32.60	645
32.54	644
32.48	643
32.44	642
32.38	641
------	----
20.00	400
15.00	285
10.00	141
9.00	109
8.00	75
7.00	39
6.00	1

800 m

min	pts.
2:08.7	945
2:08.8	943
2:08.9	942
2:09.0	941
2:09.1	939
2:09.2	938
2:09.3	936
2:09.4	935
2:09.5	933
------	----
2:10.2	923
2:10.3	921
2:10.4	920
2:10.5	918
2:10.6	917
2:10.7	916
2:10.8	914
2:10.9	913
2:11.0	911
------	----
2:12.9	882
2:13.0	881
2:13.1	880
2:13.2	879
2:13.3	878
------	----
2:40.0	569
3:00.0	397
3:30.0	201
4:00.0	54
4:10.0	13
4:11.0	9
4:12.9	1

IN SOME DISTANCE RACES AND THROWING EVENTS, ALL POSSIBLE TIMES AND DISTANCES ARE NOT GIVEN. IF, FOR EXAMPLE, IN THE SHOT PUT, THE EXACT RESULT IS NOT STATED IN THE TABLE, THE POINTS SCORE FOR THE RESULT IMMEDIATELY UNDERNEATH SHOULD BE AWARDED.

The Decathlon scoring system

In this activity, children follow the progress of the eventual Gold Medalist, Daley Thompson (GB) using the same method of scoring as for the Heptathlon. This time only the one athlete is highlighted.

1. Recall the Heptathlon activity and give the background to the Decathlon

> DO YOU REMEMBER WHEN WE FOLLOWED GLYNIS NUNN IN THE WOMAN'S HEPTATHLON, AND HOW THE ATHLETES SCORED THEIR POINTS?
>
> WELL, TODAY WE WILL FOLLOW ANOTHER EQUALLY EXCITING CONTEST WHERE ONE COMPETITOR, DALEY THOMPSON OF GREAT BRITAIN, IS PITTED AGAINST JURGEN HINGSEN, THE WORLD RECORD HOLDER, AND HIS (THOMPSON'S) PREVIOUS BEST PERFORMANCE

> THE CONTEST IS THE DECATHLON.
> HOW MANY EVENTS DO YOU THINK THIS WILL HAVE?

> TEN

> THE DECATHLON IS THE SEARCH FOR THE PERFECTLY-BALANCED, ALL-ROUND ATHLETE.
> THE MAN WHO CAN COMBINE SPEED AND STRENGTH, AGILITY AND ATHLETICISM...AND MAINTAIN A PUNISHING LEVEL OF EXCELLENCE THROUGHOUT THE TEN-EVENT, TWO-DAY COMPETITION

> THE DECATHLON DATES BACK TO THE 19th. CENTURY.
> IN 1884 A MULTI-EVENT COMPETITION WAS HELD COMPRISING 100 YARDS, SHOT PUT, HIGH JUMP, 880-YARDS WALK, HAMMER THROW, POLE VAULT, 120 YARDS HURDLE, 56 POUNDS WEIGHT, LONG JUMP AND MILE RACE...ALL IN ONE DAY!

> AGAIN THE INSTRUCTIONS ARE ON THE TAPE — SO LET'S TRY THE ACTIVITY

PREPARATION
• One worksheet (page 52) per pupil.
• A scoring table (page 52).
• A videotape player and prepared tape.
Preview the videotape and familiarise yourself with the calculations.

SCORING METHOD

The instructions on the videotape by Bruce MacAvaney, Network Ten Sports commentator, are meant for years 8–12 pupils only.

For years 4–7, pupils will use the excerpts from the complete scoring tables page 54, practising the skill of interpreting tables.

However, watching the explanation on the tape should not cause too much confusion.

Descriptions of the performances of Thompson and Hingsen are provided. Teachers may like to read these after each event to add to the atmosphere.

The descriptions are taken from D. Emery and S. Greenberg, *World Sporting Records*, The Bodley Head, London.

2. The 100 Metres (Event 1)

Thompson exploded from the blocks to set his best ever legal time for a 100 m during a decathlon, clocking 10.44 into a one metre per second head wind. Hingsen drawn in the same heat, finished almost five metres down in 10.91 and 122 points adrift. (Thompson's best ever 100 m time in a one-off individual race was 10.36 seconds.)

Score 948 points.

The steps as described on the videotape are shown below. You may, alternatively, choose to use calculators and the decimal system. In that case you could use the following steps: .4 of 27 = 10.8 (≈ 11) so subtract 11 from 959. Emphasise that the answer must lie between 932 and 959.

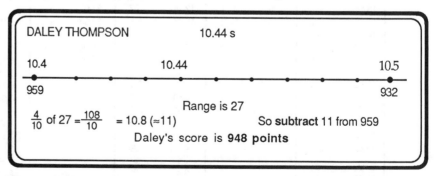

This is the last time that the videotape explains the procedures in diagrammatic form.

After each subsequent event, pause the tape for pupils to do their calculations.

The Long Jump (Event 2)

Teachers may choose to work through the steps involved in the calculations for the Long Jump scores as these involve *addition*.

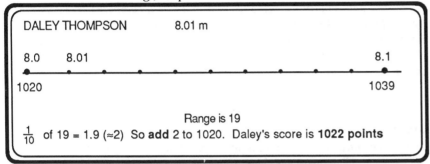

DALEY THOMPSON   8.01 m

8.0   8.01   8.1

1020   1039

Range is 19
$\frac{1}{10}$ of 19 = 1.9 (≈2) So **add** 2 to 1020. Daley's score is **1022 points**

The long jump is Thompson's best event. But going into the Olympics, Hingsen's personal record of 8.04 m was ahead of Thompson's best of 8.00 m. Hingsen got progressively better in Los Angeles with 7.50, 7.70 and 7.80. But Thompson topped him on each occasion with 7.83, 7.84 and a final round of 8.01 to not only crack his lifetime best, but also add another 42 points to his lead. A reproduction of such a jump would have given Thompson fifth place in the individual long jump event won by American Carl Lewis, only two days earlier.

Score 1022. Total 1970.

Shot Put (Event 3)

Hingsen stepped into the shot put circle with the air of a man bent on swatting a fly. During his world record in June, he had put the shot 16.42 m. Thompson's lifetime best was a relatively puny 16.10 m in open competition and he had never bettered 15.66 m in a decathlon. Hingsen won but with a disappointing 15.87 m against Thompson's 15.72. The West German's net gain was nine points. Thompson was 155 points ahead and still thundering towards a world record.

Score 831. Total 2801.

High Jump (Event 4)

Thompson had been struggling in the high jump all season. From a personal best of 2.14 m set indoors he had deteriorated to a seasonal best of 1.87 m. Hingsen had cleared 2.18 m. Here, surely, was his chance again. Instead, Thompson cleared 2.01 m at his third attempt and the German, who had received treatment for a knee injury, eventually made 2.12 m, a fine effort but one which could claw back only 77 points. Thompson led Hingsen by 78 points. Would the strain start to show?

Score 882. Total 3683.

400 metres (Event 5)

Thompson had been working hard on his 400 m in training... and it showed as he clocked 46.97 s, the second fastest of his career. Hingsen also ignored the pain of his knee injury to produce a storming 47.69 s, only 4/100ths of a second away from his personal best. But Thompson added another 36 pionts to the gap between the two of them to end the afternoon with 4622, a world record for the first day of a decathlon. Hingsen, on 4519, was 17 points short of the halfway score in his existing world record, which was clearly under threat.

Score 1950. Total 4633.

END OF DAY ONE

At this stage Jurgen Hingsen, Daley's main challenger was on 4519, 114 points behind.

Daley makes his point!

DALEY THOMPSON . . . may equal existing record.

LONDON, Thurs., AFP — English decathlete Daley Thompson is about to become co-holder of the world record nearly two years after the performance that won him the Olympic gold medal in Los Angeles.

Extended study of the finish photograph has shown Thompson's time for the 110 metres hurdles was a thousandth of a second faster than was thought.

This made the performance worth one more point, which enabled Thompson to equal West German Jurgen Hingsen's existing world record of 8,798 points.

The Los Angeles timing was investigated by the International Amateur Athletic Federation at the request of the British board and they have agreed that the original timing was inaccurate.

This clip from the Melbourne Herald tells of how, two years later, Daley Thompson was awarded one extra point for the 100m Hurdles (his time being changed from 14.35 to 14.335), enabling him to equal Hingsen's world record of 8798 points.

Day two
110 Hurdles (Event 6)

Hingsen had a distinct advantage over Thompson in the first event of the second day, holding a personal best of 14.07s, compared to 14.26 s. Again, though, Hingsen missed his opportunity, clocking a disappointing 14.29 to finish half a metre clear of Thompson in 14.34. Hingsen had gained only six points (Thompson's original time of 14.34 has since been officially amended to 14.33).

Score 922. Total 5555.

Discus (Event 7)

In the end, after all the months of preparation and hours of competition, Thompson's gold medal and share of the world record depended on one turn of the discus wheel of fortune. Hingsen had produced a lifetime best of 50.82; Thompson, after two throws, had managed only 41.24 m. The difference in points was 176... enough to give the German a commanding lead. Thompson, clearly nervous but supremely competitive, stepped in for his final attempt and hurled a life-saving 46.56 m. Thompson still led... by 33 points.

Score 810. Total 6365.

Pole Vault (Event 8)

Thompson and Hingsen are evenly matched in the pole vault. With the javelin and 1500 to come — both events in which the German had posted superior performances — Thompson knew he desperately needed to improve the slender 33 point lead. Once again, it would be his competitive temperament which would see him through. Hingsen, troubled now by a stomach upset, went out at 4.70 m, having cleared 4.50 m, well short of his personsal best of 5.10 m, Thompson went over 4.70 m at his second attempt... and promptly raised the bar to 4.90. Twice he failed. Then on the third try, with daylight to spare, he soared clear and celebrated with a backflip in the landing area. Thompson went on to jump 5.00 m. His lead was 153 points and a world record looked certain.

Score 1052. Total 7417.

Javelin (Event 9)

Hingsen, beaten by Thompson in European and World championships, was now reliving his nightmare. Depressed and disconsolate he threw 60.44 m, some seven metres short of his best. Thompson, almost leisurely, recorded 65.24 m, close to his best ever. Already he had scored 8241 points.

Score 824. Total 8241.

1500 m (Event 10)

Thompson needed to run 4:34.8 to gain a total of 8799 points and claim the world record. During the world championships a year earlier, when he had been suffering the after-effects of injury, he had clocked 4:29.72. Curiously, in Los Angeles, such an effort proved beyond him. When he reached the bell, Thompson needed a last lap of 71.6; this from an athlete who had run 63.5 at a similar stage of the European Championships to break the world record. Now he slumped to 71.8 and a final time of 4:35.00. Enough only for a share of the record (following the official amendments in 1986). Hingsen, who clocked 4:22.60, finished with 8673 points, the eighth highest in history.

Score 556. Total 8797.

Years 4 ↓ 10   VIDEO

How many points could you score?

Pupils could try some of the events and score them. Average the score and make a total as for ten events, for boys or seven events for girls. How close to Daley's or Glynis' score did you get?

HE NEEDS THREE MORE POINTS

Ideas for extension activities

Graph the tables to see the curves

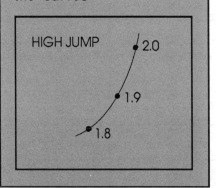

HIGH JUMP

2.0

1.9

1.8

A full set of tables can be generated using computers and linear proportion.

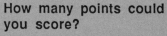

Investigate the relative abilities of athletes in different events

You could graph the athletes' performances.

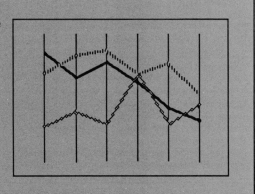

DECATHLON WORKSHEET

EVENT	PERFORMANCE	POINTS	TOTAL
1. 100 m			
2. Long Jump			
3. Shot Put			
4. High Jump			
5. 400 m			
6. 110 m Hurdles			
7. Discus			
8. Pole Vault			
9. Javelin			
10. 1500 m			
		TOTAL POINTS World Record 8798	

✂ —

DECATHLON POINTS (Correct values)

EVENT	PERFORMANCE	POINTS	TOTAL
1. 100 m	10.44	948	948
2. Long Jump	8.01	1022	1970
3. Shot Put	15.72	831	2801
4. High Jump	2.03	882	3683
5. 400 m	46.97	950	4633
6. 110 m Hurdles	14.34	922	5555
7. Discus	46.56	810	6365
8. Pole Vault	5.00	1052	7417
9. Javelin	65.24	824	8241
10. 1500 m	4:35.0	556	8797
		TOTAL POINTS **8797** World Record 8798	

(*Note the recent change to the time for the 110 metres hurdles. It is now approved as 14.33 s. See the PLAN for further information)

DECATHLON SCORING TABLE - (Years 8-12 Version)

DAY ONE

100 m s	pts.	Long Jump m	pts.	Shot Put m	pts.	High Jump m	pts.	400 m s	pts.
10.0	1073	8.2	1058	21.0	1117	2.3	1106	44.0	1110
10.1	1044	8.1	1039	20.0	1066	2.2	1025	45.0	1054
10.2	1014	8.0	1020	19.0	1013	2.1	941	....	....
10.3	986	7.9	1000	18.0	960	2.0	857	46.0	1000
10.4	959	7.8	980	17.0	904	1.9	769	46.1	994
10.5	932	7.7	961	....	....	1.8	680	46.2	989
10.6	905	7.6	941	16.0	849	1.7	588	46.3	984
10.7	879	7.5	921	15.9	842	1.6	493	46.4	979
10.8	853	7.4	901	15.8	836	1.5	394	46.5	973
10.9	828	7.3	881	15.7	830	1.4	293	46.6	968
11.0	804	7.2	861	15.6	824	1.3	189	46.7	963
....	....	7.1	840	15.5	818	1.2	79	46.8	958
12.0	580	7.0	820	....	....	1.15	24	46.9	954
13.0	390	....	....	15.0	789	1.14	12	47.0	948
14.0	228	6.0	604	14.0	222	1.13	0	....	....
15.0	88	5.0	371	13.0	130			48.0	898
15.7	0	4.0	113	12.0	32			49.0	852
		3.9	85	11.0	22			50.0	805
		3.8	57	10.0	11			....	....
		3.7	29	9.0	1			55.0	603
								60.0	433
								65.0	289
								70.0	166
								75.0	60
								76.0	40
								77.0	20
								78.0	2

DAY TWO

110 m Hurdles s	pts.	Discus m	pts.	Pole Vault m	pts.	Javelin m	pts.	1500 m min	pts.
13.0	1094	60.0	1041	5.5	1165	90	1093	3:30.0	1108
13.1	1084	55.0	958	5.4	1143	80	989	3:40.0	1002
13.2	1066	50.0	872	5.3	1121	70	880	3:50.0	905
13.3	1053	49.0	854	5.2	1098	69	868	4:00.0	816
13.4	1039	48.0	837	5.1	1075	68	857	4:10.0	735
13.5	1026	47.0	819	5.0	1052	67	845	4:20.0	660
13.6	1013	46.9	817	4.9	1028	66	834	4:30.0	589
13.7	1000	46.8	815	4.8	1005	65	822	....	....
13.8	987	46.7	813	4.7	981	64	810	4:34.5	560
13.9	975	46.6	811	4.6	957	63	798	4:34.6	559
14.0	963	46.5	809	4.5	932	62	798	4:34.8	558
14.1	950	46.4	808	....	....	61	774	4:34.9	557
14.2	939	46.3	806	4.0	807	60	762	4:35.1	556
14.3	927	46.2	804	3.5	672	....	....	4:35.2	555
14.4	915	46.1	802	3.0	528	50	633	4:35.2	554
14.5	904	46.0	800	2.5	371	40	491	....	....
14.6	897	45.0	781	2.0	197	30	330	4:40.0	525
14.7	881	44.0	763	1.5	1	20	139	4:50.0	464
14.8	870	....	....			15	25	5:00.0	408
14.9	859	40.0	686			14.03	1	5:10.0	355
15.0	848	....	....					5:20.0	306
....	....	30.0	474					5:30.0	259
20.0	449	20.0	223					5:40.0	216
25.0	209	15.0	74					5:50.0	175
26.0	173	14.0	41					6:00.0	136
27.0	138	13.0	7					6:10.0	99
28.0	107	12.82	1					6:20.0	64
29.0	77							6:30.0	31
30.0	50							6:40.0	1
31.0	24								
31.9	2								

Years 4 ↓ 10   VIDEO

DECATHLON SCORING TABLE (Years 4-7 version - no linear proportion calculations)

DAY ONE										DAY TWO									
100 m		L/Jump		Shot Put		H/Jump		400 m		110 m H.		Discus		Pole Vault		Javelin		1500 m	
s	pts.	m	pts.	m	pts.	m	pts.	s	pts.	s	pts.	m	pts.	m	pts.	m	pts.	min	pts.
10.37	968	8.10	1039	15.80	836	2.07	917	46.89	954	14.33	923	46.64	812	5.02	1057	65.61	829	4:34.8	558
10.38	965	8.09	1037	15.78	835	2.06	909	46.91	953	14.34	922	46.58	811	5.01	1054	65.53	828	4:34.9	557
10.39	962	8.08	1035	15.77	834	2.05	900	46.93	952	14.35	921	46.53	810	5.00	1052	65.44	827	4:35.1	556
10.40	959	8.07	1033	15.75	833	2.04	891	46.95	951	14.36	920	46.47	809	4.99	1050	65.36	826	4:35.2	555
10.41	957	8.06	1031	15.73	832	2.03	882	46.97	950	14.37	919	46.42	808	4.98	1047	65.27	825	4:35.4	554
10.42	954	8.05	1030	15.72	831	2.02	874	46.98	949	14.38	917	46.36	807	4.97	1045	65.19	824	4:35.5	553
10.43	951	8.04	1028	15.70	830	2.01	865	47.00	948	14.39	916	46.31	806	4.96	1042	65.10	823	4:35.7	552
10.44	948	8.03	1026	15.68	829	2.00	857	47.02	947	14.40	915	----	---	4.95	1040	65.02	822	------	----
10.45	946	8.02	1024	15.67	828	1.99	849	-----	---	14.41	914	30.00	474	4.94	1038	64.93	821	5:00.0	408
10.46	943	8.01	1022	-----	---	1.98	840	55.00	603	-----	---	20.00	223	4.93	1035	------	---	5:30.0	259
-----	---	8.00	1020	15.00	789	1.97	831	60.00	433	25.00	209	15.00	74	-----	---	40.00	491	6:00.0	136
13.00	390	7.99	1018	14.00	222	-----	---	65.00	289	26.00	173	14.00	41	4.00	807	30.00	330	6:10.0	99
14.00	228	7.98	1016	13.00	130	1.60	493	70.00	166	27.00	138	13.00	7	3.50	672	20.00	139	6:20.0	64
15.00	88	7.97	1014	12.00	32	1.50	394	75.00	60	28.00	107	12.82	1	3.00	528	15.00	25	6:30.0	31
15.7	0	7.96	1012	11.00	22	1.40	293	76.00	40	29.00	77			2.50	371	14.03	1	6:40.0	1
		-----	---	10.00	11	1.30	189	77.00	20	30.00	50			2.00	197				
		6.00	604	9.00	1	1.20	79	78.00	2	31.00	24			1.80	122				
		5.00	371			1.14	12			31.90	2			1.60	42				
		4.00	113			1.13	0							1.50	1				
		3.90	85																
		3.80	57																
		3.70	29																

IN SOME DISTANCE RACES AND THROWING EVENTS, ALL POSSIBLE TIMES AND DISTANCES ARE NOT GIVEN. IF, FOR EXAMPLE, IN THE SHOT PUT, THE EXACT RESULT IS NOT STATED IN THE TABLE, THE POINTS SCORE FOR THE RESULT IMMEDIATELY UNDER SHOULD BE AWARDED.

(An example of this is Daley Thompson's discus result - 46.56 m - see page 50).

The mathematics of darts
and
Darts 2

These activities show how video can be applied to maths education. Videotape of the 1986 Pacific Masters Darts Championship and the 1986 Embassy World Darts Championship are used as highly motivating sources for learning maths. Pupils gain an appreciation of the game, the scoring and mathematical strategies and logic needed to decide appropriate finishes. World Champion Eric Bristow — 'the crafty Cockney' is featured in both programs.

THIS ACTIVITY IS PART OF THE MCTP PROFESSIONAL DEVELOPMENT PACKAGE FROM THE CURRICULUM DEVELOPMENT CENTRE, CANBERRA

Years 4 ↓ 10 VIDEO

1986 Embassy World Champion Eric Bristow.

1986 Pacific Masters Women's Darts Champion Maureen Flowers

The structure of the two videotapes

The mathematics of darts

Outlines tactics and scoring methods and the final games of the 1986 Pacific Masters Darts Championships.

- Introduction by sports commentator, Debbie Spillane.
- The final game of the Women's Final. Pupils are invited to score.
- Debbie explains the tactics.
- Eric Bristow discusses two interesting finishes and pupils are challenged to investigate possible strategies.
- Pupils keep score in the final two games of the Men's Final, and also investigate possible finishes.

Darts 2

Shows the first, fifth and sixth sets of the finals. The competition is the best of 11 sets. Pupils are challenged to practise scoring and discuss strategies for finishing.

- The background to the Embassy World Darts Championship is told and the finalists, Eric Bristow and Dave Whitcombe are introduced.
- Pupils score the first 'leg' of the finals, pausing to subtract and investigate possible finishes.
- The commentator introduces the fifth set and pupils score all five legs.
- In the sixth and final set, children are invited to watch and enjoy the game, not keeping tally of the scores, but considering different finishes.

The mathematics of darts

This proved to be a most fascinating activity. Trials schools report pupils being very surprised and enthusiastic about the complexities of darts with its rapid mental computations and the 'logic of finishes'.

Finalists in the Pacific Masters (Women's) Darts Championship Sharon Colclough and Maureen Flowers.

FEATURES OF THE 'MATHEMATICS OF DARTS' AND 'DARTS 2'

- A realistic application.
- Use of video clips to provide provide data.
- The physical and mental demands of the sport.
- Excellence in performance in men's and women's sport.
- Challenges pupils to be quick in subtraction, multiplication and mental computation.
- Problem solving — individually in groups or as a whole class.

Preparation for 'The mathematics of darts' and 'Darts 2'

- Preview the whole of the Mathematics of Darts and the last two 'legs' of the Darts 2 tapes, although the two tapes would probably be used over two or three lessons.
- You must understand the game (see the rules at the top of the page opposite) and its subtle strategies for these lessons to be successful. This and the previewing will allow you to plan your lesson, choose which tape to use and when to pause the tape.
- If possible, bring a dart board for extra interest and discussion.
- Make copies of worksheets 1, 2 and 3 if required.

1. Create a motivating atmosphere

Encourage pupils to share anecdotes (often gruesomely humorous) and use the enthusiasm of those who do know something about the game to motivate the others.

> HOW MANY HERE HAVE PLAYED DARTS?

> DOES THE GAME OF 501 MEAN ANYTHING TO YOU?

> WHAT'S SO CHALLENGING ABOUT SCORING BACKWARDS?

> WE GOT A DARTS SET FOR CHRISTMAS BUT MUM WON'T LET US PLAY WITH IT BECAUSE WE PUT HOLES IN THE WALL

You may choose to introduce the subject by playing a game.

> WHO HAS PLAYED DARTS BEFORE AND COULD GIVE US A DEMONSTRATION?

> NOTICE HOW JANE AIMS FOR 20, NOT THE BULLSEYE.

For your classroom you could use a caneite display board or a set-up like this.

HESSIAN

ROLLED-UP SCREEN ON STAND

DON'T-COME-CLOSER LINE

Emphasise the lethal potential of darts. Many people have been killed or blinded by carelessness. Indeed darts are used as a weapon of war.

Challenge children to devise safety standards for people and property when playing, handling and storing darts.

In the videotape World Champion Eric Bristow — 'the crafty Cockney', explains the rules of 501, the parts of the dart board and some preferred shots.

You may choose to have children use calculators

---

2. Introduce the 'Mathematics of darts' videotape

> THE FIRST PROGRAM SHOWS SOME OF THE WORLD'S TOP DARTS PLAYERS PLAYING 501. YOU'LL SEE HOW YOU NEED MATHS FOR SCORING AND WORKING OUT THE STRATEGIES EACH PLAYER TAKES

> YOU'LL NEED A PEN AND WORKSHEET NUMBER ONE

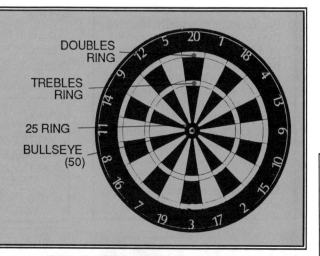

THE RULES OF THE GAME OF 501
- Each player starts with a score of 501.
- In turn, they throw three darts at a time subtracting the totals from 501.
- The winner of the game is the first to reach zero, but he/she must finish with a double or a bullseye.

The dartboard is placed 1.73 m from the floor to the bullseye and the toe line is 2.37 m from the board.

DOUBLES RING
TREBLES RING
25 RING
BULLSEYE (50)

Years 4 ↓ 10   VIDEO

3. Challenge children to beat the announcer

Play the videotape where it shows the introduction to the finals of the Pacific Masters (Women's) Darts Championship between Sharon Colclough and Maureen Flowers.

This is a major aspect of the use of the video medium — challenging children to respond directly to the data on the screen.

READY NOW?
LET'S SEE IF WE CAN TOTAL THE SCORES AND EACH ONE OF US WRITES THEM DOWN BEFORE THE ANNOUNCER CALLS THEM OUT

SHARON COLCLOUGH | MAUREEN FLOWERS
THROWS TO FINISH 501 | THROWS TO FINISH 501

RESULTS

SHARON COLCLOUGH		MAUREEN FLOWERS	
THROWS	TO FINISH 501	THROWS	TO FINISH 501
100		100	
60		85	
45		100	
100		100	
24		65	
100		56	

Continue the tape until Eric Bristow challenges pupils to:

4. Consider possible finishes for 13

At this stage we recommend that pupils do *not* do the subtractions for the games as time will not permit. Rather rely on the announcer doing the subtraction and giving the score to finish. The opportunity for the subtraction comes later in the men's final.

WE'LL PAUSE THE TAPE HERE.
NOW CONSIDERING THAT SHE MUST FINISH WITH A DOUBLE, WHAT POSSIBLE SCORES COULD SHE GET?

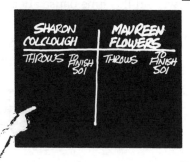

1 D6
3 D5
5 D4
7 D3

NINE DOUBLE TWO

ELEVEN DOUBLE ONE

5. Consider which strategy is best

1 D6
3 D5
5 D4
7 D3
9 D2
11 D1

I RECKON 1 D6 IS BEST 'COS ONE LOOKS EASY TO HIT AND SO DOES SIX

I'D AIM FOR A DOUBLE LIKE THREE WHICH IS WIDE RATHER THAN DEEP

I RECKON ONE DOUBLE SIX IS BEST BECAUSE IF YOU MISS DOUBLE SIX AND HIT SIX YOU STILL HAVE ANOTHER CHANCE

Play the tape to where Eric explains why 5 D4 is the ideal finish.

Eric continues, posing the question to children *'what is the highest possible three dart finish'*. Pause the tape and give children time to discover that it is 170; T20, T20, bullseye.

Pupils may gradually observe the common tactic to leave 40 or 32 to finish. This enables the players to progressively alter their strategy as they go. For example, if 40 is the target then the player obviously aims for D20.

If this misses and scores 20, then D10 can be attempted.

If only 10 is scored this leaves D5.

32 allows even more fall-back scores.

Barry Wilkshire

You may choose to have children use a calculator for this stage.

With 151 to go, Eric can finish with his next three-dart throw. He misses and leaves himself 58 to finish.

Whilst you could challenge pupils to work out a finishing score, (either T17, T20, D20 or T19, T20, D17) thus giving reason for Eric aiming for T17, we believe that the task of subtraction is sufficient challenge at this stage.

Barry Wilkshire cannot finish even after his fifth turn.

Eric tries for 18 D20 and gets it, winning the championship.

6. How could you score 125 with 3 darts?

Continue the tape where it shows games in the final of the Pacific Masters Championship between Eric Bristow and Barry Wilkshire. Eric leads 3 games to 2 in the best of 9 games competition.

Pause when the question is raised in the first game shown.

WE'LL PAUSE THE TAPE HERE.
WRITE DOWN ALL THE POSSIBLE WAYS YOU COULD SCORE 125 WITH THREE DARTS.
THEN WE'LL DISCUSS WHICH IS BEST

7. Subtracting the score from 501 to get the number to finish

Continue the tape of the match between Eric Bristow and Barry Wilkshire (Northern Territory) for the Pacific Masters Darts Championships. As before, have children record the totals of the three throws, but this time pause after Eric has his fourth turn — when he is within a winning score. Children are invited to subtract the totals from 501 for each player.

8. What are the possible finishes?

Children's worksheets should look like this below. Children work out possible finishes and enter them in the lowest box.

	ERIC BRISTOW		BARRY WILKSHIRE	
PUPILS RECORD THE TOTALS OF EACH TURN ON THIS SIDE...	THROWS	TO FINISH	THROWS	TO FINISH
		~~501~~		~~501~~
	140		24	
	25		45	
	85		60	
...AND THEY TOTAL THESE SCORES AND SUBTRACT FROM 501 TO GIVE THE AMOUNT TO FINISH AND RECORD ON THAT SIDE	100	151	41	330

9. Which finishes do you think Eric would try for and what actually happened?

Continue the videotape, pausing again after Eric has had his next turn.

ERIC DIDN'T MAKE THE 151 DID HE? HE SCORED 93. WHAT DOES THAT LEAVE AND HOW CAN IT BE THROWN?

AND WHAT STRATEGY DO YOU THINK ERIC WILL ADOPT?

58   18 D20   T18 D2

Darts 2

'Game on' calls the commentator.

Dave Whitcombe.

The split screen enables the viewers to catch the details

'Ouch!' 'Er, sorry. I still have a dart in my hand.'

Victory!

Darts 2

Darts 2 is an extension of The mathematics of darts. Children watch Eric Bristow and Dave Whitcombe at the 1986 Embassy World Darts Championship and try to beat the announcer at adding the scores, calculating the remainder and considering the best possible finishes.

1. Introduction

Recall the parts of the previous lesson that the children liked best. Also recall the personalities, rules and strategies of the game.

The features and preparation are as for The mathematics of darts (see page 56). You will also need Worksheet 3. You may also wish to make copies of an overhead projectual of the recommended finishes, page 68.

Discuss with the class the common strategy of trying to leave either 40 or 32 to finish. Point out how often D20 and D16 occurs on the recommended finishes.

TELL US WHAT IS DIFFERENT ABOUT THE OUTER RING?

WHAT SCORE DO YOU START WITH?

THE OUTER RING COUNTS AS DOUBLE

WHAT DO YOU NEED TO FINISH?

WHAT IS THE NAME OF THE MEN'S WORLD CHAMPION?

YOU HAVE TO SCORE A DOUBLE TO FINISH

HOW MANY DARTS DO YOU THROW EACH TURN?

OR A BULLSEYE

2. Play the first leg of the first set, pausing as required by the tape to consider possible finishes

The BBC announcer introduces the players and they play the first leg of the first set.

World-class players take about five turns to finish (fifteen darts). But it is quite possible to finish in the third turn.

THIS TIME WE'LL OCCASIONALLY PAUSE TO SUBTRACT AND TO FIND OUT WHETHER THE PLAYER CAN FINISH AT HIS NEXT TURN...

...AND IF HE CAN FINISH, WHAT STRATEGIES COULD HE ADOPT?

John Lowe won £102 000 for being the first person to score 501 at a major event throwing the minimum nine darts. It happened in the World Match Play Championships at Slough, England. His throws were: six successive treble 20's, treble 17, treble 18, and double 18.

3. The fifth set (optional)

If time is limited or interest wanes, you could move on to the sixth and final set.

At this stage teachers have a choice between having children work individually or in small groups to work out different solutions.

4. Sixth and final set — simply enjoy it

By this stage, children will have done a lot of mental computation. They will also have gained a good understanding of the strategies and subtleties of the game of darts. So let them simply enjoy watching the rest of the games, not bothering to keep score, but to *consider finishes* as required by the tape.

Completed sample worksheets for teacher reference are printed on page 66, only some finish as being shown. Not all darts experts would recommend the same finishes.

THIS TIME LET'S NOT BOTHER ABOUT TOTALING. LET'S ENJOY THE GAMES AND WE'LL TRY TO PREDICT THE FINISHING STRATEGIES

Children play the game

Have two or more children play a game while the rest of the class discuss tactics as they play. You could make a game of 201 for less-than champions.

NO! GO FOR A NINE THEN YOU CAN GO FOR A DOUBLE EIGHT

The least number of throws

Challenge children to work out the least number of turns to score 501. Give three examples of sets of throws which achieve this.

I GET THREE

I GET FIVE

Observing trends and patterns

Display the recommended finishes between 52 and 41. What do you notice? Are there other sets of numbers that deserve consideration?

BUT WHY NOT 1 D20 FOR 41?

Extension activities

to The mathematics of darts and Darts 2. *As with the main activities these can be attempted by individuals or in small groups or by the whole class. There are a lot of maths in the analyses.*

Should not-so-good darts players always aim for 20?

Experts aim for treble 20 so that if they miss they will score 20. However if you miss left or right you would only get a low 1 or 5. So if you are not an expert, which group of sectors should you aim for to score as much as possible?

LET'S WORK OUT WHETHER 16 WOULD BE BETTER

There is more to this question than meets the eye. For instance if you aim for 14 and just miss you will get a 9 or 11. Better than if you miss a 20. The question can be asked at many levels with increasingly sophisticated results.

Why you should use this strategy

Select three finishes from the games. Tell children to find three other ways of finishing, writing an argument as to which is preferable.

HE COULD HAVE AIMED FOR TRIPLE TWENTY BUT THAT WOULD HAVE LEFT HIM WITH A SEVEN

Where are the numbers located?

Cover the numbers on a dart board. Challenge children to remember the correct positions. Then discuss the reasons why the arrangement is as it is.

Did the designer do it randomly?

YES! BUT 20's EASY

How many darts to score...?

Younger children could list all the numbers to 60 and find out:

- which can be thrown with a single dart.
- which numbers can be scored with a double.
- which numbers can be scored with a treble.

LOOK AT HOW MANY NUMBERS CAN BE SCORED WITH BOTH SINGLES AND DOUBLES

But what if you miss the number?

Why are there so few double odd numbers in the recommended finishes.

IF YOU MISS AND ONLY GET THE SINGLE NUMBER...

Worksheet 1   # Pacific Masters Darts Championship
Women's Final

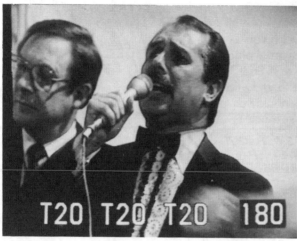

'They love the maximums' cries the commentator.

As you can see, the dart-on-dart scored 0.
How would you score it?

SHARON COLCLOUGH		MAUREEN FLOWERS	
THROWS	TO FINISH 501	THROWS	TO FINISH 501
....	....	....	....
....	....	....	....
....	....	....	....
....	....	....	....
....	....	....	....
....	....	....	....
JUST WRITE THE TOTALS – DON'T SUBTRACT			

Worksheet 2

Pacific Masters Darts Championship
Men's Final

The championship is the best of nine games.
The tape starts with Eric leading three games to two.

Game ⌐6⌐

ERIC   BRISTOW

THROWS	TO FINISH 501

BARRY   WILKSHIRE

THROWS	TO FINISH 501

POSSIBLE FINISHES FOR [   ]

Game ⌐7⌐

ERIC   BRISTOW

THROWS	TO FINISH 501

BARRY   WILKSHIRE

THROWS	TO FINISH 501

POSSIBLE FINISHES FOR [   ]

VIDEO
Years 4 → 10

Worksheet 3(a)

Darts 2

- Each game of 501 is called a 'leg'.
- The first to win three legs takes the set.
- The first to get six sets wins the match and World Championship.
- 'D20' means double 20 or 40. 'T16' means treble 16 or 48.

Set [1] **Leg** [1]

ERIC BRISTOW THROWS	TO FINISH 501	DAVE WHITCOMBE THROWS	TO FINISH 501

POSSIBLE FINISHES FOR [ ]	POSSIBLE FINISHES FOR [ ]
ACTUAL FINISHES	ACTUAL FINISHES

Set [5] **Leg** [1]

ERIC BRISTOW THROWS	TO FINISH 501	DAVE WHITCOMBE THROWS	TO FINISH 501

POSSIBLE FINISHES FOR [ ]	POSSIBLE FINISHES FOR [ ]
ACTUAL FINISHES	ACTUAL FINISHES

Set [5] **Leg** [2]

ERIC BRISTOW THROWS	TO FINISH 501	DAVE WHITCOMBE THROWS	TO FINISH 501

POSSIBLE FINISHES FOR [ ]	POSSIBLE FINISHES FOR [ ]
ACTUAL FINISHES	ACTUAL FINISHES

Worksheet 3(b)

Darts 2

Set 5   Leg 3

ERIC BRISTOW	DAVE WHITCOMBE
THROWS TO FINISH 501	THROWS TO FINISH 501

POSSIBLE FINISHES FOR [ ]

POSSIBLE FINISHES FOR [ ]

ACTUAL FINISHES

ACTUAL FINISHES

Set 5   Leg 4

ERIC BRISTOW	DAVE WHITCOMBE
THROWS TO FINISH 501	THROWS TO FINISH 501

POSSIBLE FINISHES FOR [ ]

POSSIBLE FINISHES FOR [ ]

ACTUAL FINISHES

ACTUAL FINISHES

Set 5   Leg 5

ERIC BRISTOW	DAVE WHITCOMBE
THROWS TO FINISH 501	THROWS TO FINISH 501

POSSIBLE FINISHES FOR [ ]

POSSIBLE FINISHES FOR [ ]

ACTUAL FINISHES

ACTUAL FINISHES

Set 6   Leg 1

ERIC BRISTOW	DAVE WHITCOMBE
POSSIBLE FINISHES FOR [ ]	POSSIBLE FINISHES FOR [ ]

ACTUAL FINISHES

ACTUAL FINISHES

Set 6   Leg 2

ERIC BRISTOW	DAVE WHITCOMBE
POSSIBLE FINISHES FOR [ ]	POSSIBLE FINISHES FOR [ ]

ACTUAL FINISHES

ACTUAL FINISHES

Set 6   Leg 3

ERIC BRISTOW	DAVE WHITCOMBE
POSSIBLE FINISHES FOR [ ]	POSSIBLE FINISHES FOR [ ]

ACTUAL FINISHES

ACTUAL FINISHES

Set 6   Leg 4

ERIC BRISTOW	DAVE WHITCOMBE
POSSIBLE FINISHES FOR [ ]	POSSIBLE FINISHES FOR [ ]

ACTUAL FINISHES

ACTUAL FINISHES

VIDEO

Years 4 ↓ 10

Darts 2

Solutions to Worksheet 3(a)   (For teachers)

- Each game of 501 is called a 'leg'.
- The first to win three legs takes the set.
- The first to get six sets wins the match and World Championship.
- 'D20' means double 20 or 40. 'T16' means treble 16 or 48.

Set 1   Leg 1

ERIC BRISTOW		DAVE WHITCOMBE	
THROWS	TO FINISH 501	THROWS	TO FINISH 501
60		41	
99		45	
123		180	
99		140	
	120	35	
			60

POSSIBLE FINISHES FOR [120]
T20 20 D20

ACTUAL FINISHES
20 20 T20 20
10 5 25Busts 20
0 D10 0✓

POSSIBLE FINISHES FOR [60]
20 D20

ACTUAL FINISHES
20 20 0 20
0 10 5 5

Set 5   Leg 1

ERIC BRISTOW		DAVE WHITCOMBE	
THROWS	TO FINISH 501	THROWS	TO FINISH 501
135		160	
100		60	
96		100	
105		97	
	65	48	
			16

POSSIBLE FINISHES FOR [65]
25 D20
T19 D4

ACTUAL FINISHES
9 16 20 20
0✓

POSSIBLE FINISHES FOR [16]
D8

ACTUAL FINISHES
D8
0✓

Set 5   Leg 2

ERIC BRISTOW		DAVE WHITCOMBE	
THROWS	TO FINISH 501	THROWS	TO FINISH 501
44		140	
100		95	
135		140	
174			126
	48		

POSSIBLE FINISHES FOR [48]
16 D16
D16 D8
8 D20

ACTUAL FINISHES
16 16 D8 0✓

POSSIBLE FINISHES FOR [126]
T20 T10 D18
T19 19 50

ACTUAL FINISHES
19 19 30 68

Darts 2

Solutions to Worksheet 3(b)   (For teachers)

Set 5, Leg 3

ERIC BRISTOW		DAVE WHITCOMBE	
THROWS	TO FINISH 501	THROWS	TO FINISH 501
140		100	
60		80	
140		100	
60		100	
	101	97	
			24

POSSIBLE FINISHES FOR **101**: 19 50 D16, T20 1 D20, T17 18 D16

POSSIBLE FINISHES FOR **24**: D12

ACTUAL FINISHES: 19 25 1   56 | D12   0✓

Set 5, Leg 4

ERIC BRISTOW		DAVE WHITCOMBE	
THROWS	TO FINISH 501	THROWS	TO FINISH 501
60		41	
59		95	
140		140	
100		100	
55			125
	87		

POSSIBLE FINISHES FOR **87**: T17 D18, 17 20 50

POSSIBLE FINISHES FOR **125**: 50 25 50, 25 T20 D20, T20 T11 D16

ACTUAL FINISHES: 17 20 50 0✓ | 25 20 20 60

Set 5, Leg 5

ERIC BRISTOW		DAVE WHITCOMBE	
THROWS	TO FINISH 501	THROWS	TO FINISH 501
140		60	
58		140	
100		95	
100		100	
	103	98	
		8	

POSSIBLE FINISHES FOR **103**: 20 T17 D16, T17 20 D16

POSSIBLE FINISHES FOR **8**: D4

ACTUAL FINISHES: 20 T17 D16 0✓

Set 6, Leg 1

DAVE WHITCOMBE — POSSIBLE FINISHES FOR **24**: D12
ACTUAL FINISHES: 12 D6 (24) 0✓

ERIC BRISTOW — POSSIBLE FINISHES FOR **36**: D18
ACTUAL FINISHES: D18

Set 6, Leg 2

ERIC BRISTOW — POSSIBLE FINISHES FOR **56**: 16 D20
ACTUAL FINISHES: 16 D20 (56) 0✓

DAVE WHITCOMBE — POSSIBLE FINISHES FOR **74**: T14 D16
ACTUAL FINISHES: 9 15 25 (49) 25

Set 6, Leg 3

ERIC BRISTOW — POSSIBLE FINISHES FOR **16**: D8
ACTUAL FINISHES: D8 (16) 0✓

DAVE WHITCOMBE — POSSIBLE FINISHES FOR **141**: T20 T19 D12, T20 T15 D18
ACTUAL FINISHES:

Set 6, Leg 4

ERIC BRISTOW — POSSIBLE FINISHES FOR **43**: 11 D16
ACTUAL FINISHES: 11 0 0 (11) 32

DAVE WHITCOMBE — POSSIBLE FINISHES FOR **160**: T20 T20 D20
ACTUAL FINISHES: T20 T20 20 (140) 20, 10 D5 (20) 0✓

Years 4→10

VIDEO

Recommended finishes for the darts game 501

180	4 darts	120	T20 20 D20
179	4 darts	119	T20 19 D20 or T19 T10 D16
178	4 darts	118	T20 18 D20
177	4 darts	117	T20 17 D20 or T19 20 D20
176	4 darts	116	T20 20 D18
175	4 darts	115	T20 15 D20
174	4 darts	114	T20 18 D18 or T20 14 D20
173	4 darts	113	T20 13 D20
172	4 darts	112	T20 12 D20
171	4 darts	111	T20 19 D16 or T17 20 D20
170	T20 T20 bull	110	T20 18 D16
169	4 darts	109	T20 17 D16
168	4 darts	108	T20 16 D16
167	T20 T19 bull	107	T20 10 D20 or T19 18 D16
166	4 darts	106	T20 10 D18 or T20 14 D16
165	4 darts	105	T20 13 D16
164	T20 T18 bull	104	T20 12 D16 or T18 18 D16
163	4 darts	103	T17 20 D16
162	4 darts	102	T20 10 D16
161	T20 T17 bull	101	T17 10 D20 or T17 18 D16
160	T20 T20 D20	100	T20 D20
159	4 darts	99	T19 10 D16
158	T20 T20 D19	98	T20 D19
157	T19 T20 D20	97	T19 D20
156	T20 T20 D18	96	T20 D18
155	T20 T19 D19	95	T19 D19
154	T18 T20 D20	94	T18 D20
153	T20 T19 D18	93	T19 D18
152	T20 T20 D16	92	T20 D16
151	T17 T20 D20	91	T17 D20
150	T20 T18 D18	90	T18 D18
149	T20 T19 D16	89	T19 D16
148	T20 T20 D14 or T20 T16 D20	88	T16 D20
147	T20 T17 D18	87	T17 D18
146	T20 T18 D16	86	T18 D16
145	T20 T15 D20	85	T15 D20
144	T20 T20 D12	84	T20 D12
143	T20 T17 D16	83	T17 D16
142	T20 T14 D20	82	Bull D16
141	T20 T19 D12	81	T19 D12
140	T20 T20 D10 or T20 T16 D16	80	T20 D10 or T16 D16
139	T20 T13 D20	79	T13 D20
138	T20 T18 D12	78	T18 D12
137	T19 T16 D16 or T20 T15 D16	77	T15 D16
136	T20 T20 D8	76	T20 D8
135	T20 T15 D15	75	T13 D18
134	T20 T14 D16	74	T14 D16
133	T20 T19 D8	73	T19 D8
132	T20 T16 D12	72	T16 D12
131	T20 T13 D16	71	T13 D16
130	T20 T18 D8	70	T10 D20
129	T20 T11 D18	69	T11 D18
128	T20 T20 D4	68	T20 D4
127	T20 T17 D8	67	T17 D8
126	T19 T11 D18 or T20 T18 D6	66	T18 D6 or T10 D18
125	T20 T11 D16 or T20 T19 D4	65	T19 D4
124	T20 T16 D8	64	T16 D8
123	T20 T13 D12	63	T17 D6 or T13 D12
122	T18 T18 D16	62	T14 D10
121	T19 T16 D8	61	T15 D8

60	20 D20
59	19 D20
58	18 D20
57	17 D20
56	16 D20
55	15 D20
54	14 D20
53	13 D20
52	20 D16
51	19 D16
50	18 D16
49	17 D16
48	16 D16
47	15 D16
46	14 D16
45	13 D16
44	12 D16
43	11 D16
42	10 D16
41	9 D16
40	D20
39	7 D16
38	D19
37	5 D16
36	D18
35	3 D16
34	D17
33	1 D16
32	D16
31	15 D8
30	D15
29	13 D8
28	D14
27	11 D8
26	D13
25	9 D8
24	D12
23	7 D8
22	D11
21	5 D8
20	D10
19	3 D8
18	D9
17	1 D8
16	D8
15	7 D4
14	D7
13	5 D4
12	D6
11	3 D4
10	D5
9	1 D4
8	D4
7	3 D2
6	D3
5	1 D2
4	D2
3	1D1
2	D1
1	Score is bust.

The mathematics of diving

This videotape shows seven of the best of the women's dives and their scores from the 1984 Olympic Games. It has been produced as a teaching aid, to illustrate a realistic application of mathematics as well as a particular role that video can play in maths teaching.

The spirit of the way the activity is presented, is to let the pupils experience success in finding the correct score and to feel 'qualified' to be a judge at the next competition they see.

The features of this activity

- The concept that maths is often used in sport scoring systems.
- A realistic application of maths.
- Video clips as a different way to teach maths.
- Exposure to excellence in performance and the Olympic Ideal.
- Exercises in decimals and averages.
- Use of calculators.
- A non-threatening learning atmosphere.

Equipment

- A videotape player.
- The videotape supporting this activity is
- Calculators, one between two children.
- Photocopied worksheets (pages 73-4) — one per pupil.

The eventual winner, Sylvia Bernier (Canada).

The mathematics of diving

A videotape of diving events at the Olympic Games enables pupils to use calculators and maths to learn and understand the internationally-used scoring system in a non-threatening way.

If pupils are not familiar or comfortable with calculator use, some preliminary practice in adding a list of decimal numbers may be useful. (This is probably better done on a prior session.)

Read out these sets slowly to check pupils' skills.

8.5 8 6.5 6 5.5 (Total = 49.0)
9.0 8 6.5 6 6.5 (Total = 46.5)

Trials schools found one calculator per pair of pupils preferable to one each as it naturally generates useful informal discussion.

1. Preview the videotape

It runs for 25 minutes. After the section for screening to the class — the events and credits, there is a one-minute blank, followed by a four-minute discussion of the philosophy and development of the unit, followed by another set of dives for extra practice.

2. Introduction

Give out worksheets and ensure there is one calculator per pair of pupils

I HAVE HERE A VIDEOTAPE OF THE 1984 OLYMPIC GAMES WOMEN'S DIVING FINALS. YOU WILL SEE THE BEST DIVING IN THE WORLD.

BUT DO YOU KNOW HOW THE DIVES ARE SCORED?

IT IS REALLY QUITE INTERESTING, AND VERY MATHEMATICAL

MOST OF THE INSTRUCTIONS ARE ON THE TAPE, SO LET'S GET STARTED

3. The four steps for calculating the final score

Step 1. Cross out the highest and lowest score.
(Reason: to avoid possible errors by judges.)

~~7.0~~
6.5
7.0
~~6.5~~
7.0
7.0
6.5

Step 2. Average the five remaining scores.
(Reason: To give the competitor just one score representative of all judges.)

5)34.5

Step 3. Multiply by three.
(*Reason:* All international diving scores are based upon a three-judge total.)

6.9
x3
20.7

Step 4. Multiply by the Degree of Difficulty.
(*Reason:* Some dives are more difficult than others.)

20.7
x2.9
60.03

Pupils like doing all the calculations on the calculator. There is no need to write down intermediate results.

4. Practice examples

Estimation: Pupils seem to enjoy trying to 'be the judge', and write down their opinion, for example, 5.5, 6.0 etc. However, it is not an essential part of the lesson and they may like to see several dives before feeling comfortable making their own guesses.

All the teacher needs to do each time is push the PAUSE button **twice** (after slow-motion dive),

(i) **just before** scores appear (as 'feet go into the water') to allow pupils to estimate scores,

(ii) **as soon as** the scores appear on the screen.

When the answers have been calculated, let the video run-on for pupils to verify their calculations. The dive is then shown again in slow motion. (Answers are shown at the bottom of the page.)

> Look for children who may be having difficulties. Be sure that every child participates and does the calculations correctly. Where errors occur, be sure that the pupil recognises and understands them and the solutions.

One of the scores as displayed showing name, country, degree of difficulty and final score.

JENNY DONNET	7.5
AUSTRALIA	6.5
	7.0
DD 2.9	6.5
	7.0
SCORE	7.0
60.03	6.5

5. Conclusion

There are three options.

(i) Towards the end of the tape there are three extra dives taken from the previous round of the same competition. This can fill out the lesson if the time permits, or be used in a second session if enthusiasm remains.

(ii) Problem solving — a follow-up analysis of various aspects of the scoring. (See Extension worksheet)

(iii) A fun 'Test' to run in the last five minutes of the lesson.

'O.K. Here is your test to see if you can qualify as in international judge! I'll read out the seven scores — you calculate the final score'.

Question 1. 7.5 8.5 8.0 8.0 8.5 7.0 7.5

$$DD = 2.4$$

Question 2. 8.0 7.0 7.0 6.5 7.0 7.5 6.5

$$DD = 3.4$$

> Comments from trials schools:
> *'Pupils felt they had learned something interesting and useful and many proudly reported they went home and shared their newly found knowledge.'*
> *'We set up a judging "panel" of seven pupils and compared their results with the real scores — added extra drama and participation'*
> *'Another feature our school liked was the multicultural aspect.'*
> *I like the natural way calculators fit into the activity.'*
> *'All students, including the less-able got involved and felt successful.'*

Answers:

	Final round	Previous round
J. Donnet	60.03	-
L. Qiaoxian	61.56	38.64
C. Seufert	70.47	60.48
D. Jongejans	50.40	32.76
S. Bernier	62.25	56.70
K. McCormick	67.20	63.10

Extension activities

Can you work these out too?

How much must Kelly score to win the Gold Medal?

What sets of scores would *just* give Kelly McCormick 70.45 points to win the Gold Medal?

If Kelly had chosen a dive with a D.D. of 3.2, what *average* score would she have needed to win the Gold Medal?

What are the minimum scores Li Yihua would need?

Li Yihua needed 76.9 to win the Bronze Medal. She chose a forward twist with double back somersault which has a D.D. of 3.0 What is one possible set of scores which will give her this?

I DID ONE OF THOSE DIVES WHEN SOMEONE PUT A FROG DOWN MY BATHERS

What is the maximum score possible

for various degrees of difficulty?

DD	2.0	2.4	2.6	2.8	2.9	3.0	3.1	3.5
Max. score								

What can you tell just by looking at the scores?

Below are the scores and D.D.s for three divers. Some scores are much higher than others. But be careful. The highest score may not give the highest *total* score. (Why?)

Estimate who you think will get the highest total score.

IT WOULD PROBABLY BE... BECAUSE...

Discuss your estimates with your classmates, telling why you chose that person.

Check your answer using a calculator.

Judge other performances the same way

Judge skating, ballet, acting, boxing, karate, TV shows, movies and other interests you may have.

Form groups of judges and find out how other groups rate the same performances.

EH! ONLY A TWO?

One of the major themes is recognition of the role of maths in attributing a score to a performance.

	JOE	MINH	CARLA
	8.5	7.5	7.0
	9.0	8.0	7.5
	8.5	7.5	7.0
	8.0	7.5	6.5
	7.5	7.5	5.5
	8.5	6.5	5.5
	9.0	7.0	6.0
DEGREE OF DIFFICULTY	2.4	2.8	3.5

Other ways of showing the scores.

Work out convenient ways, such as books of 'flash' cards or simply holding up fingers.

Worksheet 1   The mathematics of diving

Method
1. Cross out the highest and lowest. (To eliminate possible errors.)
2. Add remaining marks: divide by 5 . (To find the average.)
3. Multiply by 3. (Three-judge system is used.)
4. Multiply by Degree of Difficulty: DD (To reward success at difficult dives.)

Sample dive

Jenny Donnet (Australia)

1.
2.
3.
4.
5.
6.
7._____

Average score

$\div 5 =$ ☐

_____

$\times 3 \times DD =$ ☐ Final score

Practice

Dive 1: L. Qiaoxian (China)

Your guess: ☐

1.
2.
3.
4.   DD =
5.
6.
7.

→ ☐ Final score

Dive 2: C. Suefert (U.S.A.)

Your guess: ☐

1.
2.
3.
4.   DD =
5.
6.
7.

→ ☐ Final score

Worksheet 2   # The mathematics of diving

Dive D. Jongejans (Holland)

Your guess:

1.
2.
3
4.   DD =
5.
6.
7.

→ [ ] Final score

Dive S. Bernier (Canada)

Your guess:

1.
2.
3
4.   DD =
5.
6.
7.

→ [ ] Final score

Dive K. McCormick(U.S.A.)

Your guess:

1.
2.
3
4.   DD =
5.
6.
7.

→ [ ] Final score

FURTHER PRACTICE

Dive L. Qiaoxoan (China)

Your guess:

1.
2.
3
4.   DD =
5.
6.
7.

→ [ ] Final score

Dive C. Seufert (U.S.A.)

Your guess:

1.
2.
3
4.   DD =
5.
6.
7.

→ [ ] Final score

Dive D. Jongejans (Holland)

Your guess:

1.
2.
3
4.   DD =
5.
6.
7.

→ [ ] Final score

Dive S. Bernier (Canada)

Your guess:

1.
2.
3
4.   DD =
5.
6.
7.

→ [ ] Final score

Dive K. McCormick (U.S.A.)

Your guess:

1.
2.
3
4.   DD =
5.
6.
7.

→ [ ] Final score

Dive L. Yihua (China)

Your guess:

1.
2.
3
4.   DD =
5.
6.
7.

→ [ ] Final score

Simulation of the TAB

Gambling is widespread in our community. Do pupils, about to leave school, have realistic expectations about the outcomes of gambling? Trials schools say 'No!' and report a huge gap between perception and reality.

Here we attempt to show TAB gambling and its mathematical realities. There are few other opportunities for pupils to learn its costs in such an objective way.

We recommend that you inform parents about this activity either via your pupils or, for preference, directly with handouts to prevent misrepresentation occurring.

One trials school ran this activity as part of a parents' day. It generated much valuable public discussion and support.

THIS ACTIVITY IS PART OF THE MCTP PROFESSIONAL DEVELOPMENT PACKAGE FROM THE CURRICULUM DEVELOPMENT CENTRE, CANBERRA

Years 9 → 10 | VIDEO

The aims of this activity

Mathematical. Pupils will practise using percentage and other mathematical skills in a realistic situation with real form guides and real races. And, by analysing the results, children will develop some concepts of compound interest — in this case compound depreciation.

Social/Moral. Pupils will develop evidence-based awareness of the way TAB actually operates, so that their expectations are realistic if they decide to 'invest' on the TAB.

We neither wish to encourage nor discourage gambling as entertainment, but we use the maths to help children develop realistic expectations about the TAB.

Features of this activity

- Simulation of events as near to the real situation as possible.
- Highly motivating activities.
- An important social issue — being realistic about gambling.
- Based upon the contrast between popular perception and reality.
- Use of calculators.
- Concepts of compound interest — in this case, compound depreciation.
- A demonstration of mathematical modelling.

Background

The expectations of the punter

The TAB is a huge, multi-million dollar enterprise.

One recent advertising campaign which renamed the TAB agencies 'The Lucky Shop', raises interesting questions about how the public perceives the TAB.

The TAB is often suggested as a better investment agency than Lotto for gamblers, because only about 15-20% of the investment is withheld by the TAB, compared with about 40% in Lotto. However the reality of punters' behaviour is that money returned as dividends is reinvested, thus making it subject to a compounding effect.

A punter starting with $100 and betting it all on each of eight races will have it theoretically reduced to $100 x (0.8)^8 = $17. Clearly this is not the way real punters operate. (They may spread their $100 or bet on fewer races.) But it is a simplified mathematical model. However a

punter who starts with $100 and ends up with under $50 may consider himself/herself just unlucky, expecting normally to end up with $80. This lesson aims to help pupils develop a realistic expectation of these situations.

Simulation of the TAB

'Pupils were so motivated by these activities that the high level maths and quick calculations required were taken in their stride. But best of all, the lessons proved to be one of the best ways to encourage children to challenge and debunk widely held and popular myths about gambling.'

'The pupils could vividly see that the TAB never loses and that after a while the TAB would own nearly all the money'.

Comments from trials schools.

These activities worked best when divided into three separate sessions.

Session 1. Present and explore, in discussion, the TAB images — is TAB really the 'The Lucky Shop'? Can TAB lose?

Quantify pupils perceptions and expectations.

Show a horse race and simulate betting operations.

Session 2. Races 2–9 of a meeting. Use a streamlined procedure to get through 8 races. Pupils see TAB takings steadily rising while average class holdings diminish.

Session 3. (or homework) Extension analysis of compound depreciation of reinvesting winnings.

There has been wide advertising of the TAB as 'The Lucky Shop' to attract new punters. In the long run only the TAB wins. The degree of difference between perception and reality is one measure of the 'social issue' aspect of gambling. This activity hopefully will close the gap for some pupils.

Preparation

- The MCTP tape *Maths of the TAB* has two complete meetings available, one from harness racing, one from greyhounds. An alternative is to make a tape recording of races from TV sport or radio about two or three weeks in advance. This adds greatly to the 'reality ' of the simulation. Results in envelopes or dice are a poor alternative. Harness and greyhound races were chosen because of limited numbers in each race and because children found it easier to follow their selection than for race horses.

- Print enough copies of the form guide for each pupil for your taped race meeting and the Punters' Record Sheet, page 82.

- Make an overhead transparency of the Punter's Record Sheet.

- Have at least one calculator for the room — one per child is ideal.

- A clock.

Session 1.

Finding out and recording children's perception and knowledge of race meetings and betting

Children must be free to give their honest perceptions without fear of ridicule or any hint of bias by the teacher. Avoid praising what you see as good attitudes at this stage. Let attitudes be formed by their objective inquiries.

Record the answers, for we will re-examine them at the end of the program.

Quantifying children's perceptions

Distribute the worksheets and project and overhead transparency to show pupils where to enter their opinions.

Explain that they must write down what they honestly feel. That is, not to be frivolous or fanciful.

Introduce a videotape of a real race meeting

> WE ARE GOING TO RUN A SIMULATED RACE MEETING TO SHOW HOW TAB BETTING WORKS

> YOU WILL ALL START WITH A HYPOTHETICAL $100 TO 'INVEST' ANY WAY YOU LIKE. WE WILL HAVE RACES ON VIDEO.
>
> WE WILL COLLECT THE DATA AND DO THE CALCULATIONS NORMALLY DONE BY THE TAB STAFF AND COMPUTER

> WE WILL RUN ONE RACE IN DETAIL THIS SESSION AND THE REMAINING RACES NEXT SESSION

> BUT BEFORE WE START I'D REALLY LIKE TO GET YOUR GUESSES ABOUT THE LIKELY OUTCOMES.
>
> REALISTICALLY WE KNOW SOME WILL WIN, OTHERS PROBABLY LOSE

> ...IN THIS BOX WRITE THE PERCENTAGE OF THE CLASS WHO WILL WIN...
>
> ...IN THIS BOX THE AVERAGE HOLDINGS OF THE CLASS AFTER THE EIGHT RACES...
>
> ...AND IN THIS BOX HOW MUCH MONEY THE TAB WILL HAVE WON (OR LOST)

Years 9 ↓ 10   **VIDEO**

Place your bets

Hand out the form guides.

> IN FRONT OF THE NAME OF EACH HORSE ARE THREE DIGITS.
>
> THOSE ARE THE PLACES THE HORSE CAME IN THE LAST THREE RACES.
>
> BUT THEY DON'T TELL THE CLASS OF RACE OR HOW FAST

> SO STUDY THE FORM AND SELECTIONS AND PLACE YOUR BETS ON AS MANY HORSES AS YOU LIKE.
>
> BETS ARE FOR WIN AND ARE IN $5 OR MULTIPLES OF $5

Discuss how the horse most likely to win — the favourite, has a 'short' dividend (low payout) and a horse not likely to win, a 'long shot', has a greater dividend.

Pupils can calculate the expected dividend for all horses. This may also be done as an extension activity.

While pupils are recording their bets on the record sheets, draw up columns like these below on the chalkboard.

> WOULD YOU LIKE TO COME OUT AND RECORD YOUR BETS BY ADDING YOUR BET TO THE LAST TOTAL?

Total all the bets to find the Total Class Investment.

HORSE SENSE???

The reasons for choosing horses are numerous. Professional tipsters study the 'form' which means the recent performances of the horse. But even tipsters disagree. Other people look at past performances and if the horse came 8th, 4th then 2nd they say 'it is due for a win'. Other people pick horses for less obvious reasons like lucky numbers or the name has a coincidental meaning.

Calculate the amount the TAB takes

After all bets are recorded, use a calculator to find the Total Class Investment, that is, the total of all bets on this race, then eventually the total TAB takes.

> ENTER THE TOTAL CLASS INVESTMENT HERE IN YOUR RECORD SHEETS...
>
> ...THEN WE CAN CALCULATE THE 20% THE TAB TAKES. WRITE THIS DOWN HERE

> ...THEN SUBTRACT THE TAKE FROM THE TOTAL CLASS INVESTMENT.
>
> THAT LEAVES THE TOTAL PAYOUT THE TAB WILL GIVE BACK TO THE PUNTERS WHO WIN

The 20% TAB take is an approximate figure. The actual TAB take varies with types of events.

Have pupils identify their winning bets on the chalkboard as a check on accuracy. Don't worry about small discrepancies. They won't seriously affect the statistics.

'They're off'

Run the race — at least the first part up to when the horses enter the straight for the last time, on fast picture search, with the finish at normal speed.

> WELL — THE FAVOURITE WON.
> HOW MANY OF YOU BET ON IT?
> CIRCLE YOUR WINNING BET.
> WHO'S BET WAS THIS?
> WHO'S WAS THIS?

Work out your dividends

> LET'S WORK OUT YOUR DIVIDENDS.
> GET YOUR CALCULATORS. DIVIDE YOUR TOTAL PAYOUT BY THE NUMBER OF DOLLARS BET ON THE WINNER.
> ROUND THAT TO THE NEAREST FIVE CENTS

> WRITE THE DIVIDEND HERE...
> WORK OUT YOUR OWN WINNINGS. MULTIPLY THE DIVIDEND BY THE AMOUNT YOU PUT ON THE WINNING HORSE

> THEN ADD THIS AND YOUR BALANCE TO GET YOUR FINAL BALANCE

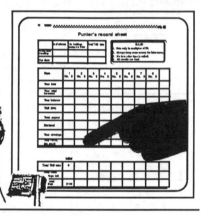

How much does the class have now?

> NOW ORIGINALLY THE CLASS HOLDINGS WERE $100 EACH BY 30 OF YOU.
> THAT MAKES $3,000.
> WRITE THAT HERE...

> ... FROM THAT SUBTRACT THE TOTAL TAB TAKE.
> WRITE THAT HERE...

> THEN DIVIDE IT BY THE NUMBER OF PUPILS IN THE CLASS — 30.
> THIS GIVES THE AVERAGE CLASS HOLDINGS.
> ENTER IT HERE

The probability is that there will be more losers than winners. Make sure that the class is well aware of this.

Rounding off the lesson and preparing for Session 2

Discuss what pupils have learned.

There is one area of concern that must be countered, that is some pupils will have 'won' and could go away with the feeling that gambling is profitable. By responsible questioning, remove any such confidences, yet do not destroy the important point of discussion in the next session.

> HOW MANY PEOPLE HAVE MORE MONEY
>
> HOW MANY HAVE LESS

> OF THOSE WHO WON, DOES ANYONE THINK THEY WILL KEEP WINNING?

> NEXT SESSION WE WILL BE HAVING THE OTHER RACES FROM THIS MEETING.
> WE'LL FIND OUT TOMORROW

Collect the sheets so that they will not be lost or forgotten for the next session.

Session 2. **The rest of the race meeting**

The class must work quickly to get through all eight races before the end of the lesson, so limit the times between each race.

> LET'S GO OVER HOW YOU FILL IN YOUR RECORD SHEET NOW...

> WE MUST WORK QUICKLY THIS SESSION.
> ALL BETS CLOSE AND THE RACE STARTS ON THE FIVE-MINUTE MARK — SO GO!
> YOU HAVE THREE MINUTES TO STUDY THE FORM AND PLACE YOUR BETS

The discussion period at the end of this session is most important. So leave at least fifteen minutes. This may necessitate running fewer races. If you do, extrapolate the TAB holdings, class holdings and the average class holdings to the last race.

To pace your lesson, a bell or gong will add realism to the start.

Compare the realities with the estimates made at the beginning

> HOW MANY PUNTERS MADE A PROFIT? HOW MANY MADE A LOSS?

> WHAT FRACTION OF THE CLASS MADE A PROFIT? HOW DOES THIS COMPARE WITH YOUR INITIAL ESTIMATE?

> DID THE TAB TAKINGS MATCH YOUR ESTIMATES?

> WHAT PERCENTAGE OF THE ORIGINAL CLASS HOLDINGS DID THE TAB TAKE?

Point out how the average of 30 pupils at one race meeting is mathematically the same as one person at 30 meetings, that is, your long-term average.

Record the results on the chalkboard for pupils to use later.

Review the original questions and perceptions

> CAN THE TAB LOSE?

> IS THERE ANY LUCK INVOLVED ON THE TAB SIDE? WILL THE TAB'S AMOUNT EVER SHRINK?

> CAN ANY OF THIS MONEY EVER BE RETURNED TO THE PUNTER AS DIVIDENDS?

> WHAT WOULD HAPPEN WITH THE MONEY IF THE PUNTER RETURNED NEXT WEEK WITH THE LEFT- OVER FROM LAST WEEK?

This question is critical to the development of the concept of compound interest (or compound loss) to be analysed in the next session.

Collect the record sheets so that they will not be lost or forgotten for the next session.

Pupils are usually very surprised that although TAB takes only 20% from each race's takings, the final percentage is much higher.

The reason for the relentless growth of the TAB share is the compounding effect produced by reinvestment. For every dollar that 'visits' the TAB, it is successively diminished.

This model is closer to the average punter's behaviour than when always betting all moneys on all races.

Session 3.

Analysis and looking back

On the chalkboard, make a chart like this (below). Children copy it into their workbooks. Analyse the percentage of all the moneys the TAB holds after each race.

> HOW DO YOU THINK PUNTERS FARE WITH THE TAB?

> HOW COME WE INVESTED $5 000 WHEN WE ONLY HAD $3 000?

> BLIMEY! AFTER A WHILE TAB WILL HAVE ALL THE MONEY

Such pupils are beginning to grasp the realities of compound interest.

RACE	1	2	3	4	5	6	7	8
TOTAL BETS INVESTED (ACCUMULATE THESE)								
TOTAL TAB TAKE								
TAB AS % OF HOLDINGS								

How does betting on the TAB relate to Compound Interest — exploring a mathematical model

This section formalises the mathematics of betting strategies and how they are subject to a compounding effect.

1. Betting all the money on every race

> LET'S FOLLOW THE FORTUNES OF $100 AS IT VISITS AND 'REVISITS' THE TAB

> WE USE A CALCULATOR TO CONTINUE TO RACE 8

> AFTER THE FIRST RACE TAB TAKES 20%, WHAT DOES THAT LEAVE?

> SECOND LEG. NOW WE HAVE $80 TO INVEST. WHAT HAPPENS TO THAT? etc. etc. etc.

RACE	1	2	3	
START	100	80	64	
BET	100	80	64	(and so on)
BALANCE	80	64	51.2	

$51.20

$80

$64

$40.96

Pupils with calculators can compute the money sequence for the eight races. **The answers are:** $100.00 $80.00 $64.00 $51.20 $40.96 $32.72 $26.21 $30.97 $16.78

Hence the strategy reduces the $100 to $16.78, and the TAB holds 83% (i.e. $83.22)

Clearly, few punters bet in this way in practice.

---

2. Bet half and keep half strategy

Pupils can fill in the table and discover that this strategy is equal to a 10% loss per race and a final holding of $43.05.

RACE	1	2	3	4	5	6	7	8
START	100	90	81	72.9	65.6	59	53.1	47.8
BET	50	45	40.5	36.4	32.8	29.5	26.5	23.9
KEPT	50	45	40.5	36.4	32.8	29.5	26.5	23.9
RETURN	40	34	32.4	29.1	26.2	23.6	21.2	19.1
BALANCE	90	81	72.9	65.6	59	53.1	47.8	43

3. What strategy did the class use on average?

Pupils with calculators could find the 'typical strategy' their class used and the loss rate by simple trial and error method.

Trials class's results ranged from $60 to $72 returned on $100. This corresponds to a loss per race of 5% average and a betting strategy of keeping back ¾ of the money. (Mathematical final balance is $66.34.) You could pose the question, *'Since you only bet a quarter of your money, is it the same as starting with $25 and betting the lot, or starting with $400?'* Of course if a punter bets all of the money on all races, one loss loses all, whereas by betting a quarter you at least play four races.

---

4. Computer extensions

Computer programs could be written to model different betting strategies. For instance, what betting strategy would return 75% after eight races?

All the above are designed to illustrate that **compound interest** and not simple interest applies in betting.

The concept of turnover

In the above model of betting all the money every race, we started with $100, finished with $16.78, but 'invested' (or turned over) a total of $100 + 80 + 64 + ... 20.97 = $416.21.

What was the 'turnover' for the other strategies explored?

Explore these figures

If the public investment or turnover was $1 358 000 000, how much 'real' money was invested?

HERE ARE THE 1986 VICTORIAN TAB FIGURES

TAB IN VICTORIA 1986-87*

TOTALISATOR INVESTMENTS $1,358,237,000

RETURNED AS DIVIDENDS $1,142,196,000

* Source TAB annual report 1987

Sportscolour
Race 9 18-10-86

Punter's record sheet

	% of winners	Av. holdings (starting with $100)	Total TAB take
A real race meeting			
Our class			

Race	1 No. $	2 No. $	3 No. $	4 No. $	5 No. $	6 No. $	7 No. $	8 No. $	
Your bets									
Your total invested									
Your balance									

Total class investment									
TAB 20%									
Total payout									
Number of $s on the winner									
Dividend									

Your winnings									
Your FINAL BALANCE									

	Initial								
Total TAB take	0								
Total class holdings left									
Av. total holdings	$100								

Simulation of the TAB
Form guides for harness racing

		'THE AGE' Ray Huxley	'THE AGE' Dennis Jose	SUN N. Donnelley	BOOKMAKER Bill Hutchison
1	7.00	VANCE GLEN SHY TYPE IMA ORPHAN	VANCE GLEN SHY TYPE CHANNEL THUNDER	VANCE GLEN SHY TYPE LIGHTNING TWO	VANCE GLEN IMA ORPHAN LIGHTNING TWO
2	7.30	ARTLIMOND BOBBY'S PET FINDSUMORE	BOBBY'S PET ARTLIMOND MAJEST. JESTER	FINDSUMORE BOBBY'S PET ARTLIMOND	MAJEST. JESTER FINDSUMORE ARTLIMOND
3	7.55	SIR VANCE MIGHTY SCOTCH ATOM BRAE	SIR VANCE HOKUM MIGHTY SCOTCH	HOKUM MIGHTY SCOTCH SIR VANCE	SIR VANCE HOKUM MIGHTY SCOTCH
4	8.20	IDAMAC IMA LOWDEN SPARECHILD	ONE HAPPY FELLA IDAMAC SPARECHILD	IDAMAC SPARECHILD IMA LOWDEN	IDAMAC ONE HAPPY FELLA SPARECHILD
5	8.45	QUITE FAMOUS TRUNKEY WEST IMATHREAT	TRUNKEY WEST QUITE FAMOUS GAME ORO	QUITE FAMOUS IMATHREAT GOSH	GAME ORO ARMCHAIR RIDE TRUNKEY WEST
6	9.15	COON. MEADOW SPARE BEAU HOW. THAT LADY	COON. MEADOW HOW. THAT LADY ABLE THOR	COON MEADOW SPARE BEAU NARRALITE	COON MEADOW SPARE BEAU NARRALITE
7	9.45	TRUE ROMAN LORD ALIAS BLACKWOOD MAC	TRUE ROMAN MINNESOTA FATS LORD ALIAS	TRUE ROMAN LORD ALIAS MINNESOTA FATS	TRUE ROMAN LORD ALIAS LESLIE ORMOND
8	10.15	SMOOTH FALCON SPAN. PERFUME IRISH BRAE	SMOOTH FALCON CALOPHYLIA SPAN. PERFUME	SMOOTH FALCON DRAST. ACTION CALOPHYLIA	SMOOTH FALCON CARDINAL WAY DRAST. ACTION
9	10.45	BLAZIN ROMEO HANOVER BOY WEIR BORN	WEIR BORN BLAZIN ROMEO HANOVER BOY	CADILLAC RANCH BLAZIN ROMEO WEIR BORN	HANOVER BOY WEIR BORN CADILLAC RANCH

Years 9 ↓ 10   VIDEO

▓ BETTING ▓

Race 1
Ev VANCE GLEN
4 Lightning Two
9-2 Shy Type
5 Ima Orphan
10 Channel Thunder
12 Dark Dreamer, Henry Bruce
20 Arco Belino
25 Times Run Out

Race 2
7-4 MAJESTIC JESTER
3 Artlimond, Findsumore
7 Bobby's Pet
8 Craig's Pride
12 Amarna, Hilarious Tune
15 Rippleite, Hilarious Gift

Race 3
7-4 SIR VANCE
3 Mighty Scotch, Hokum
10 Acacia Lad, Joe Louis, Myrnlong Looney
12 Crafty Leigh, Atom Brae, Smiley Lad

Race 4
5-2 IDAMAC
3 One Happy Fella
9-2 Sparechild, Ima Lowden
12 Demon Doon, Idol Elmo
15 Gracefield Lad, Snappy Chap
20 Rosenkaviller

Race 5
7-2 IMATHREAT, GAME ORO
4 Trunkey Westerner, Quite Famous
7 Armchair Ride, Pascinelle
8 Armbro Gold
10 Gosh
25 Adios Moth

Race 6
4-6 COONARA MEADOW
4 Spare Beau
9-2 Narralite
6 How's That Lady
15 Good Time Dancer
20 Deux Dark Ones, Super Tinge
33 Karamea Loobatross, Snow Byrd

Race 7
1-3 TRUE ROMAN
4 Lord Alias
10 Leslie Ormond
15 Blackwood Mac
15 Downsouth Clare, Admiral Aaron
20 Minnesota Fats, Wongala Supreme
33 Our Sylvania

Race 8
1-8 SMOOTH FALCON
15 Cardinal Way, Calophylia, Drastic Action
20 Amazing Choice
33 Irish Brae, Avant Garde, Spanish Perfume
100 North Hanover

Race 9
2 BLAZIN ROMEO
3 Hanover Boy
9-2 Weir Born, Cadillac Ranch, Lost Ambitions
10 Burning Gold
12 Myrnlong Glenn
20 Maleguena
50 Charisma Star

---

1. **7 O'CLOCK STAKES** **7.00**
$7400. Mobile 2380 metres.
1—114 Shy Type   J F Ryan Fr   6—444 Dark Dreamer   K R Trembath Fr
2—529 Channel Thunder   W B Clarke Fr   7—110 Ima Orphan   V J Knight Fr
3—198 Arco Belino   P J Wells Fr   8—645 Henry Bruce   N F Shinn Fr
4—381 Vance Glen   J O'Sullivan Fr   9—104 Times Run Out   F Scicluna Fr
5—133 Lightning Two   B W Alford Fr

2. **NORTHWOOD PARK STAKES** **7.30**
$3400. Mobile 1940 metres.
1—522 Artlimond   R Pace Fr   6—133 Majestic Jester   G A Lang Fr
2—322 Craig's Pride   C N Fletcher Fr   7—122 Amarna   B R Gath Fr
3—118 Findsumore   L G Hobbs Fr   8—521 Hilarious Tune   K M Dunsford Fr
4—415 Rippleite   M L O'Brien Fr   9—Bobby's Lord   Scratched Fr
5—173 Bobby's Pet   A J Buckley Fr   10—935 Hilarious Gift (Em)   G W Turner Fr

3. **R.G COCHRAN STAKES** **7.55**
$6900. Mobile 2380 metres.
1—684 Atom Brae   G A McMahon Fr   6—687 Reperio (Em)   T E Brain Fr
2—384 Acacia Lad   G J Moy Fr   7—761 Smiley Lad   T B Warwick Fr
3—423 Joe Louis   G R Conroy Fr   8—371 Hokum   Gavin Lang Fr
4—476 Crafty Leigh   A D Peace Fr   9—217 Sir Vance   J O'Sullivan Fr
5—387 Myrnlong Looney   K C Hampton Fr   10—214 Mighty Scotch   J W Niven Fr

4. **BRIGADIER PAINE STAKES** **8.20**
$5650. Mobile 1940 metres.
1—354 Idamac   J G Coburn Fr   6—124 Ima Lowden   D J Smith Fr
2—146 Snappy Chap   T A Mahar Fr   7—556 Idol Elmo   N G Gath Fr
3—933 Sparechild   N G Ingram Fr   8—435 Ambidextrous (Em)   P J Conroy Fr
4—332 Demon Doon   B R Gath Fr   9—241 One Happy Fella   J O'Sullivan Fr
5—712 Gracefield Lad   M F Dillon Fr   10—243 Rosenkaviller   G D Wilson Fr

5. **A.G HUNTER MEMORIAL** **8.45**
$25,000. Mobile 2380 metres.
1—591 Armchair Ride   V J Knight Fr   6—111 Trunkey Westerner   T B Warwick Fr
2—862 Adios Moth   Dennis Wills Fr   7—314 Gosh   J H McDermott Fr
3—64½ Henry Bruce (Em)   N F Shinn Fr   8—253 Armbro Gold   T A Mahar Fr
4—113 Pascinelle   D F Hill Fr   9—641 Quite Famous   J O'Sullivan Fr
5—111 Imathreat   M Azzopardi Fr   10—242 Game Oro   K E Pocock Fr

6. **RUSSELL T.WHITE STAKES** **9.15**
$6650. Mobile 2380 metres.
1—760 Goroke (Em)   P J Marantelli Fr   6—568 Deux Dark Ones   G D Wilson Fr
2—341 Coonara Meadow   J F Ryan Fr   7—570 Karamea Loobatross   I R Lee Fr
3—606 Spare Beau   M D O'Bree Fr   8—298 Snow Byrd   C H Powell Fr
4—244 How's That Lady   B J Barron Fr   9—912 Good Time Dancer   I A Caruana Fr
5—534 Narralite   R J Hall Fr   10—693 Super Tinge   K M Harrison Fr

7. **TROTTERS CUP** **9.45**
$10,000. Mobile 2840 metres.
1—016 Minnesota Fats   G R Conroy Fr   6—230 Our Sylvania   C W Lang Fr
2—198 Wongala Supreme   P J Conroy Fr   7—421 Lord Alias   I R Jones Fr
3—620 John Gilbert (Em)   J G Coburn Fr   8—701 Admiral Aaron   G A Lang Fr
4—167 Blackwood Mac   R N Mathews Fr   9—753 True Roman   Gavin Lang Fr
5—750 Leslie Ormond   T A S Thompson Fr   10—605 Downsouth Clare   I R Lee Fr

8. **JUDGE MITCHELL STAKES** **10.15**
$3400. Mobile 1940 metres.
1—923 Irish Brae   L P Adams Fr   6—185 Copper Shadow (Em)   V J Knight Fr
2—452 Cardinal Way   J O'Sullivan Fr   7—234 Calophylia   S K Duffy Fr
3—100 Spanish Perfume   P R McCraw Fr   8—163 Avant Garde   G D Wilson Fr
4—425 Drastic Action   R N Mathews Fr   9—311 Amazing Choice   Gavin Lang Fr
5—844 North Hanover   C W Lang Fr   10—611 Smooth Falcon   V J Knight Fr

9. **THE LUCKY LAST** **10.45**
$3400. Mobile 1940 metres.
1—856 Barrow Smith (Em)   D J Smith Fr   6—343 Lost Ambitions   J F Ryan Fr
2—136 Weir Born   V J Knight Fr   7—183 Blazin Romeo   D W Guy Fr
3—373 Cadillac Ranch   N F Shinn Fr   8—318 Maleguena   E R Hurley Fr
4—125 Burning Gold   C Clarma Fr   9—213 Myrnlong Glenn   K C Hampton Fr
5—317 Hanover Boy   A D Peace Fr   10—571 Charisma Star   W F White Fr

Simulation of the TAB
Form guides for greyhound racing

Numbers *after* each runner represent the odds.
Numbers *before* represent results in previous races.

Olympic Park dog guide

SELECTIONS
By PETER PEARSON

1—PHARAOH'S MASK, 1; MYSTIC HOPE, 2; TERIMOTO, 3.

2—BRINDLE JOY, 1; FLETCHER MISS, 2; TEM'S MONARCH, 3.

3—JOHNNY'S TORANA, 1; QUASNA, 2; OBITUARY, 3.

4—VILLAGE ROYAL, 1; COCARI, 2; HALO POINT, 3.

5—DESIRABLE LASS, 1; ROYCOTE, 2; JOYFUL CHEER, 3.

6—DARK AVENGER, 1; RIDGEWELL LASS, 2; HEATHER'S OPAL, 3.

7—LADY MONCAIN, 1; MERCY BEAT, 2; MARBUZET, 3.

8—WISHING TOP, 1; TRIUMPH, 2; JUST A SKERRICK, 3.

9—FAIR TRADE, 1; CELTIC BOY, 2; SWIFT TIME, 3.

10—PRINCESS WINNIE, 1; LORD RASHENDAR, 2; DANCING CHARIOT, 3.

1—7.25 HANDICAP — 732
- 1—14233 TERIMOTO (5) — 43.43
- 2—41532 PHARAOH'S MASK (1/3) — 43.08
- 3—56184 STAYGEN (12) — 44.28
- 4—46252 VAL'S FLYER (12) — 43.72
- 5—51177 EMOTION GIRL (50) — 43.76
- 6—27526 REVLO QUEEN (100)
- 7—72552 MYSTIC HOPE (6) — †
- 8—77253 SWANKY REMO (12) — 44.18

2—7.45 GRADE 5 — 511
- 1—68343 MICHAEL TANA (12) — 30.06
- 2—11526 HELIUM (8) — •
- 3—22P21 TEM'S MONARCH (12) — 30.31
- 4—62536 TOBIQUE LASS (15) — •
- 5—26352 BRINDLE JOY (9/2) — †
- 6—62851 MY ROBERTA (6) — †
- 7—42542 FLETCHER MISS (7/2) — †
- 8—12322 COPPER CHIEF (5/2) — 30.28
- 9—1166 PETRABAR (12) (R) — 30.80
- 10—68817 MELISSA'S DREAM (15) (R)

3—8.05 SPRINT GRADE 5 — 511
- 1—41341 JOHNNY'S TORANA (9/4) — 30.18
- 2—15412 PILBARA GOLD (10) — •
- 3—85421 MY PAL KATIE (7) — •
- 4—15321 OBITUARY (5/2) — •
- 5—25320 QUASNA (4) — 29.90
- 6—35776 OUR PLEASURE (16) — 30.62
- 7—57113 BRETT'S BOUNTY (16) — †
- 8—23383 ROYAL ASCOT (18) — •
- 9—25115 ROCKARO RES (8) (R) — †
- 10—41241 TEMANTIC (7) (R)

4—8.25 GRADE 5 — 511
- 1—11541 VILLAGE ROYAL (4/6) — †
- 2—27842 NATIONAL STAMP (10) — †
- 3—44422 COCARI (7) — •
- 4—74231 YOUTHFUL NIGHT (8) — •
- 5—47138 TERRY ETZEL (12) — 30.50
- 6—77317 MOLLY'S MATE (16) — †
- 7—72313 NASHUA STAR (6) — †
- 8—61234 HALO POINT (15) — †
- 9—23112 FEATURE (8) (R) — •
- 10—11 ALLY PALLY (20) (R) — •

5—8.45 GRADE 5 — 732
- 1—84574 ROYCOTE (2) — 44.00
- 2—57314 BLACK PRESIDENT (16) — •
- 3—64116 DUSKY CHANT (8) — •
- 4—72312 DESIRABLE LASS (7/4) — •
- 5—24131 SHARP NOTE (6) — 44.64
- 6—6352F RODWAY (12) — 45.11
- 7—21478 TAMAROO CHIEF (16) — †
- 8—14661 JOYFUL CHEER (6) — †

6—9.05 GRADE 5 — 511
- 1—51325 VALLEY DEVIL (8) — †
- 2—12336 AUTOMATISM (9) — 31.40
- 3—22452 HEATHER'S OPAL (4) — 30.88
- 4—65525 DARK AVENGER (7/2) — 30.81
- 5—12121 GALVISTON (9/2) — •
- 6—41324 RIDGEWELL LASS (7) — 30.80
- 7—62683 HIGH ROLLING (8) — 30.34
- 8—14264 BRANDON PARK (6) — 30.41
- 9—23315 DIAMOND COURIER (res) (10) — †
- 10—73261 SECOV (res) (8) — 30.60

7—9.25 FREE FOR ALL — 511
- 1—31113 DEL'S DASHER (8) — 30.54
- 2—55212 I'M SOMEONE (8) — 30.17
- 3—41312 MERCY BEAT (3) — 30.21
- 4—31513 LADY MONCAIN (2) — 30.06
- 5—12734 FINAL STRIDE (8) — 30.33
- 6—14114 MARBUZET (6) — 30.28
- 7—73381 GAME KEEPER (10) — 30.60
- 8—84111 FLYING HALO (10) — 30.61
- 9—26203 CAMONA MISS (res) (6) — 30.28
- 10—21836 PEGGY LOUISE (res) (15) — 30.41

8—9.45 GRADE 5 — 511
- 1—37831 MIDNIGHT CLEAR (7) — 31.30
- 2—13211 TRIUMPH (3) — •
- 3—13331 RED ROCK (8) — 31.10
- 4—53461 SUNSHINE KID (15) — 30.79
- 5—42418 GAMBLER'S HOME (8) — †
- 6—23613 WISHING TOP (2) — †
- 7—66152 JUST A SKERRICK (8) — 30.56
- 8—11614 SUPREME WEED (6) — †
- 9—12237 READY NOW (res) (9/2) — †
- 10—55441 BLACK STATE (res) (8) — •

9—10.05 MAIDEN — 511
- 1—75131 FAIR TRADE (5/2) — 30.93
- 2—67171 ROMANTIC MISS (6) — 30.97
- 3—23131 CELTIC BOY (7/2) — 30.47
- 4—21 CHOSEN LINE (4) — 30.84
- 5—23171 GRALINDA PRINCE (6) — 30.90
- 6—1 SWIFT TIME (8) — 30.88
- 7—1 INTERIOR FINISH (10) — 30.92
- 8—1231 FAR OUT TROUT (8) — 30.86
- 9—1 MARELDA (res) (12) — 31.38
- 10—62261 CHROME DOME LASS (res) (12) — 31.54

10—10.25 MAIDEN — 511
- 1—22841 SATANIC KATE (7/2) — 31.13
- 2—641 MEYAR TOPS (8) — 31.12
- 3—52271 PRINCESS WINNIE (7) — 31.34
- 4—33151 LORD RASHENDAR (7/2) — 30.98
- 5—61571 MAGIC ZULU (7/2) — 31.07
- 6—1 DANCING CHARIOT (7) — 31.12
- 7—24421 GIMME A BREAK (6) — 31.04
- 8—211 SELYNYA LAD (5) — 31.01
- 9—1 MARELDA (res) (12) — 31.38
- 10—62261 CHROME DOME LASS (res) (12) — 31.54

The mathematics of rowing

Using a video clip of championship rowing, pupils can, using data obtained directly from the screen, make calculations such as stroke rating, speed of the boat, and the distance moved per stroke. The activity invites teachers to assess the value of using realistic data and the active use of video.

Features of this activity

- A realistic application.
- Use of video to bring data to classroom.
- Exposure to rowing and its terminology.
- Exposure to excellence in sport.
- The maths of ratio and rates.
- Use of calculators.
- Estimation.

THIS ACTIVITY IS PART OF THE MCTP PROFESSIONAL DEVELOPMENT PACKAGE FROM THE CURRICULUM DEVELOPMENT CENTRE, CANBERRA

Years 4 ↓ 7   VIDEO

1. Show the video clip of some championship rowing events, both men's and women's events.

2. Invite pupils to explore some of the maths involved.

3. Based on hearing terms such as 'the crew has lifted their rating', invite pupils to estimate the number of strokes per minute.

4. Calculate the rating two ways.

   (i) Time ten complete strokes and convert with a calculator to strokes per minute;

   (ii) Count (estimate) the number of strokes in ten seconds and convert.

   - Which of these methods is more reliable?

   - Why not count strokes for a full minute?

5. Repeat this for about five segments from different events.

Other possibilities

How far the boat moves in one stroke.

1. Watch clip.
2. Estimate distance in one stroke.
3. Count strokes for 250 metres (the usual distance between the marker buoys).
4. Divide to find the answer and check against perception.
5. Does the winning team move the most distance per stroke?

The speed of the boat.

1. Watch clip.
2. Estimate speed (in km/h).
3. Time boat over 250 or 500 metres.
4. Convert to speed.
5. Check against perception.

Ten pin bowling

The scoring system of ten pin bowling as well as being quite mathematical has subtle and interesting rules to cover 'spares' and 'strikes'. Pupils are encouraged to learn and apply the rules and enjoy the top class play of the Australian Masters Finals (Women's and Men's).

Features of this activity
- Exposes pupils to the game of ten pin bowling.
- Teaches the nature and method of the scoring system.
- Allows pupils to practise their scoring skills in a real game.

Preparation
Prepare and run off copies of the score sheet on the opposite page for each pupil.

THIS ACTIVITY IS PART OF THE MCTP PROFESSIONAL DEVELOPMENT PACKAGE FROM THE CURRICULUM DEVELOPMENT CENTRE, CANBERRA

The champions, Warren Stewart and Leanne Moyle.

This kind of activity can be developed into an exciting and challenging maths lesson if video footage of a ten pin bowling game, or some other game with a complex scoring system, is available.

1. Use some of the video as a teaching segment.

2. Challenge pupils to see if they can accurately score a complete game. Pause after (*say*) frames 2, 4 and 9 to check on the scores to that stage. (The scores appear on the screen after four frames each time.)

3. After frame 9, or perhaps a a bit earlier, a discussion could focus on what would need to happen for each player to have a chance of winning.

4. Show the final frame and check on the final scores.

Follow up could be to practise on other videoed games of bowling, or analyse possible 'what if' scoring situations that may have arisen.

For example,

What if Bee Singha had finished with three consecutive strikes?
What if a player had ten consecutive spares?
What is the highest and lowest they could possibly score?

Some do's and don'ts in bowling
DON'T rush the foul line. A brisk walk will keep the ball on a smooth arc.

DON'T loft or bounce the ball on the lane. Both your ball and the lane will suffer.

DON'T try to throw a speed ball. Control is the most important ingredient for high scores.

DON'T get discouraged with slow progress.

DO push the ball out and down as you take your first step.

DO follow through smoothly. This will give you accuracy.

DO work on your spare shots. It is possible to bowl a 190 game without a single strike by sparing every frame.

Ten pin bowling — Scoresheet

NAME	1	2	3	4	5	6	7	8	9	10	TOTAL
Bee Singha											
Leanne Moyle											
Warren Stewart											
Steve Kiss											

Years 6 → 10   VIDEO

How to score

- Each game consists of 10 frames, each box on the score sheet represents one frame.
- You have two deliveries per frame, unless you roll a STRIKE.
- If you knock down 10 pins with your first ball in a frame you have scored a STRIKE. Mark with an 'X' on the score sheet. (You only bowl one ball for that frame.)
- A STRIKE counts 10 plus the number of pins you knock down with your next two balls (when it is your turn to bowl again).
- If you knock down 10 pins with two balls you have scored a SPARE. Mark with a diagonal stroke on the score sheet.
- A SPARE counts 10 plus the number of pins you knock down with your first ball in the next frame.
- If you fail to get a STRIKE or a SPARE you merely record the number of pins down as your score for that frame.
- The score is carried over from frame to frame.

A typical game

Eva Brick	2 7	X	4 3	8 /	9 -	7 /	X	X	5 3	6 / 8	150
	9	26	33	52	61	81	106	124	132	150	

NOTE: One line on your score sheet is one game, as in the above example.

Notes

Chapter two

Social issues in the mathematics classroom

SOCIAL

Purpose

Activities in this chapter are presented to teachers as an invitation to explore the role of social issues as part of the mathematics curriculum and as a facet of each teacher's individual repertoire of understanding about teaching, learning and curriculum design.

Rationale

The fundamental question in this area is whether or not mathematics should present itself as a pure and neutral subject devoid of any moral, ethical, or social overtones. There is an argument that if mathematics is to prepare pupils for the real world, then part of its presentation should address issues from the real world.

Schoenheimer (1975) argued that studies of mathematics are inextricably linked to the value systems of the society in which they are embedded.

I assume for example, that most mathematics teachers know the story of the Communist teacher who posed the question, 'A man buys butter at 4 roubles a kilo

> ... if mathematics is to prepare pupils for the real world, then part of its presentation should address issues from the real world.

and sells it at a profit of 25%. What does he get?' To which the pupil replied, 'Six months!' It is a reminder that when we calmly accept the straight arithmetical answer we are implicitly teaching a value-judgment; that buying a commodity and selling it again for private profit is ethically acceptable. You may very well think that it is, and I am not here constrained to agree or to disagree. My point is .... your teaching is necessarily multi-dimensional. You are not merely teaching mathematics. You are also teaching many things including ethics — mathemethics. (p. 5)

He further argued that, given the many pressing issues confronting our society, mathematics should be one of the vehicles to empower pupils to understand and take an active role in finding solutions to such problems. Indeed, is this not the singularly most important role of the school?

This emphasis is qualitatively different to the current push for the use of 'applications' in mathematics. Such efforts are often confined to making use of realistic situations as illustrations or motivators in the desire to acquire abstract mathematical skills. The purpose lies clearly towards the mathematics — the application is but a passing vehicle towards this end.

This chapter argues for a complete reversal of this purpose.

Could not mathematics be a vehicle (along with others) to bring the pupil to confront the social, moral and ethical considerations relating to some important social issue? The emphasis here is clearly on understanding and reacting to the issue, the mathematics being but a means to achieve this.

An illustration

In the activity *Mortality quiz*, Year 10 pupils explore the mathematics of the life insurance industry. The one major reason for this is to illustrate mathematically, using graphs such as at right and calculations about life insurance premiums that they are on a *statistical upslope* in terms of the chances of death. The clear intent is that this knowledge, along with knowledge from other sources, will make pupils reflective, and personally safer as a result.

The graph showing Probability of death in the next year *against* Age *has strong messages for pupils about to leave school and obtain a driver's licence.*

Maths teaching as a social issue

Ubiratan d'Ambrosio, the Brazilian mathematics educator has claimed that for many children school mathematics can have a decidedly negative effect in the sense that as a result of studying mathematics they understand less, not more about the world. On going to school, d'Ambrosio (1985, p. 37) says pupils lose the capabilities they had and are not able to replace them with 'learned skills', and they progressively acquire a sense of failure and dependency.

In Australia there is plenty of evidence to show that many intelligent children are experiencing extreme difficulty in learning school mathematics because of the mismatch between the knowledge of home and school and that of the school and the dominant society (Bourke & Parkin, 1977; Harris, 1980).

Many MCTP activities relate school mathematics to everyday concerns of children. But in some of the activities there is a deliberate attempt to encourage learners to use their mathematical knowledge and skills to investigate ethical issues. In presenting these activities, we have maintained as neutral as possible positions, but children and teachers are invited to consider the implications of important data.

Experiences from trialling

One school adopting a social issues approach claimed that mathematics studies are only relevant if they address what they saw as the major issues of our world, namely:

- war
- racism
- poverty
- pollution
- dehumanising social institutions.

Accordingly, the maths course was completely built around these issues. Certainly, this is radically different in structure and purpose to an organisation built around content themes such as algebra, trigonometry and Pythagoras.

There are many themes that could be explored in a similar way such as Housing, Crime, Smoking, Advertising, Welfare, Taxation and Insurance.

A major finding of teachers is the need to be *responsive*; i.e. to react to issues as they emerge in the media or in the local community.

Activities such as these might be quite different for pupils from their expectations of what constitutes school mathematics. For this reason it has been found effective, prior to an activity, to share with pupils the purposes

> # The maths course was completely built around the issues of war, racism, poverty, pollution (and) dehumanising social institutions.

and reasons for the differences and to seek their reactions afterwards.

Several schools went to some lengths to empower pupils to explain to parents why these activities were being studied as part of the maths program.

Where activities address issues such as road trauma or gambling, there is a great need to tread sensitively and cautiously as many pupils may come from families that have been affected by such issues.

Assessment. Given that we show pupils what we value by the way in which we assess, it is essential to carry the purposes of each activity through to any assessment procedures. For this reason a report, including findings, feelings and suggested courses of action with respect to a social issue, is preferable to a content-based testing of particular maths skills.

SOCIAL

This class modelled the 'Clown' game and were quite surprised by the actual chances of winning. (From Everybody wins.*)*

A final word

If it is true that every social issue has its mathematical dimension and that a rigorous analysis of the mathematical data is an essential, or at least a highly desirable component in the making of value-judgments, then a whole new and exciting vista opens for teachers of mathematics. Not only do they have the opportunity to make their contribution, as in moral duty bound, to an understanding of problems as diverse as cigarette addiction, resource exhaustion and the effects of tariff protection on poor countries. They can do this at the same time as they demonstrate that rationality, and rigour, relationships and relevance are crucial attributes of mathematics.

(Schoenheimer, 1975, p. 12)

References

d'Ambrosio, U. (1985). Environmental influences. In R. Morris (Ed.), *Studies in mathematics education.* Paris: UNESCO, Vol. 4, 29-46.

Bourke, S.F., & Parkin, B. (1977). The performance of Aboriginal pupils. In S.F. Bourke, & J.P. Keeves (Eds.), *Australian studies in school performance*, Vol.3, *The mastery of literacy and numeracy.* Canberra: Australian Government Publishing Service.

Harris, P. (1980). *Measurement in tribal Aboriginal communities.* Darwin: Northern Territory Department of Education.

Schoenheimer, H. (1975). Mathematics could be vital! In D. Williams (Ed.) *Perspectives in teaching mathematics.* Melbourne: Mathematical Association of Victoria, 1-13.

Activities with a social issues component in other chapters

Simulation of the TAB. (Ch. 1)

Tinker, tailor — male or female. (Ch. 11)

Carrot patch people. (Ch. 12)

'Using cubes we modelled babies and adults. We learnt that the reason why babies suffer when they are left in cars in hot days is to do with surface area to volume ratio'.

Everybody wins

Seems easy! Drop a ball down the clown's throat, and, provided you have judged it correctly, the ball will go over to the outer bin and you will collect a big prize. And even if you miss — you get something. You can't lose!

Well that's how it appears — but as with all carnival games, the odds are stacked against you. This activity helps children to understand how maths works for the carnival operator, and how appearances can be deceptive.

Should confronting social issues such as the realities of gambling be a part of a teacher's repertoire and a school maths program? Teachers are invited to trial this activity and debate this question.

Features of this activity

- A mathematical model based on the results of an experimental situation.
- Application of a popular fairground game.
- Uses maths to explore a social issue.

- Finding out why the game is so popular. (Success looks easier than it turns out to be.)
- Use of calculators.
- Use of a computer. (Optional)

This activity is best conducted around Showtime.

Years 5 ↓ 8

SOCIAL

Preparation
- One worksheet (page 98) per pupil.
- An overhead copy of the game board. (Optional)
- 32 counters per group of two pupils.
- A coin for each group.
- Calculators — one per group.
- Computer and program *Everybody wins.*

Part of mathematics is communicating your thoughts, ideas and findings to others. The pupil who wrote this report of the activity obviously enjoyed herself.

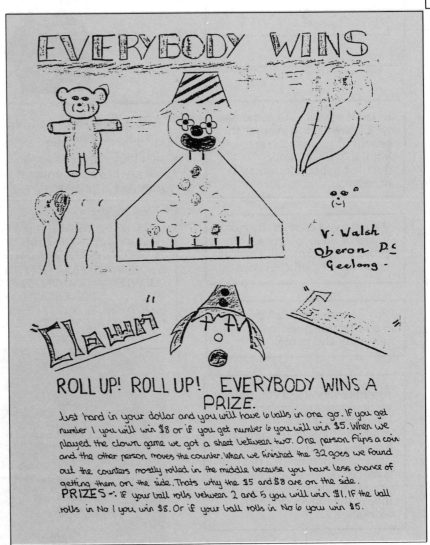

EVERYBODY WINS

V. Walsh
Oberon P.S.
Geelong.

ROLL UP! ROLL UP! EVERYBODY WINS A PRIZE.

Just hand in your dollar and you will have 6 balls in one go. If you get number 1 you will win $8 or if you get number 6 you will win $5. When we played the clown game we got a sheet between two. One person flips a coin and the other person moves the counter. When we finished the 32 goes we found out the counters mostly rolled in the middle because you have less chance of getting them on the side. Thats why the $5 and $8 are on the side.
PRIZES -: If your ball rolls between 2 and 5 you will win $1. If the ball rolls in No 1 you win $8. Or if your ball rolls in No 6 you win $5.

THIS ACTIVITY IS PART OF THE MCTP PROFESSIONAL DEVELOPMENT PACKAGE FROM THE CURRICULUM DEVELOPMENT CENTRE, CANBERRA

SAMPLE PUPIL REPORT

Everybody wins

Children quickly learn that carnival games are usually more difficult than they appear — that the odds are heavily stacked in favour of the operator. This activity shows how mathematics can explain why.

A mathematical model of the clown game.

It is not practical to make a working version of the actual game. A mathematical model of this game involves the ball being deflected by pegs in a triangular array. The model assumes the ball does not rebound or miss a row of pegs.

The arrows below show a sample 'pathway' a ball could travel, bouncing either right or left.

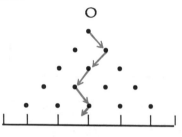

In trials schools the game was well known. However for the benefit of pupils who are not familar with it, some detailed explanation may be necessary.

An enlarged copy of the game board or on an overhead projector works well. This can be re-used by other classes.

Why 32 counters? Ask pupils to ponder this question as they play the game.

Alternatively use a computer to demonstrate the game. Load the disk into the computer, choose the program *Everybody wins* and choose demonstration mode. The ball is moved down by successive presses of the space bar. Pupils follow the moves on their worksheets.

1. Games at the Show

Generate discussion about games at the Show. (Favourites, cost of games, who won prizes, what prizes were like, who won a valuable prizes [only a few], a novelty prize [nearly all]. Why is this? [luck, it's 'rigged' etc.]).

2. The 'Clown game'

Discuss their experiences of this game.

3. Demonstrate our version of Clown

Make sure that the pupils clearly understand how the game is played so that they can focus on the outcomes. Hand out worksheets, a coin, and 32 counters to each group of two. Sketch the array of pegs on the chalkboard and stick the counters with Blue tac.

4. The three parts of the investigation

Write the heading and the three parts on the chalkboard.

> a. What our eyes tell us.
> b. Results from the game.
> c. Predicting results from a mathematical model

These three stages provide 'advance organisers' for what is to follow.

What our eyes tell us.

> NOW THAT YOU'VE SEEN A FEW TRIALS, AS A PAIR, PREDICT WHERE THE 32 COUNTERS WILL FALL

> PUT YOUR PREDICTIONS HERE

Children often tend to spread the counters evenly across all six slots.

5. Play the game

> OK! YOU ALL HAVE 32 COINS SO PLAY 16 EACH.
> ONE PERSON TOSSES THE COIN, THE OTHER MOVES THE COUNTER.
> WHEN YOU HAVE FINISHED WRITE YOUR RESULTS ON THE BOARD BESIDE YOUR INITIALS

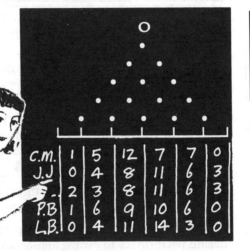

C.M.	1	5	12	7	7	0
J.J	0	4	8	11	6	3
.	2	3	8	11	6	3
P.B	1	6	9	10	6	0
L.B.	0	4	11	14	3	0

Faster groups could be encouraged to complete two sets of 32 trials, comparing the second set with the first and the other pupils' results.

The symmetry pattern now emerges, showing that the outside boxes are the least likely outcomes.

6. Patterns in the results

> CAN YOU SEE ANY PATTERNS IN THE ANSWERS?

> HOW DO THESE COMPARE TO YOUR PREDICTIONS BEFORE YOU PLAYED THE GAME?

> TRY 32 TRIALS

> LET'S SEE IF THE COMPUTER DOES ANY BETTER

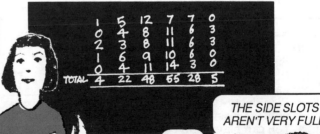

	1	5	12	7	7	0
	0	4	8	11	6	3
	2	3	8	11	6	3
	1	6	9	10	6	0
	0	4	11	14	3	0
TOTAL	4	22	48	55	28	5

> THE SIDE SLOTS AREN'T VERY FULL

> NOT MUCH

If appropriate, a discussion on averages could follow here, or be taken up as a valuable extension.

7. Mathematical predictions

Draw this chart on the chalkboard and work out the probability at each stage.

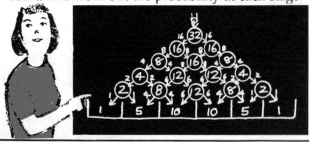

MATHEMATICIANS COULD HAVE WORKED OUT THIS PATTERN BEFORE WE STARTED.
ANY IDEAS HOW?... YES! THAT'S THE IDEA.
WHEN IT HITS A PEG, THE BALL WILL HAVE EQUAL CHANCES OF GOING IN EITHER DIRECTION.
SO OF THE 32 BALLS HITTING THE FIRST PEG, 16 SHOULD GO LEFT AND 16 RIGHT (etc)......

FAIRLY CLOSE WEREN'T THEY?
*BUT WHY WEREN'T THEY **EXACTLY** THE SAME?*

8. Compare the mathematical model with the class and computer results

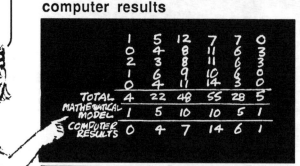

THE MATHEMATICAL MODEL DOESN'T ALLOW FOR ODD THINGS HAPPENING

IT'S A SORT OF AVERAGE

Children seem to have an intuitive idea that as the number of experiments become very large the results more closely match the predicted results.

9. Use the computer to show how large numbers of trials give results near to the mathematical model

Explain to pupils that the computer can easily do large numbers of trials very quickly. Set the program on the non-demonstration mode for 32 trials to show how fast it works. Then set a large number of trials — say 128 (multiples of 32 are best). The computer will display the results it gets and the mathematical model (1, 5, 10, 10, 5, 1) which can be compared. Then set the computer for an even longer run, say 320 or 640. Point out how the more trials conducted, the nearer the results are to the mathematical model. (320 trials take about 20 mins.)

10. Conclusions — The dilemma of the carnival operator: offer tempting prizes, but make a profit

Challenge children to be carnival operators of a clown stall. They must decide what prizes to award and arrange their prize money so as to attract customers, and also make a profit.

For most classes let children designate only one or two winning boxes. For more advanced pupils they could award prizes for all boxes.

WHICH WOULD APPEAL MORE?

|$15| | | | |$15|

| | | |$2 | $2 | | | |

RULES
• Each pupils starts with a (theoretical) twenty dollars.
• Each play costs one dollar.
• Play thirty-two games or until your money runs out.
• You can play at anybody's table.
• Play at as many tables as you like.
• Keep a record of your payouts and winnings.

Clever Claire makes a profit of $2 in 32 tries because one ball could be expected to finish in each outside box.

Income = $32
Payout = $15 x 2 = $30
Profit = $2.

Bad-luck Bob makes a loss of $8 in 32 tries because ten balls could be expected to finish in each box.

Income = $32
Payout = $2 x 20 = $40
Loss   = $8.

Trials schools report that this forms an appropriate assessment of pupil learning.

11. Writing up the experience

Children can write in groups about their stall, giving reasons for decisions they make. These projects could be presented as a wall display and, later produced as a book.

Extension activities

Throwing two dice

Give each group 36 counters.

Have them draw up a scoring grid similar to that shown below.

With each throw of the two dice, add the scores and place a counter in the appropriate grid square. By stacking the counters, a histogram is constructed. The theoretical results for 36 throws is shown.

Have the groups design appropriate prize allocations.

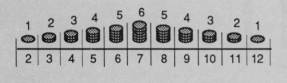

| 2 | 3 | 4 | 5 | 6 | 7 | 8 | 9 | 10 | 11 | 12 |

Number plates

In any group of twenty cars, what is the chance of at least two having the same last two digits?*

Ask the class to make predictions before going out, pencil and paper in hand, to check groups of twenty cars.

| I FOUND THREE THE SAME | I GOT TWO. TEACHER MUST HAVE RIGGED IT |

It is about 90% likely.

Explain that the maths required is really at Year 11 level, so we do the next best thing — take a sample.

Two up

Set the groups the task of finding the frequency of the three possible outcomes. A head and tail combination is twice as likely as two heads or two tails. Have pupils plan an appropriate prize allocation.

Tatts 2

Explain the game (choosing two numbers between 1 and 100) and set the groups to plan an appropriate prize allocation.

Compare your prize with the actual prize given.

Sur*prize*d?

Coin in the square (see page 117)

This Year 8-10 lesson uses the same approach to a similar carnival side show activity. You could adapt it to suit primary classes.

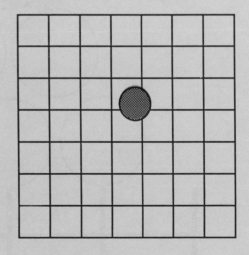

Everybody wins

Your
prediction

Danger distance

Crossing the road can be a risky business. As accident figures show us, many people fail to leave that necessary margin for error.

This activity challenges children to estimate, measure, calculate and cooperate in group tasks and, as a result of their studies, extend their thinking through thoughtful discussion.

The purpose of the activity therefore is to address, within a mathematical context, the serious social issue of road safety, and in particular the judgement of speed and distances needed by pedestrians.

BOTHER!
I'M A DECIMAL
PLACE OUT

BOMP

Years 5 ↓ 8

SOCIAL

Features of this activity

- Realistic, personal application of mathematics.
- Explores an issue of great community importance.

- Cooperative group work.
- Physical involvement.
- Timing exercises.
- Visual imagery.

Preparation

- Stopwatches — one per group of about six pupils. (Some preliminary practice with the stopwatches prior to the main session is advisable.)
- Calculators. (One per four pupils is sufficient)
- Worksheet (page 104), one per pupil.
- Measure the width of the road beside the school crossing.

THIS ACTIVITY IS PART OF THE MCTP
PROFESSIONAL DEVELOPMENT PACKAGE FROM THE
CURRICULUM DEVELOPMENT CENTRE, CANBERRA

Danger distance

How far away does an oncoming car have to be before you should cross the road?

The following lesson based on this problem has two aspects. Firstly there is the informal judgement of how far away the car is, and how fast it is going, when it will get here, how wide is the road, how fast do I travel, and will I be across before the car arrives? Secondly, there is the mathematical expression of those distances, speed and time in metres per second and kilometres per hour.

Allow one hour for the first session.

1. Introduction

Have an introduction which highlights the importance and seriousness of the issue and which draws upon the pupils' experiences and knowledge. Here are some suggestions.

Pupils' experiences

Many pupils will be aware of near misses or unfortunate accidents. Establish that the elements of safe crossing are:

- the visibility (time of day, weather, clothing, and so on),
- the speed of the car,
- how far away the car is,
- attentiveness and carefulness.

> The issue needs to be treated sensitively, yet at the same time it is important to draw out that maths has a role in road safety.

Australian pedestrian statistics
3480 injured in one year
540 killed in one year

Australian statistics

Write these facts on the chalkboard and invite pupils to comment.

2. What does 'danger distance' mean?

Hand out the activity sheets and take the pupils out to the school crossing.

> This exercise in estimation and visual imagery provides for later comparison.

> Encourage pupils to generate ideas and methods rather than instructing them.

Gather the group together.

> There are two alternative approaches offered. If you wish to involve a greater problem-solving component in this activity see page 103.

3. Setting up the 'road'

Ask pupils to walk to a point that they believe is ten metres (or to the distance corresponding to the width of the school road as measured prior to the lesson) from the side line on the basketball court.

Measure the ten metres with a trundle wheel and draw another line. This is now 'our road'.

Trials schools report a wide variety of estimates for ten metres.

Ask for times in whole seconds.

> HOW MANY SECONDS DO YOU THINK YOU WOULD TAKE JANE?.... ROBERT?

> OK! SO WRITE YOUR ESTIMATE ON THE WORKSHEET.
> THEN AFTER THAT WE'LL FIND OUT JUST HOW LONG IT ACTUALLY TAKES

Years 5↓8   SOCIAL

4. Practise operating the stop-watches

Give out at least one stop-watch to each group and practise operating it. Make sure that all children have a turn.

> TWENTY-FIVE SECONDS

> TWENTY-EIGHT SECONDS

> IT RESET ITSELF. I MUST HAVE PRESSED THE WRONG BUTTON

Teachers may wish this practice to be done on a previous day.

If stop-watches are not available, other watches with second hands are satisfactory.

It is worth spending some time on this part to ensure the next section goes smoothly.
Trials schools report that children find this very difficult. One trials school had the teacher timing each of the children for this reason.

5. Practise timing a person crossing the 'road'

> NOW I AM GOING TO WALK ACROSS 'OUR ROAD' AND YOU TIME ME

> OK! ARE YOU READY TO TIME ME? HERE I GO!

> 8.5 SECONDS

> 5.3 SECONDS

> 6.8 SECONDS

> WHAT TIME DID YOU GET?

> LET'S DO THAT AGAIN, BUT EVERYBODY IN THE GROUP CHECK THE TIMER

Discuss the answers and reasons for discrepancies and how practice is needed to sharpen reactions and techniques.

The physical involvement makes the calculations and the results more meaningful to the pupils.

There are plausible arguments for using the mean, mode or maximum time, but trials schools suggest this be left to the pupil to decide.

The conversion
60 km in 1 hour
= 60 000 m in 60 min
= 1 000 m in 1 min
= 1 000 m in 60 s
= 16.66 m in 1 s
is too difficult for most children.

6. Children work out their own personal times

Back in the classroom.

7. Working out their danger distances

This question could be explored, but trials schools found it preferable to present 60 km/h as about 17 m/s.

Trials schools chose to emphasise the meaning of 60 km/h and 17 m/s rather than the conversion.

Children make use of the activity sheet to calculate their danger distance.

OUT AT THE SCHOOL CROSSING

8. Pupils mark out their danger distance

Starting at the crossing, but keeping well back from the road, the teacher walks with a trundle wheel, calling out the metres, 31, 32...

Pupils stop at their personal danger distance, comparing this with their original estimates.

'The kids were staggered at how great the distance was!
This bit took time but it was essential.'

9. But what if...?

Discuss with children how this is an unnatural and idealistic situation. List all the things that could go wrong.

> DO YOU THINK IT WAS A GOOD EXPERIMENT?
> WHAT DID IT SHOW?
> WHAT DIDN'T IT SHOW?

> I'LL NEVER CROSS THE ROAD AGAIN

> MOST CARS GO A LOT FASTER THAN 60 k ALONG DONCASTER ROAD

> SOMETIMES WE RUN WHEN WE'RE IN A HURRY

> WHAT IF YOU SLIPPED?

An alternative approach to parts 3 to 9

You may wish to challenge the pupils to work out their own strategies. If so, you should discuss the many approaches children may choose to take and list them on the chalkboard. If you choose this alternative method, disregard steps 3, 4, 5, 6, 7 and 8.

> IN A MINUTE YOU WILL GET INTO GROUPS OF THREE OR FOUR AND WORK OUT HOW YOU COULD FIND OUT YOUR OWN SAFETY DISTANCES.
> BUT I'LL TELL YOU ONE PIECE OF INFORMATION YOU WILL NEED.
> A CAR TRAVELLING AT THE MAXIMUM ALLOWABLE SPEED — SIXTY KILOMETRES AN HOUR — GOES ABOUT SEVENTEEN METRES A SECOND

The activity as presented so far, is quite teacher-directed. This alternative approach is to hand the problem over to the class for them to solve in small groups.

However, trials schools found that few pupils succeeded by themselves.

Years 5 ↓ 8

SOCIAL

Extensions   1. Find out the actual speed cars travel and how this affects the danger distance.

2. Video a busy local road. Pupils can indicate the moment it is safe to cross. Stop tape and investigate distance.

Worksheet　　　　　Danger distance

1. I think that a moving car should be .... before I can safely cross the road outside the school.

2. I think I would take about .... seconds to cross 'the road'.

3. My actual time to cross the road was .... seconds.

4. A car travelling at 60 km/h covers .... metres in 1 second.

5. My danger distance is X  = ...metres.

A journalist hangs on to a road sign as he waits rescue from the rising flood waters in Linda, California.

Baby in the car

Babies must never be locked in a car on a hot day. Why? They will quickly dehydrate!

Why? Whilst there are physiological reasons for this, a major factor is mathematical — the smaller the volume, the greater the proportional surface area. The mathematical technique of modelling — making simplified, measurable versions of the real thing, is used here as a tool to give pupils the power to clearly see, understand and explain that the surface-area-to-volume ratio of babies is much greater than that of adults.

This activity illustrates how a social issue in the community can be responded to in the mathematics classroom.

Background

An incident similar to that in the newspaper story took place near my school. My pupils were very angry at the parents who had left a 'baby in a car'. (The baby recovered.) I took the opportunity to respond to this local event to highlight for pupils a mathematical principle involved, namely the ratio of surface area to volume.

Hence the activity is best done near the beginning of summer rather than whenever the topic of volume happens to occur.

The activity is presented in a way that tries to highlight the 'pedagogical thinking' of the author.

if, however, the minister would agree," he said.

Heat kills toddler

A two-year-old girl died yesterday when her grandmother left her unattended in a car parked in a factory where she worked for seven hours. The temperature inside the car reached over 50 degrees. A police report shows that the girl's body temperature rose above 40 degrees.

More aid to Ethiopia

Following an appeal by the secretary of the United Nations

Features of this activity

- Exploration of a real, everyday problem.
- Concept of mathematical modelling techniques.
- The mathematics of surface area, volume and the ratio between them.
- Opportunity for challenging sex role stereotypes.

- Includes history and experiences of women.
- Use of manipulative material.
- Discussion and writing about mathematics in a human context.
- Opportunity for cooperative learning in single sex groups.
- Collection and use of personal data. (Optional)

Preparation

- A copy of the worksheets (pages 109-10) for each pupil.
- Nine wooden cubes per pupil, or small group — 2 cm cubes are best.

THIS ACTIVITY IS PART OF THE MCTP PROFESSIONAL DEVELOPMENT PACKAGE FROM THE CURRICULUM DEVELOPMENT CENTRE, CANBERRA

Baby in the car

There is a mathematical principle that as volume decreases, the proportional surface area increases. Knowing this principle helps people to understand why a baby, in proportion to an adult, has a much larger skin area, which is one factor that makes it more vulnerable to dehydration. Knowing this, in turn, makes the mathematical principle real and relevant for children.

1. Introduction and purpose

Give out and let pupils read copies of the newspaper stories, and encourage pupils to recount any similar events.

'I believe maths should be partly responsive to current and local events as well as focusing on predetermined syllabi.'

'I made this the major purpose because I wanted the students to feel empowered with the possession of socially useful knowledge.'

'I'm worried that these articles might stereotype women as the main childcare agents. I want to challenge the connotation by discussing the forces and stresses that lead to such situations, with particular reference to women.'

The concept of the purpose and power of mathematical modelling is a specific feature of this activity.

YOU MAY WONDER WHY I CHOSE TO INCLUDE THIS IN OUR MATHEMATICS CLASS.

THE REASON IS THAT THERE IS A SOUND MATHEMATICAL PRINCIPLE INVOLVED — THAT SOME PARENTS DON'T UNDERSTAND.

THE PARENTS IN THE STORY CERTAINLY WERE NOT DELIBERATELY CRUEL — ONLY IGNORANT AND UNDER PRESSURE

UNFORTUNATELY IT HAPPENS ALL TOO OFTEN, AND, HOPEFULLY, ONCE YOU UNDERSTAND, YOU MAY BE ABLE TO PREVENT SIMILAR SITUATIONS

2. Discussion — clarification of variables and values

WHAT ARE THE FACTORS IN SOCIETY THAT LEAD TO PARENTS LEAVING A BABY IN A CAR?

WHY DOES A BABY SUFFER, IN A WAY THAT AN ADULT PERHAPS WOULD NOT?

EXPERTS TELL US IT IS NOT EXCESSIVE HEAT — IT IS MORE DUE TO DEHYDRATION, THAT IS, AS WE EVAPORATE MOISTURE TO TRY TO KEEP COOL.

THE PARENTS WERE NOT DELIBERATELY CRUEL, AND ASSUMED, PROBABLY CORRECTLY, THAT THEY THEMSELVES WOULD HAVE BEEN ALL RIGHT TO STAY IN THAT CAR FOR AN HOUR OR SO!

CLEARLY THERE IS AN IMPORTANT DIFFERENCE BETWEEN BABIES AND ADULTS THAT THE PARENTS DIDN'T UNDERSTAND

3. A mathematical model

Give out nine wooden cubes (2 x 2 x 2 cm are best) to each pupil or small group.

IN TRYING TO UNDERSTAND COMPLEX ISSUES, MATHEMATICIANS OFTEN CREATE SIMPLIFIED SITUATIONS TO EXPLORE AND LEARN FROM. THESE ARE CALLED MATHEMATICAL MODELS

LET'S REPRESENT THE BABY BY ONE CUBE — NOT A VERY GOOD LOOKING BABY BUT WE HAVE TO START SOMEWHERE! CAN YOU BUILD AN ADULT WHICH IS TWICE AS BIG? THAT IS A 2 x 2 x 2 CUBE?

Focusing on dehydration which is moisture escaping through surfaces

The problem could be presented as an open challenge. That is, to explore the two models and try to articulate why the baby dehydrates faster, or, it could be a structured teacher-led exploration.

Baby: one unit of volume, and six squares of surface through which moisture can evaporate.

Adult: eight units of volume, and 24 squares of surface. For each unit of volume, there are three surfaces through which moisture can escape. These can be seen directly on the model.

> 'I found it far more effective to keep the language simple and to avoid jargon such as surface area to volume ratio, in favour of using the language the pupils generated.'

	Volume	Surface area	Comparison
Baby	1	6	6 to 1
Adult	8	24	3 to 1

Pupils can readily see, and express the fact, that, in babies, for each unit of volume there is *twice as much surface for evaporation.*

4. Extending the mathematical model

> BUT THIS IS NOT A BABY — AND THIS IS NOT AN ADULT. SO DO YOU FIND THE RESULTS CONVINCING?

> HOW COULD WE MAKE A MORE REALISTIC ADULT — WILL THE SAME EFFECT STILL BE EVIDENT?

> An important aspect of modelling is to recognise weaknesses in the assumptions and to try to improve the model.

> *Lego* is another possible building medium.

With extra blocks, pupils can build a more realistic 'baby' and 'adult'. Calculate the volume and surface area for each and find if the 'baby' is still at a disadvantage.

The results from two different groups can be summarised on the chalkboard.

> 'By building several different models, pupils get considerable practice at counting or calculating volumes and surface area'.

> 'One pupil, having built a complicated "baby", said "Now I can see why mothers cover a baby's head on a cold day — there's lots of surface there for heat loss."'

> 'I like the fact that all the calculating of volumes and surface areas can be personalised.'

This makes the finding of the ratio between surface area and volume even more relevant and meaningful.

This (100 times...) rule has application in the medical and para-medical fields in relation to percentages of burnt skin victims suffer.

One kilogram of water is one litre in volume.

Humans are composed of about 84% water.

This values the experience and accumulated wisdom of women.

Babies heads are proportionately larger than adults, a fact well known to artists.

> 'I like the link here between converting mathematical findings back into everyday language.'

5. Can we obtain real data?

One school set the following as a homework research project.

Pupils calculate their own personal surface-area-to-volume ratio and compare it to that of a younger pupil or infant (the baby of a relative of friend?).

To find the approximate **surface area** of human body there are three different methods.

  a. Three-fifths times the height squared. ($\frac{3}{5}h^2$)

  b. 100 times surface area of the hand print.

  c. Twice height times thigh circumference. (2h x *th*)

To find the approximate **volume**:

> The density of the human body is a little more than water because of bones etc. One kilogram of body mass occupies about .9 litre volume.

Pupils work out the personal data for themselves and also a willing young subject. They then write a short report to present their findings.

6. Conclusion

Challenge pupils to tell how they would go about explaining these findings to parents.

Ask pupils to write an explanation and then, perhaps, present it to the class.

A part of the closing discussion can also refer to the folklore rules for the care of infants. Many of these are related to the surface area to volume ratio, such as covering the head on a cold day.

Pupils could interview parents to try to find out how they cared for their babies in hot and cold weather. Why did they take the steps they did?

Worksheet 1

Baby in the car

THE STRANGER WHO BROKE THE CAR WINDOW

It was a February heatwave. Michael Jones was driving to the shops with his six months old son. He parked his car, grabbed the shopping list, looked at his son who was now asleep and thought, *'I'll only be about twenty minutes, I won't wake him, I'll leave him in the car.'* So he wound up all the windows, locked the doors and went off to do his shopping.

A little while later, on returning to the car he saw someone smashing in the side window. He ran to the car *'What do you think you are doing'* he cried, *'trying to steal my son?'*

'Steal him' said the stranger, *'I'm trying to save his life'.*

Why did the stranger think the baby's life was endangered? Was he endangered? If so, would Michael Jones have been unsafe in the car under the same circumstances?

...on could be taken to op... ...e helipad proposal. Mrs Syh... said local objections were based on factors such as the environmental impact and the risks involved for local residents and schools.

if, however, the minister would agree," he said.

Heat kills toddler

A two-year-old girl died yesterday when her grandmother left her unattended in a car parked in a factory where she worked for seven hours. The temperature inside the car reached over 50 degrees. A police report shows that the girl's body temperature rose above 40 degrees.

More aid to Ethiopia

Following an appeal by the secretary of the United Nations

Parents warned not to leave infants in cars

With the hottest part of summer on the way, the Health Minister, Mr White, and the Transport Minister, Mr Roper, yesterday warned parents not to leave babies or pets in cars during the hot season.

One Victorian child has already died this summer after being left in a car on a hot day, and another has suffered severe dehydration.

Mr White said small children were particularly vulnerable to dehydration. He said babies should be given drinks whenever they asked for them, and at least every two hours.

Breast-fed infants also needed extra drinks, and breast milk could be supplemented with cool boiled water. "If you suspect your child has become dehydrated, try to cool him or her down with a cool drink and splashing the child with cool water," he said.

A dehydrated child should be taken to hospital quickly — not wrapped in clothes — and car windows should be kept down to allow breezes through.

The ministers also warned people not to leave pets in cars because of the risk of dehydration and death.

shoppers.

Worksheet 2

Baby in the car

WHAT PRECAUTIONS SHOULD A PARENT TAKE TO PREVENT BABIES DEHYDRATING IN HOT WEATHER?

Research the problem in your library, from medical friends or authorities. The St John Ambulance brigade would be glad to assist.

$2\frac{1}{4}$ TIMES FASTER

Nicholas Kiwi Pty Ltd used to advertise that their Aspro tablets now work '2¼ times faster'. What is the obvious way in which this could be done?

POOR DOG — LUCKY MOUSE!

A dog and a mouse fell down a mine shaft. The dog was killed, but the mouse walked away. Why?

THIRSTY-TOO KILOMETRES LONG

Why are marathon runners advised to drink at regular intervals? Is it true that most Olympic marathon runners are relatively small in stature? Why might this be so?

A HANDY THING TO KNOW ABOUT YOUR SKIN

There is a rule of thumb that your skin area is 100 times that of the skin area of your hand. Measure the surface area of your hand and calculate your total surface area. From that calculate your volume.

MORE SURFACE AREA TO GET THEM GOING

Reptiles need the sun to get them going. Many large dinosaurs had to have large fins or plates down their back. How does this relate to what we found out with our cubes?

DOES THE SAME PRINCIPLE APPLY FOR PROPORTIONS OF SURFACE AREA TO VOLUME FOR A SPHERE?

Guess, then check.

A sphere may appear to be a better model than a cube for estimating volume and surface area. But is it?

The volume of a sphere is $\frac{4}{3}\pi r^3$

The surface area is $4\pi r^2$

Maths and Lotto
When will your numbers come up?

For many people, picking six numbers out of 40 or out of 45 doesn't seem too difficult — that's only about one seventh of the numbers. But as with all gambling games, the easier it looks, the more people are convinced they can win, the bigger profit the organisers make. Do people have realistic expectations about their chances? Should they? In this activity pupils play a simplified form of lotto, work out the odds, and discover that there is often a big difference between perception and reality.

Features of this activity

- Explores an issue of social concern.
- Involves combination theory and simple ratio.
- A class simulation game is used.
- Involves a lot of intuitive probability.

- Includes concepts of mathematical expectation.
- Uses first-hand data generated by pupils.
- Contrasts perception with reality.
- Has a computer extension.

Preparation

You will need some devices for selecting numbers, such as (for preference) six numbered wooden cubes, folded pieces of paper numbered 1 to 6, dice or playing cards.

Some suitable 'prizes' like a packet of Minties.

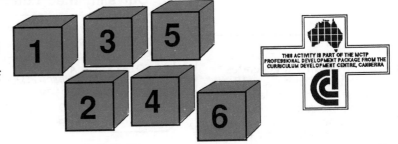

THIS ACTIVITY IS PART OF THE MCTP PROFESSIONAL DEVELOPMENT PACKAGE FROM THE CURRICULUM DEVELOPMENT CENTRE, CANBERRA

Background

The nature of our society is that there are many schemes designed to part people from their money. Are Lotto games an issue of social concern? It is not hard to find evidence of tragedy and hardship caused by a few people over-indulging in such games. It is not hard to illustrate that most people have very little perception of their real chances. Is there a role (or a responsibility) for the mathematician in schools to address this issue?

An educator's axiom

'If a person pays to participate in any scheme — they should know what to expect.'

Lotto games are a social phenomenon, extracting millions of dollars from people's pockets each week.

Do pupils, who are tomorrow's investors, (if not today's) have a realistic idea of their chances of winning and the probability of losses?

Evidence from many classes suggest that pupils hopelessly over-estimate their chances of winning. Is such a sense of unreality healthy?

The weekly exhortation *When will your numbers come up?* is never answered, but it **does have an answer** — there is a **mathematical expectation** which can be taught.

The following activity is an attempt to raise these issues in the classroom. It is not an attack on lotto games — only an argument that they provide a real issue worthy of the attention of mathematics teachers. It is to ensure that pupils have realistic expectations.

To be otherwise, is to be disadvantaged ... *Fools and their moneys are soon parted...*

Equally however ... *You can't win if you're not in ...*

The message therefore becomes: *Buy a ticket by all means, but excessive entries straining financial resources and based on unreal expectations, represent an unhealthy approach.*

Maths and Lotto. When will your number come up?

Pupils play a simplified form of Lotto — two from six. They then analyse their results which often turn out to be rather different from their initial expectations. When this is extrapolated to the real game, pupils begin to understand the overwhelming odds against them.

1. Discuss what children know about Lotto and their expectations

How many times would you expect to win lotto in a lifetime? The probability is that a typical investor will win once every 15 000 years, or about once every 200 lifetimes. (This information is for teachers only. Don't reveal to pupils until the final discussion time.)

WHO KNOWS WHAT TATTSLOTTO IS?
HOW DO YOU PLAY IT?
HOW MUCH DOES IT COST TO INVEST?
IF YOU BOUGHT A WHOLE-CARD TICKET EVERY WEEK OF YOUR LIFE, HOW OFTEN DO YOU THINK YOU MIGHT WIN?

2. Our simplified Lotto game — two out of six

The two out of six game was chosen because it generates about one winner every 15 players. So from a class of 30 players we could expect about two winners per game. (But don't let pupils know this yet.)

I WANT TO SHOW YOU SOME OF THE MATHEMATICS BEHIND LOTTO.
THE REAL GAME IS QUITE COMPLEX, SO LET'S PLAY A VERY SIMPLE FORM OF LOTTO WHICH IS MUCH EASIER TO WIN.
YOU CHOOSE TWO OF THE SIX NUMBERS

IN YOUR BOOKS WRITE GAME 1 AND THE NUMBERS FROM 1 TO 6 AND CIRCLE YOUR CHOICES.
I'LL CHOOSE 2 AND 6

3. How many winners would you expect?

Encourage pupils to take the guesses seriously. A vital aspect of the activity is to compare these perceptions with the results of the game.

One teacher collected and averaged the guesses for grades 8–11. These were as follows:

GRADE	8	9	10	11
AVERAGE	23	32	28	22

The teacher was disappointed that year 11 (who had done some combination theory) did not appear to have learned much.

I'M ABOUT TO DRAW FOR THE FIRST GAME, BUT FOR THE REASON I'LL EXPLAIN LATER I'D LIKE TO KNOW WHAT YOU THINK YOUR CHANCES ARE

WHAT DO YOUR EYES TELL YOU?
THERE ARE SIX NUMBERS IN THE BARREL.
IF YOUR TWO NUMBERS ARE DRAWN OUT, THEN YOU WIN.
IF WE PLAY THIS GAME MANY TIMES, SOMETIMES YOU WOULD WIN, OTHER TIMES YOU WOULD LOSE.
IF WE WERE TO PLAY 100 TIMES, WRITE DOWN HOW MANY TIMES YOU WOULD EXPECT TO WIN

WRITE YOUR GUESSES ON THE CHALKBOARD

4. The draw

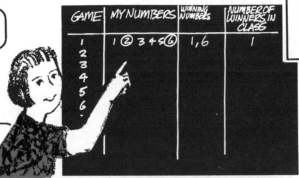

> FIRST GAME — THE WINNING NUMBERS ARE ONE AND SIX

> PLEASE WRITE THESE DOWN LIKE THIS

> HOW MANY WINNERS?

> ONLY ONE? EVERYBODY WRITE THAT IN THE LAST COLUMN

This part of the activity should take about 15 minutes and provide a good data base for later.

5. Play ten games

> I WOULD LIKE US TO PLAY TEN GAMES IN ALL BECAUSE WE NEED THE DATA FOR OUR ANALYSIS

Encourage pupils to change their numbers if they wish, although many may prefer to keep them the same. Rewarding the winner(s) at this stage with a Mintie (or similar) certainly adds motivation and interest.

Repeat this process for all ten games, giving out prizes after each game, and pupils recording the class results.

6. The analysis

Just before starting this section, a good idea is to reward all the non-winners as well.

It is important to note that the data is in a sense personal to the pupils — it was created by them, and as a result, analysis of the data will be more meaningful.

> I HOPE YOU HAVE ENJOYED THE GAME, BUT OUR REASON FOR PLAYING IT IS TO LEARN SOMETHING FROM THE MATHS INVOLVED.
> WE HAVE A LOT OF INTERESTING INFORMATION, SO LET'S SEE WHAT IT TELLS US

> MY FIRST QUESTION IS ABOUT LUCK. WE HAVE 26 PLAYERS AND WE'VE PLAYED TEN GAMES — 260 IN ALL. WE HAD 19 WINNERS.
> DO YOU THINK WE WERE UNLUCKY, THAT IS, SHOULD WE HAVE HAD MORE WINNERS?
> OR WERE WE LUCKY — THAT IS, WE DID BETTER THAN EXPECTED?
> OR ARE THE RESULTS ABOUT RIGHT?

Pupils have probably been watching the patterns of the games intently and forming judgments and predictions, however informally. This section is an attempt to document, in part, their intuitions.

Ask pupils to vote and record their votes on the chalkboard.

7. The mathematics

The following analysis is done informally, appealing more to pupils' intuitions than to formal probability.

From first principles, work out all the possible pairs.

> WE NEED TO KNOW THE CHANCES OF WINNING ONE GAME.
> YOU WIN IF YOUR PAIR OF NUMBERS IS DRAWN. SO HOW MANY PAIRS COULD YOU DRAW OUT?

> WE **CAN** ANSWER THIS QUESTION — I'D LIKE TO SHOW YOU HOW MATHEMATICS CAN ASSIST

> I'LL LET YOU WORK IT OUT.
> FOR INSTANCE THERE WILL BE...

Start the class off, but let them work out the fifteen combinations.

1,2 2,3 3,4 4,5 5,6
1,3 2,4 3,5 4,6
1,4 2,5 3,6
1,5 2,6
1,6   = 15 pairs

Years 6 ↓ 10

SOCIAL

8. Discussion — your real chances of winning

> SINCE THERE ARE 15 PAIRS YOUR CHANCES ARE...? (Answer – one in15)

> SO WHAT'S THE ANSWER TO THE QUESTION 'WHEN WILL YOUR LUCKY NUMBERS COME UP?' (Once in every 15 games)

The questions are structured to be well within the abilities of the pupils to answer, either as mental or pencil and paper arithmetic. Suggested answers are given in brackets.

15 pairs = 1 in 15 chances
26 pairs ≈ 1·7 winners per game
17 winners in 10 games

> WE HAVE 26 PLAYERS — WHAT SHOULD WE EXPECT?
> MORE THAN ONE WINNER PER GAME, BUT LESS THAN TWO.
> HOW MANY GROUPS OF 15 IN 26? (1.733...) SO WE EXPECTED ON AVERAGE ABOUT 1.7 WINNERS PER GAME.
> HOW MANY WINNERS SHOULD WE HAVE EXPECTED? (17.3)
> WE ACTUALLY HAD 19, SO OUR MATHS TELLS US WE WERE SLIGHTLY ON THE LUCKY SIDE BUT VERY CLOSE TO WHAT WE EXPECTED

The teacher could now admit that in planning for the 'prizes' (plus a few extras for the non-winners) a total of 15 to 20 winners was expected.

20 ← (17·33) → 15

> IT LOOKS LIKE A GAME OF LUCK, BUT THE ORGANISERS HAVE A RATHER GOOD IDEA OF WHAT WILL HAPPEN

> 19 WINNERS IS NOT SURPRISING.
> HAD WE ONLY THREE WINNERS I'M SURE YOU WOULD HAVE BEEN SO SURPRISED AS TO BE DOWNRIGHT SUSPICIOUS.
> IF WE HAD 150 WINNERS THEN I WOULD HAVE BEEN SUSPICIOUS.
> ACTUALLY THERE IS A WHOLE BRANCH OF MATHEMATICS DEVOTED TO KNOWING HOW SUSPICIOUS YOU SHOULD BE AS THE RESULTS GET FURTHER FROM WHAT YOU EXPECT

9. Comparison with initial guesses

The conclusion is the realisation that there is a lot more pairs than they thought there would be! If people are over-optimistic in this simple game, how realistic would their understanding of the 45:6 or the 40:6 game be?

When people have little idea of the maths involved, their guesses are most likely based on simple ratios, that is, 'two out of six means 33%'.

> IT IS INTERESTING THAT NEARLY EVERY ONE OF YOU OVERESTIMATED.
> WHAT DOES THAT MEAN FOR THE OPERATOR?
> FOR THE PLAYER?
> WHY DOES IT HAPPEN?

> THE OPERATOR WOULD FEEL HAPPY

> LET'S LOOK AT HOW THE RESULTS COMPARE WITH YOUR ORIGINAL GUESSES HERE

> THE PLAYER WILL BE DISAPPOINTED

> IF WE PLAYED 100 GAMES HOW MANY WINNERS WOULD WE EXPECT? (one winner in 15 games = 6.7 wins per 100)

ORIGINAL GUESSES

60	40	33	25	37	27
50	20	36	20	48	38
30	33	25	40	51	62
35	50	40	42	49	55
28	40

1 in 15 = 6·7 per 100

> HOW DID YOU FORM YOUR INITIAL GUESSES?

> IT LOOKS EASY BUT ITS NOT

For the operator, having a game that looks easier than it really is, is good news. For the player, the difference between reality and perception is an area that often leaves them open to disadvantage and possible exploitation.

10. Comparison with the real six-from-40 (or 45) game

The following is an attempt to present these statistics in the same way as the 6 : 2 game was developed and analysed.

> LET'S LOOK AT TATTSLOTTO WHERE YOU SELECT SIX FROM 45.
> YOU WIN FIRST DIVISION IF YOUR SIX NUMBERS ARE DRAWN FROM THE BARREL.
> SO, HOW MANY GROUPS OF SIX ARE THERE IN 45?
> YOU COULD DO IT LIKE THIS, JUST LIKE YOU DID FOR THE 6 : 2 GAME

> YOU CAN SEE THAT THERE WOULD BE A VERY LARGE NUMBER OF COMBINATIONS.
> IT'S ACTUALLY 8 145 060 DIFFERENT GROUPS OF SIX.
> THAT MEANS YOUR CHANCES ARE ONE OUT OF EIGHT MILLION FOR A SINGLE GAME

> IN REALITY, MANY PEOPLE FILL OUT A TICKET WITH TEN GAMES WHICH COSTS $2.65 (price in 1987).
> SO YOU CAN EXPECT TO WIN ONCE IN EVERY 800 000 WEEKS, THAT IS, ONCE EVERY 15 000 YEARS.

> LOTTO OPERATES IN SEVERAL DIFFERENT STATES AND ATTRACTS ABOUT $8 000 000 EACH SATURDAY.
> THAT REPRESENTS 32 MILLION GAMES AT 25 CENTS A GAME. SINCE WE EXPECT ONE WINNER EACH 8 MILLION GAMES WE EXPECT FOUR FIRST DIVISION WINNERS EACH WEEK.
> KEEP A CHECK ON HOW MANY WINNERS THERE ARE EACH WEEK.
> SEE HOW NEAR IT IS TO OUR MATHEMATICAL PREDICTIONS

```
1 2 3 4 5 6          TATTSLOTTO STATS
1 2 3 4 5 7          $8,000,000 per saturday
1 2 3 4 5 8          ≈ 32,000,000 games
      ↓                      at 25¢
1 2 3 4 5 (45)       1 in 8 million chances
8,145,060            should average
                     4 winners per week
```

> This section is the critical jump from a simple model to the real game. The experience with the simple game and the gap between perception and reality provides a base for an appreciation of the large numbers, and the low chances of winning the real game.

Years 6 ↓ 10 **SOCIAL**

11. Other discussion points

> *What would be the chances if you bought 100 tickets each week?*

Multiple ticket buying is effective — it parts customers from their money more quickly. If you purchased 100 tickets a week, that is, spent $250 a week, you could only expect to win once every 160 years.

> By showing how small the chances of winning are, hopefully, these figures will have some sort of shock value.

> *Even if Methuselah won, he would lose*

Even if you bought a ticket once a week for 16 000 years and won an expected $1.2 million, you would have spent $2 million — a nett loss of $800 000 (based on the 60% prize pool, but excluding agents' fees*).

> *Plus agents' fees.* We have only given official costs. However if agents' fees are included the returns to the investor are even bleaker, bringing the returns to the investor down from 60% to about 54%. So Methusela would have suffered a loss of over $1 million.

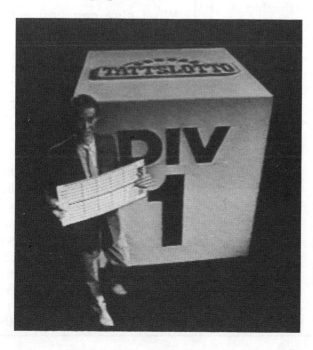

Extension activities

Are you superstitious? *Teachers report this as an absolute highlight.*

In the game two from six, pupils are quite happy to argue that each pair has the same chance of being drawn as any other pair — BUT — do they really believe this?

Pupils, as do adults, carry all sorts of strange misconceptions — the data from the ten games can illustrate this.

Since we played ten games, each pair should have been selected about 17 times, but is this the case?

Pupils could come to the chalkboard and record their selections in a table. The totals should make for very interesting discussion.

A quicker alternative is to select four sample pairs such as (1,2) (5,6) (2,5) and (3,5), tallying how many times each was selected.

Trial schools found that pairs such as (2,5) or (3,5) were selected many, many more times than 'unlikely' or extreme pairs such as (1,2) or (5,6). Why is this the case if students believe they are equally likely? — or do they?

In one trials school the pair (2,5) was picked 43 times, (1,2) was picked just 8.

One way to illustrate the point is to contrast the (2,5) with the (1,2) pair given that the class, by their choice, seems to believe the (2,5) to be much more likely.

Demonstrate the following:

'Suppose the two was the first number drawn — do you believe the number one is aware of this and goes and hides in a corner so as not to be selected while the number 5 jumped up and down trying to be picked — your own choice seems to suggest that you believe this!'

'In a real six from 45 game, no-one in their right mind would select six consecutive numbers — would they?'

An interesting exercise is to note the numbers drawn each week and to predict the number of winners. Is it true that 'unusual' or 'extreme' sets of numbers mean less winners? Conversely, does a well spaced pattern produce more than the expected four winners per week?

I'M NOT SUPERSTITIOUS, BUT THERE'S NO WAY I WOULD SELECT THE NUMBERS 1,2,3,4,5,6 OUT OF 45.

Analysis by computer

After the two from six game, a computer could be used to move towards the complexity of the six from 45 game by examining games such as two from seven, two from eight, two from nine, then three from six, three from seven, three from eight etc.. Results could be graphed to highlight the rapidly deteriorating chances of success.

Which game gives the best odds?

Give pupils a choice between playing the three from six or the two from seven game. They work out the chances from first principles and vote.

What else can you get from the data base?

The data base of numbers drawn and numbers chosen can be explored for a variety of probability features.

... not just simple ratios

The message of the activity is that Lotto is based on combination theory, not simple ratios. Pupils become aware 'that there are a lot more combinations in the barrel than I thought there were'.

Another treatment is to focus on the money flow.

Play the same activity, but this time distribute ten Smarties (or similar 'coinage') at the start. Players come out to the front and pay to enter each game. Pupils can then physically see the 40% removal for 'expenses'. You could also deduct a further 10% agent's fee. The 'prize pool' is then distributed among the winners. It is a graphic way to illustrate that you can only win at the expense of your fellow players, and to witness the relentless growth of the organisers' 'pile'.

Coin in the square

Of course you could toss a coin into one of those squares. It's almost an insult to your skills to think that you couldn't. And the odds seem to make the bet very attractive.

But as with all forms of commercial gambling, the game appears easier than it is. By the pupils modelling the real game, they find out that perceptions do not always match reality.

This activity provides a framework for teachers to discuss the place of social issues, such as gambling, in the mathematics classroom.

Features of this lesson

- A mathematical model based on the results of an experimental simulation.
- Prediction and testing the prediction by playing the game.
- Application of a popular fairground game.
- Computer extension.

- Finding why the game is so popular (achievement looks easier than it turns out to be).
- Concept of expectation.
- Group work.
- Extension for Year 10 pupils.

This lesson is best conducted around Show time.

Preparation

- Draw 36 mm squares on large pieces of paper, such as cartridge or butchers paper. Make one per group of about three pupils.

  ALTERNATIVES

  If you have an A3 photocopier print several grids per group and stick them together.

  If you can get a large sheet of clear plastic with a 36 mm grid drawn on the under-side, and big enough to cover a large table, the whole class could play on a bench which is near to the real thing.

- One worksheet (page 122) per pupil.
- One 1¢ piece per pupil.
- One only twenty-cent coin.
- Calculators (optional).
- On the chalkboard write the headings for the parts of the lesson ➡

For year ten pupils write the fourth heading.

(d) ' What mathematics tells you.'

COIN IN THE SQUARE
a. What your eyes tell you.
b. What an experiment tells you.
c. What is a fair prize?

Coin in the square

Most pupils are intrigued to play this popular carnival game in a maths class. They are surprised to find how steep are the odds against them and often declare the game to be a 'rip off'.

1. Demonstrate how to play the game

Place the grid on the table, hold up a twenty-cent coin and invite a pupil to demonstrate the game.

> Encourage the telling of anecdotes, especially those where one person wins a big prize which is normally followed by a lot of losers.

> Less academic groups responded to a more direct approach. Admit that it is a 'rip off' so that *they* will have the 'good oil' over the people who don't know. *'A fool and his money are soon parted.'*

2. It's really a very predictable mathematical game

> Telling the pupils the structure of the activity and purpose helps pupils know what is coming and to organise their thoughts.

3. 'What your eyes tell you' — How many times out of 100 do you think you'd win?

Demonstrate with a few throws on to the grid.

> Encourage pupils to take their estimation seriously — a major aspect of this activity is the difference between a person's perception and reality.

> Class averages in trials schools tend to be about 50 to 60, but this figure is clearly influenced by the introduction.

When pupils have written their guesses on the board, they should return to their seats, and copy the lesson headings and the class averages into their workbooks.

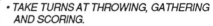

4. What an experiment tells you! — 100 throws

Give each group a grid and coins

> NOW YOU CAN PLAY THE GAME AND FIND OUT WHO HAD THE NEAREST GUESS.
>
> WOULD YOU BELIEVE ME IF I SAID THAT I KNOW WHICH OF YOU GUESSED CORRECTLY?
>
> WE CARNIVAL OPERATORS KNOW HOW MUCH MONEY PEOPLE ARE LIKELY TO WIN BEFORE WE WORK OUT HOW BIG A PRIZE TO OFFER

> OK! ORGANISE YOURSELVES INTO GROUPS OF ABOUT THREE.
>
> DRAW A FOOT LINE SO THAT EVERYBODY MUST TOSS ABOUT HALF A METRE TO THE BOARD LIKE THIS

> • TAKE TURNS AT THROWING, GATHERING AND SCORING.
> • EACH TEAM THROWS 100 TIMES, SO THAT'S THIRTY- THREE TIMES EACH (PLUS ONE).
> • IF THE COIN GOES OFF THE BOARD, HAVE ANOTHER TURN.
> • WHEN FINISHED, WRITE YOUR SCORES ON THE CHALKBOARD, THEN FIND THE CLASS AVERAGE.

5. Compare the results with the guesses

> LET'S LOOK AT THE RESULTS.
> OUR GUESSES AVERAGED OUT AT 62% BUT WHEN WE PLAYED WE ONLY AVERAGED 25%.
> WHAT A DIFFERENCE!
> WHAT HAPPENED?

> IT LOOKS EASIER THAN IT WAS

> This is a critical aspect. What does this difference mean for the operator?

> A valuable outcome for pupils is that the psychology behind such games is exposed.

> Trials schools' averages ranged from 19 to 31. The theoretical result is 25.
>
> For added interest you could write 25± 6 on a piece of paper, seal it in an envelope and give it to a pupil to open at the end of the lesson.

6. What is a 'fair' prize?

Give out the worksheet.

Accept a few guesses from the class and systematically test them against what we would expect to happen.

> IF YOU WERE THE CARNIVAL OPERATOR, WHAT IS A REASONABLE PRIZE TO OFFER FOR EACH WINNING THROW?

> Encourage comments from the class on the advisability of the various payouts.
>
> The carnival operators need to make a profit, but not too much or people will not play.

> ABOUT FIVE CENTS

> LET'S LOOK AT THAT

> SO FOUR CENTS IS A FAIR PRIZE, BUT IF THE OPERATOR NEEDS TO MAKE A PROFIT HE OR SHE MAY DECIDE TO GIVE A THREE OR EVEN TWO CENT PRIZE

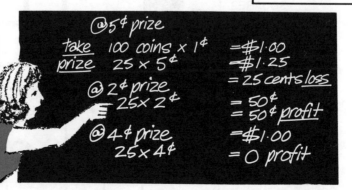

The first period will probably end at this point. The next part on the following page should consolidate the concepts learnt so far and provide practice for the mathematical and tossing skills learnt.

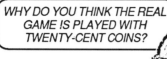

SESSION 2   **7. But the real game is with twenty-cent coins**

WHY DO YOU THINK THE REAL GAME IS PLAYED WITH TWENTY-CENT COINS?

THEY ARE BIGGER SO YOUR CHANCES ARE LESS

YOU'D TAKE TOO LONG TO MAKE ANY PROFIT OUT OF ONE-CENT COINS

HOW MANY WINS WOULD YOU EXPECT FROM 100 THROWS OF A TWENTY-CENT COIN?

HOW COULD YOU WORK OUT A FAIR PRIZE?

WE'D NEED TO DO ANOTHER EXPERIMENT

Trials schools found that after a very active group-work lesson, this follow-up lesson which allowed consolidation and skill practice, was a desirable balancing feature.

8. Fair prizes for other coins

For each coin type, pupils could conduct a quick experiment, or be told the result from 100 throws. (The theoretical results are included on the worksheet.)

Then by trial and error, pupils can complete the worksheet and;

• discover what a 'fair' prize is, that is, one that yields no profit,

• discuss and decide what prize the operator should offer to earn a reasonable profit.

Later, at the end of the lesson, pupils will be testing their predictions.

PRIZE	40¢	$2
EXPECTED PAYOUT	$2.00	$10.00
PROFIT or LOSS	$18.00	$10.00

---

9. Back to reality

Pupils often like to discuss variations of the real game and how these have been deliberately included to affect the payouts. Why is the game successful at fairs like the Royal Show?

Would it be likely to succeed at other locations.

SPECIAL HIGH-VALUE PRIZES WHICH ARE OFTEN CIRCLES, NOT SQUARES, SURROUNDED BY LOW-VALUE SQUARES

THICKER BORDERS

A SLIPPERY SURFACE TO REDUCE THE EFFECT OF THE SKILL

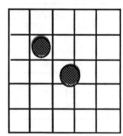

THE GENEROSITY OF THE JUDGE — ON OR OVER THE LINE

OTHER SIZE SQUARES — LARGER OR SMALLER

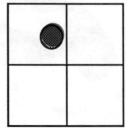

COINS GOING OFF THE TABLE

STIFF CHEDDAR MATE

10. Concluding activity

Complete the second lesson with a game to test pupils' predictions.

- Use five operators, each controlling a board with a different size coin. Payout prizes should be as decided on the worksheet.
- All start with two dollars (on paper only).
- Players can play on any board.
- Each player records his or her payouts and receipts.
- Near the end of the lesson, players calculate their profits and losses.

EXTENSION FOR YEAR TEN

Calculating the mathematical percentage

> By drawing coins in 'winning positions' pupils could be challenged to find the shape and size of the 'winning area'.

A HINT:
WHERE MUST **THE CENTRE OF THE COIN** FINISH TO BE IN A WINNING POSITION

SINCE A ONE-CENT COIN IS 18 mm WIDE, THE CENTRE IS NOT ALLOWED TO COME WITHIN 9 mm OF AN EDGE.
SO THE WINNING AREA IS AN 18 mm SQUARE

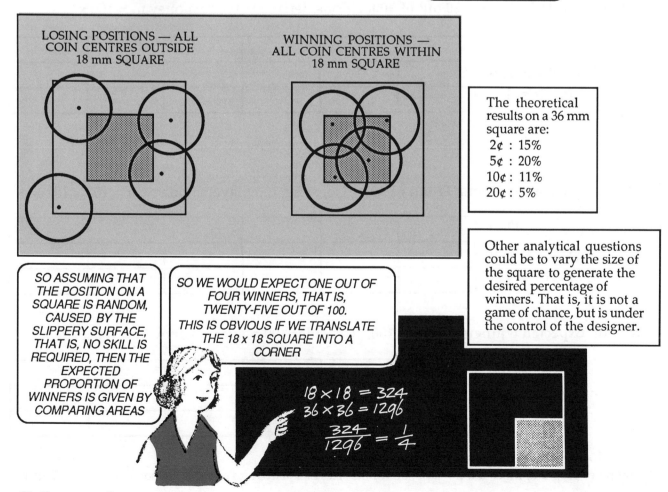

LOSING POSITIONS — ALL COIN CENTRES OUTSIDE 18 mm SQUARE

WINNING POSITIONS — ALL COIN CENTRES WITHIN 18 mm SQUARE

> The theoretical results on a 36 mm square are:
> 2¢ : 15%
> 5¢ : 20%
> 10¢ : 11%
> 20¢ : 5%

> Other analytical questions could be to vary the size of the square to generate the desired percentage of winners. That is, it is not a game of chance, but is under the control of the designer.

SO ASSUMING THAT THE POSITION ON A SQUARE IS RANDOM, CAUSED BY THE SLIPPERY SURFACE, THAT IS, NO SKILL IS REQUIRED, THEN THE EXPECTED PROPORTION OF WINNERS IS GIVEN BY COMPARING AREAS

SO WE WOULD EXPECT ONE OUT OF FOUR WINNERS, THAT IS, TWENTY-FIVE OUT OF 100.
THIS IS OBVIOUS IF WE TRANSLATE THE 18 x 18 SQUARE INTO A CORNER

$$18 \times 18 = 324$$
$$36 \times 36 = 1296$$
$$\frac{324}{1296} = \frac{1}{4}$$

Challenge pupils to analyse in a similar way the theoretical results for two, five, ten and twenty-cent coins.

Years 8 ↓ 10 SOCIAL

Worksheet

Coin in the square

For each coin, decide what would be the fairest prize to offer

1¢ coin. Expected winners: 25 out of 100. Consider 100 players. Money in = 100 x 1¢ = 100¢

Prize						
Expected payout						
Profit or loss						

2¢ coin.Expected winners: 15 out of 100. Consider 100 players: money in = 100 x 2¢ =$2

Prize						
Expected payout						
Profit or loss						

5¢ coin. Expected winners: 20 out of 100. Consider 100 players: money in = 100 x 5¢ =

Prize						
Expected payout						
Profit or loss						

10¢ coin. Expected winners: 11 out of 100. Consider 100 players: money in = 100 x 10¢ =

Prize						
Expected payout						
Profit or loss						

20¢ coin. Expected winners: 5 out of 100. Consider 100 players: money in = 100 x 20¢ =

Prize						
Expected payout						
Profit or loss						

Extension

A computer program, which allows variations of the sizes of squares and coins, is included on the MCTP disk.

Worksheet
Coin in the square

Notes

Mortality quiz

Should life insurance statistics be used to teach mathematical probability, or should the figures be used in the hope and expectation that pupils will be more aware of road realities, and that this knowledge will make them safer road users?

Both approaches are educationally sound, but this activity strongly promotes the latter.

Features of this activity

- A realistic application — the life insurance industry.
- A motivating quiz based on the pupils perceptions of the patterns of life expectancy.
- Addresses sensitive areas of personal safety, particularly road safety.

- Language linkages via explanation of quiz answers.
- Interpretation of tables and graphs.
- Intuitive probability.
- Analysis and interpretation of insurance premiums.
- Use of calculators.
- Non-threatening.

...but is it really maths?

This activity considers social issues, in particular the area of road safety and the way that smoking affects health. It is intended to stimulate discussion as to whether such ideas should be treated within a maths class and whether maths should be presented as a neutral or 'pure' subject.

Given that many mathematics curriculum documents state a primary aim as 'preparing students for the real world', such a debate or discussion would seem relevant.

If teachers accept that subjects sensitive to social themes *should* be presented in the maths classroom, an additional purpose of this activity is to act as a template, model or guide to illustrate how ideas could be converted into successful teaching.

Preparation

One copy of the two tables, pages 130-1, per pupil. You may choose to prepare the graph on page 127 on an overhead projectual with overlays for male and female.

THIS ACTIVITY IS PART OF THE MCTP PROFESSIONAL DEVELOPMENT PACKAGE FROM THE CURRICULUM DEVELOPMENT CENTRE, CANBERRA

Mortality quiz

When an insurance company charges one person $1.28 and another person $5.40 per month for the identical insurance policy you can bet your life* that they have good reasons — mostly based on statistics. This activity looks at such figures and the reasons for them.

* Couldn't resist the double entendre. Of course a life insurance policy is a bet with the insurance company on your life. (If you die, you [???] win the bet)

> ### WARNING
> Since the subject is the statistics of death, be very sensitive to the feelings of children who may have had recent bereavements or whose family or friends have had serious injuries. If you know of such a case you may choose to reschedule this activity to a more appropriate time.

1.   Safe ages and unsafe ages

The questions and the given commentary are designed to find out whether pupils are aware that different ages have different probabilities of dying.

> Trials schools reported that this question need explanation.

> The answer is based on the most recent figures available, males and females combined.

> *I HAVE AN INTERESTING FIVE QUESTION QUIZ FOR YOU, BASED ON THE LIFE INSURANCE INDUSTRY.*
> *NOW YOU PROBABLY KNOW THAT THE INSURANCE COMPANIES COLLECT STATISTICS AND, INDEED, KNOW WHAT THE CHANCES ARE.*
> *WELL THEN, WHICH DO YOU THINK WOULD COST MORE TO INSURE — A 20 YEAR OLD PERSON OR A 95 YEAR OLD?*

> *95 — BECAUSE THE 20 YEAR OLD PERSON SHOULD BE FIT*

> *GOOD! NOW HERE IS QUESTION ONE.*
> *WRITE DOWN WHAT YOU THINK IS THE 'SAFEST' AGE TO BE IN AUSTRALIA.*
> *WHAT DO I MEAN BY 'SAFEST AGE'?*
> *IT IS THE AGE AT WHICH THE CHANCES OF DEATH IN THE NEXT YEAR ARE THE LEAST.*
> *WHAT AGE DO YOU THINK IS SAFER THAN ALL OTHERS?*
> *NOW YOU KNOW THAT IT'S NOT 95, SO WHAT AGE IS SAFEST?*

2.   The class perception of the safe age

Write on the chalkboard the spread and the frequency of answers.
Then tell the class the answer.

> Trials classes showed considerable variation, giving answers from one to fifty.

> Guessing exposes current perceptions and allows them to be compared with reality.

> This question is actually included in *Trivial Pursuit.*

> *WHAT NUMBER DID YOU HAVE TRACEY?*

> *37!*   *WHO HAD HIGHER?*

> 50   45   40   42

> *WHO HAD LOWER?*

> 18   20   21   30

> *WELL THE ANSWER IS TEN.*
> *WHEN YOU THINK ABOUT IT I'M SURE YOU CAN SEE THE LOGICAL REASON FOR THIS.*
> *WE'LL DISCUSS MORE OF THESE REASONS LATER*

3. Questions based on the graph

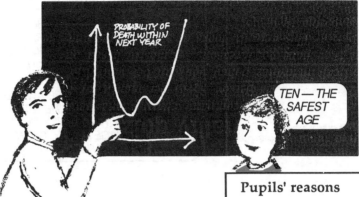

THE NEXT FOUR QUESTIONS ARE BASED UPON THE GRAPH.

IT IS NOT DRAWN TO SCALE SO YOU CAN'T WORK OUT THE ANSWERS BY LOOKING — YOU HAVE TO THINK ABOUT THEM.

NOW YOU PROBABLY KNOW THAT THE CHANCES OF DEATH IN THE FIRST YEAR OF LIFE ARE RELATIVELY HIGH.

WHAT DO YOU THINK THE FIRST LOW POINT CORRESPONDS TO?

TEN — THE SAFEST AGE

OK! HERE ARE THE NEXT FOUR QUESTIONS

QUESTIONS 2–5

2. The graph increases after ten to a local maximum, then it starts to decline. At what stage does this maximum occur?

3. The graph then goes to another low point before rising. At what age is the low point?

4. As the graph rises, it reaches the same level as the high point for question two. What age is this do you think?

5. The graph then keeps going up. (The bad news is that it doesn't come down again!) At what age do you think the chances are the same as they were in the first year of life?

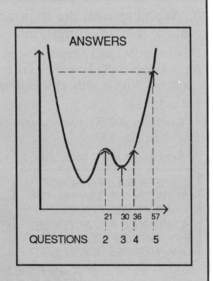

Pupils' reasons
(see step 4)

Some of the reasons given by pupils in trials schools were :

Q1. Children are past most childhood diseases, but are still under the protective umbrella of the family.

Q2. After age ten, children become more adventurous, but often lack experience and take unnecessary risks. The motor car is generally recognised as the significant factor in the maximum.

Q3. People getting older and wiser now have responsibilities — they have settled down and don't put themselves in risky situations like mountain climbing, hang gliding, racing bikes.

Q4. Age factors and diseases which develop over a long time, such as lung cancer from smoking.

Years 9 ↓ 10

SOCIAL

4. The answers, but why should they be so?

Again, one question at a time, ask for the pupils answers and write a couple of them on the chalkboard to see the spread of answers. Then give the correct answers and discuss a few possible reasons, but leave plenty of scope for further reasons to be explored when pupils form small discussion groups.

WHY DO THINK THERE IS SUCH A HIGH RISK IN THE FIRST YEAR OF LIFE?

COT DEATHS

STILLBORN BABIES

NEW BORN BABIES AREN'T ALL PERFECT AND MANY DIE SOON AFTER BIRTH

OK! NOW IN YOUR GROUPS TRY TO THINK OF REASONS WHY THIS GRAPH HAS THAT SHAPE AND WRITE THEM IN YOUR WORKBOOKS

Pupils in trials schools were very realistic and perceptive, and seemed to recognise many of the underlying reasons

This is a most important part of the lesson — the confirmation of correct guesses or the reasoning through why they could have been wrong. Group discussion seems to bring out more ideas, (via sharing) than individually.

Warn against anecdotal comparisons, pointing out how general statistics have very little predictive ability for a single individual.

After about ten minutes, have a class discussion of the possible reasons.

In the trials schools pupils clearly recognised the social intentions of the lesson, but there seemed to be no reason why they shouldn't be stated explicitly.

5 Discuss the sociological / mathematical intent of this lesson— why this topic was chosen.

DO YOU THINK PEOPLE WHO ARE JUST ABOUT TO START DRIVING ARE AWARE OF THESE FIGURES?

DO YOU THINK THEY SHOULD KNOW THEM?

DO YOU THINK THEY ARE AWARE THAT AS FAR AS THEIR HEALTH IS CONCERNED, WHEN THEY GET IN A CAR THEY 'AGE ABOUT TWENTY YEARS'?

YOU (THE PUPILS) ARE ALL ON THE UPSLOPE OF THE CURVE.

MY HOPE IS THAT BY BEING AWARE OF THE FIGURES YOU MAY TAKE ACTION TO BE A LITTLE SAFER AS A RESULT

The graph (for step 6) is dramatically displayed using an overhead projectual. For added authenticity you could plot it from the Life Tables. However a simple two-colour chalkboard diagram is sufficient.

6. Working with the insurance premiums — male / female comparisons

Distribute the data sheets. Ask questions which require analyses of the figures, especially how they are used in the insurance industry. (Use the non-smoking data at this stage.)

For example :

1. Consider 100 000 twenty year old males and 100 000 females. (See extension sheet.)

2. Repeat for forty-year olds.

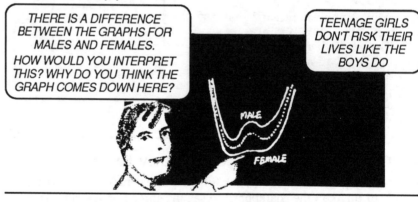

THERE IS A DIFFERENCE BETWEEN THE GRAPHS FOR MALES AND FEMALES.

HOW WOULD YOU INTERPRET THIS? WHY DO YOU THINK THE GRAPH COMES DOWN HERE?

TEENAGE GIRLS DON'T RISK THEIR LIVES LIKE THE BOYS DO

By using calculators, pupils will be able to calculate percentages, thus making for more accurate interpretations.

An overhead projectual of these charts will help focus on specific areas of the chart, thus helping pupils to locate figures.
Pupils would mark the figures under discussion.

7. Smoking and the increased death rate

Distribute the handouts. Ask questions which require analyses of the figures, especially how these are used in the insurance industry.

This section allows pupils, by manipulating some of the data, to explore the male/female comparisons and to understand more about how insurance premiums are used.

THE GRAPHS OF FEMALES ARE COMING CLOSER TO THE GRAPHS OF MALES.

LOOK AT THE 'CIGARETTE SMOKING IN AUSTRALIA' FIGURES. DOES IT PROVIDE SOME ANSWERS?

LOOK AT THE SAMPLE DEATH COVER FIGURES.

LOOK AT THE MALE AGE 20 AND THE MALE AGE 44 FIGURES.

HOW WOULD YOU INTERPRET THEM?

WHY DO YOU THINK THERE IS SUCH A DIFFERENCE BETWEEN MALES AND FEMALES AT AGE 44 BUT LITTLE DIFFERENCE AT AGE 20?

Trial teachers report that this 'busy work' with numbers is excellent reinforcement for earlier discussions.

THE EFFECTS OF SMOKING ARE CATCHING UP

Extension activities

Trends in mortality rates

Discuss the trends in mortality rates and speculate on probable and possible causes. (See the figures for 1985 and 2020.)

The mortality rates based on the three years 1980–82 can be compared with the Life Table based on the deaths in the years 1975–77. The comparisons show that during the five-year period:

more babies are surviving

The mortality rate in the first years of life fell from .01501 to .01147 for males and from .01184 to .00905 for females, a reduction of about 25 % overall.

the age 19–21 bump in the graph is going down, but...

There has been a significant reduction in the size of the male bump from .00217 to .00181 at age 19, although from ages 24 to 29 there has been a slight increase. For females the peak that occurred at about 19 has disappeared. The fall in rates in the late teens of about 18% is similar for both sexes. These are important changes at ages where many deaths can be avoided.

people are living longer

In the region of steady upward trend there have been substantial reductions in mortality rates. For males the reductions have been about 20% at age 40, 14 % at age 60 and 69% at age 90. For females the reductions have been 24% at age 40, 15% at age 60, and 69% at age 90.

THE FOLLOWING ACTIVITIES CAN BE DONE AS INDIVIDUAL PUPIL RESEARCH OR AS A CLASS ACTIVITY. YOU MAY CHOOSE TO PHOTOCOPY THIS HALF-SHEET FOR DISTRIBUTION TO PUPILS.

Giving up trying to interpret statistics is good for some people's health

In a major study in the United States, it was found that the mortality rates of ex-smokers were higher in the first year after quitting than for continuing smokers. The explanation is found in the fact that both healthy and sick individuals quit smoking. The higher mortality rate is experienced by those who quit because of illness and not by those who quit for better health. About 10% of the smokers quit on doctor's orders; this group had much higher mortality ratios than those who stopped for other reasons, and considerably biased the figures.

Discuss.

COUGH COUGH
I READ THE STATISTICS
— IT'S DANGEROUS TO
GIVE UP SMOKING

What could be causing the bump in the graph?

The graph probably indicates that under different, and biologically normal situations one might expect either:

    or

Discuss possible reasons for the aberration, and suggest reasons why one of the two graphs above (or maybe some other graph) would better reflect the normal.

Nay own yer wee bonnie laif. Yer trooth's too dangerous ye ken

Scottish figures (1930–1932), showed that married men in their twenties, thirties and forties had lower mortality rates than unmarried men. Married women of the same age groupings, however had higher mortality rates than unmarried women. On the face of it, it appears that getting married is dangerous for women!

Discuss.

...but compared to Sweden...

Compare our mortality figures with those of other countries. Compare and contrast the lifestyles to find possible reasons.

What's in it for the insurance companies?

Consider 100 000 twenty year old males and 100 000 females who insure themselves for one year.

What is the total amount collected?

What is the total payout?

Comment.

Repeat for forty-year olds.

Years 9↓10   SOCIAL

SAMPLE DEATH COVER: PREMIUM PER $1,000

Age at nearest birthday	Non-smokers		Heavy smokers		(1985 figures) Deaths per 100 000	
	Male $	female $	Male $	female $	Male $	female $
20	2.69	2.69	2.77	2.77	155	47
21	2.71	2.71	3.04	3.04	156	47
22	2.49	2.49	3.02	3.02	153	45
23	2.16	2.16	2.81	2.81	147	44
24	1.83	1.83	2.55	2.55	140	44
25	1.56	1.56	2.30	2.30	133	44
26	1.41	1.41	2.14	2.14	127	44
27	1.35	1.35	2.10	2.10	132	44
28	1.31	1.31	2.10	2.10	119	45
29	1.28	1.28	2.11	2.11	115	46
30	1.28	1.28	2.16	2.16	117	47
31	1.28	1.28	2.22	2.16	117	49
32	1.29	1.28	2.29	2.16	115	52
33	1.32	1.28	2.40	2.16	118	52
34	1.34	1.28	2.51	2.22	124	58
35	1.37	1.29	2.62	2.29	131	63
36	1.41	1.32	2.78	2.40	140	68
37	1.45	1.34	2.97	2.51	151	74
38	1.52	1.37	3.21	2.62	164	81
39	1.59	1.41	3.46	2.78	179	90
40	1.67	1.45	3.75	2.97	197	100
41	1.78	1.52	4.08	3.21	218	112
42	1.92	1.59	4.45	3.46	241	127
43	2.08	1.67	4.90	3.75	268	144
44	2.25	1.78	5.40	4.08	298	162

CIGARETTE SMOKING IN AUSTRALIA 1973 AND 1982

AGE		1973(%)		1982(%)
13 – 17	MALES	18.5	↗	21.5
	FEMALES	15.4	↗	19.0
18 – 24	MALES	48.3	↘	45.4
	FEMALES	35.1	↗	43.8
25 - 39	MALES	47.4	↘	42.2
	FEMALES	34.4	↗	35.1
40 - 54	MALES	45.7	↘	40.5
	FEMALES	33.4	↘	28.3
55 +	MALES	36.5	↘	29.3
	FEMALES	20.9	↘	20.7
	OVERALL	35%	↘	33.4

Mortality rates — a look ahead

AGE	1985 MALES	1985 FEMALES	2020 MALES	2020 FEMALES	AGE	1985 MALES	1985 FEMALES	2020 MALES	2020 FEMALES
0	.00881	.00700	.00363	.00288	60	.01494	.00704	.01210	.00478
1	.00061	.00072	.00026	.00030	61	.01634	.00774	.01333	.00526
2	.00050	.00037	.00021	.00015	62	.01789	.00852	.01470	.00579
3	.00050	.00028	.00021	.00012	63	.01963	.00938	.01624	.00637
4	.00040	.00022	.00018	.00009	64	.02157	.01032	.01797	.00701
5	.00040	.00023	.00018	.00010	65	.02374	.01135	.01992	.00771
6	.00031	.00015	.00014	.00006	66	.02617	.01247	.02212	.00847
7	.00030	.00012	.00014	.00005	67	.02887	.01370	.02457	.00930
8	.00027	.00014	.00012	.00006	68	.03185	.01506	.02730	.01023
9	.00020	.00015	.00010	.00007	69	.03511	.01659	.03030	.01127
10	.00017	.00011	.00008	.00005	70	.03861	.01834	.03356	.01246
11	.00021	.00015	.00010	.00007	71	.04237	.02032	.03696	.01380
12	.00024	.00018	.00013	.00008	72	.04641	.02256	.04062	.01532
13	.00035	.00020	.00019	.00010	73	.05071	.02508	.04454	.01703
14	.00049	.00025	.00027	.00013	74	.05527	.02789	.04872	.01894
15	.00069	.00030	.00040	.00015	75	.06013	.03099	.05319	.02105
16	.00090	.00035	.00054	.00019	76	.06536	.03446	.05802	.02340
17	.00112	.00039	.00070	.00022	77	.07097	.03831	.06322	.02601
18	.00132	.00043	.00086	.00025	78	.07700	.04264	.06883	.02896
19	.00146	.00046	.00099	.00028	79	.08350	.04758	.07490	.03230
20	.00155	.00047	.00109	.00030	80	.09056	.05321	.08152	.03613
21	.00156	.00047	.00110	.00029	81	.09807	.05956	.08828	.04044
22	.00153	.00045	.00109	.00028	82	.10597	.06667	.09539	.04527
23	.00147	.00044	.00105	.00027	83	.11427	.07444	.10286	.05054
24	.00140	.00044	.00100	.00026	84	.12312	.08278	.11083	.05621
25	.00133	.00044	.00096	.00025	85	.13266	.09164	.11942	.06222
26	.00127	.00044	.00091	.00025	86	.14491	.10239	.13045	.06952
27	.00122	.00044	.00088	.00025	87	.15829	.11441	.14249	.07768
28	.00119	.00045	.00086	.00025	88	.17289	.12784	.15563	.08680
29	.00115	.00046	.00084	.00025	89	.18885	.14283	.17000	.09698
30	.00113	.00047	.00083	.00025	90	.20628	.15959	.18569	.10836
31	.00113	.00049	.00082	.00026	91	.21759	.17220	.19587	.11692
32	.00115	.00052	.00084	.00028	92	.22806	.18488	.20529	.12553
33	.00118	.00054	.00086	.00030	93	.23747	.19750	.21377	.13410
34	.00124	.00058	.00090	.00032	94	.24559	.20990	.22107	.14252
35	.00131	.00063	.00095	.00035	95	.25230	.22196	.22712	.15071
36	.00140	.00068	.00102	.00038	96	.25791	.23357	.23216	.15859
37	.00151	.00074	.00110	.00042	97	.26276	.24458	.23653	.16607
38	.00164	.00081	.00119	.00047	98	.26719	.25492	.24052	.17309
39	.00179	.00090	.00131	.00052	99	.27155	.25879	.24444	.17572
40	.00197	.00100	.00144	.00059	100	.27596	.26302	.24841	.17859
41	.00218	.00112	.00159	.00067	101	.28042	.26730	.25243	.18149
42	.00241	.00127	.00176	.00077	102	.28494	.27162	.25650	.18443
43	.00268	.00144	.00195	.00088	103	.28951	.27599	.26061	.18740
44	.00298	.00162	.00218	.00100	104	.29413	.28042	.26477	.19040
45	.00332	.00182	.00242	.00113	105	.29880	.28489	.26898	.19344
46	.00371	.00203	.00270	.00127	106	.30353	.28942	.27323	.19652
47	.00413	.00224	.00301	.00142	107	.30832	.29400	.27754	.19962
48	.00461	.00244	.00336	.00156	108	.31315	.29863	.28189	.20277
49	.00512	.00263	.00373	.00171	109	.31802	.30330	.28628	.20594
50	.00568	.00284	.00414	.00186	110	.32296	.30804	.29073	.20916
51	.00632	.00307	.00466	.00202	111	.32795	.31281	.29522	.21240
52	.00703	.00333	.00524	.00220	112	.33298	.31763	.29974	.21567
53	.00779	.00363	.00586	.00240	113	.33807	.32250	.30432	.21898
54	.00862	.00397	.00655	.00264	114	.34320	.32743	.30894	.22233
55	.00950	.00436	.00730	.00291	115	.34837	.33240	.31360	.22570
56	.01043	.00480	.00810	.00321	116	.35360	.33741	.31831	.22910
57	.01143	.00528	.00897	.00355	117	.35887	.34248	.32305	.23254
58	.01250	.00581	.00991	.00392	118	.36419	.34757	.32784	.23600
59	.01367	.00640	.01096	.00433					

Years 9 ↓ 10   SOCIAL

Source: Australian Bureau of Statistics (1984). *Projections of Australian Mortality Rates, 1985–2020.*

The mathematics of hunger

Using a mathematical analysis of the production and distribution of such essential foodstuffs as calories and proteins, pupils are able to confront and consider some of the social and moral aspects of food availability on our planet.

Features of this activity

- An urgent and very real social issue.
- Use of real data drawn from United Nations Yearbooks and other sources.

How can such ideas be practically merged in a classroom setting?

The basic purpose is to structure a variety of mathematical investigations which inevitably and quite deliberately lead pupils to confront underlying social and moral questions. The tension thus created is partly resolved by considering strategies which are, or could be used, to improve the situation.

Outline

It is arguable that there is massive inefficiency and massive inequality in the availability of protein and calories on our planet. In particular, meat production could be considered extremely wasteful of resources purely to satisfy the western palate. How could we investigate such a claim?

- What is the daily protein requirements of humans?
- What sources of supply exist?
- What is the protein content in the various sources of supply?
- How are these produced in terms of land use?
- How are these produced in terms of protein input? For example, feeding maize to cattle.
- What are the current protein consumption rates in various countries?
- Discuss findings in terms of efficiency and equity.
- What strategies are known to be used, or could be used, to redress any inefficiencies or inequalities?

Some data on protein

A similar treatment of calories is possible.

Recommended minimal daily requirements
70 gm of protein
60% should be animal based
40% should be plant based.

Sources of protein and units/kg	
meat	145
cheese	154
eggs	209
whole rice	154
milk	180
fish	176

Western livestock consumes more grain each year than the combined populations of India and China.

Grain fed input needed* to produce 1kg animal protein	
beef	20.0 kg
pork	6.3 "
eggs	3.2 "
milk	0.6 "
*Using western farming methods	

Land usage
1 hectare cereal production yields 5 times more protein than 1 hectare devoted to beef.

SOCIAL
Years 7 ↓ 10

Poverty and health (or the *lack* of health)

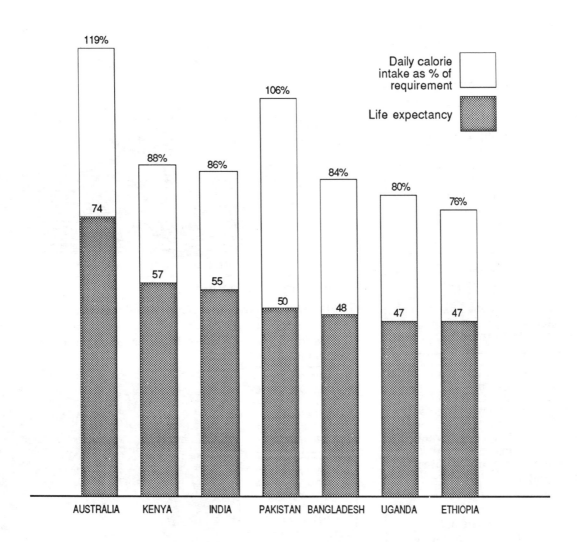

	Infant mortality rate — 1982 (per 1000 live births)	Gross National Product per capita, 1982 ($US)	Number of people per doctor (1980)
Australia	10	11 140	560
Uganda	120	230	26 810
Kenya	77	390	7 890
Bangladesh	133	140	10 940
India	94	260	3 690
Ethiopia	122	140	58 490
Pakistan	121	380	3 380

References

The United Nations Statistical Yearbook (Years 1985-1986).

Georg Borgstrom (1965), *The Hungry Planet*, McMillan.

W.S. Mooneyham (1975), *What do you say to a hungry world?* Word Books, Texas.

World Bank (1986), *World Development Report*, Washington D.C., Oxford University Press.

• Over three-quarters of all physical illness in the world could be prevented or cured by better nutrition, clean water supply, sanitation, immunisation and health education (according to WHO and UNICEF).

• The world military spending bill for 1982 was over 650 000 million US dollars — more than the combined income of 15 000 million people living in the poorest 50 countries. For the price of a single modern jet fighter plane three million people could be immunised against the major childhood diseases.

Tear Fund (1986). 'Community — compassion and justice' (Tear Fund study guide). *On Being, 13*(5), p. 5.

Public versus private transport

Public transport is frequently criticised. But what if all the train passengers used cars — how far would the line of cars stretch?

This activity encourages pupils to investigate the social issue of the public versus private transport and its impact on traffic levels, fuel usage, costs and other areas. Pupils can make predictions and their perceptions are compared with the reality of the data they collect.

Features of this activity
- Explores a social issue.
- Encourages pupil investigation.
- Involves group discussion.
- Extensions provide problems at a variety of levels.
- Most relevant for pupils living in large cities served by railway transport.

Throwing the problem over to groups encourages pupils to brainstorm for the sort of data that would be needed to be collected, and the kinds of assumptions required.

A mathematical line of reasoning such as this can stimulate and contribute to a worthwhile discussion on the issue of public versus private transport by insisting upon objective data and disciplined reasoning.

In Singapore, cars are not allowed into the central area unless they carry at least four people.

Introduction

IF ALL THE PASSENGERS FROM A TYPICAL PEAK HOUR TRAIN TRAVELLED IN CARS, HOW LONG WOULD THE LINE OF CARS REACH?'
WRITE YOUR ESTIMATE IN YOUR NOTEBOOKS

WHAT SORT OF INFORMATION WOULD WE NEED TO CONFIRM YOUR ESTIMATES?

1 km
500 m
2 km

Record the range of estimates on the chalkboard.

Collecting and analysing data

The following approach could be developed using a variety of data, either provided by the teacher or obtained by pupil investigation. The assumptions could be modified, based on pupils' experience or investigation.

HERE IS THE FLOOR PLAN OF ONE OF OUR TYPICAL RAILWAY CARRIAGES.
HOW MANY SEATS ARE THERE?

IF AS MANY PEOPLE CAN STAND AS SIT, HOW MANY PEOPLE DOES A CARRIAGE... A TRAIN... HOLD?

87   174   1044

THE AVERAGE CAR GOING TO THE CITY CARRIES 1.2 PEOPLE. HOW MANY CARS ARE EQUAL TO A FULLY LOADED TRAIN?

A CAR IS ABOUT FOUR METRES LONG. IF THE CARS QUEUE UP IN TWO LANES WITH FOUR METRES BETWEEN THEM, HOW LONG WOULD THE QUEUE BE IF ALL THE TRAIN PASSENGERS FROM ONE TRAIN TRAVELLED BY CAR?

DURING PEAK HOUR THERE ARE ABOUT 136 TRAINS RUNNING ON THE SYSTEM. HOW DOES THIS AFFECT YOUR QUEUE? TO WHERE WOULD SUCH A QUEUE STRETCH?

Railway fares are heavily subsidised. In one state the fares paid are only about 30% of the costs. To be objective, the real fare could be adjusted accordingly.

Each car 1·2 people
4 metres long
4 metres between cars
1·2 people in 8 metres

Other investigations
- A comparison of costs between train and car from various places to the city.
- A comparison of travel times.
- Fuel usage (wastage). How many litres of petrol would be used if a full trainload of people travelled by car?
- Compare government revenue in the two instances.

Chapter three

Concept learning — a first principles approach

Purpose

This chapter invites teachers to explore the effect of deliberately delaying the use of some algorithms and staying instead with a first principles approach. Concept learning is a large and complex area; MCTP has chosen to focus on just a small component of it.

Rationale

It is often said that mathematics teaching should enable pupils to understand mathematical processes rather than simply manipulate algorithms.

Many algorithms are often 'black box' mysteries to pupils. They are used to generate answers, but often seem disconnected from any logical situations they represent (as understood by the pupils).

The algorithm is an elegant end point of a series of sophisticated 'short cuts', and is intimately connected to, and representative of, the underlying mathematical principles. They are utilitarian and suited to 'answer-oriented' situations. However, their use often masks or disguises their connection to the principles.

In a recent study, Carraher, Carraher, and Schliemann (1987) showed that whereas concrete problem situations were powerful elicitors of oral computation

...the activities ... are not ends in themselves, but simply vehicles towards long-term understandings.

procedures, computation exercises tended to elicit school-learned computation algorithms. And, importantly, the school procedures were less likely to result in correct answers than were the informal, oral procedures. They concluded:

It is possible that the divorce between understanding and algorithmic calculation is a by-product of an educational system that leads children to focus not on meaning but on written numbers and rules for manipulating them when adding, subtracting, multiplying and dividing (p. 96).

Brown (1981, p. 14) believes that 'it may well be the case that a combination of reliable mental methods and the ability to use a calculator are sufficient for all practical purposes....Perhaps the present (standard) methods should be abandoned in favour of others, maybe less efficient, but more related to children's own informal methods, and hence easier to remember.'

As Constance Kamii has written:

Rather than encouraging children to think, textbooks and achievement tests emphasize correct, written forms. Teachers' guides discuss vertical and horizontal addition, but addition has nothing to do with space and is neither vertical nor horizontal. In long division, textbooks prescribe 'bringing down' a number, but division has nothing to do with directions such as up and down.

(Kamii, 1987, p. 2)

CONCEPT

Little wonder, then, that many children *appear to keep the mathematical concepts and procedures acquired outside of school quite separate from the mathematics learned at school, which they regard as sets of arbitrary rules and procedures performed on meaningless symbols'* (Putnam, 1987, p. 692).

However, work being done in a number of London schools as part of the Primary Initiatives in Maths Education (PRIME) Project indicates that given time, mental arithmetic and the effective use of calculators may replace much of the algorithmic work which currently dominates the present curriculum. Junior primary pupils in more than twenty schools are using only mental calculation and the calculator in computation work. Early reports indicate that the need for pencil and paper algorithms has not arisen as the children are becoming expert mental calculators.

Hiebert (1984) observed that *'many children experience difficulty in learning school mathematics because its abstract and formal nature is much different from the intuitive and informal mathematics the children acquire'* (p. 498). This difference is frequently responsible for the existence within the learner of parallel frameworks which are invoked according to the learner's judgement of a situation as personal or academic.

The existence of such alternative frameworks has been clearly demonstrated in the learning of science (see, for example, West and Pines, 1984). It is also clear from the following interview excerpt that students are aware of the existence of these alternative frameworks and respond with whichever they feel is most appropriate to the situation:

Cathy (13)

C: (reads) *Which of these fractions is smallest: two-fifths or three-eighths? I think three-eighths.*

I: *How did you do that?*

C: *This isn't how I did it, but it would explain it.* (Long pause while Cathy converts $2/5$ and $3/8$ to $16/40$ and $15/40$).

I: *But how did you get $3/8$ at first?*

C: *Well, an eighth is smaller than a fifth and three is just next to two.*

(Clarke, 1985, p. 242)

In Cathy's judgment, the question 'How did you do that?' required an academic response rather than a personal response. Her explanation drew on an established procedure, her actual answer derived from an estimation based on an intuitive sense of the relative size of the fractions. Both are mathematically sound, though in the situation the second was far more efficient. Yet Cathy did not feel this intuitive approach constituted a legitimate response.

Important concepts can be developed and linked using concrete materials. Here, strip graphs, pie charts, fractions and percentages are all used in representing the class data.

(*From* This goes with this.)

An illustration from *First principles percentage*

An argument presented here is that the understanding of some important mathematical ideas may in fact be inhibited not by the algorithms themselves, but by their too hasty introduction.

One way of retaining the focus on a concept is to teach ideas from first principles and delay (for a considerable time) the move into the conventional algorithm.

Consider the two approaches in this example involving percentages:

Find the simple interest on $320 for 3 years at 11.5% per annum.

Algorithmic approach

$$I = PRT/100$$
$$= 320 \times 11.5 \times 3 /100$$
$$= 36.80$$

First principles approach

11.5% means 11.5 for each 100

i.e. $11.50 for each $100

320	100	11.50
	100	11.50
	100	11.50
	10	1.15
	10	1.15
	320	36.80

Teachers trying the first principles approach report pupils naturally using short-cuts, and in a sense discovering the algorithm, but this occurs as pupils are ready, not when the syllabus dictates.

Freudenthal (1981) describes this process of the gradual increasing sophistication of shortcuts and symbolic representation as *progressive schematising*. It is a psychological progression in the mind of the learner towards the elegance of a refined algorithm. He warns of the danger of

---

...discovering the algorithm...(is learning)...the gradual increasing sophistication of shortcuts

---

denying pupils the opportunity to go through this process by the too hasty offering of rules:

Youngsters need not repeat the history of mankind but they should not be expected either to start at the very point where the preceding generation stopped.

The first principles approach might take longer, but the question to ask is whether such time is well spent. The answer to this question depends on the educational circumstances in which the problem was posed. If understanding the meaning of percentages is paramount, then the tabular non-algorithmic approach may indeed be more efficient (p. 140).

Another example from *How far is it around a circle?*

Pupils visualising, estimating and walking the circumference of circles become aware and internalise that:

(i) There is a functional relationship between radius and circumference, and

(ii) That circumference is just over 6 times the radius.

With the concept thus established, an appreciation of the precision of $C = 2\pi r$ is now more likely to develop.

The activities in this chapter are presented to assist teachers to experiment with these ideas in their own classrooms. Given any teaching situation involving algorithms, it is hoped that the teacher is then in a position to ask:

'I wonder if a first principles approach might be more effective?',

and to be able to respond appropriately. In this sense, the activities provided here are not ends in themselves, but simply vehicles towards long-term understandings.

CONCEPT

'How many paces do you think Lee Ann will take to complete the circle?'

Experiences from trialling

'I found that pupils, often used to thinking "The answer" is all-important, needed explanation and reassurance for the changed emphasis of these activities.'

'Many pupils were much more involved and committed than usual because they could see a reason for what they were doing.'

A final word

Skemp (1976) contrasts rote learning ('instrumental understanding') with meaningful learning ('relational understanding') and concludes that the former may be easier to teach and gives quick results in the short term, but is harder to remember, as well as lacking in intrinsic motivation. He uses the analogy of a person finding his way about in an unfamiliar town:

A person with a set of fixed plans can find his way from a certain set of starting points to a certain set of goals. The characteristic of a plan is that it tells him what to do at each choice point: turn right out of the door, go straight on past the church, and so on. But if at any stage he makes a mistake, he will be lost; and he will stay lost if he is not able to retrace his steps and get back on the right path.

In contrast, a person with a mental map of the town has something from which he can produce, when needed, an almost infinite number of plans by which he can guide his steps from any starting point to any finishing point, provided only that both can be imagined on his mental map. And if he does take a wrong turn, he will still know where he is, and thereby be able to correct his mistake without getting lost; even perhaps to learn from it. (p. 25)

In a simple, concrete way, these children begin to grasp the concept of a cubic metre.

References

Brown, M. (1981). Number operations. In K. M. Hart (Ed.), *Children's understanding of mathematics: 11-16.* London: John Murray.

Carraher, T.N., Carraher, D.W., & Schliemann, A.D. (1987). Written and oral mathematics. *Journal for Research in Mathematics Education, 18*(2), 83-97.

Clarke, D. J. (1985). The impact of secondary schooling and secondary mathematics on student mathematical behaviour. *Educational Studies in Mathematics, 16*(3), 231-257.

Freudenthal, H. (1981). Major problems in mathematics education. *Educational Studies in Mathematics, 12*, 491-512.

Hiebert, J. (1984). Children's mathematical learning: the struggle to link form and understanding. *Elementary School Journal, 84*(5), 497-513.

Kamii, C. (1987). Arithmetic: Children's thinking or their writing of correct answers? *Arithmetic Teacher, 35*(3), 2.

Putnam, R.T. (1987). Mathematics knowledge for understanding and problem solving. *International Journal of Educational Research, 11*(6), 687-703.

Skemp, R.R. (1976). Relational and instrumental understanding. *Maths Teaching, 77*(4), 20-26.

West, L., & Pines, L. (1984). An interpretation of research in 'conceptual understanding' within a sources of knowledge framework. *Research in Science Education, 14*, 47-56.

Activities with a concept / first principles component in other chapters

Danger distance (Ch. 2).

Baby in the car (Ch. 2).

Maths and lotto (Ch. 2).

Coin in the square (Ch. 2).

How far is it around a circle? (Ch. 4).

Algebra walk (Ch. 4).

Trigonometry walk (Ch. 4).

Three-way tug of war (Ch. 4).

Belt around the earth (Ch. 7).

Estimation of percentages (Ch. 9).

How many can stand in your classroom? (Ch. 10).

Licorice factory (Ch. 10).

Add the numbers 1 to 100 (Ch. 11).

Quadratic iteration (Ch. 13).

Area of a circle (Ch. 13).

Cats and kittens

This activity builds on the natural interest children have in cats and kittens, in exploring possible combinations of coloured kittens from single coloured parents. Children classify the various kittens and discuss and justify their conclusions.

The activity illustrates how the concept of combinations can be introduced in the junior primary school.

THIS ACTIVITY IS PART OF THE MCTP PROFESSIONAL DEVELOPMENT PACKAGE FROM THE CURRICULUM DEVELOPMENT CENTRE, CANBERRA

Features of this activity

- The use of a story to motivate children.
- Sorting and classification.
- As extensions, a range of imaginative writing tasks.
- A simple introduction to combinations.
- Problem solving.
- Class discussion.

Preparation

- Twenty cards about 20 x 10 cm to make:
    - four different coloured cats — black, white, grey and orange (or other colours if you choose),
    - sixteen kittens with combinations of the four colours.
- Four smaller cards for names (about 20 x 8 cm), plus a spirit marker.
- One copy per pupil of the worksheet.
- Unifix (optional).

CATS

KITTENS

BODY FIRST COLOUR
CHEST SECOND COLOUR

COLOUR COMBINATIONS OF KITTENS

B	W	G	O
B,W	W,B	G,B	O,B
B,G	W,G	G,W	O,W
B,O	W,O	G,O	O,G

Years K↓2 — CONCEPT

The three little kittens

Three little kittens,
  Lost their mittens,
And they began to cry,
  Oh, Mother dear,
  We sadly fear
Our mittens we have lost.
  What! lost your mittens,
  You naughty kittens!
Then you shall have no pie.
Mee-ow, mee-ow, mee-ow, mee-ow,
Now you shall have no pie.

The three little kittens
  Found their mittens,
And they began to cry,
  Oh, Mother dear,
  See here, see here,
Our mittens we have found.
  Put on your mittens,
  You good little kittens,
And you shall have some pie.
Purr-r, purr-r, purr-r, purr-r,
Oh, we would love some pie.

The three little kittens
  Put on their mittens
And soon ate up the pie;
  Oh, Mother dear,
  We greatly fear
Our mittens we have soiled.
  What! soiled your mittens,
  You naughty kittens!
Then they began to sigh,
Mee-ow, mee-ow, mee-ow, mee-ow,
Then they began to sigh.

The three little kittens
  Washed their mittens.
And hung them out to dry;
  Oh, Mother dear,
  Do you not hear,
Our mittens we have washed.
  Ah! washed your mittens.
  Then you're good kittens,
But I smell a rat close by.
Mee-ow, mee-ow, mee-ow, mee-ow,
We smell a rat close by.

Cats and kittens

1. About cats and kittens — setting the background to the activity

Gather children around in a group on the carpet.

> IN MATHS TODAY WE ARE GOING TO TALK ABOUT CATS AND KITTENS.
> WHO KNOWS THE STORY OF 'THE THREE LITTLE KITTENS'?
> SHOW ME THREE FINGERS.
> JOIN WITH ME IN TELLING THE STORY IF YOU KNOW IT...
> THE THREE LITTLE (etc.)

> ...LOST THEIR MITTENS...

> Maths is mentioned at this point to emphasise that activities such as these *are* maths, that maths is part of ordinary living.

> Some words may need clarification, for example *mittens, soiled* and *litter.*

2. Kittens that take after their parents

> WHO HAS CATS AT HOME?
> HAVE ANY OF YOUR CATS HAD KITTENS?
> HOW MANY?
> WHAT NAMES?
> WHAT COLOURS?

> WE ARE GOING TO LOOK AT SOME PICTURES OF CATS AND KITTENS IN A MOMENT.
> SO THAT WE CAN ALL SEE THEM LET'S STAND UP, JOIN HANDS AND SIT IN A BIG RECTANGLE AROUND HERE

> If there are children whose appearance is very much like their parents, and if those parents are also well known to the class, for example Aboriginal, Oriental or Mediterranean, have them come to the front of the class and tactfully discuss how they take after their parents.

3. Naming the four parent-cats

> HERE ARE FOUR CATS. LEE ANN AND PETER! YOU PICK YOUR FAVOURITE CAT AND GIVE IT A NAME

> SPELL 'BLACKY' LEE ANN

> BLACKY

> GINGER

Write the names of the cats — in our case *Blacky* and *Ginger* on the smaller cards and place them under the two chosen cats. Put the other two cats away until step 5.

4. Which kittens belong to these cats?

Put the two cats on the carpet. Place their names under them. Spread out the 16 kittens and challenge children to determine which kittens belong to the cats.

> Another method is to share the 16 kittens among the group, asking them to decide on their own kitten. If they think it belongs to the cats, they place it below the cats. They must explain their reasoning each time.

> Trials schools found that on this first try nearly all of the 16 kittens were placed, no doubt partly due to eagerness to participate. However it was interesting to note that generally the correct ones were placed first.

> WE ARE GOING TO TRY TO FIND OUT WHICH OF THESE KITTENS COULD BELONG TO THESE CATS... DO YOU THINK THIS IS ONE?...WHY?

> YES! BECAUSE IT HAS A BLACK TUMMY LIKE BLACKY

5. Which five kittens?

Again invite two children to select their favourite coloured cat and begin the task again, this time restricting the selection to five kittens.

> THIS TIME SNOWY (WHITE) AND SMOKEY (GREY) TOOK BACK FIVE KITTENS TO THEIR HOME.
> CAN YOU PICK WHICH ONES THEY WERE?

Repeat the activity for a third time, this time specifying the four kittens (towards which you are heading).

Simplistically, from two cats (say black and white) one might expect four possible combinations BB,BW,WB, and WW. But that does not account for earlier generations or multiple siring where there could quite well have been other colours which could appear in the kittens. So while you are working towards the four possible combinations, if children can justify why other colours are possible, accept them as a *possibility*, but the others are a more likely *probability*.

6. Colour in the worksheet kittens (Individual work)

Hand out the worksheets to the class. Explain that children are to use coloured pencils (or other media), colour and name the kittens that might be in their litter. Explain also that they need not colour in *all* the kittens if they so choose.

The children's work will graphically illustrate the wide range of understandings and systematic approaches to classifications.

Years K↓2   CONCEPT

7. Sharing the work

Recall the children and have them form groups and compare their litters.

> ALL OF YOU WHO HAD GREY AND BLACK CATS, SEE IF YOUR KITTENS LOOK THE SAME

Follow-up activities

- Have children relate anecdotes about their cats.
- Children could write a story about their cats, cutting out their pictures of kittens for illustrations.
- Tell stories concentrating on mathematical aspects. For example in the Three Little Kittens story, 'They lost their mittens — how many mittens did they lose?'

Extension activities

- Draw combinations of animals, for example, girelephaffs, ligers.
- Make collages of combinations of people.
- A simplified version of the MCTP activity, *Carrot patch people* could be tried, using unifix.

 CAT

 CAT

KITTEN

KITTEN

KITTEN

KITTEN

KITTEN

KITTEN

This goes with this

Pupils put their survey preferences on to a strip of paper — a simple **strip graph.** *But then this strip is bent into a circle, and* **voila** *— a* **pie graph!** *Then the strip is surrounded by 100 beads and instantly — there are the* **percentages** *for all to see!*

Rarely is there such a powerful illustration for teachers of an activity that makes important mathematical concepts and their integration so clear and understandable and in such an effective way.

Features of this activity

- The power of a concrete aid to illustrate concepts — in this case to link fractions, strip graphs, pie charts and percentages.
- The organisational structure which converts a good idea into a successful classroom activity.

- Group work.
- Use of pupils' firsthand data in a survey.
- Optional use of calculators.
- Follow-up work.
- Worksheet included.

Preparation

- Strips of cardboard or strip paper (about 2 cm x 100 cm), one per group
- '100-bead' rings, one per group.
- Sheets of butcher's paper, one per group.

From trials schools:
'I loved the idea but was just as impressed with the way it was put into practice and involved all pupils actively and efficiently.'

THIS ACTIVITY IS PART OF THE MCTP PROFESSIONAL DEVELOPMENT PACKAGE FROM THE CURRICULUM DEVELOPMENT CENTRE, CANBERRA

This goes with this

This activity is in three sections.

a. Demonstrating equivalence. The class is surveyed to find ice-cream preferences. A strip graph is made and bent to make a pie graph. 100 beads are put around it and there are the percentages.

b. Group work. Pupils generate their own data, make graphs and analyses, and present these findings back to the whole class.

Follow-up extensions. These activities are designed to reinforce the general concepts, imagery and concept of conversion from fractions to percentages.

The survey should generate no more than half a dozen categories.

Trials schools report the teacher should join the survey if needed to ensure that the class total is not an 'easy' number such as 20, 25 or 30.

'It seems better to express the results as numbers (e.g. 8 out of 27) rather than as fractions (8 twenty-sevenths).'

Being personal, data collected from the pupils tends to increase their commitment and interest.

'I felt it worthwhile to allow discussion about the data itself. For example, "Strawberry is very popular but they don't sell it at our canteen. Why might that be?" This is preferable to using totally meaningless and artificial data.'

SECTION A: DEMONSTRATING EQUIVALENCE

1. Collecting the data

Use information from a simple class survey such as 'favourite icecream flavour.'

I WANT TO SHOW YOU DIFFERENT WAYS OF REPRESENTING THIS INFORMATION AND HOW THESE DIFFERENT METHODS ARE MATHEMATICALLY THE SAME AS EACH OTHER

CHOCOLATE 8/27
STRAWBERRY 7/27
VANILLA 5/27
CARAMEL 3/27
OTHE 4/27

2. Fractions to strip graph

ANOTHER WAY OF SHOWING THESE FRACTIONS IS ON A GRAPH

LEAVE ABOUT A CENTIMETRE OVERLAP AT ENDS. (SEE NEXT STEP)

CARDBOARD STRIP 'BLU-TAC' ED ON CHALKBOARD.

INVITE CHILDREN TO COME OUT AND MARK THIS INFORMATION ON THE STRIP.

COUNTING ON IS A FEATURE OF THIS TASK.

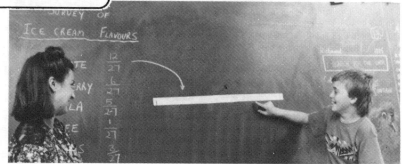

The 'heavy' paper needs to be about 80 cm — 100 cm long (to match the bead ring — see Section B step 3).

27 pupils would mean each division could be 3 cm.

LEAVE A COUPLE OF CENTIMETRES OVERLAP AT ENDS FOR NEXT STEP

It is critical to use stiff paper to ensure the shape forms a circle.

3 cm

YOU MAY NEED TO TAPE TWO STRIPS OF CARDBOARD TOGETHER TO GET 80 cm LENGTH

THAT'S LIKE A NUMBER LINE

'Every pupil could see that they were personally represented on, or "owned", a small segment of the strip graph.'

3. Strip graph to pie chart

Do this step slowly and demonstrably. The action from straight line to circle provides a visual image of the relationship.

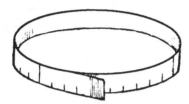

JOIN WITH BLU
TAC USING
OVERLAP. LEAVE
THE MARKINGS
ON THE OUTSIDE

Place the cardboard ring onto butcher's paper and draw a circle by tracing along the inside edge. Join the segment lines to the centre.

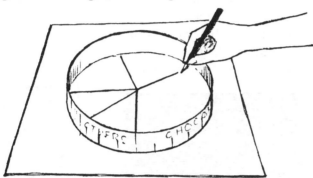

Remove the cardboard ring, and complete the pie graph by labeling it.

SO YOU CAN SEE, ALL
27 CLASS 'VOTES'
HAVE BEEN
TRANSFERRED ON TO
THE PIE CHART

4. Pie chart to percentage

Place the 100-bead loop around the pie chart. The loop should be just a bit larger than the chart.

Convert the sections on the pie chart to percentages by inviting students to count the beads. Record these findings beside the graph and on a separate chart.

PEOPLE FIND MANY
ADVANTAGES IN
SOMETIMES GIVING
INFORMATION AS A
FRACTION OF 100, THAT
IS, AS A PERCENTAGE

THAT'S 29
BEADS

I THINK IT IS
CLOSER TO 30

One school reported a successful 'physical equivalent' pie chart. Pupils sitting in a circle display their votes on a card. (Use A4 size card and textas for visibility)

PUPILS
SITTING IN
CHAIRS

RULERS OR
STRING TO
SEPARATE
SECTIONS

Several surveys can be quickly conducted and displayed this way.

Years 5 ↓ 8

CONCEPT

Coloured beads are available in bulk from most pre-school or early-childhood supply centres.

Interesting debate sometimes occurs about accuracy of counting or if someone notices the total is perhaps 98 rather than 100 due to rounding errors. However the major emphasis by far is the visual image generated of the equivalence of fractions to line graphs to percentages.

The 'hi-tech' finish is impressive but it is important that the search for accuracy does not detract from, or confuse the concrete imagery from the earlier work.

5. Calculator accuracy
(Optional)

If pupils are able, or perhaps only for a few individuals interested in the challenge of precision, the calculator can resolve the dilemma of accuracy.

I TOLD YOU IT WAS 29.629 BEADS

SECTION B – GROUP WORK

1. Generating and collecting data for the group activity

Having demonstrated the various forms of presentation, this section details how pupils, working in groups, can have first hand experience of the conversions.

Every pupil individually fills out a questionnaire on about nine surveys (see worksheet). This allows for up to nine groups to undertake their own investigation.

The prepared worksheet allows the survey to be completed in less than five minutes.

Trials found about four to seven choices in each category is effective and manageable.

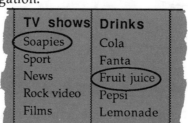

TV shows	Drinks
Soapies	Cola
Sport	Fanta
News	Fruit juice
Rock video	Pepsi
Films	Lemonade

YOU JUST HAVE TO CIRCLE YOUR CHOICE

All pupils then walk past collection boxes and 'snip off' their survey tickets into the relevant box. (e.g. ice-cream or margarine containers)

'I found this a very efficient way to collate data.'

By having say ten survey boxes, even though you have only six groups, adds flexibility and choice.

2. Pose the question

I WANT EACH GROUP TO PREPARE A REPORT TO BE PRESENTED TO THE WHOLE CLASS.
YOUR PRESENTATION MUST INCLUDE THE INITIAL FRACTIONS, THE LINE GRAPH, PIE CHART AND PERCENTAGES

LET'S CHOOSE THE 'COUNTRIES WE WOULD LIKE TO VISIT'

OK! QUICK, BEFORE ANOTHER GROUP PICKS IT

The report should also include interpretation of the results and recommendations, for example, *'We should write a letter to the TV station to tell them that hardly anyone here watches the soapies.'*

3. Group work

Each group needs a piece of butcher's paper (or A3), a 100-bead ring, and a cardboard strip and sticky tape.

If there are 27 in the class, rule up a large piece of cardboard into 27 rows (plus extra for overlap) and then cut off one strip for each group.

4. Reporting

> 9 OUT OF 27 WOULD LIKE TO HOLIDAY IN NEW ZEALAND

> THAT IS SHADED IN BLUE HERE ON THE STRIP GRAPH

> HERE IT IS ON THE PIE CHART

> IT'S A '33-BEAD' CHOICE. THAT IS, 33 OUT OF EVERY 100 PEOPLE

The completed graphs and charts could be displayed on a board (and used for reference in the future) or made into a class activity book.

Conclusion

Ask pupils their reactions to the use of the concrete aids.

'I felt it was very valuable for each group to physically handle the concrete aids — it seemed to help generate a lasting mental image.'

'I prepared some "100-bead rings" with the colours mixed at random. In others, for easy counting, I grouped the colours (in twos, fives or tens).'

The teacher moving around the groups can observe organisation, cooperation and initiative. Let groups organise themselves, but encourage all pupils to physically handle the material.

There are enough tasks in the reporting to require every member of the group to participate in many ways.

'The groups were reporting back the class's own data.'

Listening to the language (not always formal) gives interesting insight into pupils' understandings.

Years 5↓8   CONCEPT

One benefit of the repetition of the use of the 27 is that pupils nearly all realised that each vote was worth about 4 beads and saw relationships such as $^{10}/_{27}$ as about 10 lots of 4 beads — approximately 40%.

'I sent the project material home with pupils to show their families as a form of reporting.'

'I wanted to strengthen in pupils, the value of using concrete aids to get away from seeing maths as very abstract.'

Follow-up (Suggestions from trials schools.)

To strengthen the use of concrete aids, the resultant mental imagery and the value of percentages.

For reinforcement

I wanted to get away from always using 27, so I successfully repeated the whole activity, but this time deliberately used a range of denominators.

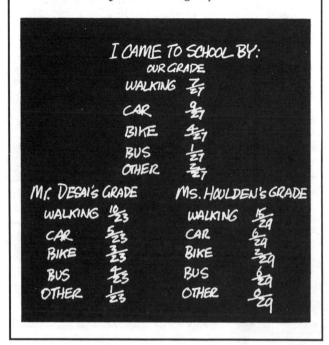

For converting fractions to percentages

This highlights the use of percentages to compare fractions.

> HERE ARE THE SURVEY RESULTS OF TWO CLASSES

> CONVERT THESE FRACTIONS TO PERCENTAGES. WHAT DO THESE FIGURES TELL YOU?

Would a shopkeeper or travel agent be interested in such information?

For imagery — estimating the number of beads.

Present any sets of fractions such as 8 out of 21, 9 out of 11, 15 out of 21, 4 out of 28, 4 out of 7.

> I WANT YOU TO VISUALISE A PIE GRAPH OF 8 OUT OF 21

> GOT IT?
> NOW ESTIMATE THE NUMBER OF BEADS ON THE EIGHT SECTION AND WRITE IT DOWN

> THE ANSWER IS 38%. RECORD HOW MANY YOU WERE 'OUT'

1. Try five practice problems.
2. Give out the answers, add up errors and discuss estimation strategies.
3. Give a retrial and look for improvement.

Repeat this activity from time to time to reinforce the imagery involved.

Sample survey sheet

This goes with this

TV shows	Drinks	Favourite number from 1 to 10		Fast food groups	The area I would like to visit most	Chocolate Bar	My favourite colour	I came to school by;	The number of brothers and sisters I have
Soapies	Cola	1	6	Pizza	Europe	Mars Bar	Red	walking	0
Sport	Fanta	2	7	Hamburger	U.S.A.	Cherry Ripe	Blue	car	1
News	Fruit juice	3	8	Chinese	Antarctica	Violet Crumble	Green	bike	2
Rock video	Pepsi	4	9	Chicken	Asia	Polly Waffle	Yellow	bus	3
Films	Lemonade	5	10	Fish and chips			Other	other	more than 3
				Pies					

TV shows	Drinks	Favourite number from 1 to 10		Fast food groups	The area I would like to visit most	Chocolate Bar	My favourite colour	I came to school by;	The number of brothers and sisters I have
Soapies	Cola	1	6	Pizza	Europe	Mars Bar	Red	walking	0
Sport	Fanta	2	7	Hamburger	U.S.A.	Cherry Ripe	Blue	car	1
News	Fruit juice	3	8	Chinese	Antarctica	Violet Crumble	Green	bike	2
Rock video	Pepsi	4	9	Chicken	Asia	Polly Waffle	Yellow	bus	3
Films	Lemonade	5	10	Fish and chips			Other	other	more than 3
				Pies					

Volume of a room

The traditional method of teaching the volume of a room would be to give the formula—width x length x height, then measure the dimensions and multiply them together. This activity illustrates how adding a variety of additional teaching strategies enhances the quality of the learning environment. The approach we present here encourages pupils to visualise a cubic metre and allows them to explore the problems of 'filling' the room with actual cubes. No formula — just a development of mental imagery and the appreciation of quantity. This provides a sound basis for understanding the concept of volume and later for understanding the formula — for pupils of all ability levels.

THIS ACTIVITY IS PART OF THE MCTP
PROFESSIONAL DEVELOPMENT PACKAGE FROM THE
CURRICULUM DEVELOPMENT CENTRE, CANBERRA

Years 4 ↓ 8

CONCEPT

Features of this activity

It demonstrates how a 'traditional' approach to this topic can be enriched by the deliberate inclusion of desirable teaching and learning features such as mental imagery, estimation, problem solving, physical involvement and the creation of a non-threatening environment.

Preparation

Metre-long sticks and joiners to construct enough cubes to go along the width and length of the classroom plus two more (for height). Assemble one and have it out of sight — maybe lying flat. A source for the rods and joins is *Edudomes* PO Box 82 Montrose VIC 3765.

JOINERS MADE FROM
SOFT PLASTIC
TUBING RIVETED OR
BOLTED TOGETHER

Comments from trials teachers

'All pupils became interested and involved. There was no fear of failure for anyone.'

'Producing the real cubic metre was a highlight for both pupils and for me.'

'I really believed all pupils benefited greatly from the activity — it was something for all ability levels.'

'Most students greatly underestimated. I was really surprised.'

Volume of a room

The teacher uses visual imagery and estimation as strategies to focus on the number of cubic metres of volume in the classroom. This is followed by problem solving including construction of cubic metres, to find the correct answer.

Finally a discussion compares the answer with pupils' initial perceptions and focuses on the concept of filling space.

1. Which unit to measure the room?

> WE HAVE DONE A LITTLE BIT OF WORK ON VOLUME AND YOU'VE MET SOME OF THE UNITS OF VOLUME SUCH AS LITRE AND CUBIC CENTIMETRE.
> TODAY'S ACTIVITY IS ABOUT MEASURING THE VOLUME OF LARGER THINGS SUCH AS THIS ROOM...

> ...NOW WHICH UNIT SHALL WE USE — A CUBIC CENTIMETRE OR WHAT?

> A CUBIC CENTIMETRE IS TOO SMALL

> SO'S A LITRE

> A CUBIC METRE

The use of mental imagery is a deliberate attempt to access and start the activity from each pupil's current perceptions.

Encourage pupils to take care with, and pride in, their estimation skills, because later the correct answer will be worked out.

By writing their guesses on the chalkboard, children tend to take their guesses more seriously.

A major advantage for the teacher is that it produces a collective data base of the class's current understandings and perceptions.

'At this stage the kids didn't know the formula, so their guesses were totally based on visual imagery.'

Being able to change guesses allows pupils a chance to review their thinking. Many significant insights occur at this stage. *'I'll have to rethink my ideas of size.'* *'That table's about a cubic metre size.'*

2. Mental imagery and estimation of the volume of the room

> YOU ALL KNOW HOW LONG A METRE IS, DON'T YOU?
> WELL, I WANT YOU TO IMAGINE A BOX OR CUBE WHERE EACH SIDE IS ONE METRE LONG.
> CAN YOU SEE IT IN YOUR MIND'S EYE?
> NOW LOOK AROUND THE ROOM.
> IMAGINE ALL THE FURNITURE GONE.
> THINK HOW MANY OF THESE ONE CUBIC METRE BOXES WOULD FILL THE ROOM

> ...WHEN YOU HAVE DECIDED ON A NUMBER, WRITE IT HERE ON THE CHALKBOARD

Estimate
50   55
75   60
100   110
130   150
135   130
90

3. Show the real cubic metre and let them guess again

> HERE IS A MODEL OF A CUBIC METRE. HOW DOES IT COMPARE WITH THE IMAGE YOU HAD IN YOUR HEAD?

> HAVE A LONG LOOK AT THE REAL CUBE AND HOW MANY OF THEM WOULD FIT IN HERE.
> IF YOU WOULD LIKE TO CHANGE YOUR ESTIMATE WRITE YOUR NEW ONE HERE

4. A list of suggestions for solving the problem

Write them on the blackboard.

> LOOK AT THE RANGE OF GUESSES WE HAVE, FROM 10 TO 350 CUBIC METRES

> HOW CAN WE FIND OUT?

> YOUR SUGGESTIONS
> Find out how many cubes go over the front wall and how many faces rows of them there will be.
>
> Find out how many cubes will cover the floor.

Rather than giving the formula (L x W x H), present the problem and hand it over to the pupils. Allow children to use their problem-solving abilities.

5. Work through the suggestions with the pupils

There will be a few ways. One advantageous method was to start in the middle of the room and four groups of pupils constructed cubes to radiate out from the four faces of the original cube. An extra cube can be built on top of the central cube to get an idea of height.

'I found the concrete approach allowed pupils to more easily visualise the filling of the room with rows and layers of cubes.'

> THAT'S NINE LONG AND EIGHT WIDE SO SEVENTY-TWO WOULD COVER THE FLOOR.
> THEN YOU'D NEED ABOUT 3 LAYERS OF THAT SO THAT'S ABOUT 200 CUBIC METRES

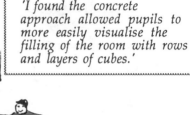

By laying the stick cube flat pupils find a two-dimensional representation of a cube and other shapes.

6. Discussion and comparing the answers with the estimates

> WELL THE ANSWER IS ABOUT 200 CUBIC METRES

> DID SEEING THE REAL CUBES HELP ANYONE?

> ISN'T THAT INTERESTING. WHY DO YOU THINK SO MANY OF US UNDERESTIMATED?

> GEE! THERE'S A LOT MORE THAN I FIRST THOUGHT THERE WAS

Many pupils underestimate, often by a wide margin. Do not disparage wide guesses *'we all make wrong guesses'*. Rather encourage pupils to appreciate how much power they will have as they acquire more accurate mental images.

Discussion should focus on whether pupils have a better appreciation of filling space and a knowledge of the cubic metre and its uses in measuring air, water, soil and rocks.

Extensions

Would the average customer or sales person have an accurate image of a cubic metre?

Discuss

A CUBIC METRE OF SAND PLEASE

OK!

A visual demonstration of one million

Place a cubic centimetre in the middle of the stick cube. Ask how many of these would go into the cube. One trial class rounded up all the MAB blocks in the school and managed to fill about one third of the cube.

A THOUSAND

TWO THOUSAND

FIFTEEN HUNDRED

How much water you can use before you pay excess rates

Find out how much water you may use before you pay excess rates. Then get a mental image of how big a swimming pool or tank you would need to hold this amount of water. (Most water-suppliers measure in cubic metres. One cubic metre = one thousand litres)

WE USE **THAT** MUCH!

Find out how much water Captain Cook needed for his voyage to Australia.

He had a crew of twenty-seven, each of whom needed two litres a day. Sometimes it would be four or five weeks before they would be able to get fresh supplies.

YO HO HUM AND A BARREL OF WATER ..... HO HUM!

Estimation with fractions

This simple, yet effective activity, where pupils compete against themselves, focuses on the concept of fractions without the impediment of 'rules without reasons'.

Features of this activity

- Focuses on the concept of fraction.
- Estimation skills—builds confidence to 'have a go'.
- Includes a problem-solving segment on how to check estimates.
- Highly motivating and personal for pupils.

- Measurement.
- Calculation of fractions of whole numbers.
- Caters for a wide range of abilities.
- Includes an outdoor activity extension.
- Progress is obvious to pupils.
- Non-threatening.

Preparation

- A metre rule or tape measure.
- One ruler and one copy of each worksheet (pages 159-60) per pupil.

THIS ACTIVITY IS PART OF THE MCTP
PROFESSIONAL DEVELOPMENT PACKAGE FROM THE
CURRICULUM DEVELOPMENT CENTRE, CANBERRA

Comments from trials schools

'Good for getting the feel of fractions'.

'All pupils found that they had improved, and this was a very good start to fractions'.

'Pupils were motivated to learn more'.

'Slower pupils should not be expected to do the calculations'.

'I really valued the non-threatening structure which allowed all to become involved'.

Years 5 ↓ 8

CONCEPT

---

1. Estimating two-fifths of the width of the chalkboard

> YOU ALL HAVE A RATHER GOOD KNOWLEDGE OF FRACTIONS; YOU'VE BEEN LEARNING TO ADD AND SUBTRACT FOR YEARS.
> I WOULD LIKE TO SHOW YOU A SLIGHTLY DIFFERENT ACTIVITY THAT CONCENTRATES MORE ON THE MEANING OF A FRACTION.
> THE LESSON IS ACTUALLY AN ESTIMATION COMPETITION WHERE YOU COMPETE AGAINST YOURSELF!

For junior classes, you could start with easier measures such as one quarter or half.

Challenge pupils to estimate two-fifths of the distance from the left side of the chalkboard. Invite three pupils to put their marks with their initials.

> WATCH CAREFULLY AND I'LL ASK YOU ALL TO VOTE ON WHICH YOU THINK IS THE CLOSEST

> NO! IT SHOULD BE FURTHER THIS WAY

It is interesting to note how often the third pupil picks a point that is half way between the previous two. You could discuss why this is clever, but do not be critical.

By voting on the issue, pupils feel personally involved and motivated to find out which is the best estimate. Most pupils take pride in their ability to estimate.

'I found the voting idea kept all the class watching carefully and personally involved.'

Be prepared to accept several strategies. For instance folding a length of string into fifths or stepping out a marked length of a chalkboard ruler until, by trial and error, there are five equal parts. Discuss the strengths and weaknesses of each method.

If you receive no response at all, provide some leading questions. For example, *Could you work out one fifth?*

In some trials schools stages 1, 2 and 3 were repeated using another fraction such as five-eighths to give pupils more confidence.

PROVIDING ANSWERS FOR THE WORKSHEET

A fast method, and one which gives quick feedback, is to have children mark their lines, then read out the correct positions (60, 24, 80, 96, 45) for pupils to copy down and mark on to their lines. This will save pupils from getting flustered about computation, and let them concentrate on the concept of fraction rather than the number crunching.

OR

Pupils do the computation, but remind them that all lines are 120 mm. Then children can calculate the errors or measure them directly and compute the total error.

2. Checking the estimation

Ask for various strategies and accept all solutions that will work.

HOW CAN WE DETERMINE WHICH MARK IS CLOSEST?

GET A PIECE OF STRING THE LENGTH OF THE BOARD AND FOLD IT INTO FIVE

STEP OFF A CERTAIN LENGTH OF THE BIG RULER AND KEEP ADJUSTING THE LENGTH UNTIL YOU GET FIVE PARTS ACROSS

MEASURE THE WIDTH, DIVIDE BY FIVE AND MULTIPLY THAT BY TWO

3. Discuss the strategies

Calculate the correct length, measure and mark it on the chalkboard and compare it with the estimates.

WELL THE EXACT MEASURE IS 145 cm WHICH IS...
... HERE.
THAT'S PRETTY CLOSE TO YOUR MARK SUE.
HOW DID YOU ESTIMATE SO WELL?

A HALF IS EASY TO JUDGE AND TWO-FIFTHS IS JUST UNDER A HALF

4. Individual work

Distribute Worksheet 1, and work through question 'a' with the class.

Emphasise that this is the purpose of the whole activity — to learn how to make good estimates — *it is a very valuable skill.*

'I have two worksheets for you — the first one is to let you see how good you are already, and later in the lesson the second one is to let you find out if you have improved'.

LENGTHS OF THE LINES ON THE WORKSHEET
NB. Your photocopier may stretch or shrink the lines so check the answers.

a — 60	f — 30	k — 60	p — 40
b — 24	g — 20	l — 100	q — 114
c — 80	h — 48	m — 54	r — 42
d — 96	i — 100	n — 88	s — 56
e — 45	j — 75	o — 42	t — 60

5.   How do you do your estimating? What methods do you use?

As in step 3, have those with low total errors share their methods with others. This forms the basis for possible improvement in the further exercises.

> FOUR-FIFTHS
> IS ONE-FIFTH
> FROM THIS
> END

> Trials schools found that some classes handled this stage better in small groups.

> The challenge usually motivates pupils to make a serious attempt to improve their score. Of course, even the pupils who did well in the first trials will have quite a challenge to better their performance.

6.   Reducing your total error (Improving your estimating)

Distribute Worksheet 2.

> LET'S SEE IF YOU CAN
> REDUCE YOUR TOTAL
> ERROR.
> WE'VE LEARNT A BIT FROM
> EACH OTHER

> Some trials schools paired fast pupils with those weak in division, thus giving the fast pupils practice at communication skills and helping to better pace the lesson.

> 'I had an enjoyable and useful discussion with the class about whether they enjoy this type of activity and why'.

Years 5 ↓ 8   CONCEPT

7.   Conclusion

Find out whether most (if not all) of the class has improved.
Use this result to re-emphasise the purpose of the activity which is *to think about the size and meaning of a fraction, rather than the calculations.*
If some pupils haven't improved, or want to improve further, worksheets 3 and 4 are available (or re-do Worksheets 1 and 2 but substitute different fractions).

Extension activities

More lines — more estimating

Use Worksheets 3 and 4 for further practice or for homework.

The same activity can be done on many scales.

Two-fifths of the way home

Pupils estimate the point at which they are (say) two-fifths of the distance from home to school, then check using a map.

THE POST BOX IN
PETTY'S LANE IS
ABOUT ONE-THIRD
OF THE DISTANCE
TO SCHOOL

LET'S CHECK
ON THE MAP

Street-directory companies sometimes allow strictly limited photocopying of their maps for educational purposes. For instance, in Melbourne, Melway Publishing Pty. Ltd. gives permission to individual teachers to photocopy any of the Melway maps in the Melway Street Directory of Greater Melbourne (etc.), subject to the following conditions:

1. This permission is valid until 31 December 1993, unless cancelled by Melway Publishing Pty. Ltd..
2. Photocopying is to be solely for school class purposes.
3. Where possible , teachers are requested to use current editions.
4. The following acknowledgement is requested: 'Reproduced with permission from Melway Street Directories, Edition ..., Map ...'

Lines between the desks

Mark convenient lengths (e.g. 2–6 m) in rows between desks or in the corridor.

Fractions of lengths of walls etc.

In the schoolgrounds, estimate fractions of lengths of walls, between fence posts or any identifiable points.

Worksheet 1

		DISTANCE OF YOUR ESTIMATION FROM LEFT SIDE	CORRECT DISTANCE	ERROR
a	$\frac{1}{2}$			
b	$\frac{1}{5}$			
c	$\frac{2}{3}$			
d	$\frac{4}{5}$			
e	$\frac{3}{8}$			
			TOTAL ERROR	

Worksheet 2

		DISTANCE OF YOUR ESTIMATION FROM LEFT SIDE	CORRECT DISTANCE	ERROR
f	$\frac{1}{4}$			
g	$\frac{1}{6}$			
h	$\frac{2}{5}$			
i	$\frac{5}{6}$			
j	$\frac{5}{8}$			
			TOTAL ERROR	

Worksheet 3

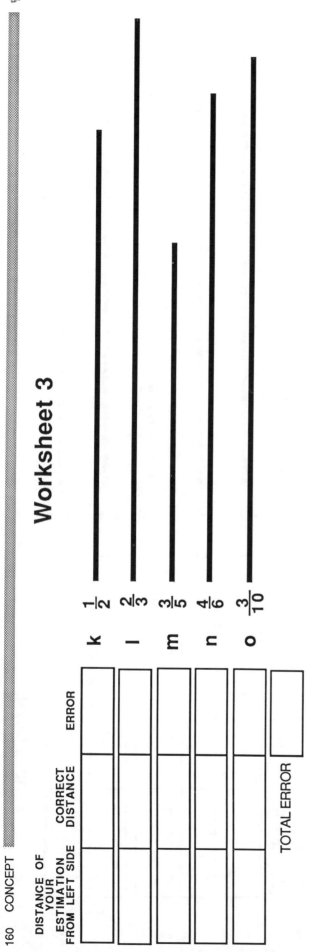

k $\frac{1}{2}$

l $\frac{2}{3}$

m $\frac{3}{5}$

n $\frac{4}{6}$

o $\frac{3}{10}$

DISTANCE OF YOUR ESTIMATION FROM LEFT SIDE   CORRECT DISTANCE   ERROR

TOTAL ERROR

Worksheet 4

p $\frac{1}{3}$

q $\frac{3}{4}$

r $\frac{2}{5}$

s $\frac{4}{10}$

t $\frac{3}{8}$

DISTANCE OF YOUR ESTIMATION FROM LEFT SIDE   CORRECT DISTANCE   ERROR

TOTAL ERROR

First principles percentage

It is just as important for pupils to understand what they are doing (the concept), and to be able to explain it to others, as to simply get the right answer. With a first principles approach as their confidence grows, pupils naturally find shortcuts, and these shortcuts ultimately become a refined and powerful algorithm. In this activity the teacher is encouraged to let this happen naturally, and not to prematurely introduce an algorithm.

Five worksheets present a graded sequence of difficulty, with suggestions for several more for the teacher to develop. And since a first principles approach and verbalisation ability are valued, any assessment strategies should also value and reflect these and not merely reward the obtaining of correct answers.

Features of this activity

- Focus on developing skill via first principles calculations.
- Calculations are based on an understanding of the meaning of each problem.
- Any shortcuts that pupils develop are encouraged, but the shortcuts must come from pupils' own observations. Formalising a shortcut into a prescribed algorithm is not advocated.
- Extensive use of simple ratios.

- The sets of problems are presented in a graded set of increasing sophistication.
- Difficult problems can be solved by breaking them down into understandable, logical and manageable steps, while retaining a focus on the concept.
- Verbalising the reasoning behind calculations.
- Optional calculator use.
- Estimation — upper and lower limits.

Years 8 ↓ 10

CONCEPT

HE'S HEAVILY INTO ALLIGORITHMS

First principles percentage

Background and organisation

- The spirit of this activity is that understanding of the concept of percentage is the primary aim and not (at this stage) the skill ability to generate answers using a formula.

- The basic approach is that at each stage of a problem pupils work out and articulate the underlying logic at a first principles level.

- The role for the teacher is to **promote** and **value** this process to pupils. That is, at this stage, *it is more important to understand what you are doing, and to be able to explain it to others, than to just get the right answer!*

- Experience has shown that pupils naturally start to use shortcuts as their confidence grows, and that these shortcuts ultimately become a refined and powerful algorithm. But it is argued strenuously here, that the teacher let this happen naturally for all pupils, rather than prematurely introduce an algorithm.

- The five worksheets are in a graded sequence of difficulty, with suggestions for several more which the teacher could develop.

- At each stage of the activity, emphasis is given to pupils' ability to articulate their reasoning and to explain their thinking to others.

- Since a first principles approach and verbalisation ability are valued, any assessment strategies should also value and reflect these and not merely reward the obtaining of correct answers.

Introduction

Hand out the first five worksheets.

Share with pupils the educational dilemma between

- getting answers, and
- understanding the ideas and being able to explain them to others.

'In these problems I'm much more interested in listening to you explaining how you get the answer than in the answer itself.'

Work through one or two problems similar to those in Set 1, emphasising the setting out and verbalising.

Small-group work

Let pupils in small groups work through the worksheets at their own rates.

Three themes, *Verbalisation, Estimation* and *Calculators* can be exploited throughout the activity.

> *'I found several pupils, who normally could not use the formula, solving quite complex problems with ease.'*

Verbalisation

To promote this, it is effective for the teacher:

- to encourage pupils to practise explaining each problem to a partner and for that partner to listen critically,
- for the teacher, in moving around the class, to constantly value and to ask for verbalisation of the reasonings of pupils,
- in checking answers, to ask for volunteers to explain to the whole class, from the blackboard, at least one problem from each set,
- build verbalisation into the assessment and share this intention with pupils.

Estimation

Particularly in the harder problems, trials found that for many pupils it was beneficial to set up an upper and lower limit for each problem. This seemed to provide 'guide rails' for pupils and prevent them getting 'lost' in the calculations.

Calculators

In the development of short-cuts, the calculator can be effectively used. Typically a pupil's book may look like:

8.5% of $650

650	
100	$8.50 (6 lots)
50	4.25
	55.25

> Schools found it was not necessary to interrupt pupils to introduce the new ideas within each worksheet.

Set one   **Working out percentages**

> Think out aloud! For instance tell your workmates what '3%' means.

Find 3% of $400.
3% means 3 for every $100. —

> You should always write this line down.

400

100	3
100	3
100	3
100	3
	12

> It is set out like this to show how many 100s and to record 3 for each 100.
> So *you* set out the problem on your worksheet like this too.

Answer: $12.

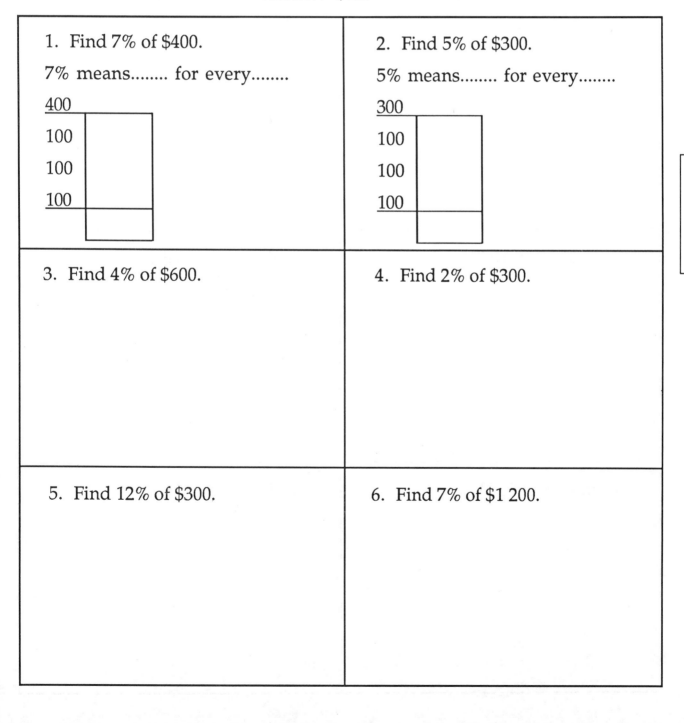

1. Find 7% of $400.

7% means........ for every........

400

100	
100	
100	

2. Find 5% of $300.

5% means........ for every........

300

100	
100	
100	

3. Find 4% of $600.

4. Find 2% of $300.

5. Find 12% of $300.

6. Find 7% of $1 200.

Set two   **Working out percentages**

Find 3% of $250.
3% means 3 for every 100
(and $1.50 for $50, i.e. half).

$$\begin{array}{r|l} \underline{250} & \\ 100 & 3 \\ 100 & 3 \\ \underline{50} & 1.50 \\ \hline & \boxed{7.50} \end{array}$$

> A simple ratio comparison means that if there are 3 for each 100, how much should we get for 50?

Answer: $7.50.

1. Find 4% of $3.50.	2. Find 6% of $150.
3. Find 5% of $250.	4. Find 8% of $350.
5. Find 6% of $850.	6. Find 9% of $350.

Set three
Working out percentages

Find 2.5% of $400.

2.5% means $2.50 for every $100.

```
400
100 |  2.50
100 |  2.50
100 |  2.50
100 |  2.50
     | 10.00
```

Answer: $10.00.

> Tell your workmates what 2.5% could mean. ($2 plus a half a dollar, *that is, 50 cents* for each $100.)

> *Estimation:*
> Upper limit 3% of $400 = $12.
> Lower limit 2% of $400 = $8.

---

1. Find 3.5% of $200.

3½% means........ for every........

200

100

100

2. Find 4.5% of $300.

---

3. Find 2.5% of $600.

4. Find 6.5% of $300.

---

5. Find 3.5% of $500.

6. Find 12.5% of $400.

Set four   Working out percentages

Find 3% of $320.
3% means 3 for every 100.
That's $3 for every $100.
or 3 cents for every 100 cents ($1).
So $10 will give 30 cents.

> **Estimation:**
> Upper limit 3% of $400 = $12.
> Lower limit 3% of $300 = $9.

> The extra challenge here is using
> ratio to find out how much for $10.

320

100	3
100	3
100	3
10	.30
10	.30
	9.60

> It is easier to go up
> from 3 cents per $1 to
> 30 cents per $10 than
> down from $3 for $100.

Answer: $9.60.

1. Find 4% of $240.

4% means

240

100

100

10

10

10

10

2. Find 6% of $330.

3. Find 3% of $460.

4. Find 5% of $410.

5. Find 7% $220.

6. Find 4% of $210.

Set five   **Working out percentages**

Find 2.5% of $350.
2.5% means $2.50 for every $100.

350	
100	2.50
100	2.50
100	2.50
50	1.25
	8.75

Answer: $8.75.

> *Estimation:*
> **Upper limit 3% of $400 = $12.**
> **Lower limit 2% of $300 = $6.**

1. Find 2.5% of $450	2. Find 3.5% of $250
3. Find 3.5% of $350	4. Find 7.5% of $550
5. Find 4.5% of $350	6. Find 3.5% of $750

Years 8 ↓ 10   CONCEPT

Set six

4.75% of $250
4.75% means 4.75 for every 100.

250	
100	4.75
100	4.75
50	2.38
	11.88

$2.38 is half of $4.75 to nearest cent.

Answer : $11.88

Problems

1. 8.75% of $350.
2. 9.25% of $550.
3. 14.65% of $250.
4. 11.25% of $350.

Set seven

8% of $230.
8% means $8 for every $100
or 8 cents for every 100 cents ($1)
i.e. 80 cents for every $10

230	
100	8
100	8
10	.80
10	.80
10	.80
	18.40

Answer: $18.40

Problems

1. 7.5% of $340.
2. 12.5% of $170.
3. 9.5% of $410.
4. 6.5% of $290.

Set eight

Putting it all together

8.75% of $243.
8.75% means 8.75 for every 100
i.e. $8.75 for $100
or 8.75 cents for 100 cents
or 87.5 for $10.

243	
100	8.75
100	8.75
10	.87
10	.87
10	.87
10	.87
1	.09
1	.09
1	.09
	23.25

to nearest cent

Shortcuts become more apparent at this stage.

Answer: $23.25

Problems

1. 6% of $315
2. 12% of $242
3. 8.5% of $723
4. 13.5% of $496

Set nine

Using a calculator

8.75% of $243.
8.75% means $8.75 for every $100.
How many $100's do we have?
More than 2? Less than 3?
i.e. we have 2.43 lots of 100.
i.e. 2.43 lots of 8.75.

To understand the logic behind the algorithm needs considerable first-principles practice.
That is, the algorithm can evolve naturally out of pupils experience and desire to get answers quickly.

Problems

1. 3.5% of $512.
2. 11.5% of $751.
3. 13.5% of $945.
4. 17.5% of $856.

Set ten

Word problems

Select or create word problems in which these types of calculations are embedded.

Backtracking

If you told someone that, by the end of the very first lesson on this topic, the pupils in your class were quite easily solving such equations as

$$5 \left(\frac{3n-2}{2} + 3 \right) - 4 = 51$$

the retort might be something like 'Where did you get the magic wand?' The magic indeed lies in the knowledge that if children understand that algebra is a summary of things they already know, then many problems disappear.

Features of this activity

- A concrete base for understanding algebraic equations.
- First principles approach; that is, building understandings by working through concepts, step by step, rather than using a 'black box' approach.

- Quite complex equations are solved by the pupils.
- A picture-story approach for understanding the order of operations.
- Forging a link between algebra and reality.

Preparation

Each pupil will need a copy of the worksheet.

Entry skills

Some experience with algebraic symbols and knowledge of order of operations.
All problems in this initial activity avoid fractions or negative integers.

Trials schools reported that at the end of the second period, 'Just-for-fun' problems such as

$$2 \left[\frac{2(3n+1)-1}{5} - 2 \right] = 6$$

were solved with great ease. After this, typical textbook problems such as
$$x + 3 = 18$$
$$2x + 1 = 13$$
appeared trivial indeed.

Years 7↓8   CONCEPT

Backtracking

Backtracking is a process of finding an unknown number, 'n' by working backwards from the result, using children's natural problem-solving skills. It breaks complex algebraic equations down into stages — parts of a picture story, and asking 'first principles' type questions such as 'What number would you need to multiply by three to get six?'

i.e. | ? | x3 | 6 | *This is shown in association with the actual algebraic equation (3n = 6).*

1.   Pick a number — any number!

I WANT YOU TO WRITE ANY NUMBER FROM ONE TO NINE ON THE BOARD SO THAT THE WHOLE CLASS KNOWS IT — THEN RUB IT OUT SO THAT I DON'T. IN A FEW MINUTES I WILL TELL YOU WHAT THAT NUMBER IS

EVERYBODY GOT THAT?

2.   Now do these operations

EVERYBODY COPY THESE BOXES INTO YOUR WORKBOOK AND DO THESE CALCULATIONS

MULTIPLY BY TWO....

...THEN ADD THREE...

... THEN MULTIPLY BY TWO...

...FINALLY TAKE AWAY ONE

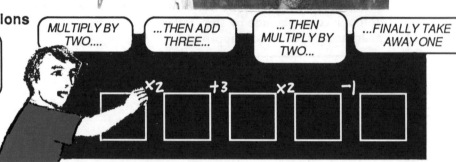

The series of boxes is a pictorial record of a 'story' that happened to the starting number. It is deliberately as non-symbolic as possible, and there is no mention of words such as 'flow chart' to burden the learning task.

At this stage there is absolutely no attempt to define the return operations, + 1 and ÷ 2. The method here uses the 'intuitive logic' of children to unravel a plot. The questions are of the form 'What number *must* have been before...?'

3.   The answer

NOW TELL ME YOUR ANSWER, AND I WILL BE ABLE TO FIGURE OUT THE ORIGINAL NUMBER

IT'S 25

4.   Backtracking

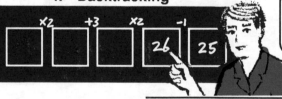

IF THE LAST THING YOU DID WAS TO TAKE AWAY ONE, THE LAST NUMBER MUST HAVE BEEN...*26

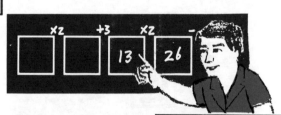

THEN THE NEXT, WORKING BACKWARDS, MUST BE...13. BECAUSE .... THAT'S WHAT WAS NEEDED TO MAKE 26 WHEN IT WAS MULTIPLIED BY TWO. DO YOU REMEMBER HAVING 13 AT THAT STAGE?

AND THAT NUMBER MUST HAVE BEEN ...TEN IF YOU ADDED THREE TO GET 13

SO OUR ORIGINAL NUMBER MUST HAVE BEEN....FIVE

5. Algebra

This section is very brief and incidental, presented almost as an 'afterthought'.

| MATHEMATICIANS CALL THIS BACKTRACKING 'ALGEBRA' | WE CALL THE NUMBER WE DON'T KNOW 'n' | SO HERE THE NUMBER MUST BE ...2n | AND THE NEXT NUMBER MUST BE ...2n+ 3 | AND THE NEXT NUMBER MUST BE ...2(2n+ 3) | AND THE NEXT NUMBER MUST BE ...2(2n+ 3) −1 | AND FINALLY WE INCLUDE THE ANSWER ...3 |

Build up the equation as you tell each step.

so **n**

becomes 2n
then   2n + 3
then 2(2n + 3)
then 2(2n + 3) − 1
finally 2(2n + 3) − 1 = 25

At this stage, no emphasis is given to the algebraic equation. It is just the first link in a process which will take time to develop.

6. Now the pupils' turn to backtrack from the mystery number

This time the pupils choose the operations (x 3, − 2, ÷ 2, + 3 in this example).

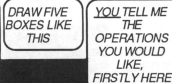

| IT'S YOUR TURN. I HAVE A MYSTERY NUMBER. SEE IF YOU CAN WORK BACKWARDS TO FIND IT | DRAW FIVE BOXES LIKE THIS | YOU TELL ME THE OPERATIONS YOU WOULD LIKE, FIRSTLY HERE | MULTIPLY BY THREE TAKE AWAY TWO DIVIDE BY TWO ADD THREE |

Up to this point the lesson will have taken about 15 minutes.

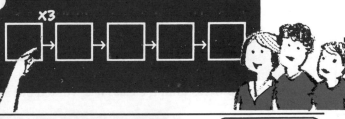

THEN THE ANSWER IS 11. SEE IF YOU CAN FIND MY STARTING NUMBER

7. Expressing the operations in algebra

In a non-threatening manner, let the class 'help' you to quickly summarise the algebra 'story'. Again pause between each step to allow children to volunteer the answer before you give it.

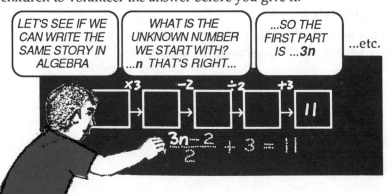

| LET'S SEE IF WE CAN WRITE THE SAME STORY IN ALGEBRA | WHAT IS THE UNKNOWN NUMBER WE START WITH? ...n THAT'S RIGHT... | ...SO THE FIRST PART IS ...**3n** | ...etc. |

It is interesting to note that complex equations such as

$$2(2n + 3) − 1 = 25$$

$$\frac{3n−2}{2} + 3 = 11$$

be given to pupils at their first algebra lesson. Yet when presented in this non-threatening way all pupils at the trials schools understood the problem and were able to work out the correct answers. Even the convention of writing 2n to mean n x 2 caused no problems.

11 ÷ 3 — Don't go!
Have the pupil whisper the number to you so that you are able to help the pupil head off problems such as if the class chooses a divisor which doesn't produce a whole number.
In those cases have the pupil tell the class to give another number because that number doesn't divide 'evenly'.
Also it prevents confusion if the pupil has miscalculated the answer.

8. Finding Yani's secret number
- Let a pupil (or small group) decide the next number.*
- The pupil draws the boxes (about five) on the chalkboard.
- The rest of the class decides the operations.
- The pupil works out the answer and writes it in the last box.
- The class then backtracks.

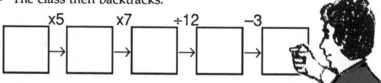

* With the whole class 'helping' you, summarise the operations using algebra. Now try some practice problems, such as the first five on the worksheet.

9. Starting with the algebra, recreate the picture story
Towards the end of the lesson, if the class appears to be ready for this stage, let them try to recreate the story from the algebraic fraction.

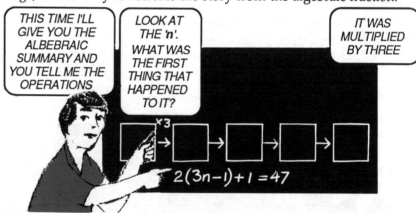

THIS TIME I'LL GIVE YOU THE ALBEBRAIC SUMMARY AND YOU TELL ME THE OPERATIONS

LOOK AT THE 'n'. WHAT WAS THE FIRST THING THAT HAPPENED TO IT?

IT WAS MULTIPLIED BY THREE

$2(3n-1)+1 = 47$

Continue the process until the class has worked out all the boxes and symbols.

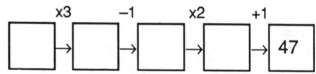

Trials schools reported with surprise and pleasure how easily pupils were able to *reconstruct* the order of operations.

One trials school reported success in having pupils work in pairs in the following way.
- One pupil chooses a number and secretly writes it down.
The second pupil draws five boxes and gives four operations — fewer for less-able pupils.
- Pupil one works out the final number* and gives it to the second pupil who uses backtracking to work it out.
The pupil with the secret number should not accept subtraction if it produces a negative number, or division if it does not produce a whole number.
- Players take turns to hold the secret number.

10. (Second period) Follow-up exercises with the worksheet

In the second, or follow-up period a mixture of problems may be presented. Some start with the picture story, then the pupils write the algebra. Others start with the algebra. You could use the worksheet on the opposite page.

The teacher should leave pupils in no doubt as to the ultimate aim — to be able to read and solve the problems, given only the algebra.

11. Conclusion

Point out the typical textbook problems such as $t + 7 = 10$. Pupils are usually very pleased how trivial these appear.

Worksheet
Backtracking

Backtrack to find the starting number, and then 'write the story' in algebra:

1. ☐ ^{x 2} ☐ ^{− 5} ☐ ⁺³ ☐ 14   Algebra:

2. ☐ ^{− 3} ☐ ^{x 5} ☐ ^{+ 3} ☐ ^{÷2} ☐ 4   Algebra:

3. ☐ ^{+ 2} ☐ ^{÷ 3} ☐ ^{+ 1} ☐ ^{x 2} ☐ 8   Algebra:

4. ☐ ^{+ 8} ☐ ^{− 4} ☐ ^{x 5} ☐ ^{− 6} ☐ 29   Algebra:

5. ☐ ^{+ 6} ☐ ^{÷ 4} ☐ ^{− 7} ☐ ^{+ 5} ☐ 5   Algebra:

Use backtracking diagrams to work out the starting number in each of the following:

6. $(2n - 3) \times 3 = 21$ ☐ ☐ ☐ 21

7. $\dfrac{7n - 2}{10} + 2 = 6$ ☐ ☐ ☐ ☐ 6

8. $5(n - 2) - 3 = 42$ ☐ ☐ ☐ 42

9. $\dfrac{2(n - 1)}{3} + 5 = 16$ ☐ ☐ ☐ ☐ 16

10. $\dfrac{6n + 7}{4} + 1 = 12$ ☐ ☐ ☐ ☐ 12

11. $2(n + 3) = 16$

12. $\dfrac{3n - 2}{5} = 2$

13. $\dfrac{n - 3}{2} + 6 = 11$

14. $\dfrac{6n - 1}{5} = 1$

15. $\dfrac{20n - 10}{3} + 2 = 12$

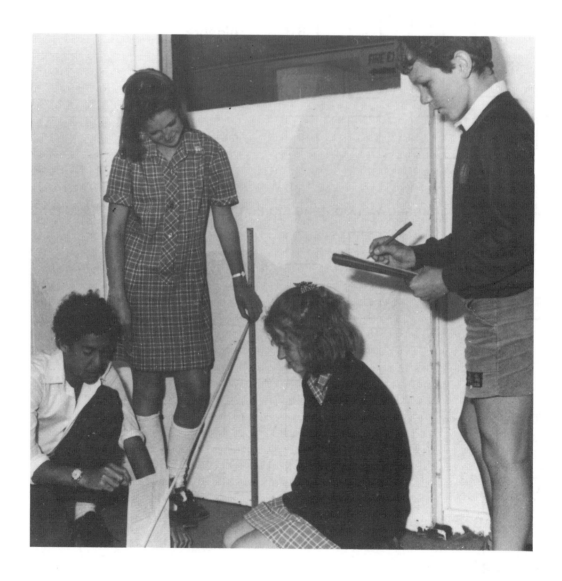

Sliding ladder

If you know the angle that a ladder makes with the ground, you can work out how far it is up from the ground and out from the wall.

That's trigonometry!

This activity, which encourages pupils (using metre sticks) to create and measure large triangles, illustrates the power of concrete aids and group work in the development of elementary trig. concepts.

Features of this activity

- Introduction to trigonometry in a concrete way.
- Pupils work cooperatively in groups to gather information.
- Graphs are used to develop the concept of sine and cosine as functions of the angles.
- Measurement.
- Calculation.
- Historical background.

Preparation

- Either two 1 metre rules per group of about four pupils or a 1 metre rule and a 1 metre long stick per group.
- Photocopy enough protractors and tables from page 178 for one per group.
- Photocopy enough graphs from page 178 for each pupil. (Put two on an A4 page.)
- Metric graph paper, one sheet per pupil. (Optional.)
- Scientific calculators and sine and cosine tables (if possible).

THIS ACTIVITY IS PART OF THE MCTP PROFESSIONAL DEVELOPMENT PACKAGE FROM THE CURRICULUM DEVELOPMENT CENTRE, CANBERRA

Sliding ladder

Sines and cosines have the undeserved reputation of being a fearful mystery. They shouldn't be, because they are not! In fact, in this quite straightforward, concrete form, they are easy to understand.

1. Trigonometry means 'measuring triangles'

> TRIGONOMETRY IS MADE FROM TWO WORDS, TRIGON — A TRIANGULAR POLYGON AND METRE — MEASUREMENT — 'MEASURING TRIANGLES'

2. The type of problem trigonometry can solve

> HERE'S THE KIND OF PROBLEM TRIGONOMETRY CAN SOLVE — EASILY!
>
> IF YOU LEAN A THREE-METRE LADDER AGAINST A WALL AT AN ANGLE OF 67° TO THE GROUND, HOW FAR UP DOES IT REACH, AND HOW FAR OUT IS THE BASE?

3. Just how could you do it?

> OK! HOW **COULD** IT BE DONE?

> YES! I'LL SHOW YOU A MOST INTERESTING WAY

> YOU COULD MAKE A SCALE DRAWING

4. Measuring 'S' and 'C'

Show pupils the group set-up, each member having a specific function. Tell them to measure at each five degrees mark and record the lengths **S** (vertical) and **C** (horizontal).

> Work in groups of two, three or four.

5. Graph the results

When a few groups have completed the table, start them off plotting the **A** (angle) and **S** and the **A** and **C** values on the graph paper.

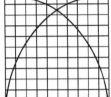

6. Discuss the graphs and the patterns in the results

THE GRAPHS SHOW THAT THE VALUES ARE SYMMETRICAL

THAT IS, **SINE** FOR 15°
   = COSINE FOR (90 −15)° or 75°

THAT IS, **SINE** FOR **A**
   = COSINE FOR **90 − A**

The two major patterns are:
1. non-linear changes, and
2. symmetry.

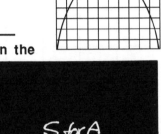

S for A
= C for (90−A)°

7. The history of sine

THE WORD 'SINE' CAME ORIGINALLY FROM THE ARABIC WORD 'JAIB' MEANING CURVE.

IN THE 12th CENTURY GERARD OF CREMONA TRANSLATED IT INTO LATIN CALLING IT 'SINUS' — THE MEASURE OF THE AMOUNT A BOW BENDS

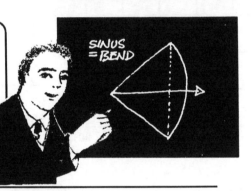

SINUS = BEND

8. The sine's cousin (oops) cosine

IF THAT'S A RIGHT ANGLE WHAT DO WE CALL **THAT** ANGLE IN RELATIONSHIP TO **THAT** ANGLE?

WELL THE SINE OF THAT **COMPLEMENTARY** ANGLE IS CALLED THE **COSINE**

COMPLEMENTARY ANGLE

To know about complementary angles is not a necessary entry skill. It can be introduced informally at this stage.

9. Using your graphs

BACK TO THE ORIGINAL QUESTION — HOW FAR UP THE WALL WILL A 3 METRE LADDER REACH IF IT IS AT AN ANGLE OF 67°

THE SINE OF 67° IS .92

SO THE ANSWER MUST BE THREE TIMES THAT — 2.76 m UP THE WALL

If you have a scientific calculator demonstrate its use. Similarly with books of log tables.

Give further exercises with other size ladders.

Emphasis: The immediate and concrete reinforcement consolidates faith in the math accuracy.

To be even more concrete a variety of length sticks could be used.

Pupils (i) **measure** the stick, say 1.45 m, (ii) **prop it up** at any angle, (iii) **measure** the angle, (iv) **calculate** the length of the wall which becomes a prediction, (v) **measure** the length to verify the prediction.

Worksheet

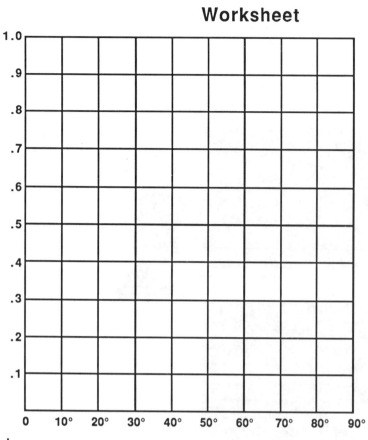

Angle	Sine	Cosine
0		
5		
10		
15		
20		
25		
30		
35		
40		
45		
50		
55		
60		
65		
70		
75		
80		
85		
90		

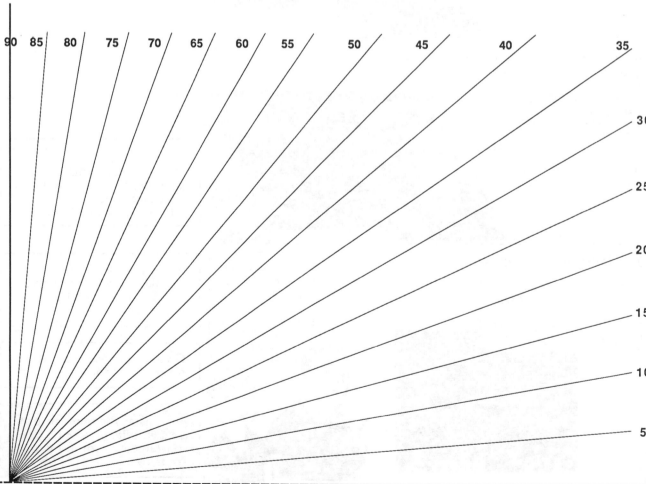

FOLD HERE

419

Pupils are presented with a number which they are told is the answer to a range of problems. They are challenged to (initially) find as many pairs of four digit numbers, whose difference is this number. The task is tackled by small groups, with much of the discussion focusing on the underlying concepts of operations, in this case, subtraction. The activity contrasts for teachers, the 'traditional' approach of pages of sums with a far more open group activity which achieves the old aims and a whole lot more.

Features of this activity
- Emphasis on understanding of operation concepts.
- Open-ended challenge for pupils.
- Small group work.
- Problem solving with a wide range of possible approaches.
- Discussion.
- Number patterns are explored.

YOU'VE DONE MANY SUBTRACTION PROBLEMS BEFORE, BUT TODAY I'M GOING TO GIVE YOU THE ANSWER TO A SUBTRACTION AND, IN GROUPS OF FOUR, I WANT YOU TO COME UP WITH AS MANY CALCULATIONS AS YOU CAN THAT HAVE THIS ANSWER

TO MAKE IT MORE CHALLENGING, I WANT THE TWO NUMBERS TO BE BOTH FOUR DIGIT ONES

Preparation
One calculator per group of four.

A competitive aspect is optional, but appears to add interest, and the competition being between groups seems to reduce any individual threat.

Years K↓3 CONCEPT

WORKING IN A GROUP ALLOWS YOU TO SHARE IDEAS.
SEE HOW MANY YOUR GROUP CAN FIND IN JUST FIVE MINUTES.
THERE IS A CALCULATOR FOR EACH GROUP FOR CHECKING YOUR ANSWER AS YOU GO

BE CAREFUL TO RECORD YOUR FINDINGS IN A SYSTEMATIC WAY

AWAY YOU GO

The teacher who first developed this activity had expected that pupils would have developed their problems by putting any four digit number in the second line and adding this to 419 to give the top line. However, few groups used this strategy. In fact, it was often the case that pupils were not aware of this important relationship.

The most common strategy was to begin with 6419 — 6000 (or a similar one), and vary this in a consistent way, such as adding 1, or 100, to both numbers and so on.

Ask for each group to report on how many they found, but just as importantly, the process they used in generating their list of problems.

6419 – 6000	1419 – 1000	????		
7419 – 7000	1420 – 1001	−1000		
8419 – 8000	1421 – 1002	419		
"	1422 – 1003	So it's 1419		
"	"			
"	"			

'What a simple, yet powerful idea. My children were doing much of the same old problems, but with a new purpose and a new understanding.'

This approach can easily be applied to other operations with smaller or larger numbers and so has application at a range of levels from about year 2 to 10.

'By watching and listening to pupils I gained much insight into their levels of comprehension.'

Weighing it up

*Judging which is heavier, a pencil or a ruler, is not too difficult a task. But sequencing a **range** of objects by weight, is much more challenging and involves valuable problem solving.*

Features of this activity

- Estimating relative weights.
- Comparing the weights of different objects.
- Ordering the weights of different objects.
- Problem solving.
- Language, indicating an understanding of concept (heavier than, lighter than, about the same, almost as heavy as, a bit more than...).

Preparation

In a large box, put as many objects of various weights from a pencil to a small book as you can 'put your hands on at the time'. You could have many of the same objects. Here are some examples. Ruler, cup, tin, scissors, cassette, ball, block, hair-brush, container, perfume bottle, small toy or doll, plate, coaster, beret, glove, corrector fluid, stapler, comb, toothbrush, hardware items such as a hinge, bolt, knob, curtain fixture etc..

- Two copies per pupil of the worksheet on the next page.
- Balances for comparing the mass of two objects.

1. Posing the problem

Hold up one large, light object and a small, heavy object.
Ask the class to predict which is heavier..... How could we check?
Encourage a pupil to do so for the group.

WHICH IS HEAVIER?

HOW COULD WE CHECK?

2. What if we had six?

Ask pairs to collect six different objects from the box. They then try to physically arrange them in order of heaviest to lightest (their estimates).

Handing the problem over to the group encourages creative strategies, discussion and cooperation.

I'VE TAKEN SIX DIFFERENT THINGS FROM THE BOX. FIRST I WILL JUDGE WHICH IS THE HEAVIEST

HMM! THAT'S LIGHTER THAN THAT, SO IT'LL GO THERE

3. Children record their guesses on the worksheet

4. Ordering the objects

Find the correct order of weights using a balance and enter the results in the worksheet.

'I asked children to predict which would be the heavier of two objects from two different lists. They quickly saw that if the lists had common objects, they could sometimes be certain without cheating.'

'The children really enjoyed comparing the correct order with their guesses.'

THAT'S HEAVIER THAN THAT, BUT IT'S NOT AS HEAVY AS THAT ONE, SO IT MUST GO THERE IN THE ORDER

IT LOOKS WRONG! THAT ONE LOOKS LIGHTER THAN THAT ONE. LET'S TRY THEM

Discuss the results, maybe finding the heaviest or the lightest of all the objects. 'Did anybody have anything lighter than this pencil?'
If time permits you could rank the weights of all the objects and test the ranking by comparing weights of two samples.

5. Extension

You could test pupils' ability to discriminate by providing sets of objects with progressively smaller differences between their weights.

Years K↓7   CONCEPT

Worksheet

Name......................

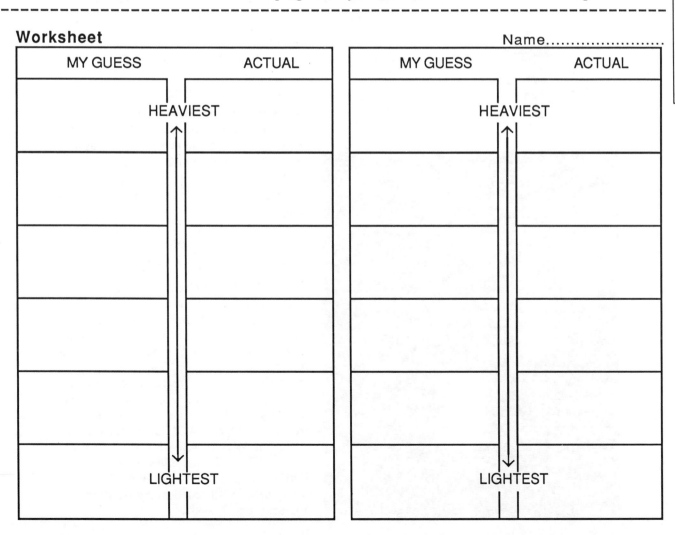

Cordial relations

Ratio is a difficult concept to understand. Much of the mathematics used at school and in the community assumes that children understand it. This primary classroom activity uses the experiences of children as frequent cordial drinkers, and their concepts of weak and strong cordial to explore ratio. Children are encouraged to verbalise their thinking on a range of problems, devise further problems, illustrate these and provide written solutions to them.

Features of this activity

- Gentle introduction to concepts of fraction and ratio.
- Emphasis on writing and verbalising reasoning.
- Variety of methods of solutions are discussed.
- Visual imagery is evoked.
- Story-shell introduction.
- Group work.
- Investigation.

The tasks from which this activity were devised were developed by Gerald Noelting ('The Development of Proportional Reasoning and the Ratio Concept', *Educational Studies in Mathematics*, 1980, vol 11, pp. 217-253).

THIS ACTIVITY IS PART OF THE MCTP PROFESSIONAL DEVELOPMENT PACKAGE FROM THE CURRICULUM DEVELOPMENT CENTRE, CANBERRA

Preparation

- *Equipment.* Twelve same-size clear plastic cups, two large bowls, a bottle of orange cordial and a large supply of water.
- Make up five glasses of 'normal' strength cordial mix, five glasses of water, one glass of very strong cordial mix and one glass of weak cordial mix.

NORMAL   WATER   STRONG WEAK

- Place two tables at the front of the classroom. These tables must be clearly labelled 'A' and 'B' to prevent confusion.

Cross-age tutoring

One school found that this activity lends itself to cross-age tutoring. After years 5/6 have been given the activity, the pupils taught it to prep–year 2 classes.

'This task lends itself beautifully to this arrangement as it allows for a varying complexity of thought. Startlingly enough, some years 1 and 2 children explained their reasoning equally clearly as my 5/6s'.

Early concepts of ratio

'Ideas of ratio are essential to any discussion of relative sizes. This is a notoriously difficult topic to treat in secondary mathematics, yet the underlying ideas are simple and to some extent obvious to even very young children. Perhaps if ideas like ratio are treated informally at an early age, the basic notions and concepts will be given time to grow before a formal treatment.' Stacey, K. & Groves S. (1986) 'Problem Solving Activities in Years Prep, One and Two' in N.F. Ellerton (Ed.), *Mathematics: Who Needs What?* Melbourne: Mathematical Association of Victoria, pp. 329-332.

1.   Making sure pupils know what the terms 'strong' and 'weak' cordial mean

Invite one pupil to pick the strong from the weak cordial drink by tasting and describing the differences.

HERE ARE TWO CORDIAL DRINKS, ONE IS STRONG AND ONE IS WEAK, WHO COULD TELL THE DIFFERENCE?

THAT'S THE WEAK ONE—NOT ENOUGH CORDIAL

THIS IS THE STRONG ONE—IT'S GOT MORE FLAVOUR

> This part of the lesson is to ensure that children understand the concepts of different strengths and to create interest in the following parts of the lesson.

2. Tell the following story to 'justify' their tasks

I WANT YOU TO IMAGINE THAT WE TIPPED ALL THESE (pointing to table A) INTO THIS BOWL...

... AND THAT WE TIPPED ALL OF THESE (pointing to the cups on table B) INTO THIS BOWL.
NOW, A DIFFICULT QUESTION FOR YOU.
WOULD TABLE 'A' HAVE THE STRONGER MIX?
OR
WOULD TABLE 'B' HAVE THE STRONGER MIX?
OR
WOULD THEY BOTH BE THE SAME STRENGTH?

Place the glasses of cordial and water on the tables as shown, (below) as you tell the story. Give everybody the chance to write down their predictions, then discuss the responses. Ask one child to sample the bowls as a test.

> Children's concepts are soundly developed when they are encouraged to verbalise their reasoning.

Years K ↓ 6   CONCEPT

3.   Which is stronger, or are they the same?

Present the following combinations, pausing between each combination for the pupils to write down A, B or the same, and then discussing each combination.

> Trials schools found that many very young children lacked the concept of 'equal' in this context.

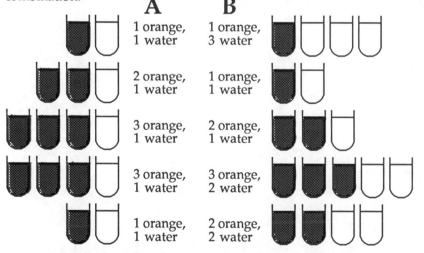

A	B
1 orange, 1 water	1 orange, 3 water
2 orange, 1 water	1 orange, 1 water
3 orange, 1 water	2 orange, 1 water
3 orange, 1 water	3 orange, 2 water
1 orange, 1 water	2 orange, 2 water

> Encourage children to see different ways of looking at the problem and emphasise the range of different methods.

The importance of writing

Noeline Reeves, in a pamphlet as part of the 'Reading Around Series', No.3, *Children Writing Maths*, gives four reasons for involving children in writing about mathematics.
* Writing to learn.
* Writing to understand.
* Writing for others.
* Writing for imagination.

4.   Over to the class!

Divide the class into groups of four. Challenge each group to:
* devise a similar problem,
* draw a picture of the problem in their books,
* work out the answer to their problem (and agree on it) and write the reasons in their books,
* 'demonstrate' their problem to the class who attempt to solve it.

> The teacher's role here is to talk to the groups, encouraging them to express their solution strategy in detail.

> Writing, like talking, can facilitate a distillation of mathematical relationships in the writer's mind. *'Through talking and writing and representing new ideas to ourselves in our own preferred way, we internalise new ideas and make them our own'*
>
> Boomer, G. (1986). From catechism to communication: Language, learning and mathematics. *Australian Mathematics Teacher, 41(1),* pp. 4–5.

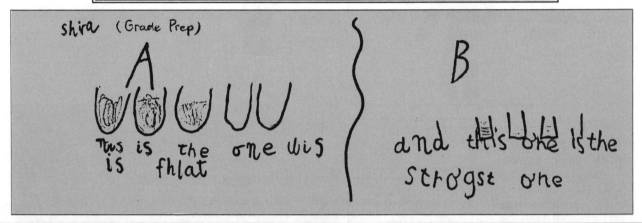

Shira (Grade Prep)

A

This is the one wis is fhlat

B

and this one is the strogst one

Christine (Grade 1)

B

A

They Both have 3 Cups

A has 2 Cordials andf B has 1 Cup of Cordial

~~B has~~

A is Strong Becduse it has more Cordial

David (Grade Two)

A = B

Two cups of jucie and two cups water in 'A'. Three cups of jucie and two cups of water 'B'. 'B' is stronger because it has more jucie.

Contents

Chapter four

Physical involvement in mathematics learning

Purpose

This Chapter invites teachers to explore ways of deliberately involving pupils physically in the learning process and to consider its long-term effect on the quality of that learning.

One of the widely expressed comments of teachers to MCTP has been:

'Without changing what I teach, I'd like to teach it a whole lot better!'

Such comments indicate a desire to improve the quality of the learning environment. One possible contributor to an improvement in quality might be the deliberate use of *physical involvement*. That is, to so structure the learning that it requires the physical participation of pupils.

This package is prepared and presented to assist teachers wishing to actively explore this issue in their own classrooms and as a result to incorporate this feature into an expanded teaching 'repertoire'.

... an attempt to go deeper into the psychology of learning and to explore the cognitive effects of physical involvement.

Physical involvement

CURRENT PRACTICE

Hopefully, as a result of trialling and analysing MCTP activities, given any teaching situation, the teacher is in a position to ask and effectively respond to the question:

'In this topic, I wonder if I could involve the pupils physically in the learning process?'

In this sense the activities provided are not ends in themselves, but simply 'vehicles' towards long-term understandings about teaching and learning.

The activities should not be confused with merely adding an outdoor component to lessons to add interest and realism. They are an attempt to go deeper into the psychology of learning and to explore the cognitive effects of physical involvement.

PHYSICAL

'What the body does the mind finds hard to forget' — some illustrations

In *Regular polygons*, string is used to illustrate the meaning and properties of regular polygons. Tests for equal angles and sides are also developed.

In this way pupils can create, experience and discuss a large range of types of polygons in a very short time. In this sense the outdoors and physical involvement can be a very efficient learning environment.

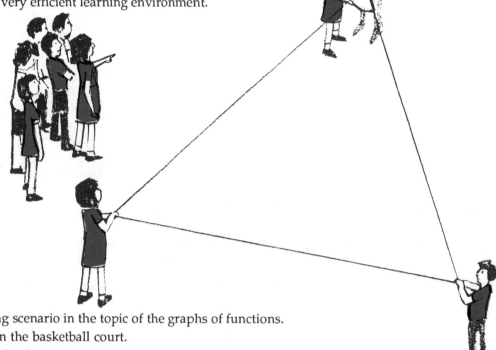

Consider the following scenario in the topic of the graphs of functions.

The class is outside on the basketball court.

Axes are drawn as in the diagram — numbers are placed one 'walking pace' apart, that is, about 50 to 60 cm.

Nine pupils are needed on the grid, others watch and record.

> *'Look at the number between your feet. Multiply it by itself. When I say ready-set-go, I want you to walk that many paces forwards (or backwards)'.*

On the sound of 'go' a lovely model of $y = x^2$ appears.

Several linear graphs or parabolas can be thus 'drawn' with pupils physically experiencing the creation of the graphs, and the numerical relationships involved.

A more complete description of the activity, *Algebra walk*, is part of this chapter.

Rationale

The question to ask is whether there is any qualitative advantage in this approach compared with more traditional teaching.

One answer, based on the success of trialling and comments from teachers from the algebra example opposite, is that *a very strong visual image remains with the participants and that this image can be 'tapped' in follow-up formal work inside the classroom.* It is easy to use phrases such as *'Remember yesterday when...' or 'Imagine you were standing on − 4, what would the instructions be?' ' How would you move?'* etc.

The strength and usefulness of the image is clearly related to the degree of physical involvement. Gagne and White (1978) proposed that people's long-term memory stores should be considered to contain four types of elements; verbal knowledge, intellectual skills, images and episodes. Episodes are memories of events in which the individual took part.

Mackenzie and White (1982), in investigating three styles of excursions involving a varying degree of physical involvement but a fixed amount of new information being presented, found that the pupils in the three groups differed in their production of *episodes*, and this largely explained a difference in long-term retention. Pupils who had been actively involved, physically, demonstrated far greater long-term recall of knowledge and skills.

> # Pupils who had been actively involved, physically, demonstrated far greater long-term recall of knowledge and skills.

It is interesting to note that there was little difference between the groups in short-term recall. Given that pupil achievement in mathematics is frequently assessed *immediately* after the teaching period with a written test, teachers who make use of active physical involvement in mathematics teaching, may not see immediate results for their efforts, and may be tempted to dismiss the use of this strategy as not sufficiently productive.

The *Algebra walk* episode creates a cognitive image which can be recalled and exploited. Another feature seems to be that pupils have a degree of 'personal investment' in the experience, which adds to the durability and usefulness of this cognitive image.

Becker (1985) talks of kinesthetical experiences or reminiscences of our own movements which can be reproduced in memory:

> *We remember former movements we carried out, and accompanying mental images. They can help to associate concepts or certain components of what is to be learned with reminiscences of that kind, and thus facilitate the accessibility of memory contents and to reinforce connections between them (p. 167).*

J.S. Cangelosi (1985) describes how a Grade 1 teacher used a school yard and a soccer ball to help his pupils discover the defining attributes of a circle. The teacher placed a soccer ball on the ground and marked a line segment about 15 metres from the ball. The teacher then called the names of two children in rapid succession, who, on hearing their names , raced from their places and tried to be the first to pick up the ball. The ball was replaced after each race. After several races, the pupils began to complain that the game was not 'fair'. They discussed how the game could be made more fair, and decided that everyone would have the same distance to run if the teacher indicated the starting positions *around* the ball. 'Circles are around something, always the same amount away', one of the pupils said.

It is not easy to find in the literature a definitive 'principle of learning' which satisfactorily explains why physical involvement in the above illustrations adds to the quality of the learning, yet the teachers who have trialled and reported on such activities are in no doubt whatever that it does.

Trial teachers also mention realism, meaningfulness, interest and commitment as variables that seem to be relevant.

PHYSICAL

Addition of vectors comes alive with a three-way tug of war.

Experiences from trialling

Going outdoors, sometimes unusual for pupils in a mathematics learning environment, needs particular emphasis on classroom management. Suggestions from teachers include:

• give pupils a clear indication of the reasons and *advantages* for the physical or outdoor component;

• clarify the outline of the organisation with pupils, i.e. where we will work, how long it will take, what we will do when we return indoors.

• give pupils an opportunity afterwards to reflect upon and feedback to the teacher their impressions and attitudes to this form of learning.

References

Becker, B. (1985). How can we use knowledge of cognitive psychology in classroom instruction? In T.A. Romberg (Ed.), *Using research in the professional life of teachers.* Maddison: Wisconsin Centre for Educational Research.

Cangelosi, J.S. (1985) A 'fair way' to discover circles. *Arithmetic Teacher, 33*(3), 11-14.

Gagne, R., & White, R.T. (1978). Memory structures and learning outcomes. *Review of Educational Research. 48*(2), 187-222.

Liske, J.F., & Evans, A. (1986). *Education goes outdoors.* New York: Addison Wesley. (This book contains a chapter in which 14 schoolyard math investigations are described).

Mackenzie, A.A., & White, R.T. (1982). Fieldwork in geography and long-term memory structures. *American Educational Research Journal, 19*(4), 623-632.

A videotape titled *Maths the Mind Cannot Ignore* addresses this issue in part and is available from the Mathematical Association of Victoria, 191 Royal Pde, Parkville 3052.

Activities from other chapters with a physical component.

Snippets (Ch. 1)

Danger distance (Ch. 2).

Volume of a room (Ch. 3).

Footsteps over Australia (Ch. 7).

Eight queens (Ch. 8).

Mallet (Ch. 9).

Pupil growth (Ch. 9).

How many can stand in your classroom? (Ch. 10).

Mirror bounce (Ch. 10).

Money trails (Ch. 11).

Spirolateral walk (Ch. 11).

The shape of things (Ch. 11).

How long to see a million dollars? (Ch. 11).

Speed graphs (Ch. 12).

Head turning (Ch. 12).

Maths in motion

These activities have as a central idea, children being physically involved by acting as numbers.

Groups of children, wearing their number cards, act out the roles and discuss the various tasks with each other while the rest of the class encourages and offers advice. The tongue-in-cheek story that goes with it makes the activity live for children, letting them bring forward all sorts of creative, non threatening ideas.

Children will enjoy repeating these activities straight after the first 'performance,' the next day and/or weeks later.

Features of these activities

- Physical involvement.
- Able to be used with small groups or the whole class.
- Fantasy settings and story telling are used.
- Use of language.
- Problem solving.

- Number recognition, sequencing, place value and number facts.
- Mental imagery. Concepts and skills are recalled when mental images these activities are formed at a later date.

Preparation

- At least one set of number cards, from 0 to 10. For the *Call the number* activity you will need one number card per child. (Laminating the cards will preserve them.)
- A means of attaching these to the child, for example, shoulder straps (as shown), pins, tape or bulldog clips.
- You may choose to make additional labels — *Mrs. Number* and *Red sports car.*

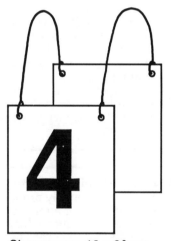

Size: approx. 12 x 20 cm

Normie Nine?

When you introduce the number children to the class, have them invent new names. For instance, Sunny One, Tricia Two, Francesca Five and so on.

HOW ABOUT TWEEDLE DUM TEN?

Maths in motion

Mrs. Number's family (In what order should my number family be?)

The aims are to have children understand such concepts as: *next number, last number, more than , less than.*

Have children discuss ways of helping Mrs. Number organise her family.

The children not participating at this stage can give advice and help. They can judge if the solution is a good one or not.

Keep discussing and arranging until the Number Line sequence is gained. Try as many of the children's ideas as possible.

If no one comes up with the Number Line sequence get them to remember back to the line the children were in when you were introducing the Number family.

If this is still not successful you will have to pose some leading questions, for example, 'What is the next number we say when we are counting?'

Once the children have become reasonably proficient at arranging the numbers in number line sequence they can then discuss the problem... 'How quickly can you get into line?' Discuss 'before' and 'after' numbers.

1. Have the numbered group line up in order behind you. Tell the following story and have children act it out.

WHENEVER THE NUMBER FAMILY GO ON AN OUTING THEY ALWAYS GO IN A LINE IN THE RIGHT ORDER.

ONE DAY, WHILE GOING SHOPPING, THEY HAD TO CROSS THE PEDESTRIAN CROSSING.

DON'T FORGET— LOOK RIGHT, LOOK LEFT, LOOK RIGHT AGAIN.

OK NOW CROSS...

2. Children jump back into an unordered bunch.

...BUT WHEN THEY WERE ONLY HALF-WAY ACROSS, A BRIGHT RED RACING CAR CAME SPEEDING AROUND THE CORNER.

THE DRIVER DIDN'T SEE THE CHILDREN.

SO Mrs.NUMBER SCREAMED 'RUN BACK QUICKLY!'...

3. Children try to suggest a strategy. Normally children suggest starting at '1' and working up.

...WHEN THEY HAD GOTTEN OVER THEIR SHOCK Mrs.NUMBER TOLD HER CHILDREN TO GET INTO LINE.

BUT THEY COULDN'T REMEMBER WHERE THEY BELONGED IN THE LINE.

NOW HOW COULD THE CHILDREN FIND THEIR PLACES?

4. Challenge children to find more efficient strategies. Change the number cards on to other children and play the game...'How quickly can you get into line?'

FIND OUT WHERE EACH NUMBER GOES

FOUR GOES BEFORE FIVE

HOW CAN WE GET THEM ALL TO HELP AT THE SAME TIME?

NINE'S MORE THAN EIGHT

A little help from the teacher

No — this isn't five raised to the power of one. This teacher invented yet another activity. 'Find a larger number and climb gently on its back.'

'You (two) should be on the other side of the street', cries number nine.

Smallest to largest

Line up eleven children from shortest to tallest.

Give the shortest the number '1' and the tallest the number '10'.

Place the numbered cards, jumbled up, in front of the children.

Ask class to predict who will be first and last to get their right number.

Tell children to get their correct numbers.

Discuss why some people get them before others.

> I MUST BE NINE 'COS I'M BEFORE TEN

> I MUST BE ONE 'COS I'M AFTER YOU

> I'M TWO 'COS I'M AFTER ONE

Where do the rubbish bins belong?

Tell the numbered children that they are the rubbish bins in (your) street.

Tell the tale of how the wind blew them all down to the end of the street.

The rest of the class clap to simulate the noise of the wind clattering the bins, while the 'bins' huddle in disorder at the 'end of the street'.

Then challenge 'bins', with the help of the rest of the class to find their right places before the 'garbo' (the teacher) comes.

To reinforce the idea of odds and evens, children can tell the class what they are — e.g. 'I'm six and I'm even.'

Step forward and bow

This can be an activity for the whole class if cards are available.

Children line up and when their number is called, they take one step forward and bow.

> MORE THAN TWO BUT LESS THAN FOUR

> WE'RE MORE THAN TWO BUT LESS THAN FOUR

Other instructions may be:
- Numbers bigger than six.
- Three.
- Odd numbers.
- Numbers starting with 'T'.

Get behind the number

Using one group of numbered pupils, call certain groups of people to fall in behind the numbers you call until only one child is left in the class. (Ideal for a pre-recess activity)

> GET BEHIND TWO IF YOU HAVE BROWN HAIR

Other instructions may be:
- ... if your birthday is in April.
- ... if you are wearing yellow.
- ... if you are wearing a digital watch.

Call the number

Suitable for the whole class divided into groups from eight to eleven children.

One child throws up a bean bag, calls a number then returns to his or her place.

The catcher repeats the activity.

Bob down when you're called

As you count with the class, the appropriate children bob down. Other instructions might be:

- Count backwards 10, 9, 8...0.
- Even numbers.
- Odd numbers.
- From five down.

AS I CALL OUT YOUR NUMBERS BRING YOUR CARDS TO ME —
FOUR!
NINETY-EIGHT
ALL THE ODD NUMBERS...

A packing-up activity

Form big numbers

Have the numbers 1 2 3 4 5 6 7 8 9 walk around while the music plays. When the music stops children quickly form groups of three numbers. The teacher then calls out either 'highest' or 'lowest' and groups arrange themselves to make the highest or lowest possible number in the fastest time.

This activity can be very noisy with the excitement and encouragement of the rest of the class.

LOWEST

Who would have to turn into another number? (Place value)

As with the last activity, children form up into groups of three numbers when the music stops.

Ask children which numbers would have to change, and to what, to change the total number to such as:

- Make twenty more.
- Make a hundred more.
- Make five more.

MAKE ONE HUNDRED MORE

JANICE WOULD HAVE TO CHANGE TO A FIVE

Make even larger numbers

Take any seven (or six, five or four) numbers. Children move around and when the music stops they form numbers, each three from the right holding hands.

The whole class reads the number.

Challenge pupils to move to make either the highest or lowest numbers

THREE MILLION, SEVEN HUNDRED AND TWENTY-FOUR THOUSAND, ONE HUNDRED AND FIFTY-SIX

HIGHEST

Bingo bodies

Most children will have played some form of Bingo in the past. This version encourages teachers to involve their pupils as 'physical counters' in playing the game. Quick mental computation, estimation, number facts and use of the calculator all combine in an enjoyable problem-solving activity. A traditional skill-based task is enriched by the injection of a range of features.

Features of this activity

- Active physical involvement.
- Mental computation and estimation.
- The calculator used to test predictions.
- Group problem solving.
- Number properties are reinforced.
- The activity provides a clear-cut distinction between situations when calculators are used and not required.

Preparation

- Five counters per pupil.
- One copy of each Gamesboard (pages 200-1) per pupil.
- Enough calculators for about half the group.
- One copy of answer sheet. (For teacher, page 199)
- Pupils could be sent out to draw with chalk two 4 x 4 grids without the numbers on the netball court. Alternatively, wooden sticks will do the job.

50 cm SIDED SQUARES

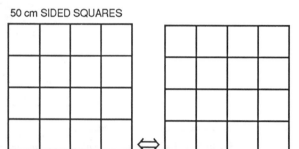

3 m APART

THIS ACTIVITY IS PART OF THE MCTP
PROFESSIONAL DEVELOPMENT PACKAGE FROM THE
CURRICULUM DEVELOPMENT CENTRE, CANBERRA

PHYSICAL
Years 5↓7

Bingo bodies

Pupils recall the popular game Bingo and are given the gamesboards and rules for our mathematical version. In pairs, pupils play one or two games, then move outdoors and play a friendly competition between groups.

1. Introduction

Generate a discussion about Bingo — the features of the game, how one wins and so on.

Having the outside grids drawn up prior to the session will help the activity run smoothly.

Encourage the children to do the explaining. Emphasise the different winning directions, ten in total.

AS THE NUMBER COME UP, YOU CROSS THEM OUT OR COVER THEM UP.
YOU ARE TRYING TO GET THEM IN A ROW.
THEN YOU CALL BINGO

66 — THAT'S 'CLICKETY CLICK'

11 IS CALLED 'LEGS ELEVEN'

2. Outline the session

Hand out the introductory game sheet.

YOU'LL NEED FIVE COUNTERS OF A SINGLE COLOUR.
AS JULIE EXPLAINED, WE'LL COVER NUMBERS WITH COUNTERS AND TRY TO GET FOUR IN A ROW

WE'LL NEED A DIFFERENT COLOUR FROM OUR PARTNER

Bingo bodies rules

Each of the sixteen numbers on the board is the product of two numbers written in the circles at the bottom. In turns, you will find the two factors that make a number on the grid, tell your opponent and then place one of your counters on that number. If you use up all five counters and the game is not finished you can remove a counter(s) to elsewhere.

3. Read out the rules

SO, SINCE 77 = 11 x 7, YOU WOULD SAY '11 TIMES 7 IS 77' AND PUT YOUR COUNTER ON 77

Limited to just five counters, children are encouraged to develop strategies, and so seek the factors of a particular square rather than work out answers randomly.

Those who finish early can try a second grid.

4. Children play a game or two

YOU'VE BLOCKED ME. I'LL TRY A DIAGONAL. 105 IS 7 x 15

I NEED 220. IT MIGHT BE 20 AND SOMETHING...

Allow children sufficient time to complete at least one of the introductory grids before asking them for the strategies they are using to find the factors.

5. Summary of strategies

IF THE NUMBER ON THE BOARD IS ODD, THEN BOTH FACTORS MUST BE ODD

IF THE NUMBER ON THE BOARD FINISHES WITH A ZERO OR FIVE THEN...

I KEEP ONE FACTOR FIXED AND MULTIPLY BY THE OTHERS IN TURN

IF THE NUMBER I GET IS SMALLER THAN WHAT I WANT, I CHOOSE A LARGER FACTOR

'They enjoyed explaining their strategies. A lot of very useful number concepts came out at this point.'

'Children were keen to learn from each other because of the competition which was to follow.'

Steps 1 to 5 should not take any more than 15 minutes. These strategies will be employed by the children outside.

6. Setting up the 'outdoor' teams inside

Break the group into four random teams. Each team will need to choose a leader. Hand out the outdoor gamesboards and calculators.

YOU WILL BE THE COUNTER. WHEN YOU DISCOVER THE FACTORS, THE CAPTAIN WILL PLACE YOU ON THE 'BOARD'

THE NUMBERS ARE MORE COMPLICATED NOW. CALCULATORS WILL HELP, BUT YOUR STRATEGIES WILL HELP YOU DECIDE WHICH NUMBER TO TEST ON THE CALCULATOR

WE'LL USE NETBALL BIBS TO DISTINGUISH OUR TEAM

Because the numbers in the grid are more difficult, calculators should be provided. It is intended that the children should see the appropriateness of mental computation in the introductory grids and the use of calculators now, so the numbers were carefully chosen.

The children will see that the strategies they developed will still be important when using calculators.

Years 5↓7

PHYSICAL

7. Preparing to play

Take the teams outside to the 'four square' courts (or similar) and with a piece of chalk construct four by four grids. (This is better done prior to the lesson.) Do not write the actual grid numbers on the ground or give the factors missing from the circles until all is ready to start.

Children are expected to be able to reconcile their gamesboard grid with that on the ground. To clarify this, step on to one of the grid squares and ask the children to tell you what number is in that one on the gamesboard. Move around to different squares on the grid until children are able to make the connection.

8. Bingo bodies

Assign two teams to each of the marked-out grids. Ensure that children can identify one team from another (netball bibs, sleeves rolled up, jumpers on, etc. ...) and then read out the factors to start the game. Children fill them in on the gamesboard.

A team that is able to get four in a row should yell *Bingo!*

Pupils then play other games on the gamesboard.

9. Conclusion/extension

- Have the teams produce another gamesboard for the next time.
- Game can easily be adapted for addition, division, decimals, fractions, word meanings,... depending upon year level.
- Make gamesboards without providing the factors. The numbers should be small for this is a more difficult task.

'I was pleased with how well they visualised the numbers after a while. It was excellent spatial training.'

ONCE THE CAPTAIN HAS PUT YOU ON THE GRID, YOU MUSTN'T HELP WITH CALCULATIONS UNLESS YOU ARE TAKEN OFF

YOU HAVE TO IMAGINE WHERE THE NUMBERS ARE FROM YOUR ACTIVITY SHEET. WHERE IS 420?

'It was quite a struggle the first game. Lots to understand and remember. But the second game was marvellous and much easier.'

All counter numbers (the factors) and solutions are on the teacher's answer sheet.

'Being outside, on a large physical scale seemed to generate more discussion and enthusiasm than the equivalent indoor version.'

'Kids enjoyed the game so much that they have been playing the game at lunchtimes with other children. It's a great one for an odd fifteen minutes.'

'As they made up their own, we had an endless supply of grids.'

Bingo bodies   Teachers' answer sheet

Introductory problems

140 **7x20**	77 **7x11**	84 **12x7**	48 **4x12**
240 **12x20**	300 **15x20**	220 **11x20**	90 **6x15**
132 **12x11**	24 **6x4**	66 **6x11**	42 **7x6**
72 **6x12**	180 **12x15**	60 **4x15**	105 **7x15**

(6) (12) (7)
(4) (20) (15) (11)

350 **5x70**	770 **11x70**	105 **5x21**	55 **5x11**
231 **11x21**	143 **11x13**	490 **7x70**	1470 **21x70**
65 **5x13**	147 **7x21**	910 **13x70**	77 **7x11**
273 **13x21**	84 **4x21**	52 **4x13**	91 **7x13**

(7) (5) (11)
(4) (70) (21) (13)

Outdoors 1

420 **12x35**	1085 **23x46**	204 **12x17**	437 **19x23**
805 **23x35**	713 **23x31**	1058 **31x35**	323 **17x19**
527 **17x31**	1610 **35x46**	589 **19x31**	276 **12x23**
874 **19x46**	552 **12x46**	391 **17x23**	665 **19x35**

(12) (19) (31)
(46) (17) (23) (35)

Outdoors 2

1312 **32x41**	195 **13x15**	270 **15x18**	1066 **26x41**
576 **18x32**	390 **15x26**	3381 **13x26**	472 **32x46**
832 **26x32**	1886 **41x46**	533 **13x41**	468 **18x26**
598 **13x46**	234 **13x18**	615 **15x41**	738 **18x41**

(13) (15) (41)
(46) (32) (18) (26)

Outdoors 3

588 **21x28**	3402 **63x54**	987 **21x47**	434 **14x31**
1764 **28x63**	294 **14x21**	2961 **47x63**	651 **21x31**
868 **28x31**	1316 **23x47**	392 **14x23**	1134 **21x54**
658 **14x47**	1512 **28x54**	1323 **21x63**	1674 **31x54**

(14) (21) (47)
(63) (31) (54) (28)

Outdoors 4

273 **13x21**	270 **15x18**	1029 **21x49**	224 **7x32**
1568 **32x49**	126 **7x18**	544 **15x32**	378 **18x21**
637 **13x49**	315 **15x21**	672 **32x21**	234 **13x18**
576 **18x32**	147 **7x21**	882 **18x49**	735 **15x49**

(7) (13) (18)
(49) (15) (32) (21)

Years 5↓7   **PHYSICAL**

Bingo bodies

Gamesboard 1

Introductory problems

140	77	84	48
240	300	220	90
132	24	66	42
72	180	60	105

(6) (12) (7)
(4) (20) (15) (11)

350	770	105	55
231	143	490	1470
65	147	910	77
273	84	52	91

(7) (5) (11)
(4) (70) (21) (13)

Outdoors 1

420	1085	204	437
805	713	1058	323
527	1610	589	276
874	552	391	665

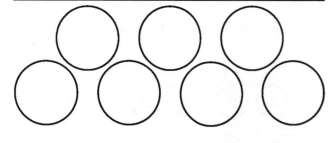

Outdoors 2

1312	195	270	1066
576	390	3381	472
832	1886	533	468
598	234	615	738

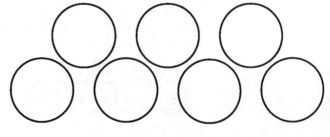

Bingo bodies

Outdoors 3

Outdoors 4

588	3402	987	434
1764	294	2961	651
868	1316	392	1134
658	1512	1323	1674

273	270	1029	224
1568	126	544	378
637	315	672	234
576	147	882	735

Make your own

PHYSICAL Years 5→7

An octahedral 'sculpture'.

Seventy pupils at a maths camp 'sheltering' in their four-ninths, three frequency icosa-geodesic dome.

Platonic solids

A Platonic solid is a polyhedron where all the faces and angles are the same. Only five Platonic solids exist. They are named after Plato, a famous Greek geometer and philosopher.

This activity challenges teachers to evaluate the effectiveness of letting pupils explore these shapes using large-scale physical group experiences.

Features of this activity

- A physically active two-lesson sequence.
- Develops the concepts of Platonic solids by building their skeletons, and leads to Euler's rule.

- It involves use of metre-long sticks and joiners to create large scale models.
- Concepts of rigidity and symmetry are developed incidentally.
- Cooperative work in groups.

Preparation

- You will need about 150 one-metre long sticks (9.5 mm dowelling is best) and about 75 joiners.

JOINERS MADE FROM SOFT PLASTIC TUBING

These can be easily made or there are commercially available kits. A source for the rods and joins is *Edudomes* PO Box 82 Montrose VIC 3765.

- Much room is needed for this activity, therefore it is best done outdoors. If that's not possible a hall is next best.

It can be conducted in a normal classroom using the arrangement shown.

Position the work tables against the walls, thus creating space for four work areas.

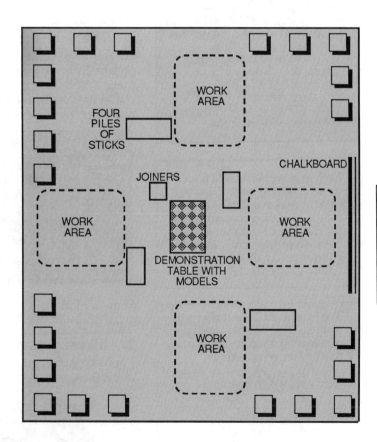

THIS ACTIVITY IS PART OF THE MCTP PROFESSIONAL DEVELOPMENT PACKAGE FROM THE CURRICULUM DEVELOPMENT CENTRE, CANBERRA

Years 5 → 9

PHYSICAL

Platonic solids

This activity is designed to 'get to know' the family of five Platonic solids and to develop pupils' visual imagery and the appreciation of basic structures and their stability.

> LATER WE WILL BE BUILDING SOME MATHEMATICAL MODELS LIKE THESE.
> BUT THIS LESSON WE WILL BE FINDING OUT HOW SOME STRUCTURES ARE MADE AND WHY THEY ARE SO STRONG

> WE HAVE TWO GROUPS OF SOLIDS. THIS GROUP IS SPECIAL FOR A PARTICULAR REASON

> WE CALL THEM PLATONIC SOLIDS AFTER AN ANCIENT GREEK MATHEMATICIAN CALLED PLATO. THERE ARE ONLY FIVE PLATONIC SOLIDS. I'D LIKE YOU, TO GET TO KNOW THEM, ONE BY ONE

> WE ARE GOING TO BUILD THEM AND, HOPEFULLY, FIND OUT SOME INTERESTING THINGS ABOUT THEM

1. Platonic solids and other geometric shapes

Have models of Platonic solids on one side of the table and other solids such as cylinders, rectangular prisms and pyramids on the other side.

> ALL THE FACES ARE THE SAME ON THOSE SOLIDS

> AND SO ARE THE ANGLES

Encourage children to describe the solids in their own language. Do not force the use of correct terms such as 'regular polyhedron', but restate any clumsy or inadequate terminology children may use with the correct term so that children get used to hearing them.

Each group could build about three tetrahedrons. They are easy to make and take only four joiners and six sticks. But for the rest of the models, because of the limitation of equipment, there must be whole-group models.

Trials schools found that other shapes were inadvertently constructed, most common being the square pyramid.

If this happens, challenge the class to pick what is wrong with this. Note its instability when it is put on its side.

Enter the number of fitting positions to the table on the chalkboard.

2. The first Platonic solid — the tetrahedron

As you investigate the tetrahedron with the class, make a table on the chalkboard as in the worksheet and enter the numbers.

> THE FIRST AND SIMPLEST PLATONIC SOLID IS CALLED A TETRAHEDRON

> THE WORD TETRAHEDRON COMES FROM TWO ANCIENT GREEK WORDS 'TETRA' MEANING FOUR AND 'HEDRON' MEANING FACE

> AFTER BUILDING, CAREFULLY COUNT THE VERTICES, FACES AND EDGES AND ENTER THESE ON THE WORKSHEET

NAME	TYPE OF FACE	No. FACES	No. CORNERS	No. EDGES	FIT POS
TETRAHEDRON	△	4	4	6	

Show a model or describe the tetrahedron and challenge each pair of pupils to build one.

3. Investigating the properties of the tetrahedron

Pupils construct tetrahedrons and find out about their rigidity even when turned at angles.

> TRY TURNING IT ON ALL SIDES. IS IT RIGID IN ALL DIRECTIONS?

> IF I DRAW A CHALK TRIANGLE AROUND THE BASE, IN HOW MANY DIFFERENT POSITIONS COULD YOU PLACE THE TETRAHEDRON ON THAT BASE?
> (3 x 4 = 12 POSITIONS)

4. The cube or hexahedron (The second member of 'our family'.)

WHICH OF THESE SHAPES DO YOU THINK IS THE NEXT PLATONIC SOLID?

WITHOUT LOOKING AT IT, CAN YOU REMEMBER
HOW MANY FACES? (Six)
HOW MANY CORNERS? (Eight)
HOW MANY EDGES? (Twelve)

THE ANCIENT GREEK WORD FOR SIX IS 'HEX'.
SO WHAT DO YOU THINK THE OTHER NAME FOR THE CUBE COULD BE? (Hexahedron)

OK! EACH GROUP, LEAVE ONE TETRAHEDRON STANDING BUT USE THE STICKS AND JOINERS TO MAKE A CUBE

Again, as the faces, edges and corners are counted, enter the numbers to the table on the chalkboard. Pupils enter these on their worksheets.

NAME	TYPE OF FACE	No. FACES	No. CORNERS	No. EDGES	FITTING POSITIONS
TETRAHEDRON	△	4	4	6	12
CUBE	▢	6	8		

THE CUBE

5. The properties of the cube

Pupils will discover the instability of the cube.

RIGID STRUCTURES ARE NORMALLY BASED ON TRIANGLES.
SEE HOW THIS SQUARE COLLAPSES BUT THE TRIANGLE IS RIGID

Also the cubic metre is the common unit by which soil, sand, rocks and water are measured.

IT WON'T STAND UP

Choose one tetrahedron and a cube to save as a record.

Show how, when laid flat, the sticks create a two-dimensional image of the cube.

6. The octahedron
(Third Platonic solid)

THE NEXT PLATONIC SOLID IS THE OCTAHEDRON. HOW MANY SIDES DO YOU THINK IT WOULD HAVE? (Eight)

SEE IF YOU CAN MAKE IT. ALL OF THE SIDES ARE TRIANGLES

BUILD IT AND FIND OUT HOW MANY FACES, CORNERS, EDGES AND FITTING POSITIONS IT HAS, AND ENTER THEM ION THE WORKSHEET

QUITE STRONG ISN'T IT? WHAT SHAPE DOES IT LOOK LIKE?

A DIAMOND

YES, THE DIAMOND IS THE WORLD'S HARDEST SUBSTANCE.
THE STRENGTH OF A DIAMOND LIES IN THE WAY IN WHICH ITS ATOMS ARE HELD IN A TRIANGULAR WAY

To fit these activities into two periods you may have to stop the class when one or two groups have successfully completed their octahedrons.

'My class later built a "magic sculpture" by linking all the octahedrons together.'

'Pupils naturally wanted to stand the octahedron on a point — rather than let it sit on its triangle base. This created interesting discussion about symmetry.'

THEY'RE ALL TRIANGLES

EACH CORNER HAS FIVE STICKS

7. The icosahedron   (Fourth Platonic solid)

Whilst it is possible to pose the construction of the icosahedron as a problem (Construct a polyhedron with 20 faces, 12 corners and 30 edges), it is a sufficient challenge to place a model in the centre of the room and challenge groups to recreate one.

8. Properties of the icosahedron

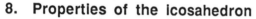

WHICH WAY DO YOU THINK IS BEST TO REMEMBER THIS SHAPE?
ON THE FLAT OR ON A POINT?

ON THE POINT LIKE A DIAMOND

WHO CAN SEE TWO FLAT, PENTAGONAL SHAPES IN THERE?
YOU CAN?
CAN YOU FIND ANY OTHERS.
HOW MANY?

'There are 12 in all, but "proving" this was most worthwhile.'

THERE'S ONE THROUGH THERE AND ONE THROUGH THERE

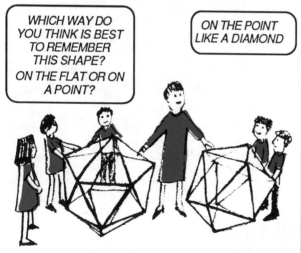

I'VE TAKEN OFF THE BOTTOM PIECES AND IT GIVES A ONE-FREQUENCY GEODESIC DOME.
DOMES ARE BASED ON TWO SHAPES — SPHERES AND TRIANGLES WHICH ARE VERY UNLIKE A NORMAL BUILDING BASED ON CUBOIDS

9. Euler's rule

THERE IS AN INTERESTING RELATIONSHIP BETWEEN THE NUMBER OF FACES, CORNERS AND EDGES OF THOSE SHAPES. IT'S CALLED EULER'S RULE

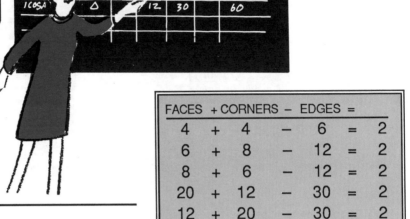

NAME	TYPE OF FACE	No. FACES	No. CORNERS	No. EDGES	FITTING POSITIONS
TETRAHEDRON	△	4	4	6	12
C...	☐	6	8	12	24
OCT.	△	8	6	12	24
ICOSA	△	12	30		60

Pupils could be challenged to discover the connection and then to test it on other polyhedra.

FACES	+ CORNERS	– EDGES	=	
4	+ 4	– 6	=	2
6	+ 8	– 12	=	2
8	+ 6	– 12	=	2
20	+ 12	– 30	=	2
12	+ 20	– 30	=	2

10. The dodecahedron (Fifth Platonic solid)

Discuss the model, the shapes of the faces and its possible rigidity — considering the fact that the faces are not triangular. Count the faces, corners and edges and find out whether Euler's rule still pertains. If time permits, have groups try to build one, if only to show that it is hopelessly unstable.

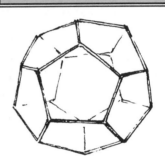

- -

Worksheet

NAME OF PLATONIC SOLID	TYPE OF FACE	No. FACES	No. CORNERS	No. EDGES		FITTING POSITIONS

Years 5 ↓ 9

PHYSICAL

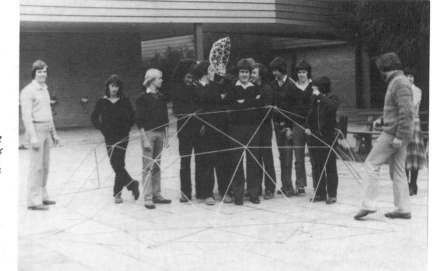

*Stages in the
growth of
geodesic domes*

How far is it around a circle?

Too often, pupils calculate the circumference of a circle without understanding the meaning of π — they simply plug in the formula and hope for the best. So when a miscalculation is made the mistake is not always apparent.

But in this activity, by stepping out the radius and the circumference of many circles and comparing the two rough measures, pupils develop a mental image and intuitive feeling of the relationship — a sound basis for understanding the formula C = 2πr.

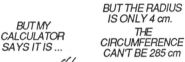
BUT MY CALCULATOR SAYS IT IS...

BUT THE RADIUS IS ONLY 4 cm. THE CIRCUMFERENCE CAN'T BE 285 cm

Features of this activity

- Physical involvement helps develop intuitive understanding of this important proportional relationship.
- Involves estimation and mental imagery.
- An active, outdoor, small-group activity.
- Develops the concept of π in an informal intuitive manner.

Preparation

- Each pupil should make a copy of the table at the right in his or her workbook. The radii are deliberately mixed up to try to have pupils concentrate on each problem individually, rather than pattern from one to the next, as would happen if the radii went 4, 5, 6...
- One eight-metre length of string for each pair of two pupils.

Radius	4	7	6	10	8		
My guess							
Accurate							

THIS ACTIVITY IS PART OF THE MCTP PROFESSIONAL DEVELOPMENT PACKAGE FROM THE CURRICULUM DEVELOPMENT CENTRE, CANBERRA

Years 5↓8 **PHYSICAL**

How far is it around a circle?

Physical involvement is used in this activity in the belief that if the pupil actually walks both the radius and circumference, then the pupil will develop a 'feel' for the relationship between them, in a way not possible using pencil-and-paper activities in the classroom.

1. Demonstrate to the whole class

Have children gather together. Make sure each group has a notebook (with the table), pen and string.

> THE PERSON WHO WILL STAY AT THE <u>CENTRE</u> STANDS STILL AND HOLDS THE END OF THE STRING

> THE <u>WALKER</u> STANDS BESIDE THE CENTRE PERSON, THEN TAKES FOUR PACES, LETTING OUT THE STRING

The walker marks the starting position, then paces and counts while the centre person pivots.

> IF THE WALKER KEEPS WALKING FORWARD HANGING ONTO THE STRING WHAT PATH WILL SHE MAKE?

> HOW MANY PACES DO YOU THINK LEE WILL TAKE AROUND THAT CIRCLE?

> ... FIVE, SIX SEVEN...

Surprisingly it is not always obvious to pupils that the path will be a circle. Also it is an opportunity to include terminology such as radius and circumference.

The guesses are an indication of pupils' perceptions. The correct answer is of course approximately 25. The range of guesses is amazing and worth pointing out to the class. Note how many guesses are under 25, and how many are over.

If pupils have made a guess, they will usually be interested in the accuracy of that guess. However, it is more beneficial for all pupils to experience the walk themselves, especially those whose guesses indicated a rather poor perception.

2. Group work

Pupils break into pairs and work through the problems (including the first four-pace problem) and some they make for themselves. Point out that they should make a guess before each walk and take turns at being centre and walker.

3. Discussion

When most of the groups have completed the table, move the class back inside.

> CAN YOU SEE A RELATIONSHIP BETWEEN THE DISTANCE AROUND THE CIRCLE, AND THE DISTANCE OUT FROM THE CENTRE?

> DOES THIS RELATIONSHIP WORK IN ALL CASES?

> WERE YOUR GUESSES BECOMING MORE ACCURATE?

> IT SEEMED ALWAYS TO BE ABOUT SIX

> EVEN WITH BIG STEPS

> During the trials, pupils were interested in the effect of using consistently small or large steps. They were intrigued to discover that the relationship did not change as step size changed.

4. Extension (Optional second period)

The worksheet is designed to help pupils achieve an even more accurate ratio than six.

If sources of errors are recognised and controlled, it is possible to be surprisingly accurate in determining that the ratio is a bit over six. For example, if pupils use a radius of three paces, then the walk may well produce 21 due to small errors. However a radius of ten paces usually gives a walk of about 60 – 65, much closer to the correct ratio because errors have less influence.

> There may be much discussion about the different answers the pupils get, and about any errors of measurement that could produce these. Trialling found that most results were $C = 6r$ or $C = 7r$.
>
> However the accuracy of the value is not important to this lesson. The important mathematical idea here is the existence of the proportional relationship between C and r.
>
> The overall result is that each pupil will usually become aware that the circumference is about six times the radius.
>
> This is a good background on which to build an appreciation of the formula $C = 2\pi r$.

> In one trials class the teacher collected results for a radius of 10. These were averaged and produced a result of 62.8, that is, a ratio of 6.28.
> $(2\pi \approx 6.25)$

Extension worksheet How far is it around a circle?

The distance around the circle is one of the following.

     a. Just less than six times the radius.

     b. Exactly six times the radius.

     c. Slightly more than six times the radius.

The following activities may help you to decide.

---

1. Which radius would better help you decide?

If you repeated the walking activity, which radius, a two-pace radius, or ten-pace radius would better help?

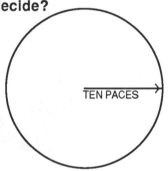

---

2. Do the circle-walking activity using heel-to-toe paces

- Try to be as accurate as possible.
- Don't let the centre move.
- Keep the string tight.

Radius					
Circumference					
6 x radius					

---

3. Try using a trundle wheel

Tie one end of the string to a stake in the centre and the other to the handle of the trundle wheel, near the axle. Enter your measurements in the table above.

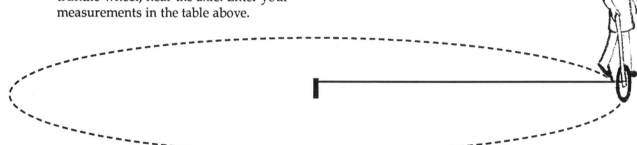

CONCLUSION:— The distance around a circle is .... times the radius.

Algebra walk

'Multiply the number between your feet by two. Add one. Now step that out.' Quite a simple, achievable task for nine pupils. But instantly, for all to see, pupils quickly form lines as on a graph — a concrete example of the seemingly difficult linear function, $y = 2x + 1$. The activity generates a powerful image which forms a sound basis for formal learning and a vivid illustration of the power of physical involvement.

'Every now and then you find an activity that is so simple, elegant and powerful you would wonder why it is not enshrined in the *Teaching Almanac of Good Ideas*'.

Features of this lesson

- Concept of linear relationships.
- Imagery upon which formalisation can be built.
- Provides a model for later reference.
- Personal and physical involvement.
- Group work.
- Brief time required.

Preparation

You need a set of axes drawn in chalk on an outdoor (for preference) area. Each unit needs to be about one average walking step (approximately 50 cm).

Comments from trials schools
'This made graph drawing easier than I have ever found it — the imagery is very powerful.
The best feature is the dynamic imagery it creates for pupils. This imagery proves to be invaluable later when developing abstract models on the chalkboard. The images are vividly recalled using phrases like "remember when we were outside — what would the instructions be for $y = 3x + 1$. How would the person on +4 move?"'

Years 8 ↓ 10

PHYSICAL

Algebra walk

Each child stands on a number on the x axis. The teacher gives the equation as a simplified command, the pupil makes a quick calculation and steps into position. Instantly a graph of the equation appears. This activity provides a sound, concrete basis for understanding linear function.

1. Linear graphs

Nine pupils are needed on the grid — the others are on the side watching, predicting and recording.

> LOOK AT THE NUMBER BETWEEN YOUR FEET.
> MULTIPLY IT BY TWO.
> ADD ONE.
> GOT IT?
> WHEN I SAY 'GO' WALK THAT MANY PACES, EITHER FORWARDS OR BACKWARDS.
> GO!

All of a sudden a beautiful model of a graph of the linear function $y = 2x + 1$ appears with all sorts of fascinating imagery and involvement, upon which skill development and understandings can be built.

'It was spectacular to observe, and very non-threatening for pupils.'

'I never found the classwork so easy as I did after the outdoor segment. I'll use it every year from now on.'

The power of group learning

Almost every time the activity was trialled we found something like the following happened — without a single word from the teacher.

On the word 'Go', the –4 pupil confidently marches forward while his or her compatriots retreat to the opposite sector.

But after a rapid assessment of the situation, there is a scurry back into formation — suitably 'advised' by colleagues. That is followed by a quick, informal discussion about multiplying by negative numbers.

This is an excellent example of the power of group learning. Trials teachers rated this self-correcting aspect as a highlight of the lesson.

However if pupils on the negative numbers (especially) become too confused, more direct help could be given.

> EH! WHAT ARE YOU ALL DOING BACK THERE?

> WHEN YOU MULTIPLY A NEGATIVE WITH A POSITIVE YOU GET A NEGATIVE

> THIS IS THE NEGATIVE — YOU'RE IN THE POSITIVE

> YOU FORGOT. YOU'RE A NEGATIVE NUMBER

2. Other linear graphs

Try other equations such as the following.

$y = 2x - 1$ $y = 4x + 4$ $y = 3x + 1$

$y = x - 3$ $y = 2x - 3$ $y = 4 - x$

Several lines can be quickly constructed, with different teams being placed on the line, or changing position within the line.

If appropriate, gently guide more capable pupils to the negative numbers.

> Point out how the pupil on zero has a comparatively easy job.

> Up to the end of these exercises, the activity normally takes about 15–20 minutes.

> Consolidate this stage by giving many examples until the images and understandings are clear, rather than rushing to the formal pen and paper stage.

> 'The concept of gradient is very apparent in the spaces between pupils.'

Years 8 ↓ 10

PHYSICAL

Extension activities

1. Simultaneous equations, $y = 2x + 1$ and $y = -x + 7$

WE ARE GOING TO FIND OUT WHERE TWO LINES INTERSECT

*FIRST LINE —
LOOK AT THE NUMBER BETWEEN YOUR FEET.
MULTIPLY BY TWO.
ADD ONE.
READY?
GO!*

*SECOND LINE —
LOOK AT THE NUMBER BETWEEN YOUR FEET.
MULTIPLY BY MINUS ONE.
ADD SEVEN.
READY?
GO!*

There is no need to burden the learning task by mentioning the terms such as simultaneous equations at this stage.

In future lessons these activities could be used to introduce work-book activities or as a fun way to check answers during skill development.

To distinguish the lines you could select lines of pupils who have the same characteristics such as one line of boys, the other girls; one line of dark haired pupils, the other light; pupils with white shirts, the others blue etc.

2. Quadratics, $y = x^2 - 2$

*LOOK AT THE NUMBER BETWEEN YOUR FEET.
MULTIPLY IT BY ITSELF.
THEN TAKE AWAY TWO.
HAVE YOU WORKED THAT OUT?
GO!*

'The symmetry and other patterns within quadratics were beautifully displayed.'

3. Quadratics, y = x(x + 3) − 5   [or y = x² + 3x − 5]

> LOOK AT THE
> NUMBER BETWEEN
> YOUR FEET.
> MULTIPLY IT BY A
> NUMBER THAT IS
> THREE BIGGER.
> THEN TAKE AWAY
> FIVE.
> HAVE YOU WORKED
> THAT OUT?
> GO!

> This is easier than
> the more formal
> instructions
> *'Multiply your
> number by itself.
> Then add three
> times the number.
> Then take away
> five.'*

4. Solving quadratic equations, y = (x + 2)² − 7 = (x² + 4x - 3)
= x(x + 4) − 3

> 'A 20 m yellow
> rope really
> highlighted the
> curve and
> allowed pupils
> to focus on
> intercepts.'

> 'I put the basic
> y = x² on the grid
> and then we
> moved all over
> the place. For
> example two
> paces left
> produces
> y = (x + 2)²
> and so on.'

PHYSICAL Years 8 → 10

The obvious mistakes made by pupils lead to discussion and a greater understanding of the concept.

The classic parabola $y = x^2$.

Trigonometry walk

Sine and cosine are often difficult concepts for children to understand. But by having children create large triangles using string, and by stepping out the lengths of the sides, strong mental images, vital for understanding the concepts are formed.

Features of this activity

- An outdoor, physical activity.
- Concept of a trigonometric function.
- Introduces the unit circle approach to trigonometry.
- Group work.
- Involves estimation.
- Uses calculators.

Preparation

- You will need a basketball court or courtyard.
- About 15 m of string per group of about four to six pupils.
- One large protractor per group.
- Chalk.
- A scientific calculator that has sine, cosine and tangent functions).
- One copy per pupil of the worksheet on page 223.

Why 'walk' rather than measure?

It is certainly possible to lay out an outside unit circle with a radius of (say) ten metres and for pupils to measure, instead of walking, each of the lengths.

This would seem to improve on the traditional 'pencil and paper' introduction by the deliberate inclusion of the features of large scale and outdoor components, and would provide accurate results.

However, there seems to be subtle but important extra benefits when pupils 'walk' the lengths. In particular, the features of estimation and personal physical involvement are added. Freed from the constraints of measuring with instruments, students seem to focus more on the relationships and are better able to 'internalise' the experience for later recall.

The purpose of this activity is to invite teachers to explore and debate just these sorts of issues. It is after trialling and seeing the effects on pupils' learning, that we have a base of experience upon which to have a productive debate.

PHYSICAL Years 9 → 10

Trigonometry walk

By children physically experiencing (by walking) the sine, and later the cosine of a triangle, a strong mental image of the relationship between angle and length is created. This cognitive image can then be used in formal situations back in the classroom, that is, the episode can be relived as a concrete basis for understanding sine and cosine.

1. Demonstrating the method

Mark out a ten-pace radius, quarter circle.

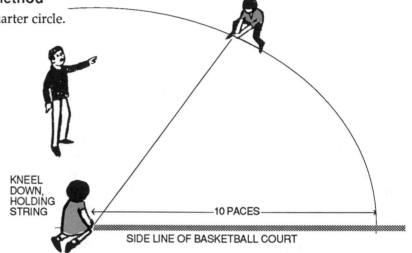

> *WE WILL BE MEASURING LENGTHS BY STEPPING THEM OUT, SO YOUR STEPS MUST BE ALL THE SAME SIZE.*
>
> *MARK A POINT ON THE SIDE LINE AND TAKE TEN VERY EVEN STEPS.*
>
> *FROM THAT POINT WE WILL DRAW A QUARTER CIRCLE*

KNEEL DOWN, HOLDING STRING

10 PACES

SIDE LINE OF BASKETBALL COURT

2. What happens to the sides of the triangle as you go along the quarter circle?

The walker creates right-angled triangles as he or she walks the circle. It is important for watching pupils to visualise these triangles as the angle at the centre changes.

> If the walker is stopped once or twice on his or her walk, the triangle could be highlighted with string.

> *'Pupils seemed to get a strong visual image that there is an infinite number of triangles, and that each is different.'*

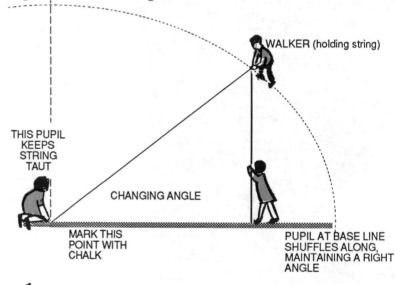

WALKER (holding string)

THIS PUPIL KEEPS STRING TAUT

CHANGING ANGLE

MARK THIS POINT WITH CHALK

PUPIL AT BASE LINE SHUFFLES ALONG, MAINTAINING A RIGHT ANGLE

> *WATCH THE TRIANGLES THEY CREATE.*
>
> *ONE SIDE IS ALWAYS THE SAME.*
>
> *BUT WATCH WHAT HAPPENS TO THE PERPENDICULAR AND THE BASE*

> *THE PERPENDICULAR KEEPS GETTING LONGER*

> *THE BASE KEEPS GETTING SHORTER*

3. The step as point one of a unit of measurement

IF WE MADE THE RADIUS ONE UNIT AND THE RADIUS IS TEN STEPS LONG, HOW LONG IS ONE STEP?

ONE TENTH OF A UNIT, THAT'S .1

Have one pupil step this out as you pose the question. The pupil should arrive at the chalk line if the steps are uniform—a good test of stepping skills.

1 OF A UNIT ←——→

←———————— ONE UNIT ————————→

4. Finding one sine value (say 20°)

This time the position of the stepper is determined by the angle. One person holds the rope at the 20° position while other pupils do the measuring.

Trials schools report that it is better to focus on the sine separately from the cosine, rather than treating them together.

OUR TASK IS TO MEASURE THE LENGTH OF THE VERTICAL (THE SINE) TO WITHIN ONE TENTH OF A STEP

1, 2, 3, 4 — ABOUT 3.4 PACES

THAT'S .34

LET'S TRY TWENTY DEGREES

COUNT THE STEPS

DO YOU THINK IT IS EXACTLY .34?

20°

MATHEMATICIANS HAVE WORKED OUT THE MEASURES VERY ACCURATELY AND I'LL SHOW YOU AFTER YOU HAVE MADE YOUR MEASURES

The class will probably be willing to accept that .34 is not exact, but it is reasonably close.

If you think that pupils need another example to fully understand the method, repeat the exercise using (say) 58°.

5. The tables and the task

Give out the worksheets and have the pupils form groups of four to six.

NOW YOU KNOW HOW TO DO IT, HERE IS A TABLE. FIND OUT THE SINE AT EACH TEN DEGREES. NOTE THAT TO CONVERT PACES TO SINE — DIVIDE BY TEN

NOW YOU HAVE SEEN ONE EXAMPLE (FOR 20°), IT IS YOUR TURN. FIND THE SINE VALUES FOR EACH 10° FROM 0 TO 90

Some trials schools had friendly competitions to find the group with the least errors total.

Years 9 ↓ 10   PHYSICAL

Trials teachers reported this moment as a highlight for them. As the trig. values 'pop out' of the calculator, it could be seen that the numbers had real meaning for the pupils.

These perceptions, so critical for a sound grasp of the relationships of lengths, seem to be in direct proportion to the experience of 'walking the lengths'.

The collective set of triangles merge to form a dynamic mental image, that is, each pupil can replay the episode in his or her mind and 'see' the lengths changing.

In this way, trigonometric functions should have more meaning than the abstract set of numbers in tables.

It is preferable to leave these observations at the concrete level at this stage. Trials schools reported that by going too fast, by dropping such 'gems' as $\sin A = \cos(90 - A)$, spelled the 'beginning of the end' for many pupils.

6. The calculated lengths. How accurate were you?

> NAOMI, YOU FIND THE EXACT LENGTHS TO WITHIN TWO DECIMAL PLACES USING THE CALCULATOR. EVERYBODY ELSE, WRITE THEM IN YOUR TABLE

> WORK OUT YOUR ERRORS

> SINE 10° IS...

7. Discussions about the pattern of lengths

> WHAT DID YOU NOTICE ABOUT THE LENGTHS?

> IT INCREASES A LOT IN THE BEGINNING, THEN IT SLOWS DOWN

> AFTER THIRTY DEGREES IT'S ALREADY HALFWAY TO THE TOP

> THE BIGGEST IT CAN GET TO IS ONE

8. The horizontal or cosine

In a similar way to the sine, pupils walk the triangles and fill in the second table.

> WHAT DID YOU FIND OUT ABOUT THE BASE OR COSINE?

> THESE LENGTHS GET SMALLER AS THE ANGLE GOES UP

> IT GOES SLOWLY AT FIRST AND THEN SPEEDS UP

> BEFORE THIRTY IT'S HARDLY GOT STARTED

> IT'S SORT OF OPPOSITE TO THE OTHER ONE

EXTENSIONS

This activity is a lovely illustration of how the tangent value increases dramatically as the angle approaches 90°.

Tangents

This model works equally well for tangent as well as sine and cosine. The side of the basketball court is a tangent to the circle.

To find tan 20°, simply walk along the tangent until the 20° mark is reached. Make a table, as for the sine, but replacing the word sine with cosine. Complete the table, from 0° to 90°.

Other trig. ratios

It may be stretching the value of this activity, but the ratios of sec, cosec and cot are also evident as illustrated.

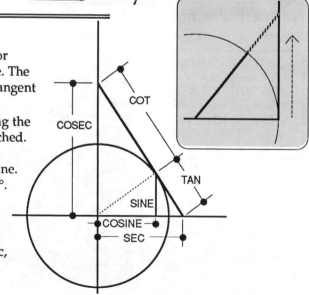

COT

COSEC

TAN

SINE

COSINE

SEC

Worksheet   Trigonometry walk

SINE

Angle	0°	10°	20°	30°	40°	50°	60°	70°	80°	90°
Paces (to nearest tenth)										
Sine (Paces + 10)										
Correct										
Error										

COSINE

Angle	0°	10°	20°	30°	40°	50°	60°	70°	80°	90°
Paces (to nearest tenth)										
Cosine (Paces +10)										
Correct										
Error										

- ✂

SINE

Angle	0°	10°	20°	30°	40°	50°	60°	70°	80°	90°
Paces (to nearest tenth)										
Sine (Paces + 10)										
Correct										
Error										

COSINE

Angle	0°	10°	20°	30°	40°	50°	60°	70°	80°	90°
Paces (to nearest tenth)										
Cosine (Paces +10)										
Correct										
Error										

Years 9↓10   **PHYSICAL**

'Hold it there at 40°.'

Finding sine 50°.

Outdoor Pythagoras

This teaching approach, uses real triangles, lets pupils devise their own individual problems, predict the answer using Pythagoras, and enjoy the fruits of the confirmation of their predictions.

Teachers are encouraged to contrast this approach with the typical 'text-book' treatment and to debate its educational merit.

Features of this activity

- A cheerful alternative to the textbook.
- A skill-development lesson.
- An outdoor segment.
- Triangles used are real and visible, not abstract.
- Estimation.

- Immediate reinforcement for the calculations they do.
- Encourages use of calculators.
- The exercises are created by pupils, not from text.
- Non-threatening.

Preparation

Metre-long sticks and measuring tapes or metre rulers for each group of two or three pupils.

THIS ACTIVITY IS PART OF THE MCTP
PROFESSIONAL DEVELOPMENT PACKAGE FROM THE
CURRICULUM DEVELOPMENT CENTRE, CANBERRA

Years 9 → 10

PHYSICAL

Outdoor Pythagoras

After a teacher demonstration of the method, pupils work in small groups, creating triangles by propping up a metre-long stick against a wall.

After estimating the height, they measure the base and by using Pythagoras calculate the height.· The height is then measured and compared with the estimation and calculation.

A short introduction like this helps describe what the lesson hopes to do, and how it is organised.

Introduction

I WANT TO PROVE TO YOU HOW ACCURATE PYTHAGORAS IS IN CALCULATING THE MISSING SIDE OF A TRIANGLE

INSTEAD OF COPYING TRIANGLES OUT OF A TEXT BOOK, WE CAN MAKE REAL TRIANGLES BY PROPPING A METRE STICK AGAINST A WALL

Non-threatening

The opening line of the lesson is:

'I want to show you how accurate Pythagoras is ...'

The title implies a sharing with pupils, through their experience, of the accuracy and power of a bit of mathematics. The spirit is also implied in the title. The way the teacher acts is to nurture the pupils to an appreciation of the accuracy and power of the Pythagoras Theorem, not to present them with the task of learning a skill which many pupils will perceive as — *'Here's another bit of maths I'm likely to fail.'*

Hence the conclusion (and any assessment) should be in the same spirit, of establishing whether the pupils are indeed convinced.

I WANT TO DEMONSTRATE HOW TO DO ONE PROBLEM, THEN I AM GOING TO ASK YOU TO DO FIVE MORE, AND YOU'LL PROBABLY BE ABLE TO DO THESE OUTSIDE

...AND BEST OF ALL, INSTEAD OF HAVING TO LOOK UP THE ANSWERS IN THE BACK OF THE BOOK, YOU CAN CHECK YOUR ANSWER DIRECTLY ON THE TRIANGLE

Prop a stick against a wall in any position.

HOW HIGH DO YOU THINK THAT IS? WRITE YOUR ESTIMATION IN YOUR NOTEBOOK

I THINK IT'S JUST UNDER 60 cm, SAY 58 cm

IF WE MEASURE THE BASE, WE CAN USE PYTHAGORAS TO PREDICT HOW HIGH UP THE WALL IT REACHES

THEN WE WILL BE ABLE TO CHECK BY ACTUALLY MEASURING SO YOU DON'T HAVE TO LOOK UP THE BACK OF THE BOOK

Estimation

This is promoted to be an awareness-raising and motivating aspect. If the pupil is encouraged to look at the triangle and ask *'What length does it look like?,'* then this raises an expectation and reference for the following calculations. Motivation is gained by encouraging pupils to see how close they can estimate to the correct measure. Estimation also enables a greater focus on the underlying relationships between the sides that can otherwise be masked under a welter of calculations.

THE BASE IS 83.1 CENTIMETRES

Have one or two pupils measure the base, accurate to one decimal place, (e.g. 83.1 cm) with a ruler or tape. Once you move the metre stick you 'destroy' the triangle.

YOU SET OUT
THE WORKING IN
YOUR BOOKS
LIKE THIS

Try to scale the diagram to look like the real triangle.

Calculators

The calculations involved offer an ideal opportunity for utilitarian use of calculators. Pupils in trials schools responded very positively to their use.

MATHEMATICS HAS
TOLD US THAT THE
STICK IS BETWEEN 55
AND 56 cm UP THE WALL.
SEE HOW
MATHEMATICS GIVES US
THE POWER TO PREDICT
ANSWERS

THE
PREDICTION
IS 55.1 cm

NOW WE
CAN CHECK

Look suitably relieved (?) when the measurement does support the prediction, or quite concerned if there is a difference, leading to the need to check everything.

Don't be over concerned with accuracy unless it is an advanced class. The major emphasis is for all pupils to experience the power of making the prediction using Pythagoras, and then enjoying the success of seeing their prediction to be correct, or at least close.

The introduction and demonstration so far, should take only about ten minutes.

Years 9 → 10

PHYSICAL

Concrete embodiment

The traditional treatment after the teacher's introduction is to practise multiple abstract problems from the text book. This activity only requires pupils to do five problems, but in each case the triangle they create is a physical reality — they can see, touch and measure the three sides of each triangle. Textbook problems, often not drawn to scale, are abstract and often near to meaningless for many pupils.

It can be argued that just five real concrete examples embody as much or more learning than pages and pages of textbook problems.

Pupils tend to use rough notes outside, then write proper copy as soon as they arrive back inside.

Pupils seem to genuinely enjoy the reinforcement of seeing the prediction come true — a sense of power? Also, each triangle is of their own creation which seems to add to the commitment.

Group outdoor work

After initial demonstration by the teacher, groups of two or three pupils are liberated to work in a specified location outdoors. The outdoors offers the advantages of space and physical freedom. Trying to create the same activity indoors can be very crowded and noisy. As long as pupils have a clear set of instructions — they do five problems, and with a specified location and time limit, there are few problems of lack of control. In addition, as pupils finish and return to the classroom they have an immediate task to write up their results.

Group work, as distinct from an individual exercise, is beneficial in terms of the discussion that takes place between pupils when creating and carrying out each problem. As the teacher circulates between groups you will hear many instances of such things as problem clarification (*What do we have to do?*), problem solving (*That's nowhere near correct — we must have done something wrong!*) and many other instances for productive dialogue normally denied to pupils in a formal skill-based setting.

In small groups, pupils do five problems

Give the groups a clear set of instructions and liberate them into a defined working area such as a courtyard.

Each group needs a metre stick and a ruler or tape.

I WANT YOU TO DO FIVE PROBLEMS.
SET THEM OUT AS IN THE DEMONSTRATION EXAMPLE.
YOU'VE GOT 20 MINUTES — THAT'S FOUR MINUTES PER PROBLEM.
REPORT BACK TO CLASS WHEN YOU'VE FINISHED

REMEMBER WHAT TO DO?
• PROP UP THE STICK IN ANY POSITION.
• WRITE DOWN YOUR ESTIMATION OF THE HEIGHT.
• MEASURE THE BASE.
• CALCULATE THE HEIGHT.
• CHECK BY MEASURING

While groups are working

• Collect into one group those pupils who are not coping, for extra demonstration. However if this group gets to be 80% of the class it's time to go back inside.

• Discuss accuracy with interested groups. Many pupils are quite eager to hunt down the source of even a half-centimetre error. List possible sources of errors.

• Suggest they measure height, and calculate base, instead of vice-versa.

• Trials schools report creative groups constructing extreme situations such as:

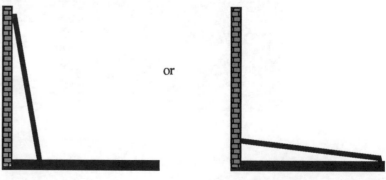

or

Back in class

- Set out workings in books.
- Perhaps discuss errors and how groups explained these.
- Review the results in light of purpose.
- Ask class what benefits or enjoyment they received from creating their own triangles, instead of working from the book.

Conclusion

I wanted to convince you how accurate Pythagoras' theorem is.

Ask the class if they are indeed convinced. That is, the spirit of the lesson is about establishing the accuracy of the theorem, not about punishing pupils for incorrect calculations. Perhaps pupils could write a short report as an alternative assessment to a skills calculations test.

Extensions

- Use sticks of various lengths.
- Predict the measurement of a stick of unknown length by measuring base and height. Then measure to check accuracy.
- Triangles can be formed in a horizontal as well as vertical plane.
- Extend to larger, real situations in the room or outside.

For senior classes

Use the metre rods to establish the accuracy of the cosine rule, by measuring and calculating different combinations of angles and lengths.

> Having clearly defined tasks as they arrive back keeps the focus of attention to the task rather than last night's episode of *Dallas*.

> **Positive reinforcement**
> In text book lessons, after the calculations, the only authority to which pupils can appeal for feedback is the 'back of the book', the answer itself having little or no meaning.
>
> In this lesson, after calculation, the answer is verified by direct measurement. In this way, the calculated answer has real meaning and pupils receive immediate positive feedback from the measurement check.

> **Power shift**
> A small but interesting aspect of the lesson is that five problems, rather than being set by a remote authority are created by the pupils. This gives them a measure of control over their learning which they enjoy.
>
> Many groups do two or three standard examples then, while still charged with enthusiasm, explore more extreme settings.

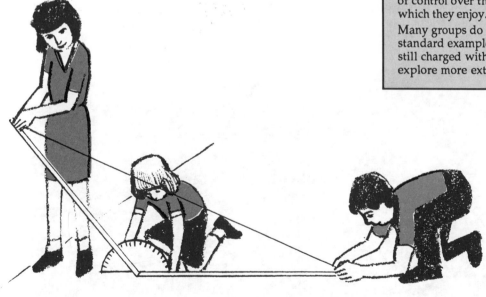

Years 9 ↓ 10

PHYSICAL

In Eight queens *(see* Computers, Chapter eight*), pupils are challenged to model this famous chess puzzle, by positioning eight players, each acting as a chess 'queen', so that none can be 'captured' by any other. The physical activity is then modelled by computer.*

Estimating lengths

Pupils' concept of length can quickly become more accurate through this physical activity. They are challenged to estimate different lengths, then immediate feedback is obtained by measuring and the analysis of errors.

Teachers are encouraged to debate the educational value of the features built into this activity.

> I'M 1.23 m OUT

> 19 m IS RIGHT HERE

> MY MARK IS AT 17 m 26 cm

The steps

- Mark a starting point.
- Make another mark at an estimated 19 m away.
- Calculate the error, record and graph it.
- Do the same for the other distances.

Features of this activity

- Application of measurement skills.
- Establishes mental images of length.
- Immediate feedback, allowing pupils to check their estimations and refine their concept of distance.
- Self esteem is raised with improved performance.
- Group work.
- An outdoor activity with physical participation.

You will need:

- A tape measure — one per group.
- A table in pupils' workbooks like the one below. Explain how both it and the graph paper is to be used.

DISTANCE	ACTUAL	ERROR
19 m		
23 m		
14 m		
36 m		
18 m		

- Graph paper

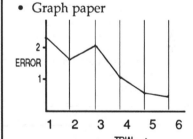

(A finished graph may look like this. Do the errors get less?)

This activity is best done outdoors in groups of two to five. Class results can also be combined.

'Pupils definitely had a much greater "feel for" and confidence with units of measurement after this activity.'

'The graphs created excellent discussion'.

Years 5 ↓ 8

PHYSICAL

Regular polygons

The concept of regular polygons is developed by children physically creating these with string.

- Three pupils form a triangle and shuffle until the sides are thought to be equal.
- They then devise tests for equal lengths and equal angles.
- Add pupils to extend to other polygons.

Features of this activity
- Development of the concept of regular polygons and their properties.
- Develops estimation skills.
- Cooperative learning and sharing of ideas.

You will need:
20 m lengths of string and large protractors for each group.

A test for equal lengths.

This is an extremely efficient way to quickly illustrate a range of shapes such as isosceles and scalene triangles, rhombuses, parallelograms and so on.

Extensions
1. Try to explain the patterns of the angles 60°, 90°, 108° ...
2. Explore similar patterning in the external angles.

Add pupils to extend to other polygons.

ALL THE SIDES ARE EQUAL, BUT THE ANGLES AREN'T. SO IT'S A POLYGON BUT NOT A REGULAR POLYGON

PHYSICAL
Years 5 ↓ 10

How long is your pace?

This activity through physical involvement increases pupils' awareness of how pace length changes under different conditions.

1. Pupils estimate the lengths of seven different types of paces and enter them in a table like the one below.
2. Ten paces are taken, measured, averaged and recorded in the table.
3. The results are plotted on a graph like the one at the bottom of the page.

Points for discussion

- Do normal walking paces vary throughout the day?
- Why use ten, rather than one?
- Should you have a standing start or should you already be in motion?
- Jessie Owens was reputed to have a stride length at full pace of 2.65 m (8'10"). Mark this out on the ground for observation and comparison.

Features of this activity

- Develops the concept of length.
- Estimation.
- Averaging.
- Graphing.
- Involved the use of personal data.

You will need:

Measuring tapes and chalk.

This activity relates closely to Snippet 1, page 32.

A surprising result for most pupils is the very large increase once people start to run.

HERE IS YOUR TEN-PACE LENGTH

	Estimate	Measure
Walking normally		
Walking quickly		
Jogging		
Running		
Running very fast		
Long bounding steps		
Walking backwards		

Years 6↓9 **PHYSICAL**

Graph with vertical axis marked 0, 50, 100, 150 and horizontal axis marked: NORMAL WALK, QUICK WALK, JOG, RUN, FAST RUN, BOUNDING, BACKWARDS

The 40 second walk

This activity, through repeated physical trials allows pupils to intuitively develop the relationships between distance, time and speed.

Features of this activity

- Develops the relationship of time to walking pace (speed) and distance.
- Estimation.
- Graphing.

You will need:

Stopwatches and chalk.

Groups of about six to eight work best. More than that seems to produce a 'follow-the-leader' situation.

Repeat for five trials, recording times and graphing errors.

Use the group results as a basis for discussion. For example: Why did everyone under-estimate?

Graph the results.

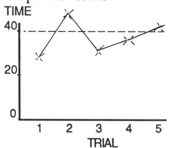

YOUR CHALLENGE IS TO WALK TO THAT TREE AT A STEADY PACE TAKING EXACTLY FORTY SECONDS

TRY TO DECIDE 'IN YOUR MIND' HOW FAST YOU WILL HAVE TO TRAVEL

NO SPEEDING UP OR SLOWING DOWN ONCE YOU HAVE STARTED — GO!

(WHISPER) THIRTY-FIVE THIRTY-SIX THIRTY-SEVEN

I DID IT IN THIRTY-ONE SECONDS. I WAS TOO FAST

THIS ACTIVITY IS PART OF THE MCTP PROFESSIONAL DEVELOPMENT PACKAGE FROM THE CURRICULUM DEVELOPMENT CENTRE, CANBERRA

Walk the plank

Such concepts as − (⁻2) are normally difficult for children to understand. However this physical outdoor game embeds the concepts without complicated terminology.

A game normally takes five to ten minutes using seven marks in each direction.

FACE THE SHARK.
WALK TWO PACES
BACKWARDS

FACE THE
BOAT.
TAKE ONE
PACE
FORWARDS

START

DANIELLE GOT TO
THERE BY FACING THE
SHARK AND TAKING
TWO PACES
BACKWARDS.
WHAT OTHER WAY
COULD SHE HAVE GOT
THERE WITH THE SAME
NUMBER OF STEPS?

BY FACING THE
BOAT AND
TAKING TWO
PACES
FORWARDS

BOAT

Features of this activity

- The concept of directed numbers.
- Formal symbols (+ −) not needed.
- Establishes strong mental pictures from the physical involvement.
- Non-threatening.

You will need:

Two big dice marked like this.

1. *Direction* —boat or shark.

2. *Walk forwards or backwards*
   F1, F2, F3, B1, B2, B3.

Keep challenging pupils to give the alternate way of getting to the same place, for example that

| B | F3 | ≡ | S | B3 |

$$-3 \equiv -(^{+}3)$$

Years 7 ↓ 8   PHYSICAL

THIS ACTIVITY IS PART OF THE MCTP
PROFESSIONAL DEVELOPMENT PACKAGE FROM THE
CURRICULUM DEVELOPMENT CENTRE, CANBERRA

Incentre of a triangle

Through physical activity, pupils experience the meaning of incentre. Teachers are encouraged to trial and debate the effectiveness of this approach.

Features of this activity
- Shows many important properties of triangles.
- Develops intuitive appreciation of concepts such as bisection, intersection, angle of incidence and angle of reflection.

You will need:
Large mirrors with safe edges.

Definition
The incentre of a triangle is the intersection of the angle bisectors.

- Each pupil holds his or her mirror at an angle where the other two pupils can see each other.
- A fourth pupil finds the place where he (or she) can see himself (or herself) in all mirrors.
- Challenge all pupils to devise a test to prove that it is the incentre.

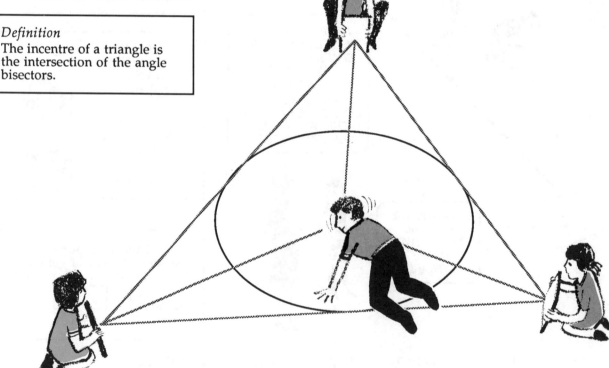

THIS ACTIVITY IS PART OF THE MCTP PROFESSIONAL DEVELOPMENT PACKAGE FROM THE CURRICULUM DEVELOPMENT CENTRE, CANBERRA

PHYSICAL Years 8 ↓ 10

Circumcentre of a triangle

Pupils cooperatively find the circumcentre of a large triangle (three points) using realistic, practical methods. This physical approach increases the likelihood of the concept of circumcentre being retained by pupils.

Features of this activity

- A realistic problem.
- Cooperative learning.
- Practical, non-instrumental construction.

You will need:
String and pegs.

Setting out the circumcentre and the triangle

Two groups could compete against each other, firstly hiding a 'treasure', (a coin, paper clip or the like) then trying to find the other team's treasure.

Place a peg into the point where you want the circumcentre to be. Then drive into the ground three stakes equidistant (10-15 m) from the peg. (These form the triangle.)

Bury a 'treasure' where you remove the peg, leaving no visible evidence.

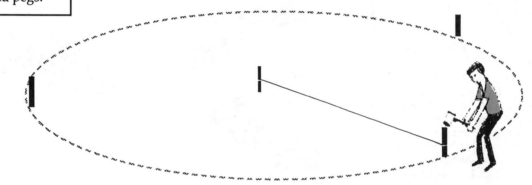

Finding the circumcentre

Using two long and equal lengths of string, the second group constructs perpendicular bisectors to locate the circumcentre.

Test that it is the circumcentre by measuring to each corner of the triangle.

> Allow pupils to place a 'guess marker' which can later be compared to the accurate position.

> THE CIRCUMCENTRE LIES SOMEWHERE ON THIS LINE

> NOW WE HAVE TO FIND THE PERPENDICULAR BISECTOR OF ANOTHER SIDE

> *Definition*
> The circumcentre of a triangle is the point where the perpendicular bisectors of the sides meet.

> This activity is surprisingly accurate even in rough bushland.

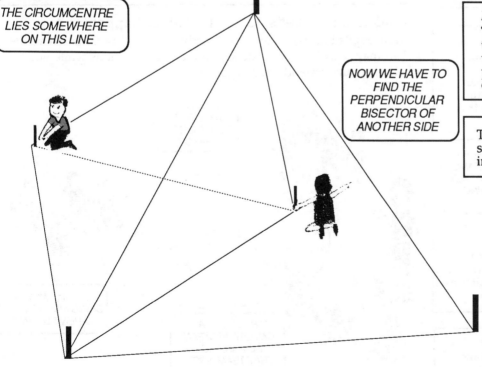

Years 8 ↓ 10

PHYSICAL

THIS ACTIVITY IS PART OF THE MCTP PROFESSIONAL DEVELOPMENT PACKAGE FROM THE CURRICULUM DEVELOPMENT CENTRE, CANBERRA

The three-way tug of war

This tug of war provides a physical experience from which understandings about vectors develop. Whilst the normal tug of war relies on brute strength, this three-way version is a contest of tactics and ability. Teachers are invited to construct this outdoor group activity with traditional approaches.

Addition of vectors and the concept of equilibrium may well present problems for pupils whose only experience of the concept is making copies of diagrams like this.

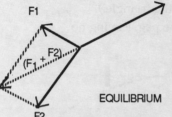

On the other hand, when the learning comes from personal experiences and perceptions, pupils are more likely to see relevance in the subject and apply the concepts both in and out of the classroom.

Many pupils lack an intuitive feel for vectors and, in particular, for the addition of vectors.

Our task is to relate the concept to pupils' experience and to provide activities which supplement them.

A best-of-three-games contest provides maximum learning benefits, allowing time for tactics to develop. Five games produce an exhausted maths class unable to participate in follow-up discussions.

IT LOOKS LIKE THIS TEAM'S MUCH STRONGER BUT THEY ARE STILL NOT WINNING. WHY?

The physical experience demonstrates that while F3 is equal and opposite to the resultant of F1 and F2, a similar result is true for both F1 and F2.

This activity has also been successfully used to teach the angle concept to a grade six class, as a rugby training exercise and as a party game.

You will need:
- Three thick, strong ropes about six metres long.
- A flat area at least 20 x 20 m. Draw the circle as shown.

Divide the class into three. Don't worry about balancing the strengths of the teams, because children soon discover that if one team looks like winning, the other two combine forces by narrowing their shared angle (increasing their sum of the vectors) to return the knot to the centre.

3 m RADIUS CIRCLE DIVIDED INTO EQUAL PARTS

A team wins if the trailing (centre) rope passes the circumference at their sector.

'Hold it there! Let's look at what is happening!'

Warn pupils that you may occasionally order rest periods where the class may relax (maybe sit down) in the same positions while you help them understand what is going on.

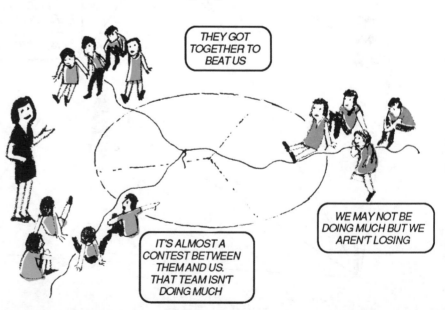

THEY GOT TOGETHER TO BEAT US

WE MAY NOT BE DOING MUCH BUT WE AREN'T LOSING

IT'S ALMOST A CONTEST BETWEEN THEM AND US. THAT TEAM ISN'T DOING MUCH

Chapter five

Pupils writing about mathematics

Purpose

In recent years, many teachers have been enthusiastically adopting the basic concepts of the process/conference approach to writing. In process writing, pupils are in control of what they write, how they will write and what materials are to be used. Drafting, and subsequent discussion with peers, teachers or parents followed by editing, allow improvements and refinements in the piece of work.

This process allows the teacher to gain deeper insights into children's degree of understanding, while they are able to work at their own rates and levels. This has proved highly motivational, and has been found to reduce fear of failure. Many teachers are exploring the potential of this process in the mathematics classroom (see, for example, Byrne, 1986; Mett, 1987).

This MCTP chapter invites teachers to 'explore the territory', with a view to assessing the value to mathematics learning of such an approach. A range of activities across K-10 is presented to support such exploration.

Rationale

How does writing about mathematics enhance learning?

• Mathematical experiences can be 'captured' for later recall.

• Pupils can use 'natural' language, arising from real contexts.

The...writing...illustrated the children's capacity to go beyond the goals and expectations within which we often constrain them.

• Writing, like talking, can facilitate a distillation of mathematical relationships in the writer's mind. *'Through talking and writing and representing new ideas to ourselves in our own preferred way, we internalise new ideas and make them our own'* (Boomer, 1986, pp. 4–5).

• Pupils' work provides a springboard for further discussion about the concepts being explored.

• For many children, writing is an enjoyable, creative experience.

• Writing can take place as a cooperative group task.

• The written piece of work can assist teachers in formal and informal assessment.

Try this experiment with a young child or a class. First cover four counters with a piece of paper, and place three counters next to the paper. Say, 'I have seven counters altogether; you can see three. How many do I have hidden?' Later, present the written problem $3 + \Delta = 7$. Many children will correctly reason that four counters are hidden, but will answer 10 for the written problem.

Formal representations of mathematics should be the end product of previous mathematical writing experiences. The 'right' way to write mathematics has to be built up from the children's resources of language and earlier representations. It seems inconsistent that at the stage children are being given time and opportunity to come to terms with print and being encouraged to approximate whilst they acquire skills, they are also being encouraged to produce perfect mathematical text.

(Reeves, 1986, p. 1)

WRITING

Pengelly (1986, p.16) argues that our challenge is 'to find ways for children to investigate mathematical ideas, to support children in finding ways to represent those ideas and to trust that children will work towards formal mathematical thinking and methods of communication.'

Del Campo & Clements (1987, p. 12) argue that all modes of communication represented in the table at right should be present, often, in mathematics classrooms. *'Imagining' has been included as an expressive form of language because 'by imagining one can communicate with oneself.'*

Modes of communication

MODE	RECEPTIVE LANGUAGE (processing someone else's communication)	EXPRESSIVE LANGUAGE (your own language)
SPOKEN	listening	speaking
WRITTEN	reading	writing
PICTORIAL	interpreting diagrams, pictures	drawing
ACTIVE	interpreting others' actions	performing demonstrating
IMAGINED	—	imagining

Mett (1987) has described how senior school students were trained to write about calculus. Three kinds of writing were expected of the pupils:

1. *Journal writing* — each day the pupils wrote about accomplishments, reactions, and puzzling questions. The mere act of writing helped to clarify ideas and sort out problems.

2. *Class writing* — every day the pupils wrote, for five to ten minutes on a topic which they had been considering (or were about to consider). Then, pupils listened to, and commented upon, what others had written.

3. *Assigned projects* — here, polished, well-researched writing was expected of the pupils. The projects were graded for content and quality.

It is interesting to note that practising scientists in research and development corporations report that over 30 percent of their time is spent writing (Lampe, 1982).

Robinson (1986, p. 83) points out that the child's language is important to mathematics teachers because *'it provides the teacher with a window into the child's mind. It is mainly by getting the child to talk and write about his or her understandings that the teacher can have any idea where the child is in regard to understanding mathematics, so talk and writing are absolutely essential to the mathematics teacher.'*

Some illustrations

Jennifer Corrie (1986) asked children in pairs to write about particular mathematical terms. Tan Fook and Miranda (Grade 2) produced the example at right for 'Equals'.

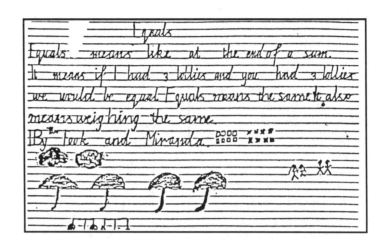

In *Children writing about calculators*, the teacher hands out calculators to young children, with no other instructions than to see what they could discover. The process writing which follows graphically illustrates the children's capacity to go beyond the goals and expectations, within which we often constrain them. The example at right relates to a child's discovery about the square root key ('the tick').

The hypothesis that the square root key *'makes the numbers go less'*, though not correct for numbers between 0 and 1, provides an opportunity for the teacher to encourage the child or a group of children to explore this statement together. The level of sophistication will naturally vary with the age of the pupils. (Young children show a fascination for calculators in general, and solar power and the square root key in particular.)

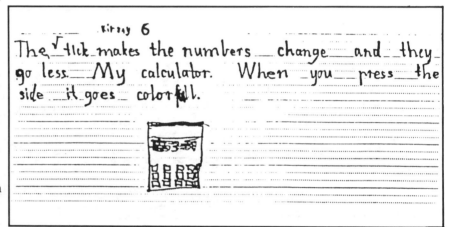

Noelene Reeves (1986, p. 3) gave examples of children constructing class books which illustrated particular concepts. Possibilities included *What We Know About Fractions*, *The Day We Cooked Dinner at School* and *Our Book of Tall Things*. A class book about *Half* included the following.

You can write it as a word or a sign.

Half means one part out of two.

If you fold a piece of paper over so that the corners match and cut it you have two halves.

You can't have any size pieces, they have to be exactly the same.

Sometimes half is more like 1, like when you have 6 things and you give half of them to a friend. You both get 3 but it's still half.

Half is sharing something into two equal parts.

It can be one thing or lots of things but the shares have to be the same.

You can put two halves together and make 1 again.

If you add more than two halves together you get more than 1. 5 halves is like having 2 pieces of paper and a half as well but you would need the sticky tape.

If you half fill a jug with water you can have a top half and a bottom half. You can say the jug is half full or half empty. The water comes to the middle.

The line across the soccer field is in the middle and makes two halves. You have half time at football and that comes in the middle of the match.

Sally is 8 and her brother John is 16. John is twice as old as Sally. Twice means two, so does double. Doubles and halves are partners.

In music, a crotchet is half a minim and quavers go twice as fast as a crotchet...

In *Mortality quiz*, an activity in the *Social issues* chapter, pupils are presented with a five question quiz, focusing on *'safe'* and *'dangerous'* ages. This activity uses mathematics to explore the social issue of road safety. They are asked to consider various key points on the graph at right, with a view to assigning an age to each one. Following this, and the presentation of the actual figures, pupils are broken into groups.

Each group is required to write about the reasons for the graph being as it is, based on their collective experiences. These reports are then shared with the rest of the class, and discussed further.

Del Campo & Clements (1987, p. 19) sounded a note of caution about the move to apply the language principles of *'process writing'* and *'conferencing'* to the mathematics classroom. They warned that the emphasis can quickly shift from a mathematics activity to a language-only one, if the teacher is focusing too much on the importance of generating a quality piece of literature, rather than assisting the child to learn more about mathematics and move to increasing mathematical elegance. The example at right, where the child was asked to develop a story using a certain group of fractions is clear evidence of the possible pitfalls.

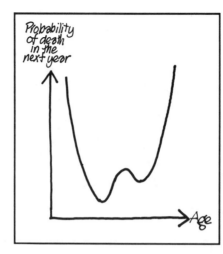

Activities from other chapters with a writing component

Mortality quiz (Ch. 2).

Sum stories (Ch. 6).

Four cube houses (Ch. 11).

References

Boomer, G. (1986). From catechism to communication: Language, learning and mathematics. *Australian Mathematics Teacher, 41(1)*, 2-7.

Corrie, J. (1986). Material presented to the 1986 Key Group Conference, April, Lorne.

Del Campo, G., & Clements, M.A. (1987). *Children hearing, watching, reading, writing, talking, drawing, imagining, acting out, practising and creating mathematics.* Paper presented at the tenth annual conference of the Mathematics Education Research Group in Australasia (MERGA), at James Cook University (Townsville), July 1987.

Lampe, D. R. (1982). Writing in an R & D Group: The Invisible Activity. *The MIT Report, Industrial Liaison Program of the Massachusetts Institute of Technology 10*, 1-2.

Mett, C. L. (1987). Writing as a learning device in calculus. *Mathematics Teacher, 80(7)*, 534-537.

Pengelly, H. (1986). *Learning to write mathematics by writing mathematics.* Adelaide: South Australian Education Department.

Reeves, N. (1986). Children Writing Maths, *Reading Around Series No. 3*. Melbourne: Australian Reading Association.

Robinson, I. (1986). Exploring Mathematics in Classrooms. In N. F. Ellerton (Ed.), *Mathematics: Who needs what?* Melbourne: Mathematical Association of Victoria, 80-85.

Children writing about calculators

Calculators are distributed to children with no other instructions than to see what can be discovered. The process writing that follows graphically illustrates children's capacity to go beyond the goals and expectations within which they are often constrained.

Features of this activity
- Open exploration.
- Discussion between pupils and between teacher and pupils.
- Uses a 'Process writing' (including sharing and conferencing) approach to maths.
- Children's work is bound into a book.

Some work with five year old children encouraged the authors to explore the results of children writing about calculators. The process, as used in four classes with ninety children aged from five to eight was as follows.

1. The teacher gathered the grade together, and, prior to giving children calculators, asked them to **share their knowledge of calculators** — what they look like, whether they have used one at home or at school, what they are for, how they work and so on.

2. The following **instructions were** then **given**. 'I'm going to give you each a calculator. I'd like you to spend some time finding out about your calculator, how it works and some of the things it can do. Share some of the things you find out with your neighbour, and in a little while, I'll be asking you to write about some of the things you have found'.

3. The teacher then **gave each child a calculator** and they returned to their seats. The calculators were a mixture of solar and battery-powered models of various sizes.

4. The children were then given **time to explore** the calculator, and to share their discoveries with a neighbour.

5. They then **wrote a first draft**, giving details of at least one thing they had discovered. These were also shared with neighbours.

6. The children then **discussed their findings** with the teacher, and adjusted their first draft, as necessary.

7. Children were then encouraged to **illustrate their work**.

8. The teacher ran a class discussion, where several pupils showed their work and **shared their discoveries**.

9. Using the infant typewriter, the work was typed, illustrated by children, and **the work was 'published'** in a binder.

10. This book was **put in an accessible place** in the classroom.

The level of interest and enjoyment surprised both the authors and the teachers. Children were prepared to spend up to an hour and a half on the process, far more than had been planned. Their interest was only halted by the bell for recess.

THIS ACTIVITY IS PART OF THE MCTP PROFESSIONAL DEVELOPMENT PACKAGE FROM THE CURRICULUM DEVELOPMENT CENTRE, CANBERRA

Years K↓4 | WRITING

What they wrote about

Solar Power

This was a source of absolute fascination, with children moving enthusiastically around the room eager to share their discoveries.

'A calculator is exciting. When it is dark, it goes off. When the sun comes up, it goes on.' (Ross, aged 6)

'When you shut the cover on the sunlight calculator it turns off, and when you put your hand over the top. They change colours when you press zero. They change purple, yellow and blue, red and brown.' (Sarah, 8)

'I think this is amazing. When I take the calculator and put my hands over each other, then all of it goes off.' (Chris, 6)

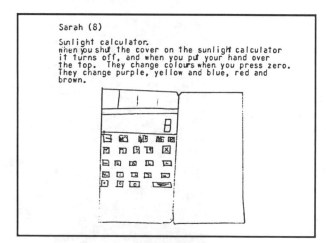

Sarah (8)

Sunlight calculator.
when you shut the cover on the sunlight calculator
it turns off, and when you put your hand over
the top. They change colours when you press zero.
They change purple, yellow and blue, red and
brown.

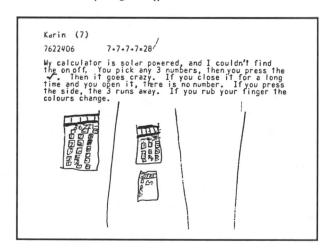

Karin (7)

7622406   7+7+7+7=28

My calculator is solar powered, and I couldn't find
the on off. You pick any 3 numbers, then you press the
√. Then it goes crazy. If you close it for a long
time and you open it, there is no number. If you press
the side, the 3 runs away. If you rub your finger the
colours change.

The Capacity and Role of the Calculator

Children drew many conclusions about the calculator, based on their exploration. (Most were accurate!)

'You can make many, many sums. Kylie and I found out that if you go a long way from the calculator you can't see the numbers.' (Jade, 6)

'I found out about memories and I memorised my phone number.' (Danielle, 7)

'Memorise is Rm. Calculators are like mini-computers except you cannot play games. You can learn sums on them too.' (Emily, 8)

'On my calculator I discovered that it could do this really hard sum. I didn't know that it could do hard sums. My partner took it away and I could still see it.' (Sarah, 6)

Emily (8)

Memorise is Rm. Calculators are like mini computers
except you cannot play games. You can learn sums on
them too. There are 24 buttons on one, and they are
+/- mrc m= AC √ 789 x ÷ 456% C/CE 123 - 0. =. +

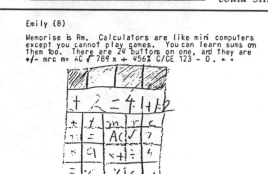

'I found that when you put the sum on the screen and pushed the equal button lots of times other answers came up on the screen.' (Sharni, 6, discovering the constant function).

'..I found out it didn't do the sum, it just told the answer.' (Jacqui, 6)

Large numbers and the movement of numbers across the screen

Children were fascinated with large numbers and many related them to concepts of interest to them.

'We pressed 100 + 100 = 200,   300 + 900 = 1200. When you press 3 and 900 it equals 903.'
(Troy, 6)

'While I was playing with the calculator, I saw the numbers walk out of their life.'
(Michael, 5)

'I pressed one button, and it was staying in front.' (Shenna, 5)

'When I pressed the calculator, the numbers went backwards.' (Bree, 5)

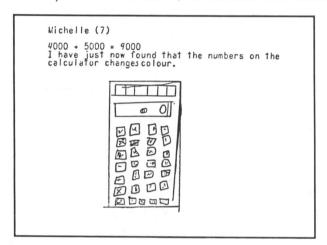

Michelle (7)

4000 + 5000 = 9000
I have just now found that the numbers on the calculator changes colour.

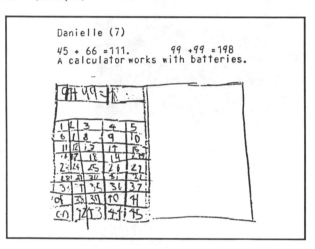

Danielle (7)

45 + 66 =111.   99 +99 =198
A calculator works with batteries.

Number patterns

Towards the end of the initial sessions, pupils were starting to explore the patterns.

'We found out that 1+2+3+4+5 + 1+2+3+4+5 = 30.' (Joshua)

'What I'm making is a pattern. It goes like this.

1 2 1 2 12 21 12 21 12.' (Carla, 6)

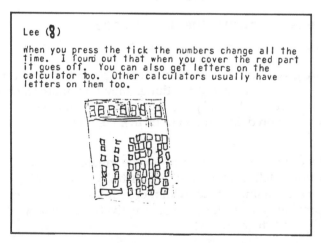

Lee (8)

When you press the tick the numbers change all the time. I found out that when you cover the red part it goes off. You can also get letters on the calculator too. Other calculators usually have letters on them too.

The square root key

Though at a simple level, children showed considerable fascination with the square root key ('the tick').

'I found that the tick with the short line makes lots of numbers.'
(Brielle, 6)

'You pick any three numbers, then you press the √ . Then it goes crazy.'
(Karin, 7)

Positive attitudes/motivation

The children thoroughly enjoyed the non-threatening open nature of the exploration, and worked enthusiastically for up to one and a half hours.

'1437912345 I like calculators because they are fun to play with.' (Kathleen, 5)

'A calculator is exciting. It has numbers and buttons.' (Ross, 6)

'I pressed 1000000 + 1000000 and it equalled 2000000. It was fun using the calculators. My calculator can do anything.' (Andy, 6)

'I tried a shared between. It was a nought but it was fun.' (Michelle, 6)

Daniel (6)

The dinosaur lived for 20001249 and I wil tell you how I did it- by multiply.

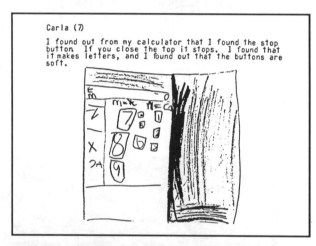

Carla (7)

I found out from my calculator that I found the stop button. If you close the top it stops. I found that it makes letters, and I found out that the buttons are soft.

Some reflections following the experience

Where to from here?

As the children are given further opportunities to explore and discover, to share, write about and draw about the things they find, more teacher guidance may be required to channel pupil curiosity to the number patterns that can be explored, leading on to further concept development.

The fascination that some children showed for the square root key (admittedly at a low level), highlights the possibility of extending children by bringing them into contact with more sophisticated concepts than they have previously met, thereby constructively stimulating both their curiosity and their interest.

It appeared that the standard school calculator with four operations, memory and square root is as suitable for the first years of primary school as it is for the later years. Large, well-spaced keys and solar power ensure easy use by young children.

This article has described the first experiences of some young children with the pocket calculator. The challenge is to find activities and experiences which will build on the enthusiasm obviously generated and maintain the calculator's status as a fascinating tool with which to explore number.

Tell me a story (Primary)

This activity links maths, creative writing and drama, showing children that interpreting a graph can just be like telling a story. It invites teachers to contrast the effectiveness of these alternative strategies with more traditional means of developing the skills of graphical interpretation.

Features of this activity

- Develops the concept of line graphs.
- Group discussion.
- Children develop their stories as a shared writing experience.
- Informal evaluation using reading and drama.
- The approach used encourages girls' participation.

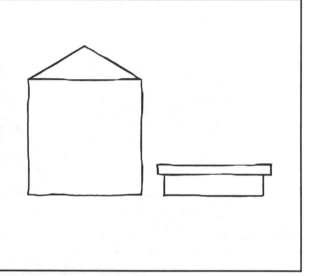

Preparation

- One copy per pupil of the graph on page 251.
- Make a sketch like the one at right on the chalkboard or on an overhead projectual or chart.

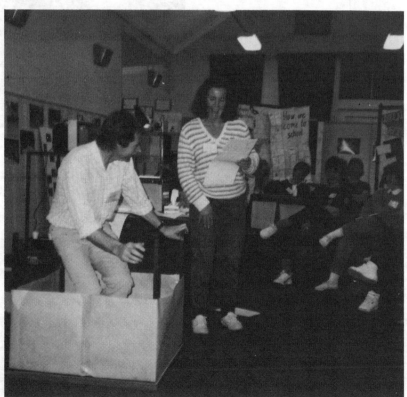

Teachers from an In-service act out a bath scene.

WRITING

Years 5 ↓ 7

Tell me a story (Primary)

The class discusses examples of how a line graph can be read, and what the line indicates is going on. The children are given another graph, and, working in pairs, they dramatically present and/or write their own interpretations of the graphs.

GETTING STARTED

The holiday house, the tank and the graph

With the class watching, complete the drawing as shown.

> YOUR FAMILY HAS JUST BOOKED THIS FARM HOUSE BY THE SEA, FOR A HOLIDAY. PEOPLE SAY THE HOUSE IS SHABBY, BUT THE RENTAL IS VERY LOW AND THE BEACH IS GREAT

> TODAY WE WILL BE WRITING ABOUT YOUR HOLIDAY EXPERIENCES, AND WE WILL USE THE GRAPH TO HELP US

The graph provides a visual image to help children with the next step.

Silently draw this graph next to the house.

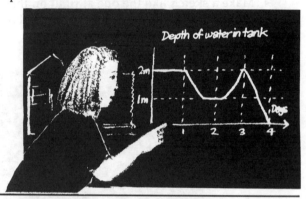

Some trials schools found that, because children in some classes became restless at this stage, it may be preferable to prepare the whole drawing and graph, then explain it gradually.

Class discussion

Ask the group for information from the graph.

Point out that their answers describe the graph, but that our task is to *explain* the changes.

Record children's responses on the graph.

> WHAT DEPTH OF THE WATER IS IN THE TANK AT THE BEGINNING OF THE HOLIDAY?
> ... MIDDAY ON THE SECOND DAY?
> ... AT THE END OF THE FOURTH DAY? *etc.*

> WHAT DID YOUR FAMILY DO ON THE FIRST DAY?

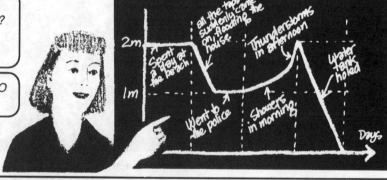

The comments on the graphs shown are from trials schools.

The *curved* part requires special discussion — only a small increase in the morning, larger in the afternoon, greatest in the evening.

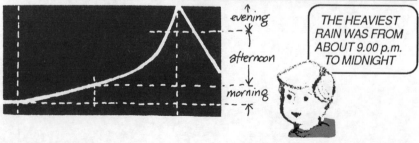

> THE HEAVIEST RAIN WAS FROM ABOUT 9.00 p.m. TO MIDNIGHT

PUPILS MAKE THEIR OWN INTERPRETATION OF A GRAPH

Tell me a story

Hand out the bath graph to the children.

Establish that the children can 'read' the graph by asking a few specific questions.

> *THIS GRAPH RELATES TO THE WATER LEVEL IN A BATH*

> *WHAT HAPPENS TO THE LEVEL OF THE WATER WHEN YOU CLIMB INTO THE BATH?*

> *HOW DEEP WAS THE BATH AT TEN PAST SIX?*

> *THIS ACTIVITY IS NOW IN TWO MAIN PARTS. WORKING IN PAIRS, I WANT YOU TO WRITE A CREATIVE STORY WITH A SUITABLE TITLE. WHEN YOU ARE FINISHED, I WANT YOU TO 'ACT OUT' THE STORY FOR THE REST OF THE CLASS*

As the children work, move around the groups
- answering questions,
- conferencing ideas,
- encouraging a balance between creativity and mathematical accuracy,
- encouraging both pupils in the pair to contribute ideas.

The assessment used here is informal and non-threatening as the teacher encourages tactful appraisal of the strengths (and any weaknesses) of each report.

Non-competitive assessment allows many girls to feel more comfortable.

Groups who finish early can be invited to prepare their play — one member to read, one to do the acting.

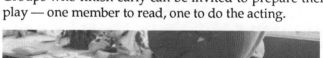

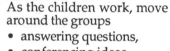

Years 5↓7

WRITING

Discussion and evaluation

- Provide time for children to discuss their reaction to each group's story.
- The rest of the class could 'assess' each explanation by following the story on their copy of the graph.
- Videotape each group's play. This could be taken home to share with parents.
- Make a book. Illustrate some of the stories with photographs.

Extension and follow-up activities

1. Tell children a story and ask them to prepare a graph.
2. Apply the approach to other topics — car trips, athletic performances, pocket money.

   Column graphs may also be used, particularly with lower grades.
3. Read some picture story books related to the theme (and which could be graphed). For example, *Mr. Archimedes Bath* — Pamela Allen. (Collins, 1985); *Who Sank the Boat?* (Nelson, 1985).

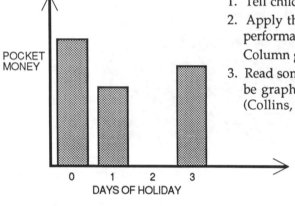

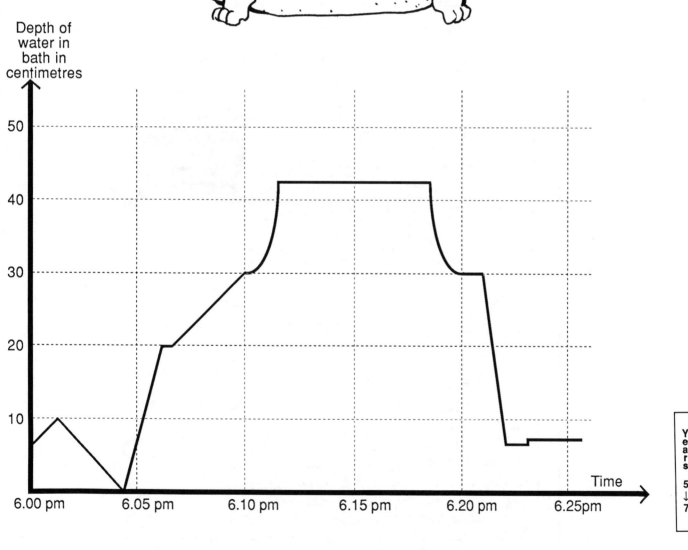

Depth of
water in
bath in
centimetres

50

40

30

20

10

Time

6.00 pm   6.05 pm   6.10 pm   6.15 pm   6.20 pm   6.25pm

Some writings from the trialling of Tell me a story *(Primary) at grade 6m, Whittington P. S. Vic.*

The oo far man   *Joy and Michelle*

A man was at the tip. When he came home he felt all yukky and sticky from being at amongst all the rubbish. He wanted a bath but found the tap had been dripp Ant. The level of the water was about 5cm high. He turned on the tap and the level of the water was at ten cm. The time was 6:03. He did a belly whacker and the water went all over the floor. There was no bath water left in the bath. He ran the water again and it went up to at least 20cm. Then the water runs slow up to 30cm because the plug was not in properly. The big fat man got into the bath and the bath water rises up to about 4. He stays in the bath for until 18 mins past 6. Then he got out and the water went down at about 30cm high. Then he

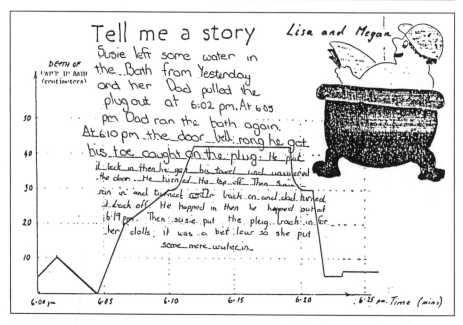

Tell me a story   Lisa and Megan

Susie left some water in the Bath from Yesterday and her Dad pulled the plug out at 6:02 pm. At 6:05 pm Dad ran the bath again. At 6:10 pm the door bell rang he got his toe caught on the plug. He put it back in then he got his towel and answered the door. He turned the tap off. Then Susie ran in and turned water back on and dad turned it back off. He hopped in then he hopped out at 6:19 pm. Then susie put the plug back in for her dolls; it was a bit low so she put some more water in.

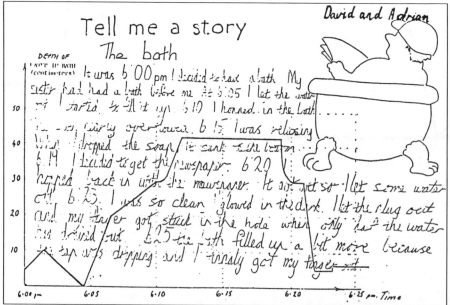

Tell me a story   David and Adrian

The bath

It was 6 00 pm I decided to have a bath. My sister had had a bath before me. At 6:05 I let the water and started to fill it up. 6:10 I hopped in the bath. It was nearly overflowed. 6:15 I was relaxing when I dropped the soap it sank like lead. 6:19 I decided to get the newspaper. 6:20 I hopped back in with the newspaper. It was not wet so I let some water off. 6:25 I was so clean I glowed in the dark. I let the plug out and my finger got stuck in the hole when only half the water had drained out. 6:25 the bath filled up a bit more because the tap was dripping and I finally got my finger out.

Tell me a story (Post Primary)

This group activity revolves around a graph which models cars travelling on a road. There are lots of opportunities for creative interpretation, for talking and sharing, for story telling, and for creative presentation of findings through writing or acting.

Compare this to the typical textbook approach where pupils work individually on a series of one-dimensional exercises. The activity is a powerful illustration of a quite different teaching approach to this topic.

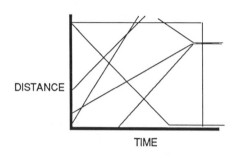

Features of this activity

- The capacity of a graph to model a real situation.
- Groups creatively prepare and present hypothetical stories based on a graph.
- The approach used encourages girls' participation.

- An application of linear graphs.
- The lesson uses group discussion to a large extent.
- Creative group reporting, including verbalisation of mathematical observations.

Preparation

Each pupil needs a copy of the worksheet on page 256.

Comments from trials schools

'It was entertaining for kids and allowed them to be creative.'

'It was a pleasant change from their usual lessons — it made a number of good points in a fun situation.'

'A terrific way to end the topic.'

Pupils act out the happenings of the blue car.

The graph used in this activity is taken from M. Swan (1985), Traffic — an approach to distance-time graphs, *The Language of Education and Graphs*. Nottingham: Joint Matriculation Board and Shell Centre for Mathematical Education, and is reprinted with kind permission.

Years 9 ↓ 10

WRITING

Tell me a story (Post primary)

After a teacher demonstration of method, a graph with many lines representing cars at a particular part of a road, and at a particular time is distributed. Working in groups, pupils discover many things happening, and are asked to tell the story of one of the cars and what a passenger in that car might have seen and done. The approach used in this activity encourages girls to be involved in a context which is usually oriented to boys (i.e. cars).

> A GRAPH CAN TELL YOU A 'STORY' ABOUT AN EVENT.
> THE MATHEMATICS OF THE GRAPH CONTAINS INFORMATION ABOUT THE REALITY OF SOME SITUATION

1. Introduction

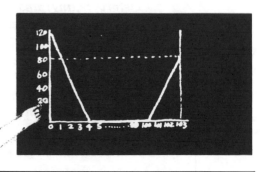

> HERE'S A TELEPHONE BOX BESIDE A ROAD. AND THIS GRAPH REPRESENTS A CAR COMING UP TO THE TELEPHONE BOX

No deceleration or acceleration is incorporated in the graphs. No direction is necessarily implied.

TEACHER-LED DISCUSSION (MAXIMUM 5-10 MINUTES.)

2. What can this graph tell us about the movements of the car?

Bring out concepts of direction, distance, time and speed.

> THE CAR STARTS OUT 120 METRES FROM THE TELEPHONE BOX — IT ARRIVES FOUR SECONDS LATER, TRAVELLING AT 30 METRES PER SECOND.
> AFTER NINETY-SIX SECONDS (MAYBE MAKING A PHONE CALL) THE DRIVER LEAVES AT A SLOWER SPEED OF 20 METRES PER SECOND

Since group work is an important part of the lesson, it is worth emphasising this to pupils.

Structuring group discussion rather than pen and paper questions, allows for open-ended discussion, creative thinking and writing, use of pupils' own language and experiences in car travel. This is particularly valuable for girls.

3. Group discussion

Organise the class into groups of four or five pupils. Hand out copies of the worksheet.

> YOU'VE JUST ANALYSED ONE CAR AND ITS MOTION — HERE IS A SITUATION WITH SEVERAL CARS

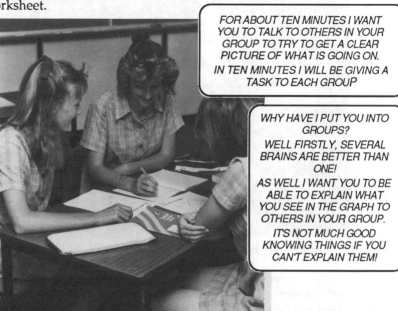

> FOR ABOUT TEN MINUTES I WANT YOU TO TALK TO OTHERS IN YOUR GROUP TO TRY TO GET A CLEAR PICTURE OF WHAT IS GOING ON.
> IN TEN MINUTES I WILL BE GIVING A TASK TO EACH GROUP

The teacher's role during the group discussions.
- Visit each group.
- Encourage pupils to talk about what they can 'see' in the graph.
- Help pupils 'read' such things as speed, cars passing each other, and so on.
- Remind pupils of future tasks.
- Sow the seeds of creative interpretation.

Pupils become increasingly willing to ascribe 'reasons' for the green car travelling three times faster than the 'putt-putt' blue car.

> WHY HAVE I PUT YOU INTO GROUPS?
> WELL FIRSTLY, SEVERAL BRAINS ARE BETTER THAN ONE!
> AS WELL I WANT YOU TO BE ABLE TO EXPLAIN WHAT YOU SEE IN THE GRAPH TO OTHERS IN YOUR GROUP.
> IT'S NOT MUCH GOOD KNOWING THINGS IF YOU CAN'T EXPLAIN THEM!

4. Tasks for each group

After ten minutes, allot a car to each group in the class.

> *YOUR GROUP ARE ALL TRAVELLING IN THE BLUE CAR.*
> *WHAT CAN YOU SEE GOING ON AROUND YOU ... IN FRONT OF THE CAR?*
> *...THROUGH THE REAR VISION MIRRORS?*

> *PREPARE A GROUP REPORT GIVING THE HIGHLIGHTS OF YOUR TRIP FOR THESE FOURTEEN SECONDS.*
> *YOU HAVE TEN MINUTES TO PREPARE THE REPORT.*
> *THEN EACH GROUP WILL HAVE ABOUT TWO MINUTES TO PRESENT IT*

> *MAKE THEM INTERESTING, BUT ACCURATE*

> A sample report could be simulated by the teacher. Such a report could highlight possibilities but should not stifle creativity. Make sure there is enough time for the reports — ten or fifteen minutes for reporting should suffice.

5. Group reports

From your visit to each group, you can make a judicious decision on which group to invite to present the first report.

There is probably no need for every group to present a report. Some will be enthusiastic to do so, but after three reports, remaining groups may prefer to supply additional observations.

> *FOR THE REST OF THE CLASS, YOUR TASKS ARE TO LISTEN FOR ANY INACCURACIES — ESPECIALLY FOR ANY REFERENCES TO THE PARTICULAR CAR TO WHICH YOU WERE ASSIGNED, AND TO JUDGE THE OVERALL ACCURACY OF THE REPORTS*

> While pupils are preparing reports the teacher should visit each group to:
> - ensure that ideas are being recorded,
> - encourage a balance between creativity and mathematical accuracy,
> - stimulate ideas if discussion is slowing down, and encourage all members of the group to share in the presentation, rather than leave it to one spokesperson.

> The assessment used here is informal and non-threatening as the teacher encourages tactful appraisal of the strengths (and any weaknesses of each report).

> Non-competitive assessment allows many girls to feel more comfortable, particularly when considering the subject matter.

Sample reports

a. Pupils presented the report with their chairs arranged to simulate car seats. Each pupil contributed comments.

> *'We left the telephone box and jumped into our green Ferrari and raced off towards home at 36 metres per second (108 km/h).*
> *That blue car twenty metres ahead of us is going pretty slowly!'*
> *Time = 1. (intoned by the car microcomputer)*
> *'As we passed the blue car (30 metres from the phone box) we could see an orange car up ahead, a red car parked by the side of the road, and 50 metres ahead there was this large black truck coming towards us.'*
> *Time = 2 .*
> *'Did you see that orange car nearly sideswipe the parked car as it passed?'*
> *Time = 3 and a bit.*
> *'Hey, look! The red car belongs to Mr. Smith our maths teacher. He's got a flat tyre' (sympathetic mutterings) ... (The saga continues.)*

b. Applying a different approach, one group used the chalkboard ledge and coloured pens to produce a 'puppet show' of the cars in motion.

Extensions
- One school reported some keen pupils producing a computer-graphics picture of the cars in motion.
- Interested groups may like to create another graph, or extend the worksheet graph.

Tell me a story

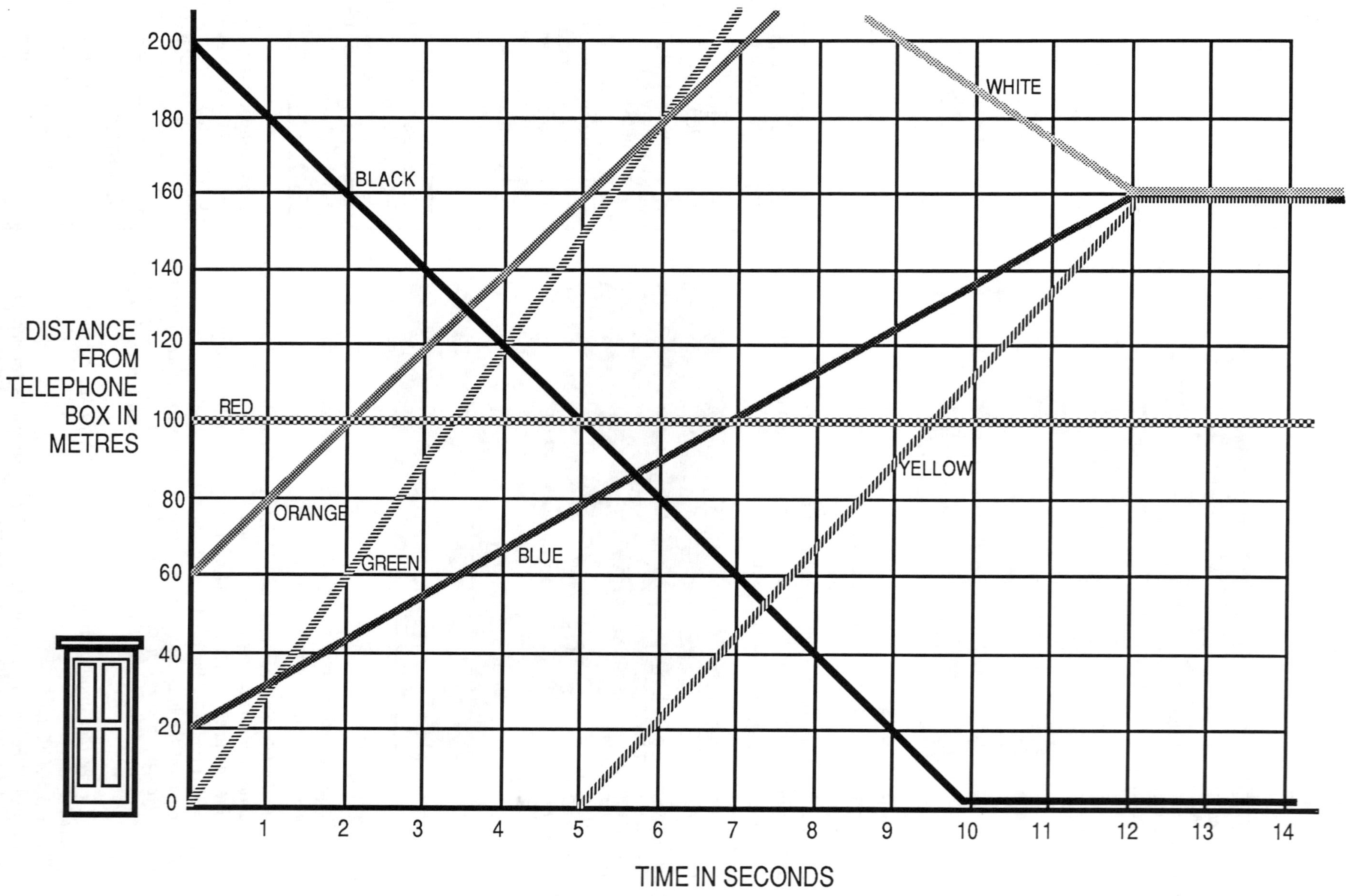

DISTANCE FROM TELEPHONE BOX IN METRES

TIME IN SECONDS

WHITE
BLACK
YELLOW
BLUE
GREEN
ORANGE
RED

Favourite number

Children are invited to think about their favourite number and to write about and illustrate its mathematical properties. This activity enables children to communicate their knowledge of number patterns and properties, in order to expose their understandings or misconceptions, with a view to further discussion with other pupils, the teacher or the whole class. It also encourages teachers to explore the area of children's writing of mathematics, showing how a simple idea can develop into a powerful learning experience.

1. Tell us all about your favourite number

> I WANT YOU TO THINK ABOUT YOUR FAVOURITE NUMBER BETWEEN 1 AND 20.
> IF YOU DON'T HAVE A NUMBER, THEN JUST PICK ONE THAT LOOKS LIKE IT MAY BE INTERESTING

> I WANT YOU TO WRITE AND DRAW ABOUT SOME OF THE THINGS THAT MAKE IT INTERESTING TO YOU.
> IT MAY BE YOUR FAVOURITE BECAUSE ITS YOUR AGE OR SOMETHING LIKE THAT, BUT I BET YOU CAN 'THINK' OF SOME MATHS IDEAS ABOUT IT AS WELL

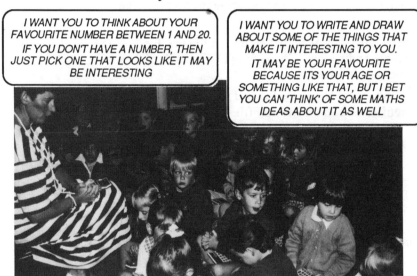

2. Writing about mathematical concepts

Trials teachers encouraged their pupils to also take the same approach to important mathematical concepts. Some examples were 'equals', 'odd', 'even', and 'one half'. Once again, this showed how sophisticated many children's concepts were.

3. Follow-up

Teachers found that the children's writing and illustrations provided a 'springboard' for discussion. The discussion occurred between:

- pupils,
- pupil and teacher,
- teacher and the whole grade.

Through this discussion of their writing and drawing, pupils learnt from each other, and several had misconceptions clarified.

Features of this activity

- Children communicating mathematics through writing and drawing.
- Discussion between pupils and between the teacher and the pupil.
- Open ended structure.

Preparation

A list of mathematical terms could be made for use in step 2.

Trials found that children produced some very articulate and accurate descriptions of the properties of their numbers.

Teachers commented that this activity enabled different children to come to the same task and respond at a wide range of levels.

'Children who often have a negative view of mathematics were pleased to be able to use their language skills in a maths setting.'

'I was pleasantly surprised by their imaginative and insightful creations.'

ST JAMES, HOPPERS CROSSING
GRADE 2

Anne! cam! **12**   27.11.86

The number 12 is the most fantastic number because there is 12 month's in a year. You can divide 12 up into three groups of four. A clock goes up to 12. 12 can be a dozen and when you spell hippopotamus there are only 12 letters in it. the 12th letter in the alphabet is L. Also 30 − 18 = 12 and 12 + 12 = 24. I would say the number 12 is the best number in the hole wide world.

Equals

Equals means like at the end of a sum. It means if I had 3 lollies and you had 3 lollies we would be equal. Equals means the same it also means weighing the same.
By Took and Miranda

Inflationary language

Features
• Creative writing.
• Fun!
• Problem solving.

In this activity, children are encouraged to use Victor Borge's 'Inflationary Language' as a stimulus for creative writing. They generate a list of 'number words', to perform 'operations' on them, and challenge the rest of the class to crack the code. The mathematical content is fairly minimal, but it's a lot of fun!

A brief explanation of the inflationary-language process

In order to synchronise language with the world surrounding us, Victor Borge invented an 'Inflationary Language'.

There are many words in the English language that contain numbers, for example, <u>fore</u>sight, <u>to</u>day, cre<u>ate</u> and so <u>forth</u>. By adding one to each of these numbers, an inflationary language is created.

So that <u>wonderful</u> by adding one would be <u>twoderful</u> and <u>today</u> would be <u>threeday</u>, <u>create</u> would be <u>crenine</u>, and so on and so fifth.

1. Either explain the process of inflationary language, or play a tape recording of the story. Tape reference: Victor Borge, *'Inflationary Language'*, from *Borgering on Genius*, Polydor Ltd.

2. Pupils working in pairs, generate a list of 'number words' — about twenty should be sufficient.

3. By considering these words, pupils decide on a theme that can be developed into a brief story.

4. The story is written 'normally' first.

5. Deciding on a fairly simple operation, such as plus two or minus one, pupils rewrite and illustrate the story in its new form.

6. The pairs read their stories to the class, who are encouraged to 'crack the code' and explain the story.

A sample list of 'number' words

1. wonderful wonder won Juan
2. tootle tulips too to into toot tomb today tonight toupe´
3. free freeze fr' he's a jolly good fellow Mr. Guthrie
4. before California Forbes forehead air-force fort fortitude ford formerly fortunate
8. commemorate create intoxicated relegate great mate gate rebate demonstrate late
9. benign canine quinine nein
10. tennis intend attention tension centenary

Chapter six

Mental arithmetic

Purpose

We need to do more mental mathematics. But many children do not enjoy or learn from traditional mental arithmetic lessons in which they *'write answers to a large number of unrelated brief questions, as a result of which a few feel superior and the rest feel varying degrees of discomfort'* (McIntosh, 1980, p. 14). 'Mentals' are often done only for the purpose of starting a session- not as a special area worthy of attention in its own right.

This chapter encourages teachers to explore a new approach to mental arithmetic, one based on frequent short sessions, with activities which provide interesting and positive experiences for all children.

Rationale

Probably the most important purpose of mathematics teaching identified by teachers and the general community is 'to prepare pupils to solve problems encountered in everyday life'.

In schools, 'numeracy' often only means proficiency with the conventional paper-and-pencil algorithms. These conventional methods have been taught because they are believed to provide life skills that are essential for functioning in the adult world. Yet there is increasing evidence that these are not necessarily the skills that people use in the wider community.

Maier (1977) claimed that adults solve most everyday calculations

> **This confidence (in having command over numbers and mathematical symbols) appears to influence children's general attitude towards mathematics.**

by applying methods quite different from those taught in school mathematics classes. Referring to these unconventional and often untaught procedures as 'folk math', he wrote:

> *Some of the general differences between school math and folk math are clear. One is that school math is largely paper-and-pencil mathematics. Folk mathematicians rely more on mental computations and estimations and on algorithms that lend themselves to mental use. When computations become too difficult or complicated to perform mentally, more and more folk mathematicians are*

turning to calculators and computers. In folk math, paper and pencil are a last resort. Yet they are the mainstay of school math (p. 86).

After identifying the mathematics required in higher education, employment,and general adult life, the authors of the British report *Mathematics Counts* (Cockcroft, 1982) suggested that mental calculation should be given a far more prominent position in mathematics programs than it has been accorded recently. The report concluded that the *'decline of mental and oral work within mathematics classrooms represents a failure to recognise the central place which working "done in the head" occupies throughout mathematics'* (p. 75).

Wandt and Brown (1957) found that at least 75% of adult calculations are mental. In contrast, in mathematics classrooms the reverse is probably the case, with emphasis almost entirely on written computation. One other interesting aspect of this research is that adults were found to do many more mental-exact calculations than mental-approximate ones.

MENTAL

J.A. Hope (1986) has carried out a series of investigations into the main differences between skilled and unskilled mental calculators. He has argued that an over-reliance on written methods can lead to 'calculative monomania' — the tendency to ignore number relationships useful for calculation and, instead, resort to more cumbersome and inappropriate techniques. He cites the following examples.

$$\begin{array}{r} \overset{0\,1}{\cancel{4}} \\ -6 \\ \hline 0\,8 \end{array} \qquad \begin{array}{r} 3\overset{5\,1}{\cancel{6}\cancel{0}} \\ -359 \\ \hline 0\,0\,1 \end{array}$$

$$\begin{array}{r} \overset{9\;9\;9\,1}{\$1\cancel{0}\cancel{0}.\cancel{0}\cancel{0}} \\ -\;99.95 \\ \hline 000.05 \end{array} \qquad \begin{array}{r} 125 \\ \times 1000 \\ \hline 000 \\ 000 \\ 000 \\ 1\,2\,5 \\ \hline 1\,2\,5\,0\,0\,0 \end{array}$$

Although each of these tasks could have been solved by an elementary mental calculation, the conventional algorithm was employed despite its apparent unsuitability. When queried about the lengthy approach to these problems, the pupil replied *'that's what we have to do in school'*.

In contrast, one young skilled mental calculator used the following strategies, which exemplify a strong understanding of the properties of number.

---

8 x 99
I did $800 - 8 = 792$

25 x 480
Well, 25 is 100 divided by 4. So I divided 480 by 4 to get 120 and multiplied that by 100.

23 x 27
I did 25^2, which is 625, and subtracted 2^2, or 4.

While these methods show considerable sophistication, such informal and self-developed methods are in fact widely used by primary children (McIntosh, 1978, 1979). Unfortunately, they are often not given overt emphasis and status in classrooms, so that children sometimes think they are somehow wrong or inferior, when they are often much more appropriate.

Children can perform standard written computational procedures digit by digit without a meaningful holistic view of the numbers or the operations involved. Mental computation and estimation require pupils to look at numbers as compositional wholes and to form flexible strategies for dealing with numbers. Pupils gain a feeling of power over numbers and mathematical symbols. This confidence appears to influence children's general attitude towards mathematics.

(Barnett, 1987, p. 2).

Hope and Sherrill (1987) pointed out that skilled mental calculators make different uses of their long term and short term memory systems from unskilled mental calculators. In a research study they found that 86% of unskilled mental calculators used pencil and paper algorithmic procedures when asked to find, mentally, the value of something like 51 x 49. That is to say, they imagined the numbers set out like

$$\begin{array}{r} 51 \\ \underline{\times 49} \end{array}$$

and proceeded to carry out a long multiplication, only their mind was their piece of paper. By contrast, only about 22% of skilled mental calculators used this method; rather, they tended to adopt a variety of unconventional, but efficient mental strategies like:

$$51 \times 49 = 50 \times 49 + 1 \times 49 = 5 \times 490 + 49$$
$$= 2450 + 49$$
$$= 2499$$
$$\text{or } 51 \times 49 = (51 \times 7) \times 7 = 357 \times 7 = 2100 + 350 + 49$$
$$= 2499$$

Hope calls for a much greater emphasis on mental calculation in the classroom. The focus of instruction, he says, should be on developing a broad knowledge of number properties and relationships useful for calculation purposes.

Textbook authors should provide children with the necessary encouragement to calculate mentally.

Why ask children to use pencil and paper for calculation exercises such as $57 - 8$, $199 + 156$, 1000×26, and $3535 \div 35$?

Children should be encouraged to look for calculation shortcuts and to use pencil and paper, or a calculator, only when absolutely necessary. They should be encouraged to use mental methods to abbreviate their written calculations whenever possible.

(Hope, 1987, p. 340)

Such an emphasis, Hope claims, will lead children to be more efficient calculators with a greater understanding of the structure of numbers. James Hiebert (1987), in an article on *'Decimal fractions'*, asks how pupils will ever learn to give reasonable estimates to decimal calculations (e.g. 6.4×19.8) if they haven't gone beyond 'mental pencil and paper' representations.

It should be noted that the equally important and closely related area of Estimation is the title of another MCTP chapter.

...at least 75% of adult calculations are mental. In contrast, in mathematics classrooms the reverse is probably the case, with emphasis almost entirely on written computation.

The focus of this chapter

The activities described in this chapter are somewhat different from the normal mental arithmetic session which tends to be a series of short, one-step calculations emphasising speed and accuracy, with answers written by the children. This is perfectly valid as part of the program for improving mental computation, but it tends to be a testing rather than a learning activity, and fails to deal with many important features in mental computation, including creating a mental armoury of a variety of methods of approaching computation, using an increasing network of connections between number facts and relationships, the ability to check a result by using a different method, and the ability to perform a string of logical operations mentally rather than a single-step process.

Moreover, the traditional methods neglect the reality of the classroom context of a mixed ability group of children, all of whom need to participate at very different levels and in which it is often the child who most needs reinforcement and involvement who is locked out of the activity. Indeed, it is remarkable how many 'mental arithmetic games' which form a regular (and much enjoyed) classroom activity actually eliminate early the weak and give continued practice to the able — a valid competitive situation but hardly a valid educational one.

The activities contained in this chapter are designed to complement, extend and partly replace traditional mental arithmetic methods and to strengthen those areas neglected by them.

Experiences from trialling

These activities tend to work best under the following arrangements:

• A series of brief sessions — no more than 15 minutes — several times a week with a small group or the whole class.

• Problems or tasks may be written on the board or oral, but the answers must be oral. Any writing will be done by the teacher, thus ensuring that children concentrate on the mental activity.

• It is often better to hear and discuss several answers to a few questions, rather than only hear one answer to a large number of questions.

• It is important to select problems and tasks in which the whole group can become involved, rather than to reinforce the success of some and the sense of failure of others. The activities therefore should be enjoyable and positive learning experiences.

An excerpt from *How did you do it?*

A grade 4 teacher writes the following problem on the board: 46 + 25. Children are asked to solve this problem mentally.

The problems are written across the board, rather than down. Trial schools report that this is more likely to encourage pupils to move from standard algorithmic approaches.

The problems need not be particularly original — the solutions will almost certainly be! Avoid giving too complicated calculations — the purpose is not to see if they can do it, but how they tackle it. However, it shouldn't be so simple that it becomes automatic.

Having firstly agreed on the correct answer, ask for volunteers to explain their methods.

Teachers report that it is important to establish the answer first, (only a side issue); otherwise pupils will be waiting for it. Also, if the first few pupils to answer have impressive methods, but wrong answers, the activity can fall flat. By being fairly casual about the answer (*'so let's just have the answer... fine. Now then let's ...'*), pupils can then really focus on the processes involved.

As the pupils relate their methods, try to summarise these on the board. Teachers need to be careful not to 'rate' these methods.

The criteria for deciding whether a method is okay are:

* **does it work?**
* **is the pupil happy with it?**

'How did you do it?'

Some solutions to 46 + 25

* *Counted on hands:*
46, 47, 48,........71
* *Counted by 20:*
20, 40, 60,.......61, 62, 63,.......71
* *Counted on one hand only:*
46, 47, 48,........71
* *Verbalised:*
  40 + 20 = 60
 6 + 5 = 11,
 60 + 11 = 71

(This boy actually gave two different methods, two minutes apart).

* *Verbalised:*
40 and 20 together are 60,
....counted by ones, 66, 67, 68,
.......71
* *Verbalised:*

4 and 2 are 6, 5 and 6 are 11, so it's 71

Emphasise the variety of interesting, acceptable methods. If there is one that is particularly impressive and pupils understand it, invite them to apply it to another problem.

In summary, congratulate the class on their variety of interesting methods, and point out that most of the maths we use outside the classroom is mental, and these methods will be very useful.

Activities with a Mental Arithmetic component in other chapters

Mathematics of darts and Darts 2 (Ch. 1).

Map of Australia (Ch. 7).

Calculator snooker (Ch. 9).

References

Barnett, C. (1987). *Developing mental math and estimation in early grades.* Paper presented to the National Council of Teachers of Mathematics Annual Conference, Anaheim.

Committee of Inquiry into the Teaching of Mathematics in Schools (1982). *Mathematics counts* (Cockroft Report). London: HMSO, 74-5.

Hiebert, J. (1987). Decimal fractions. *Arithmetic Teacher, 34(7),* 22-23.

Hope, J. A. (1986). Mental calculation: anachronism or basic skill. *Estimation and mental computation,* 1986 Yearbook of the National Council of Teachers of Mathematics. Reston, (Va.): NCTM.

Hope, J.A. (1987). A case study of a highly skilled mental calculator. *Journal for Research in Mathematics Education, 18(5),* 331-343.

Hope, J.A., & Sherrill, J.M. (1987). Characteristics of unskilled and skilled mental calculators. *Journal for Research in the Mathematics Education, 18(2),* 98-111.

Maier, E. (1977). Folk math. *Instructor,* 84-89,92.

McIntosh, A. (1978). Some subtractions: what do you think you are doing? *Mathematics Teaching, 83(2),* 17-19.

McIntosh, A. (1979). Some children and some multiplications. *Mathematics Teaching, 87(2),* 14-15.

McIntosh, A. (1980). Mental mathematics--some suggestions. *Mathematics Teaching, 91(2),* 14-15.

Wandt, E. & Brown, G.W. (1957). Non-occupational uses of mathematics. *Arithmetic Teacher, 4,* 151-54.

MCTP gratefully acknowledges the major contribution of Alistair McIntosh in the development and documentation of the activities in this chapter.

Sum stories

Some times it is hard to relate the learning tasks in mathematics to real-life situations. This activity turns that problem around by presenting a calculation to children and challenging them to invent real-life situations in which the calculations might arise. This has the effect of letting children see the relevance of mathematics and think about applications for their school work. For teachers it helps to give meaning to courses which sometimes appear less-than relevant.

Features of this activity

- Emphasises relevance of arithmetic to real life.
- Shows that the same symbols can refer to many different situations.
- Encourages creativity by children
- Motivates and involves children of a wide ability range.
- Can be used regularly without repetition.
- Leads to discussion between teacher and children.
- Provides useful assessment information for teacher.

To make mental arithmetic lessons most effective

Considerable trialling in schools has shown that these mental arithmetic activities tend to work best under the following arrangements:

- A series of brief sessions — no more than 15 minutes — several times a week with a small group or the whole class.

- Problems or tasks may be written on the board or given orally but the answers must be oral. Any writing will be done by the teacher, thus ensuring that children concentrate on the mental activity.

- It is often better to hear and discuss several answers to a few questions, rather than only hear one answer to a large number of questions.

- It is important to select problems and tasks in which the whole group can become involved, rather than ones which reinforce the success of some and the sense of failure in others. The activities therefore should be enjoyable and positive learning experiences.

Comments from trial schools:

'I thought the children would have given a wider range of situations. But when the activity was repeated, more creative ideas flowed.'

'Children were initially slow to suggest stories. However, after the first couple, everyone was keen to participate and share their stories. The second session was even more successful, as the children knew what was expected of them. Stories were more varied and the process was often reversed. For example 3 + 4 = 7 to 7 = 3 +... or 4 + ... = 7'

THIS ACTIVITY IS PART OF THE MCTP PROFESSIONAL DEVELOPMENT PACKAGE FROM THE CURRICULUM DEVELOPMENT CENTRE, CANBERRA

Years 3 ↓ 6

MENTAL

Sum stories

The teacher writes a calculation on the chalkboard and children suggest a variety of 'real-life' situations in which the calculation would occur. This activity challenges pupils (and teachers) to relate daily computations to their applications.

Introduction

> WE ALL USE NUMBERS (SUMS ARITHMETIC, MATHEMATICS AND CALCULATIONS) TO HELP US FIND THE ANSWER TO PROBLEMS IN REAL LIFE.
> FOR EXAMPLE, I BUY A CHOCOLATE BAR FOR 45 CENTS AND I GIVE 50 CENTS.
> HOW MUCH CHANGE DO I EXPECT?
> WHAT CALCULATIONS DO I HAVE TO DO?

> OFTEN WE CONCENTRATE ON ANSWERS, BUT FOR TODAY'S LESSON, ANSWERS ARE NOT VERY IMPORTANT.
> I'M GOING TO ASK YOU TO THINK REALLY HARD ABOUT WHERE ELSE A PROBLEM LIKE THIS MAY COME UP

$$50 - 45 =$$

> FIVE CENTS

> 50 TAKE 45

It is important that the focus of the activity is on the situation, not on the answer to the calculation. Bring in the answer at this stage, either by giving it yourself, *'The answer is five, but that's not important at the moment'* or by asking the class to supply it *'Before we go on to this morning's challenge'*.

> NOW SUPPOSE I'M PLAYING CRICKET AND I'VE SCORED 45. HOW MANY RUNS DO I NEED TO REACH 50?

> WHAT DO YOU NOTICE?

$$50 - 45 =$$

> FIVE

> IT'S THE SAME CALCULATION AS FOR THE CHOCOLATE PROBLEM

Posing the problem

Make sure everyone is involved by giving the children the responsibility of deciding whether each story fits the calculation.

Note that 'real life' situations include space pictures, fantasy and all the make-believes or ridiculous situations which are a 'real' part of children's lives.

If children produce two or three stories on the same theme (money and lollies seem to appear frequently), get a change of direction by asking: *'Who can think of a different kind of story which fits?'* or *'Who can think of a story about ... animals, sport, home ...?'*

> NOW, WHO CAN THINK OF ANOTHER SITUATION TO WHICH THIS CALCULATION ON THE BOARD MIGHT REFER — SOME MORE TIMES WHEN I WOULD NEED TO WORK OUT 50 – 45?

> WHO AGREES WITH THAT ONE? EVERYONE? WELL DONE JOHN

> QUITE RIGHT ELIZABETH. NOW, CAN WE THINK OF ONE THAT ISN'T ABOUT MONEY?

> THERE WERE 50 CHILDREN AND 45 WERE GIRLS. HOW MANY WERE BOYS?

> MY DAD IS 45 YEARS OLD. HOW LONG BEFORE HE IS 50?

> I HAD 50 MARBLES BUT NOW I ONLY HAVE 45. HOW MANY HAVE I LOST?

> I HAD 50 CENTS AND I SPENT 45 CENTS. HOW MUCH DO I HAVE LEFT?

> *'There is a high level of involvement. Some very humorous, creative responses.'*

Developing and assessing the situation

Provided the calculation is at the appropriate level and of the kind which children use, or have been using in your class, suggestions should flow readily. If they do not, it is a clear, and useful, indication that the children have difficulty in relating that particular abstract calculation to real life. This should be remedied either at once or by planning in subsequent lessons.

If children's responses are restricted in some way, this is another useful indication of where adjustments should be made. For example in the subtraction situation described, it is common for children to offer many 'take away' situations but very few 'comparing' situations. ('I have 50 Swap cards, Jason's only got 45. How many more do I have?') This may indicate that children have not been given many comparison problems, or that the associated language does not come as readily to them.

> *'I tried to make a conscious effort to involve all the class, both boys and girls over a number of sessions.'*

Incorrect responses are also useful openings for discussion by children. How many notice it is incorrect? What calculation is appropriate for that story? Could it be adapted to make it correct?

Do not let the session drag on too long. Usually five to ten stories are enough for any particular example.

Examples of calculations which have been used at different levels

4 + 3	6 x 3
87 + 92	57 x 1.42 (a calculator was used to establish the answers),
1 + ½	18 ÷ 3
7 − 4	21 ÷ 4
1.5 − 0.5	½ x ½

However any calculation which children are handling in your class can be treated in this way. *(If it can't, it might be wise to consider why the children are doing it.)*

> *'I've really had to rethink some of my content, when the class and I realised that we couldn't find examples to which it related. For example, some of the fractions, decimals etc.'*

Apart from the informal assessment mentioned, children could be asked occasionally to write down 3 to 5 situations ('as varied as possible') relating to a given calculation.

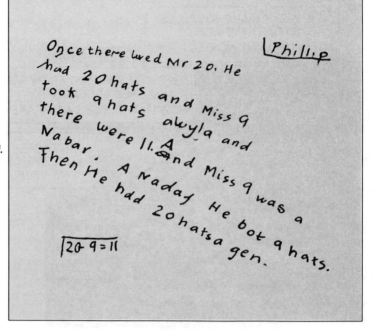

Phillip, grade 2, shows that he not only realises that 20 − 9 = 11, but also that (20 − 9) + 9 = 20.

Once there lived Mr 20. He had 20 hats and Miss 9 took 9 hats akyla and there were 11. And Miss 9 was a Nabar. A Naday He bot 9 hats. Then He had 20 hatsa gen.

20 − 9 = 11

Here Phillip gives a pictorial version of his story for 20 − 9 = 11.

These samples are by courtesy of the Association of Independent Schools of Victoria and the Catholic Education Office of Victoria — taken from G. Del Campo and M. A. Clements (1987), *A manual for the professional development of beginning mathmaticians.*

The sum combined with the vernacular 'I reckon' indicate the non-threatening nature of this approach.

6 − 5 = 4

ST JAMES
(HOPPERS CROSSING)

Belinda.
GRADE PREP

my mum got me six cakes and I ate 2 cakes and tbhat leaves for 1 reckon

Today's number is...

This activity is designed to open up the range of learning experiences by turning the calculation around — telling the children the answer and challenging them to invent the question.

And since there is an infinite number of possibilities the teacher can focus on any type of calculation he or she chooses for the class.

Features of this activity

- Allows participation in computation at level of individual children.
- Encourages creative thinking with numbers by children.

- Very flexible and adaptable by teacher.
- Encourages discussion between teacher and children.
- Can be used daily without repetition.

To make mental arithmetic lessons most effective

Considerable trialling in schools has shown that these mental arithmetic activities tend to work best under the following arrangements:

- A series of brief sessions — no more than 15 minutes — several times a week with a small group or the whole class.

- Problems or tasks may be written on the board or given orally but the answers must be oral. Any writing will be done by the teacher, thus ensuring that children concentrate on the mental activity.

- It is often better to hear and discuss several answers to a few questions, rather than only hear one answer to a large number of questions.

- It is important to select problems and tasks in which the whole group can become involved, rather than ones which reinforce the success of some and the sense of failure in others. The activities therefore should be enjoyable and positive learning experiences.

Comments from trials schools

'Less able children are keen to participate because they are able to do so at a level that is comfortable for them. More able children really enjoy giving examples that show clearly their understanding and ability.'

'I enjoy these sessions because the children's involvement is high, and I never know exactly where the session will end up. Sometimes wonderful things can result from the activity that require extra time to be spent on follow-up activities. It may involve children in predicting and testing their predictions using calculators or whatever.'

THIS ACTIVITY IS PART OF THE MCTP
PROFESSIONAL DEVELOPMENT PACKAGE FROM THE
CURRICULUM DEVELOPMENT CENTRE, CANBERRA

Years 4 ↓ 7 **MENTAL**

Today's number is...

The teacher writes a number on the chalkboard. Children create a question for which this number is the answer.

The teacher writes these calculations in a carefully ordered way and structures subsequent responses and discussion.

Introduction

The purpose of this is to relax the children so that even the least confident will feel able to offer a simple calculation without fear of being ridiculed, while making all children see that they have a role to play even when another child is offering a calculation.

YOU ARE PROBABLY USED TO ME ASKING THE QUESTIONS AND YOU WORKING OUT THE ANSWERS.

TODAY WE'LL DO IT THE OTHER WAY ROUND.

I'M GOING TO WRITE AN ANSWER ON THE BOARD AND YOU GIVE ME QUESTIONS TO WHICH THAT IS THE ANSWER.

I'LL WRITE YOUR QUESTIONS ON THE BOARD AS YOU GIVE THEM.

YOU CAN MAKE THEM AS SIMPLE OR AS COMPLICATED AS YOU LIKE, BUT WE'LL STICK TO CALCULATIONS ONLY

OH YES, AND IF YOUR CALCULATION DOESN'T GIVE THIS ANSWER, I'LL BE SO BUSY WRITING IT UP THAT I PROBABLY WON'T NOTICE. SO IT'S UP TO ALL OF YOU TO SPOT THE MISTAKES FOR ME

Starting off the activity

RIGHT! NOW TODAY'S NUMBER IS 15.
WHO CAN GIVE ME A CALCULATION TO WHICH THE ANSWER IS 15?
YES MINH?

10 + 5 ...I'LL WRITE THAT UP.
I HOPE YOU ARE CHECKING TO SEE THAT IT'S RIGHT, BECAUSE I'LL WRITE IT UP UNLESS YOU TELL ME NOT TO.
ANOTHER?

12 + 3... 9 + 6... 16- 1...AH, THAT'S A DIFFERENT ONE, I'LL WRITE THAT IN ANOTHER COLUMN

...4 x 2 + 7...THAT'S AN INTERESTING ONE, SUE.
I HOPE SOMEONE'S CHECKING IT

The teacher's role here is to encourage participation by the reticent pupils and adventurousness by the confident ones, without putting undue emphasis on either, while abdicating the role of checking the calculation entirely to the children. If a wrong calculation is unchecked, it is best not to point it out immediately (thus taking over the role from the children) but to put it on the blackboard and then, a little later, say *'I think one of these isn't right. Has anyone spotted it?'*

Structure the placing of the children's calculations on the board so as to cluster similar types of responses together for future developments. It has been found most convenient to group them under the headings shown below.

After 15 to 20 responses have been accepted, the chalkboard may look something like this:

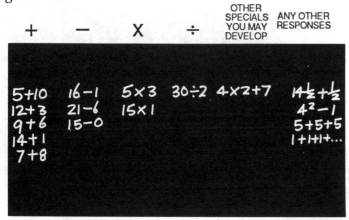

'The children love it. They become very engrossed in working out complicated equations — trying to catch their teacher unawares. They often use fractions, decimals and powers. They would go on forever if given the opportunity,'

Developing the activity

At this point the teacher may decide to put some restrictions on the responses and to concentrate on one of the groups. The following suggestions have all proved fruitful with children: it is not suggested that more than one of these be followed up on any one day.

Note that at no time has the teacher explained why these have all been placed together. It is up to the children to make the connection.

Possibility 1 (Additions)

The teacher's role here is the (difficult) one of being neutral and drawing out reasons for opinions from the class, and an agreed solution for this occasion. It would be quite reasonable for tomorrow's decision to be different.

NOW BEFORE WE GO ON, DO YOU THINK WE CAN GO ON FINDING MORE ONES LIKE THIS FOREVER?

HOW MANY DIFFERENT ONES DO YOU THINK THERE ARE?
I'LL GIVE YOU A MINUTE OR SO TO MAKE UP YOUR MINDS, THEN EVERYONE MUST GIVE THEIR OPINION.
RIGHT! ANY OFFERS? JIM?

ANY MORE?
NOW WHO AGREES WITH JIM?

WITH MARIA...?
JIM, YOU DEFEND YOUR ANSWER

SO MOST OF YOU AGREE WITH LINDA...
YES ROB?

WHAT DO WE THINK ABOUT THAT?

Possibility 2 (Subtractions)

SOME MORE LIKE THESE PLEASE

HOW MANY DO YOU THINK THERE ARE LIKE THESE?

$21 - 6,... 15 - 0,... 25 - 10$

WE CALL THAT AN INFINITE NUMBER

HUNDREDS
THOUSANDS

$115 - 100$

ONE MILLION AND FIFTEEN TAKE ONE MILLION

A TRILLION TRILLION AND 15 TAKE...

15.1 TAKE 0.1?

WHY SHOULDN'T WE ALLOW DECIMALS?

In one trials school, fascinating discussion arose as to whether 5 x 3 is the same as 3 x 5. Following a lively discussion, the teacher challenged the group to make up stories about these two which might indicate the difference. (See the MCTP activity *Sum stories* for more information on this approach.)

Possibility 3 (Multiplications)

Possibility 4 (Divisions)

Possibility 5 (Combinations)

Other possibilities

A major aim and outcome is to *expand* the awareness of pupils of the range of possibilities, yet to do this in a non-threatening manner.

Developing and assessing

This idea can be used two or three times a week (for about 15 minutes a session), using a different number each day and developing a different aspect depending on the responses of the children. *It is important not to impose a direction or to continue with the activity if interest begins to wane.*

You can get an idea of the value to individual children of this activity by getting them to write as many calculations as they can in a given time which makes a given number. If you do this at intervals, you can assess whether the number and range of ideas increases.

Extensions for secondary

The idea could be extended for older pupils in many ways.

e.g. If $a + ab$ is the answer, what is the question?

How did you do it?

This activity, which is suitable for pupils of any age from middle primary upwards, encourages pupils to verbalise their reasoning as they mentally solve a problem. Pupils (and teachers) are frequently surprised by the variety and sophistication of the methods articulated by this process. Pupils are able to 'watch themselves thinking', see that there are many (successful) ways to tackle problems, and that they use different sorts of approaches when pen and paper are not available or necessary.

Features of this activity

- Children are encouraged to explore many strategies.
- Group discussion and learning.
- Appropriate mental arithmetic strategies are used.
- Non-threatening.

To make mental arithmetic lessons most effective

Considerable trialling in schools has shown that these mental arithmetic activities tend to work best under the following arrangements:

- A series of brief sessions — no more than 15 minutes — several times a week with a small group or the whole class.

- Problems or tasks may be written on the board or given orally but the answers must be oral. Any writing will be done by the teacher, thus ensuring that children concentrate on the mental activity.

- It is often better to hear and discuss several answers to a few questions, rather than only hear one answer to a large number of questions.

- It is important to select problems and tasks in which the whole group can become involved, rather than ones which reinforce the success of some and the sense of failure in others. The activities therefore should be enjoyable and positive learning experiences.

THIS ACTIVITY IS PART OF THE MCTP PROFESSIONAL DEVELOPMENT PACKAGE FROM THE CURRICULUM DEVELOPMENT CENTRE, CANBERRA

I ASKED JOHNNIE MISS

How did you do it?

The teacher gives a mental arithmetic problem and the answer is quickly established. Then children are asked to describe the strategies they used. The ensuing discussion tends to give children confidence to use mental arithmetic and expand their repertoire of strategies.

The teacher will need to consider carefully the level of difficulty. Children will be attempting to solve it mentally. Some possibilities might be 37 + 15 (adding and subtracting two-digit numbers), or 23 x 4 (multiply or divide by a one-digit number), or 1 + 2 + 3 + 4 + 5 + 6 + 7 + 8 + 9 + 10 (or variations of these).

Teachers report that it is important to establish the answer first, (the correct answer is only a side issue) otherwise pupils will be waiting for it. Also, if the first few pupils to answer have impressive methods, but are wrong, the activity can fall flat. By being fairly casual about the answer ('So let's just have the answer..... fine, now then let's ......'), pupils can then really focus on the processes involved.

Write the problems <u>across</u> the board, rather than down. Trial schools report that this is more likely to encourage pupils to move from standard algorithmic approaches.

Write a problem on the chalkboard.

The problem need not be particularly creative, the interest lies in the methods of solution, which often turn out to be surprisingly creative. Avoid giving calculations which are too complicated — the purpose is not to see if they can do it, but **how** they tackle it. However, don't make the problem so simple that the answer becomes automatic. The example shown below is suitable for year 3.

Having agreed on the correct answer first (*'Everyone say what the answer is'*), ask for volunteers to explain their methods.

As the pupils relate their methods, try to summarise these on the board. Teachers need to be careful not to 'rate' these methods. The criteria for deciding whether a method is OK are:

- Does it work?
- Is the pupil happy with it?

TODAY I'M NOT AS INTERESTED IN THE ANSWER — WHAT IS IT BY THE WAY?... 71.
OKAY, BUT RATHER IN ALL THE DIFFERENT WAYS YOU DID IT IN YOUR HEADS

$46 + 25 =$

Some of the strategies pupils at trials schools used

Counting fingers on
one or two hands.

46,47 48,........71

Counting by 20's.

20, 40, 60,.......61, 62, 63,.......71

*FORTY AND TWENTY ARE SIXTY.
SIX AND FIVE ARE ELEVEN.
SIXTY AND ELEVEN ARE SEVENTY-ONE*

*FORTY AND TWENTY
TOGETHER ARE SIXTY.
66, 67, 68,...71*

This child actually gave two
different methods, two minutes apart.

*FOUR AND TWO ARE SIX.
FIVE AND SIX ARE ELEVEN,
SO IT'S SEVENTY-ONE*

*CONGRATULATIONS ON THE
VARIETY OF INTERESTING
METHODS YOU FOUND.
MOST OF THE MATHS WE
USE OUTSIDE THE
CLASSROOM IS MENTAL,
YOU WILL FIND THESE
METHODS VERY USEFUL*

$46 + 25 =$

Emphasise the variety of interesting, **acceptable** methods. If there is
one that is particularly impressive and pupils understand it, invite
them to quickly apply it to another problem. But avoid the
temptation to then launch into another complete lesson on this subject.
Children find these kinds of extension ideas helpful, but mental
arithmetic should be presented in short bursts.

'At first the children view the answer as all-important. It takes a few sessions before they realise that it is the method used that is under consideration. I believe this is a very valuable teaching strategy because children are exposed to different ways of doing a particular computation.'

As we explain our methods to others, we clarify our own understandings. How often do teachers testify to not having understood a concept until they had to teach it.

Most children and adults carrying out an addition in their heads choose to add the units last, unlike the standard algorithm.

'Children were totally absorbed. They were quite interested in seeing how other children obtained their answers — they contributed their procedures willingly.'

'Many have dropped less-efficient methods and are now employing better ones with confidence. Without this valuable discussion between children, this would not have occurred.'

A concern of teachers that this process could confuse children was not evident in trial schools. Children will only take on a new method if it is easier to understand and they feel they can use it.

'I lke the way children clearly learned new approaches. Yet this happened apparently informally and in a non-threatening atmosphere.'

Years 3↓8   MENTAL

Other examples

The next two examples outline a range of typical responses to the given problems.

In one trials school, a fascinating discussion arose as to why 7 x 16 could not be 113.

The random spread of the numbers encourages a variety of methods.

In summary

This activity illustrates a variety of acceptable methods, it gives children a chance to watch themselves thinking, they realise that they have perfect control over the methods they use in their head, and it encourages them to use mental arithmetic on occasions when they might otherwise have reached for the pen and paper algorithm.

Think of a number

Children are asked to think of any number between one and ten. Then the teacher gives a succession of arithmetical operations to perform on the number and, to the surprise of the children, tells them the resultant number.

The beauty of these exercises is that they can be tackled at many levels, and the apparent 'magic' provides excellent motivation for analysing what is really happening.

Many primary teachers have commented that teaching this activity gave them a new confidence in approaching algebra and helped to generate a wealth of other suitable pre-algebra activities.

Features of this activity

- Stimulating to children, promotes curiosity.
- Can be adapted to practise a variety of mental computation.
- Children can choose a number according to their confidence.
- Can lead to valuable follow-up work, leading to patterns of numbers and early algebraic ideas.
- Allows teachers to find a (rare) use for algebra.
- Very brief and useful to fill one to five minute gaps.

To make mental arithmetic lessons most effective

Considerable trialling in schools has shown that these mental arithmetic activities tend to work best under the following arrangements:

- A series of brief sessions — no more than 15 minutes — several times a week with a small group or the whole class.

- Problems or tasks may be written on the board or given orally but the answers must be oral. Any writing will be done by the teacher, thus ensuring that children concentrate on the mental activity.

- It is often better to hear and discuss several answers to a few questions, rather than only hear one answer to a large number of questions.

- It is important to select problems and tasks in which the whole group can become involved, rather than ones which reinforce the success of some and the sense of failure in others. The activities therefore should be enjoyable and positive learning experiences.

Comments from trials schools
'Perhaps one of the most valuable aspects of this activity is the lead up to patterns of number and the applications of simple algebra.'

'This activity allows children to work on the one activity at different levels depending on the number selected. Very able children in my class enjoy investigating the patterns of numbers to see why it "works" in later follow-up activities.'

Years 4 ↓ 8

MENTAL

Think of a number

Children think of a number between one and ten. The teacher gives a succession of arithmetical operations which children perform on their numbers. To the surprise of the children, the teacher gives the answer everybody has (or should have achieved). Discussion follows on the reasons for what is observed.

'Do you think I can make you all think of the same number?'

> EACH OF YOU THINK OF A NUMBER BETWEEN ONE AND TEN.
> YOU CAN START WITH ANY NUMBER, BUT I'M GOING TO MAKE YOU THINK OF EIGHT.
> DO YOU THINK I CAN DO IT?
> ... NOW, ARE YOU READY FOR MY INSTRUCTIONS?
> DON'T FORGET YOUR NUMBER !

> ADD EIGHT TO YOUR NUMBER.
> TAKE AWAY THE NUMBER YOU FIRST THOUGHT OF.
> EVERYONE WILL TELL ME WHAT YOU ARE THINKING OF **TOGETHER**

> ..EIGHT! YES ISN'T THAT SURPRISING?

> EIGHT!

The effect of calling out the number together adds to the impact.

> HERE'S A MORE COMPLICATED ONE

> THINK OF A NUMBER BETWEEN ONE AND TEN.
> MULTIPLY YOUR NUMBER BY THREE.
> ADD SIX.
> TAKE AWAY THE NUMBER YOU FIRST THOUGHT OF.
> DIVIDE BY TWO.
> TAKE AWAY THE NUMBER YOU FIRST THOUGHT OF

> NOW ALL TOGETHER — THE ANSWER YOU HAVE IS...

> ISN'T THAT SURPRISING?

> THREE !!!

'It was amazing to observe the excitement and interest that this simple trick generated. It was a great basis on which to build what was to follow.'

> DID YOU ALL START WITH THE SAME NUMBER?

> HOW DID I MAKE YOU THINK OF THREE? ANY IDEAS?...

> WE'LL LOOK INTO THAT LATER. MEANTIME, THINK OF A NUMBER BETWEEN ONE AND TEN

> I HAD FOUR

> I HAD SEVEN

Trials schools found that a brief discussion here was appropriate and that the children were excellent at verbalising their explanations.

To start at the finish

The remainder of this activity contains some simple and adaptable examples, gradually increasing in complexity and adaptability. But first, let us take the example used in the previous paragraph and look at it further, looking at what happens to different numbers if chosen.

	WHAT HAPPENS TO PARTICULAR NUMBERS			WHAT HAPPENS TO x
a. Think of a number	2	5	7	x
b. Multiply by 3	6	15	21	3x
c Add 6	12	21	27	3x + 6
d. Take away your number	10	16	20	2x + 6
e. Divide by 2	5	8	10	x + 3
f. Take away your number	3	3	3	3

We see that all three numbers chosen produce 3 at the end. But, more importantly, look at the last column. Here x is chosen, which simply means 'any number'. If you have some remnants of algebra left, you can follow the effect of each instruction on x, and verify that it also produces 3. That is, start with any number and you will end in 3. Any number at all, not just numbers between 1 and 10. If you have a calculator, try 17, 143, 73.1. They will all produce 3.

From here on there are varieties of specific instructions which will work for you. In each case, the algebra of the instructions is given, and if you follow these, you will soon be able to make up instructions of your own. If you don't like the algebra, simply ignore it and use the sets of instructions given. Check them yourself first by choosing a number and going through the computation. This will help you to decide if they are sufficiently easy or complex for your class.

Some of the later ones, which use two numbers, are very surprising indeed.

Some examples that work

1   a. Think of a number   x
       b. Multiply by 2   2x
       c. Add the number you thought of   3x
       d. Divide by the number you thought of —
           Answer is 3.   3

       (In b, you can give the instruction to multiply by another number instead of 2. The result will be one more than this number).

2.   a. Think of a number   x
       b. Multiply by 2   2x
       c. Add 4   2x + 4
       d. Divide by 2   x + 2
       e. Take away the number you thought of —
           Answer is 2.   2

3.   (This is the general case of number 2)

       a. Think of a number   x
       b. Multiply by (any number you select)   nx
       c. Add (twice the number you selected in b)   nx + 2n [= n(x + 2)]
       d. Divide by (number selected in b)   x + 2
       e. Take away the number you thought of —
           Answer is 2.   2

Years 4 → 8

MENTAL

4. a. Think of a number x
    b. Add 6 $x + 6$
    c. Multiply by 2 $2x + 12$
    d. Add the number you thought of $3x + 12$
    e. Divide by 3 $x + 4$
    f. Take away the number you thought of —
       Answer is 4.   4

5. a. Think of a number x
    b. Multiply it by itself x^2
    c. Take away one $x^2 - 1 = (x + 1)(x - 1)$
    d. Divide by one less less than your number $x + 1$
    e. Take away your number — Answer is 1.   1

6. a. Choose any number x
    b. Add the next number $x + (x + 1) = (2x + 1)$
    c. Add 9 $2x + 10$
    d. Divide by 2 $x + 5$
    e. Take away your number — Answer is 5.   5

7. a. Choose any two numbers between 1 and 9 a, b
    b. Multiply the first by 5 $5a$
    c. Add the second number. $5a + b$
    d. Double the result. $10a + 2b$
    e. Take away the second number —
       Answer contains your two numbers in order. $10a + b$

8. a. Choose two numbers less than 10 a, b
    b. Multiply the first by 5 $5a$
    c. Add 7 $5a + 7$
    d. Multiply the result by 2 $10a + 14$
    e. Add the second number $10a + b + 14$
    f. Take away 14 — Answer contains your two
       numbers in order. $10a + b$

How to make up your own

Provided your algebra could cope with the last section, you can make up your own, in this way:

   a. Think of a number x
   b. Add 5 $x + 5$
      No particular reason for choosing 5
   c. Multiply by 3 $3x + 15$
      Again no particular reason. But now we look at
      the resulting algebra, $3x + 15$. At some stage we
      want to divide this by some number to bring the
      total down. We don't want to divide by 3 since
      we have just multiplied by 3. We notice that
      adding the original number would produce
      $4x + 15$, and in order to divide by 4, we would
      then need to alter the 15 to a number divisible
      by 4. *One possibility is:*
   d. Add the number you thought of $4x + 15$
   e. Take away 3 $4x + 12$
   f. Divide by 4 $x + 3$
      *Now we can take away our number and leave
      the 3*
   g. Take away the number you thought of —
      Answer is 3.   3

More than, less than

Pupils estimate a variety of distances and other measures by 'bracketing' their estimates. Group consensus is required at each stage. Pupils are encouraged to articulate their reasoning. The power of outer limits when estimating is exposed. This activity has potential for extension into time, volume, capacity and area, and so encourages teachers to take a structured, detailed approach and apply it in a range of other areas.

Features of this activity

- Group challenge, discussion and decision making.
- Encourages articulation of mathematical concepts.

- Estimation.
- Involves mental imagery – relating sizes of things to objects of known size.

To make mental arithmetic lessons most effective

Considerable trialling in schools has shown that these mental arithmetic activities tend to work best under the following arrangements:

- A series of brief sessions — no more than 15 minutes — several times a week with a small group or the whole class.

- Problems or tasks may be written on the board or given orally but the answers must be oral. Any writing will be done by the teacher, thus ensuring that children concentrate on the mental activity.

- It is often better to hear and discuss several answers to a few questions, rather than only hear one answer to a large number of questions.

- It is important to select problems and tasks in which the whole group can become involved, rather than ones which reinforce the success of some and the sense of failure in others. The activities therefore should be enjoyable and positive learning experiences.

THIS ACTIVITY IS PART OF THE MCTP
PROFESSIONAL DEVELOPMENT PACKAGE FROM THE
CURRICULUM DEVELOPMENT CENTRE, CANBERRA

A comment from a trials teacher.
'Excellent — why didn't someone come up with this years ago?'

More than, less than

Children are asked to look at the length of a room and give upper and lower limits of a measurement. These are gradually narrowed to a range with which the whole class agrees.

Why we need to have good estimation skills

> WE OFTEN NEED TO ESTIMATE.
> SOMETIMES OUR ESTIMATES ARE VERY PRECISE, OTHER TIMES ONLY ROUGH BOUNDS ARE GIVEN.
> FOR INSTANCE, HOW LONG WOULD IT TAKE TO GET TO MY FRIEND'S HOUSE?
> YOU MIGHT SAY, I'LL BE THERE BETWEEN ONE AND TWO O'CLOCK.
> WILL I HAVE ENOUGH MONEY FOR THE THINGS I'VE CHOSEN ONCE I GET TO THE CHECKOUT?
> YOU WILL ESTIMATE IT'LL COST BETWEEN $15 AND $20 AND SO ON

> WE ARE GOING TO DEVELOP A NUMBER OF ESTIMATES OF THIS KIND, WHERE WE BRACKET OUR ESTIMATES, THAT IS, FIND AN AGREED RANGE.
> IT MIGHT SEEM FAIRLY ROUGH, BUT YOU MAY BE SURPRISED HOW ACCURATE IT TURNS OUT TO BE

It is essential to produce a very small starting lower bound, in order for the activity to fulfill its potential. Trial schools have found that expressions like *'if your life depended on it'* help to convey the message that you are looking for an extreme lower bound. Other teachers have actually started the ball rolling: *'Well, it's obviously greater than one metre and less than a million metres.'*

This consensus builds up a 'team approach' to the problem.

An easily-agreed-upon lower limit

Identify a distance inside or outside the classroom. The length of the classroom side wall may be a good starting point.

> CAN YOU GIVE ME A MEASUREMENT THAT IS CERTAINLY LESS THAN THE LENGTH OF THIS ROOM?

> DOES EVERYONE AGREE THAT THE ROOM IS **DEFINITELY** LONGER THAN ONE METRE?
> (One hopes so!)

> ONE METRE (giggle)

An easily-agreed-upon upper limit

> BETTY, CAN YOU GIVE ME A MEASUREMENT THAT IS CERTAINLY MORE THAN THE ROOM'S LENGTH?

> IS EVERYONE HAPPY WITH THAT?
> SO, EVERYONE AGREES THAT THE LENGTH OF THE CLASSROOM IS BETWEEN ONE AND ONE HUNDRED METRES

> ONE HUNDRED METRES

Emphasise that this is *absolutely* true, i.e. this answer is correct, even though we will 'come closer' in good time. Write the numbers on the chalkboard as shown above.

Explain why you say that

Encourage pupils to justify their answers. Attempting to explain our reasoning in maths helps to clarify our understanding or lack of it.

> JENNY, WOULD YOU LIKE TO IMPROVE ONE OF THOSE ESTIMATES

> WHY DO YOU SAY SO? CAN YOU CONVINCE THE REST OF THE CLASS?

> IS THERE ANYONE WHO IS <u>NOT</u> HAPPY WITH THAT?

> I'M SURE THAT THE DISTANCE IS LESS THAN 50 METRES

Children may want to pace out the length, or use similar physical strategies. But explain that part of the challenge here is to estimate by comparing to mental pictures of lengths well known to them.

An acceptable range

> VINCE, IT'S YOUR TURN

> DOES EVERYONE AGREE WITH THAT?

> I THINK IT'S DEFINITELY MORE THAN THREE METRES

If an estimate is given that is not acceptable to the group (say, more than eight metres), it is written down below the first column and crossed out to emphasise that it effectively forms a limit on future estimates.

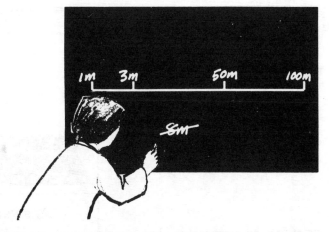

Naturally, if the discussion subsequently agrees on more than seven metres, that's it. You stop — because there is nowhere to go.
Eventually, there will be two (unanimously accepted) figures between which the estimate lies.
They may be 6 m and 11 m.
Calculate the midpoint (in this case, 8.5 m). Ask several pupils to actually measure the room.

Often, a stage will be reached where one or more pupils will not accept a suggestion. For example, someone may offer eight metres as a lower bound, and a dispute arises. Encourage the pupil(s) who object, to explain their reasoning. This may take the form of *'I'm not sure that any more than seven metre-long rules would fit along that wall'*, or *'when we measured the blackboard the other day it was 3.2 m, and I'm not sure that the wall is much more than two blackboards'*, for example.

> *'They saw the need for estimates to be thoroughly thought out. A random guess was of little value.'*

It is surprising how often the midpoint is very close to the actual distance. However, the pupils need to realise that 'between 6 and 11 metres' is perfectly reasonable.

Years 4↓8   MENTAL

One trials teacher showed the class a sheet of grid paper briefly, and then asked the students to 'bracket' the number of squares on it. (Their final bounds were 99 and 200, while the actual number of squares was 432!) This was useful for alerting the teacher to a weakness.

Extensions

On other occasions, present similar problems for discussion regarding outer limits. Any measurement or number calculation could theoretically be used in this process.

Some examples:

• Beads in a jar
• The number of cubic metres in the room
• The number of pages in a book
• Estimating bounds on the number of seconds elapsed, while children's eyes are closed

These examples will involve a varying amount of mental arithmetic. The beads in the jar, for example, might involve 'about 15 in a layer, about 20 layers, 150..... 300'.

In secondary schools, it is feasible for calculator problems like 3.64 x 1.89 to be bound by 3 x 1 and 4 x 2, i.e. between 3 and 8. Whilst fairly rough, this is easier than more precise rounding-off. There is no sense in 'homing in' on the correct answer, as obviously this is better done with a calculator.

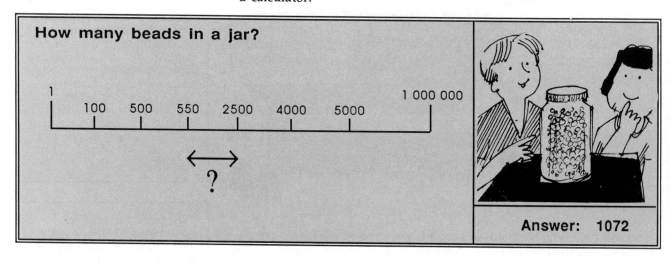

How many beads in a jar?

Answer: 1072

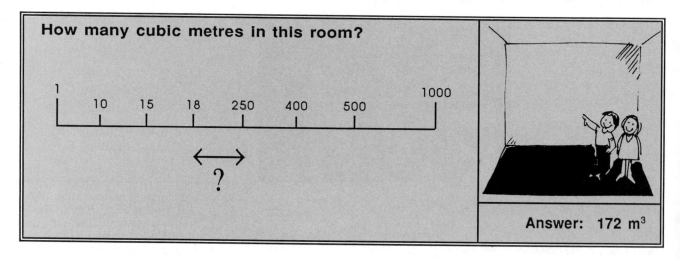

How many cubic metres in this room?

Answer: 172 m³

Find my number

An enjoyable game of 'What is the number I am thinking about?' reveals to the teacher a wealth of mental arithmetic, challenges and strategies.

Features of this activity

- Encourages thought about numbers.
- Emphasises properties of numbers.
- Can lead to useful discussion and extensions.

To make mental arithmetic lessons most effective

Considerable trialling in schools has shown that these mental arithmetic activities tend to work best under the following arrangements:

- A series of brief sessions — no more than 15 minutes — several times a week with a small group or the whole class.
- Problems or tasks may be written on the board or given orally but the answers must be oral. Any writing will be done by the teacher, thus ensuring that children concentrate on the mental activity.
- It is often better to hear and discuss several answers to a few questions, rather than only hear one answer to a large number of questions.
- It is important to select problems and tasks in which the whole group can become involved, rather than ones which reinforce the success of some and the sense of failure in others. The activities therefore should be enjoyable and positive learning experiences.

Comments from trials schools teachers

'This activity encourages discussion — not just child-teacher, but even more importantly child-child.' Another pleasing aspect is that no child is placed 'on the spot' which can lead to decreased confidence and the idea that he/she is no good at maths.'

The game is good because we all get to do or ask a question if we want to or don't want to.
It makes you think and it is good for your division.

This activity is very interesting and makes us think before we ask questions. I enjoy the activity find the number because its fun. No writing involved.

We should have at least one every maths lesson. We don't have to write pages of work

I enjoy it, it makes you think and use your brain but it is really only a game!

THIS ACTIVITY IS PART OF THE MCTP PROFESSIONAL DEVELOPMENT PACKAGE FROM THE CURRICULUM DEVELOPMENT CENTRE, CANBERRA

Years 4 ↓ 8   MENTAL

Find my number

The teacher mentally selects a number between 1 and 15. Children collectively try to find out what the number is by asking questions to which the teacher, at first, only answers 'yes' or 'no'. Children learn to refine their questioning techniques to home in on the number in the least number of questions.

The rules of the game

The choice of 50 as the upper limit is arbitrary. With younger children, 15 or 20 is appropriate. With older children 100 is most useful.

As this is assumed to be the first time this game has been introduced, do not emphasise finding the number with the fewest questions. This can be introduced later as an additional challenge when children have confidence in thinking of questions.

Asking groups rather than individuals to produce questions has two advantages — it generates discussion of the situation in the group, and gives more frequent involvement to individuals.

Writing the questions and answers on the board is very important to keep all children in touch with the challenge. Try to write the essence of the question briefly.

'Children were able to ask questions which reflected their varying levels of mathematical understanding.'

I'M GOING TO THINK OF A NUMBER BETWEEN 1 AND 50.
YOU ARE SITTING IN YOUR FOUR GROUPS AND EACH GROUP IN TURN CAN ASK ME A QUESTION.
I CAN ONLY ANSWER 'YES' OR 'NO'.
LET'S SEE WHETHER YOU CAN FIND MY NUMBER

RIGHT, I'VE CHOSEN MY NUMBER.
I'VE WRITTEN IT DOWN SECRETLY IN CASE I FORGET IT.
ANGELA, YOUR TABLE CAN ASK ME THE FIRST QUESTION

IS IT MORE THAN 30?

YES.
I'LL WRITE IT ON THE BOARD

More than 30? YES

NEXT QUESTION, SAM'S TABLE

IS IT EVEN?

NO!
WHY DO YOU LOOK DISAPPOINTED, JIM?
BECAUSE YOU WERE WRONG?
WHAT DO YOU THINK ABOUT THAT, JANE?

'NO' GIVES YOU JUST AS MUCH INFORMATION AS 'YES'

More than 30? YES
Even? NO

NEXT QUESTION, LARA'S TABLE

IS IT A PRIME NUMBER?

YES

More than 30? YES
Even? NO
Prime? YES

Second phase – What are the possible numbers?

NOW I WANT YOU TO TELL ME WHAT NUMBERS ARE STILL POSSIBLE AND I'LL WRITE THEM ON THE BOARD SO THAT WE ALL AGREE.
NOW WHAT'S THE SMALLEST NUMBER IT CAN BE?

31

YES!
WHAT IS THE NEXT NUMBER?

33

NO, WHY CAN'T IT BE 33?

BECAUSE 33 ISN'T PRIME

WHAT'S THE NEXT POSSIBLE NUMBER?

When there are five to ten possible numbers left it has been found very helpful to get the class to name them and to put them on the chalkboard. This makes everyone clarify their thinking and ensures that all children are able to be involved in the final questions.

DO WE AGREE?

More than 30 ? YES
Even ? NO
Prime ? YES

31, 37, 41, 43, 47

NOW, STEPHEN, YOUR TABLE.

YES!
SO WHICH NUMBERS CAN I CROSS OFF?

More than 30 ? YES
Even ? NO
Prime ? YES
Contains 3 ? YES

IS THERE A THREE IN IT?

41 AND 47

7, 41, 43, 47

HOW MANY MORE QUESTIONS ARE YOU GOING TO NEED?

ONE IF WE ARE LUCKY

GOOD ANSWER DOUG, CAN YOU EXPLAIN THAT?

NOW, MYRIAM, LET'S SEE IF YOUR TABLE IS GOING TO BE LUCKY

IS IT 31?

YES!
WELL DONE.
YOU FOUND MY NUMBER IN FIVE QUESTIONS TODAY.
WE'LL SEE HOW YOU DO TOMORROW

After a few games, discuss with the class what makes a 'good' question.
If the first question is 'Is it 37?' and that is the answer, it appears like a very good question but, in fact, it is only a very lucky question. Most, but not all, children will agree that a good question is one which splits the numbers in half, so that 'yes' and 'no' are equally useful answers.

More than 30? YES
Even? NO
Prime? YES
Contains 3? YES
31? YES

31, 37, 41, 43, 47

Years 4↓8 MENTAL

EXTENSIONS
How many questions are needed, if all questions are 'good' ones?

Clearly, if there are two numbers left, one question will eliminate one of them. If up to four numbers are left, one questions can eliminate two of them, and one more will leave one number only. With up to eight numbers, one question can reduce this to four numbers ...

Thus	2	numbers	1	question.
Up to	4	"	2	questions
"	8	"	3	"
"	16	"	4	"
"	32	"	5	"
"	64	"	6	"
"	128	"	7	"

So a number up to 50 can be found in six questions while seven questions should be sufficient for a number up to 100.

In general the rule can be stated as 'n' questions are enough for up to 2^n numbers'. Since $2^{10} = 1024$, this leads to the very surprising conclusion that only ten questions are needed to home in on a number up to 1000. This might be a possible challenge for an able group, who might even devise a flow chart suitable for finding any number up to 50.

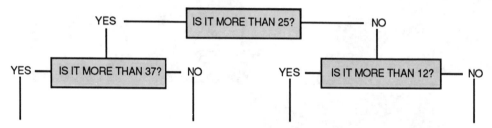

This in turn can lead on to discussion of binary arithmetic and binary coding, where information is stored in a yes/no format.

Assessing your pupils

Look for a development in the confidence with which questions are asked, and an increase in their range and relevance.

Try the game sometimes (up to 20) without writing questions and answers on the board.

Another way to assess children's progress is to make up examples like the following and give them to children to work out individually.

> My number is between 1 and 30.
>
> It is even.
> It is greater than 18.
> It is prime.
> It is divisible by 3.
>
> What is my number?

Hangman

Hangman, which is normally thought of as a language game, can also be an excellent way to involve children in mathematics.
The activity uses a code making machine (encoder) to convert words by mathematical processes, to coded and vice versa.
Quick mental computation is also a feature.

Features of this activity

- Mental arithmetic — addition, subtraction, multiplication and division.
- Constant enjoyable challenges throughout the activity.

- Success attainable using many strategies.
- Group and individual work.
- Assists spelling and investigates letter frequency.

Preparation

Copies of Worksheets 1 and 2 on pages 294-5.

THIS ACTIVITY IS PART OF THE MCTP
PROFESSIONAL DEVELOPMENT PACKAGE FROM THE
CURRICULUM DEVELOPMENT CENTRE, CANBERRA

Years 4 ↓ 7   MENTAL

Hangman

The well-known game of Hangman takes on a new challenge for children when the words are mathematically coded with the help of an encoder/decoder. Children soon find that their rewards, the answers, are achieved most efficiently by doing the mental maths.

The intention here is to build on children's own experiences.

In trials schools children came up with Morse code, semaphore, Braille, sign language, post codes and secret codes.

Understanding how the code-making machine works is a key requirement for playing *Hangman*.

This part of the lesson should not be rushed, so that all children understand the process.

This last example illustrates the *counting on* beyond 26.

1. Introduction

> TODAY WE WANT TO START BY TALKING ABOUT DIFFERENT KINDS OF CODES. WHAT CODES DO YOU KNOW?

2. Using the code making machine

Explain that most codes are made by using mathematics. Very simple mathematics can make words unrecognisable.

Hand out Worksheet 1 and explain how the code-making machine works.

> WE'LL USE ADDITION CODE

> IF WE USE THE RULE 'ADD 5' THEN 'A', THAT'S ONE, ADD FIVE — SIX, THAT'S 'F'. LOOK AT 'W'. WHEN WE ADD FIVE, WHAT WOULD THAT BECOME?

Have all children work through these examples (below) using their code-making machine (encoder).

a. Coding by addition (add 3)

A → X (counting back 3)

P → M (counting back 3)

$$1 - 3 = ^{-}2$$
or
$$27 - 3 = 24$$

$$16 - 3 = 13$$

> WHY DOES A → X? (DECODER GOES BACKWARDS AS WELL AS FORWARDS)

b. Coding by subtraction (subtract 5)

A → F

W → B

$$23 + 5 → 28$$
$$28 = 2$$

$$1 + 5 → 6$$

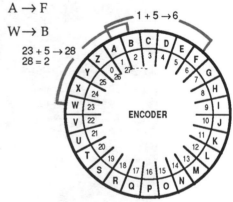

c. Coding by multiplication (multiply by 3)

G → U

O → S

Z → Z

$$26 \times 3 = 78 → 26$$
or
$$0 \times 3 = 0$$

$$7 \times 3 = 21$$

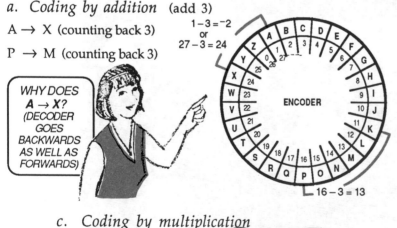

ENCODER

$$15 \times 3 = 45$$
$$45 → 19$$

d. Combinations

These are deliberately developed later after the easier ones above have been mastered.

2. Making a secret code

Choose one of the children's given names, and, step by step, have all the children code this name using the rule **+7** in the first square on the worksheet. (We have used MATHEW to illustrate what we mean.)

Using the rule **+7**, MATHEW became THOALD.

Bring out MATHEW. Say, *'This is (Mathew'???)* Walk the child seven paces forward. Stop, and say *'Now he is called THOALD. If we want to change THOALD back to MATHEW what do we do?'* (Walk 7 paces back)

> Do not explain the decoding process to the children at this stage.
> This could spoil it for those children who will discover for themselves that the way to reverse +7 is, in fact, to subtract 7.
> Understanding the secret clue is needed in order to complete the next step.

> Acting out this sequence has proved successful to assist children's understanding of this process.

THIS IS THE SECRET CLUE THAT YOU WILL NEED LATER

M	A	T	H	E	W
13	1	20	8	5	23
20	8	27	15	12	30
T	H	O	A	L	D

+7

> Do not give any further numbers or tell children to reverse the process. Allow them to discover the answer for themselves.

---

3. Break a code

Use Worksheet 1, part B.

Work the first three numbers 26, 21, 22, with the class. Children then go away in pairs to decode the message.

REMEMBER THE SECRET CLUE. WHEN WE GO TO THE CODED WORD WE ADD SIX AND WHEN WE WANT TO DECODE WE ......

T	O	P		T	E	A	C	H	E	R
20	15	16		20	5	1	3	8	5	18
26	21	22		26	11	7	9	14	11	24
Z	U	V		Z	K	G	I	N	K	X

+6

SUBTRACT SIX

4. Class activity — Hangman with codes

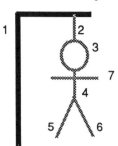

Bring the class together with their decoder sheet. Draw a diagram on the chalkboard to show the seven steps to a hanging. Teacher plays Hangman with the grade.

Write 'W Q E V X' on the board (which is the coded word for 'SMART' using the rule +4).

The children's task is to discover the word without knowing the coding rule. Invite them to choose a letter. If it is contained in the original word you write it above its coded equivalent. If it is not contained in the uncoded word they will have taken the first step in being hanged.

For example, if the letter **M** is offered, write it above the Q in WQEVX as follows:

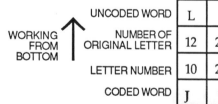

YOU ALL KNOW THE GAME HANGMAN DON'T YOU?
WE'LL PLAY IT NOW AND YOUR TASK IS TO DISCOVER THE WORD.
I'LL GIVE YOU THE WORD IN CODE BUT YOU WILL HAVE TO DISCOVER THE CODE.
LET'S SEE WHO IS FIRST TO BREAK THE CODE.
OUR FIRST CODED WORD IS WQEVX

A?

YES, THE THIRD LETTER IS A

Trials schools have found that it is worthwhile filling in the numbers for the first example only.

Encourage children not to guess answers but to work them out using the decoder.

If now the letter B is offered, the first step in Hangman is enacted.

Trials schools have also found that children need more problems to consolidate their understanding, and as well, they want to keep playing the game.

Put the coded words on the chalkboard one by one.

Answer

S	M	A	R	T
19	13	1	18	20
23	17	5	22	24
W	Q	E	V	X

Play Hangman

The following games allow the children to happily practise number facts while enjoying the game.

	UNCODED WORD	L	Y	N	C	H	E	D
WORKING FROM BOTTOM ↑	NUMBER OF ORIGINAL LETTER	12	25	14	3	8	5	4
	LETTER NUMBER	10	23	12	1	6	3	2
	CODED WORD	J	W	L	A	F	C	B

Code used was – 2

		P	L	A	N	E	T
NUMBER OF ORIGINAL LETTER		16	12	1	14	5	20
LETTER NUMBER		or 6 32	24	2	or 2 28	10	or 14 40
		F	X	B	B	J	N

Code used was **x 2**

		F	O	U	R
NUMBER OF ORIGINAL LETTER		6	15	21	18
LETTER NUMBER		18	or 19 45	or 11 63	or 2 54
		R	S	K	B

Code used was ÷ 3

Group activity

The teacher cuts up Worksheet 2 and gives two squares to each group. Groups work out the code.

Two squares are sufficient for each group. The last squares on the sheet are more difficult.

When the groups have completed this task, each group makes up their own coded words using sections of the Worksheet 1 in preparation for playing Hangman with the class.

Bring the class together on the floor. Have each group nominate a representative and select their best coded word to play Hangman with the rest of the class.

Discussion

When groups have completed the worksheets ask a member of each group to tell the class the method they used to solve a particular problem.

While this will probably include searching for the number patterns between corresponding letters, it is also likely to involve the letters they chose first.

Trials schools have found that the children usually choose the vowels first. However the letters T, N, R, S, H, D and L are all more common than letter U.

Follow on

This is now a valuable opportunity for another problem-solving activity. Each group can be challenged to devise a plan to determine the ten most common letters.

Allow each group to carry out their planned investigation and prepare a class presentation of their findings.

Extensions

- Read Conan Doyle's book *The Dancing Man* in the Sherlock Holmes series.
- Have children write coded messages using lemon juice which becomes visible under heat.

Worksheet 1

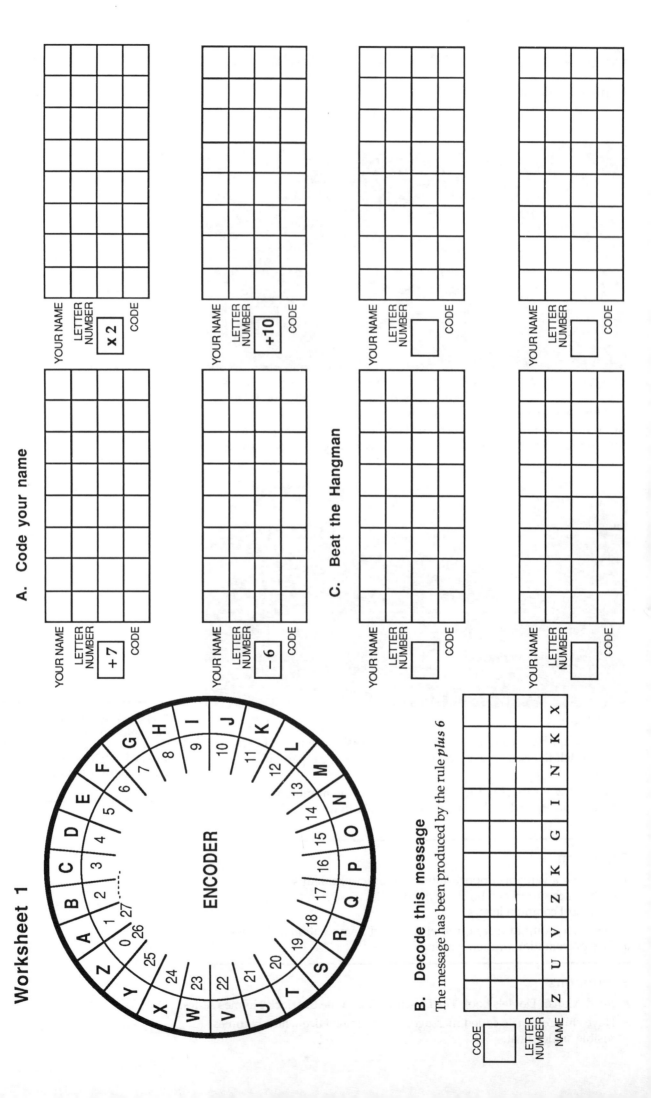

A. Code your name

YOUR NAME							
LETTER NUMBER							
+7 CODE							

YOUR NAME							
LETTER NUMBER							
x2 CODE							

YOUR NAME							
LETTER NUMBER							
−6 CODE							

YOUR NAME							
LETTER NUMBER							
+10 CODE							

B. Decode this message

The message has been produced by the rule *plus 6*

CODE							
LETTER NUMBER							
NAME	Z	U	V	Z	K	G	I	N	K	X

C. Beat the Hangman

YOUR NAME							
LETTER NUMBER							
CODE							

YOUR NAME							
LETTER NUMBER							
CODE							

ENCODER

Worksheet 2

+2	x3

CODE

LETTER
NUMBER

NAME | F | C | L | U | O | | | |

-3	x2

CODE

LETTER
NUMBER

NAME | P | D | P | L | J | | | |

+2	-2

CODE

LETTER
NUMBER

NAME | A | Q | W | V | J | | | |

-12	x2

CODE

LETTER
NUMBER

NAME | D | Z | O | B | S | H | | |

+8	-2

CODE

LETTER
NUMBER

NAME | J | I | L | O | M | | | |

+5	-3

CODE

LETTER
NUMBER

NAME | Z | E | X | J | M | F | L | K |

+7	x3	+2

CODE

LETTER
NUMBER

NAME | F | C | L | U | O | | | |

-3	-12	x2

CODE

LETTER
NUMBER

NAME | P | D | P | L | J | | | |

+5	-2	x2

CODE

LETTER
NUMBER

NAME | A | Q | W | V | J | | | |

+10	x2	-12

CODE

LETTER
NUMBER

NAME | D | Z | O | B | S | H | | |

-2	x3	+8

CODE

LETTER
NUMBER

NAME | J | I | L | O | M | | | |

x4	-3	+5

CODE

LETTER
NUMBER

NAME | Z | E | X | J | M | F | L | K |

Years 4↓7

MENTAL

Brief descriptions of other mental activities

1. Use different story forms when there are occasions for quick recall of basic facts (e.g. +, –, x, ÷). Instead of a list of 20 or more random calculations, vary the form. Instead of 8 – 5 = ? , use a variety of language and story forms. For example:

- What is the difference between 8 and 5?

- Eight take five equals?

- I have $8, you have $5, how much more have I got than you?

- I went to sleep at 5 a.m. and woke at 8 a.m. How long did I sleep?

2. Do not always have the missing number at the end. For example: 8 + ? = 12. Ask children to read this aloud. Often they have not been given a form of words, and yet this is necessary to help understand the problem. For example:

- Eight and what makes twelve?

- What do I add to 8 to make 12?

3. Give one form of a number relationship and ask for all the alternative forms (usually 8 in all). For example, given 2 + 3 = 5, children produce:

$$3 + 2 = 5, \quad 5 = 3 + 2, \quad 5 - 3 = 2, \quad 5 - 2 = 3, \quad 2 = 5 - 3, \quad 3 = 5 - 2,$$
$$5 = 2 + 3 \text{ (how do you say this if you read '=' as 'makes'?)}$$

4. Ask questions requiring more than one step. Often mental arithmetic questions require only one single step or calculation. In reality, we often need two or more steps which require further skills, and this needs practice, for example:

- I double a number and take away 3. The answer is 15. What was my number?

- Add 3 x 6 to 5 x 7.

- Start with 7. Add 2, multiply by 4 and halve the result.

- What is the smallest number after 100 which is divisible by 7?

5. Putting a set of numbered cards into order. Prepare in advance a set of cards for each team (A team of six requires a set of six cards). Arrange the class in teams of six to eight children, each team in a line.

If there are six children in each team, a simple set of cards for each team could be:

(a) 10 11 12 13 14 15

Cards are shuffled and one card is given to each child in the team. Cards must be exchanged up and down the line until all cards are in numerical order. This has to be done in silence. Children can only look at and exchange cards with their neighbours.

Some other possible sets of cards are :

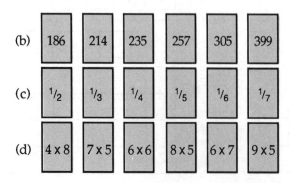

(b) 186 214 235 257 305 399

(c) ¹/₂ ¹/₃ ¹/₄ ¹/₅ ¹/₆ ¹/₇

(d) 4 x 8 7 x 5 6 x 6 8 x 5 6 x 7 9 x 5

6. What card comes next?

Prepare a set of cards in advance with at least one card for each member of the class. Here are steps for preparation of a set of five cards.

(a) Make a whole set like this.

(b) Write a different number on each card in random order.

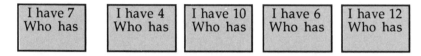

(c) Write a calculation below which leads on to the next card.

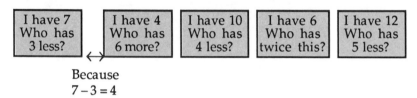

Because
7 − 3 = 4

Shuffle the cards and give one (or more) to each child. Any one child reads out his or her card. The child who has its successor raises his or her hand and reads out the other card. Keep cards in an envelope for later use.

7. Counting aloud

Counting aloud in classes frequently involves counting from zero in multiples of a particular number. This means only a limited range of numbers are counted. This activity suggests some variations from that approach.

Some possible variations include:

- Start with, e.g. 3 and add on successive 5s: 3, 8, 13, 18,.....
- Start with, e.g. 81 and subtract successive 3s: 81, 78, 75, 72, ...
- Start with 1 and double successively: 1, 2, 4, 8, ... as far as possible.
- Start with, e.g. 256 or 384 and halve successively.
- Start with 0, but say 'now add 3', 'now add 4','now add 2', 'now add 6', etc. Ask for the total at various intervals.

Organisational hints

Children could be seated in a circle, and asked to provide the next number in turn. Any situation where pupils are asked to respond quickly has a possible element of threat. Some possibilities for reducing this, as well as working to create a classroom environment where children are not afraid of giving the wrong answer) include:

- de-emphasising speed initially, or
- emphasising speed, but encouraging the notion of 'having a go',
- forming three or more groups, seated in circles, to move through the counting patterns.

Start with one person in each group. *'We're all going to start at 7, count on by 12s. First group over 200.'* Clearly, the arrival at the correct answer (211) is easily checked. Alternatively, the pupils could check the solution with a calculator— a reasonably challenging task. Alternatively, the group can be given a set time (e.g. one minute), and the group reaching the highest number in that time wins.

This team competition allows children to support each other.